PROSTITUTION, WOMEN AND MISUSE OF THE LAW

PROSTITUTION, WOMEN AND MISUSE OF THE LAW

The Fallen Daughters
of Eve

HELEN J. SELF

FRANK CASS
LONDON • PORTLAND, OR

First Published in 2003 in Great Britain by
FRANK CASS PUBLISHERS
Crown House, 47 Chase Side, Southgate
London, N14 5BP

and in the United States of America by
FRANK CASS PUBLISHERS
c/o ISBS, 920 NE 58th Avenue, Suite 300
Portland, Oregon, 97213–3786

Website http://www.frankcass.com

British Library Cataloguing in Publication Data:

Self, Helen J.
Prostitution, women and misuse of the law: the fallen
daughters of Eve
1. Great Britain. Committee on Homosexual Offences and
Prostitution   2. Prostitution – Law and legislation – Great
Britain
I. Title
364.1'534'0941

ISBN 0-7146-5481-7 (cloth)
ISBN 0-7146-8371-X (paper)

Library of Congress Cataloging-in-Publication Data:

Self, Helen J., 1937–
Prostitution, women and misuse of the law: the fallen
daughters of Eve / Helen J. Self.
p.   cm.
Includes bibliographical references and index.
ISBN 0-7146-5481-7 (cloth) – ISBN 0-7146-8371-X (pbk)
1. Prostitution – Great Britain.   I. Title.

KD8077.S45 2003
344.41'0544–dc21
2003043990

Typeset by Servis Filmsetting Ltd, Manchester

Printed in Great Britain by MPG Books Ltd, Bodmin, Cornwall

Contents

Acknowledgements

The writing of this book has extended over seven years during which time the focus of the work has changed and changed again, finally returning via the Wolfenden Committee papers to where it began. Many people have helped and encouraged me on the way and I would like to thank them all for their optimism and assistance.

The book is based upon my PhD thesis. I am grateful to my original supervisor Richard de Friend (then Pro-Vice-Chancellor of the University of Kent) for allowing me the space to pursue an obsession despite my own limited knowledge and his heavy schedule of work. During 1996–97, Richard was assisted by Dr Deborah Cheney of Kent Law School, who kindly supported me through the transitional period when Richard moved on to become Director of the College of Law, London. The inspiration that caused me to incorporate an analysis of the Wolfenden Committee papers was a lecture at London Guildhall University delivered in 1999 by Professor Frank Mort. He is not aware of this but I thank him all the same.

In approximate order of appearance I must first thank Jane Godwin (retired legal indexer) for her invaluable assistance in helping me understand the intricacies of case law. I am indebted to my friend Beverley Grey (great-niece of Josephine Butler) for her generous sifting out of primary source material and for access to her personal collection of Josephine Butler papers. My knowledge of the more recent history of the Josephine Butler Society and its fight to reform the Street Offences Act 1959 derives from this source. Judith Taylor, the Aylesford Priory Librarian, gave me invaluable help with the section on theology and allowed a heretic to sit and work in the quiet peace of the monks' library. Many other friends and acquaintances have encouraged me to persevere and given me the benefit of their knowledge and advice. My journey has also been lightened by Paterson and Co., Solicitors, through financial help as well as being the source of much irreverent laughter.

Members of the Charing Cross Police Clubs and Vice Unit have been friendly and supportive, in particular Ron Holmes, who allowed me to sift through his own collection of papers on prostitution. The police, including Dr Tim Brain, Chief Constable of Gloucestershire, have been generous with their time and helped me to establish a more rounded understanding of the problems surrounding the regulation of prostitution. Attending the National Police Vice conferences has widened my circle of knowledgeable friends and given me the courage to submit articles to the *Police Review*. This has enabled me to use my historical knowledge to illuminate the present so that the subject does not rest in a vacuum.

Since historical research relies so heavily upon archival collections the student depends upon the goodwill of archivists and librarians. Much of my research time was spent in the old Fawcett Library, where David Doughan's energy and encyclopaedic knowledge of women's history was a constant source of amazement. The Castle Street 'Wash House' has since been transformed into the new 'Women's Library' and now holds the Fawcett Library collection. I would like to thank the supporting staff of the old library, who constantly raced up and down the long corridor seeking out boxes of papers at one end and answering the bell at the other. I am equally obliged to the ever-helpful staff of the Kent County Library, Springfield, who must have winced at the constant stream of requests for books on prostitution, inter-library loans and books from the British Library collection. My husband Brian has been patient and supportive, helping me with preliminary script reading and putting up with my constant abstraction. He has not only made cups of tea but shopped, cooked meals and accepted my monopoly of the computer.

Finally I owe a special debt of gratitude to Professor Gerry Rubin of Kent Law School, without whose good counsel, patience and scholarship I would have abandoned the project.

My thesis is dedicated to my mother, Dr Constance Rover, who has been my inspiration, my mentor and my friend. Her life has spanned most of the twentieth century and while she likes to describe herself as an 'old-style feminist'. I prefer to think of her as the pioneer voice of the second wave. Her books, *Women's Suffrage and Party Politics in Britain, 1866–1914* (1969) and *Love, Morals and the Feminist* (1970) are still constantly cited. I cannot hope to emulate her level of scholarship but dedicate my work to her with admiration and with love.

Abbreviations

AIDS	acquired immune deficiency syndrome
AMSH	Association of Moral and Social Hygiene
BSBC	British Social Biology Council
CEMWC	Church of England Moral Welfare Council
CDA	Contagious Diseases Acts
CLA	Criminal Law Amendment
CLRC	Criminal Law Revision Committee
ECP	English Collective of Prostitutes
HL Deb.	House of Lords Debate
IAW	International Alliance of Women
IB	International Bureau
JBS	Josephine Butler Society
JBET	Josephine Butler Educational Trust
LN	League of Nations
LCC	London County Council
NCW	National Council of Women
NUWW	National Union of Women Workers
NVA	National Vigilance Association
PD	Parliamentary Debates
PRO	Public Record Office
ROW	Rights of Women
EUROPAP	European Network for HIV/STD Prevention in Prostitution
UN	United Nations
VSOC	Vagrancy and Street Offences Committee
WL	The Women's Library, London

Introduction

Whoever has walked through Regent Street, Queen Street and other offshoots from the Quadrant, must have observed a great number of bold-looking overdressed women, unmistakably foreign, displaying a profusion of showy jewellery and wearing indescribable bonnets. Who then are these strangers whose cheeks appear to bloom with rude health, who seem from their leering looks and indiscriminate smiles of invention to be so happy? Who apparently possess such large stores of gold and jewellery and who array themselves in velvet and satin? They are a portion of the fallen daughters of Eve. The outward impression will not, however, bear the test of examination. Their diamonds are false, their gold is neither that of Australia or California, it is manufactured in Birmingham. The roses on their cheeks vanish at the visitation of a few drops of rain, the healthy colour disappears and a cadaverous complexion with repulsive features present themselves [*sic*] to the beholder. They have long lost their sense of shame and modesty, they do not even think their impure calling is against the morals of society or opposed to the laws of virtue; they have descended to that depth of degradation at which they regard their profession somewhat in the same light as the tradesman regards his retail business.[1]

According to the actor Peter Ustinov, we develop our prejudice towards others through those institutions that we most respect, that is, the Church, the school and the family. The consequence of this early indoctrination can be the creation of widely held opinions that are notoriously difficult to influence. The following work addresses one such area of prejudice.

Through this introductory chapter I will familiarise the reader with the themes and arguments of my book and demonstrate how particular attitudes of ingrained prejudice towards prostitutes have impacted upon law and government policy. I will refer to a succession of government inquiries, including the major Wolfenden inquiry in 1957, which legitimated the continued labelling and stigmatisation of certain women for behaviour that was lawful if

conducted by others, and argue that widely held prejudice (historical, philosophical and legal) has been built into the legislation, creating a climate of vulnerability for the women involved.

The author of my opening quotation illustrates a variety of familiar but
unsubstantiated assumptions about the prostitute. The object of disgust is
female and in this case she is foreign, which deepens the contempt. Outwardly
she is well dressed, happy and healthy, but below the surface she is sickly and
degenerate. She is the harbinger of death and the destroyer of virtue. Such
themes reappear in articles and reports with predictable monotony and with
many subtle variations. Behind the rhetoric can be found considerable anxiety
over the increasing freedom and wilfulness of young women. For example, in
1899 Canon Scott Holland mourned the changing scene: 'Men become free
from the checks of local associations, girls distance us without a moment's
notice.'[2]

Besides these fears there was always an element within society who were
anxious to restrain and, if possible, to incarcerate the restless women.[3] In 1912
the Penal Reform League[4] had its own strategy for reform. There should be
conveniently situated 'Rest Homes' or hospitals where prostitutes could be
'sorted out' and sent on to appropriate institutions. These would include
country hospitals, farms and industrial settlements. 'Some women might
remain for long, even all their days.' Happy industry, music, dancing and
opportunities for study were to be among the distractions that would encourage trustworthiness, self-reliance and resourcefulness 'with joy of heart'.[5]

The more pragmatic F. S. Bullock, Chief Constable of the Metropolitan
Police CID,[6] suggested that the fear of prostitution and trafficking had been
greatly exaggerated. He wrote of the climate of religious moralising that per-
vaded society and had created an 'atmosphere charged with hostility',
although he thought it would be rash to assume that the morals of the British
were any better than their neighbours. Nevertheless, he was concerned for the
young women who were testing their freedom and realised that the reason
that drove a woman to allow herself to become 'an article of commerce' was
the desire for a more comfortable livelihood than could be found working for
low wages. 'It is the economic condition of women which drives them to this
sad condition.'[7]

During the First World War official attitudes towards promiscuous women
hardened as it was feared that they would spread disease and loosen the
marital ties of the soldiers. At the same time, some medical experts sought to
establish their credentials by psychoanalysing and pathologising the prostitute. The physician A. F. Tredgold described the behaviour of a well-
developed and attractive girl of 16 who, he alleged, had been 'recklessly'
spreading disease to soldiers. She absconded from a variety of homes and hospitals until she was finally detained, and a place was found for her in a secure
institution by the London County Council. She may well have stayed there for
the rest of her life.[8]

In 1927 the Medical Officer for Health for the LCC wrote a report on the state of common lodging houses in London and filled a page and a half with contradictory statements. Prostitutes, he wrote, still formed a very considerable proportion of the common lodging house population. They were mostly between the ages of 25 and 35. Many had been orphaned when young, had received little education and had worked for a few years in poorly paid occupations. Even so, they were more opulently dressed than other residents and occupied the best beds in the graded house. They could be observed sitting in a cosy kitchen enjoying roast mutton and green peas, while the poor match girl lunched on bread and margarine at the back of the house. The Salvation Army workers never ceased urging these women to give up their life of sin, but 'naturally enough the poor girl who is defying public opinion surrounds herself with a barbed wire entanglement of lies, phantasies, insolence and blasphemy to protect her from the antagonism of her kind. Moreover, her looks, her speech, her very walk become unconsciously stamped with the hallmarks of her trade.' Extreme intolerance of discipline was another alleged feature.[9] Here we have a typical mixture of irritation, envy and disgust. The most contemptible and unintelligent women from the bottom strata of society had somehow managed to secure for themselves a level of comfort far above their station.

The papers of the League of Nations Advisory Committee on the Traffic in Women and Children are a bottomless source of this type of analysis and invective. The International Union of Catholic Women (1930) found that 'psycho-physiological and moral data are necessary to pierce through all the reflexes and currents of the subconscious' and reported that prostitutes displayed 'fecklessness and a marked blunting of the moral faculties'. But with regard to higher faculties, 'the repetition of vicious[10] acts had strengthened in them a kind of automatism all the stronger if due to hereditary tendencies'. Their *will* had become almost entirely atrophied, 'they nearly always showed in their whole physical appearance marks of their unfortunate habit', and 'their looks, attitudes, gestures, their very reflexes betray moral disruption'. Not surprisingly, the Union regretted that the women spent too short a time in prison to allow for reform.[11] By 1943 Dr Tage Kemp (Director of the University Institute of Human Genetics, Copenhagen) claimed that he had conducted extensive research into the causes of prostitution and confidently announced that 'chronic physical disease of a more or less disabling character is one of the important causal factors'. In evidence he provided a long series of afflictions, many of which few people outside the medical profession will ever have heard of, including salpingitis, cholelithiasis, nephrolithiasis and bilateral oophorectomy. Other conditions were cited, such as rickets, rheumatic fever, gastric problems and severe burns, without mentioning their relationship to impoverished diet and bad living conditions.[12] By 1945 Dr Edward Glover of the Institute of Scientific Treatment of Delinquency, London,[13] had lightened the analytical approach. In his opinion prostitution was due to regressive symptoms, it represented a 'primitive stage in sexual development' and was the 'displacement of unconscious infantile sexual wishes'.[14]

Throughout all these papers there are comparisons between the 'normal' and the 'abnormal' woman. The normal woman was the chaste wife, mother or daughter, whereas the abnormal woman was characterised by her inability to distinguish between right and wrong. Many of the sufferers, it was said, displayed abnormally 'erotic' tendencies, and new words such as 'hypersexualism' were invented to describe their 'condition'. Their quest for an accurate definition meant that the borderline between prostitution and promiscuity was frequently breached. Consequently, promiscuous women were then subdivided into absurdly improbable categories, such as those formulated by Sybil Neville Rolphe, who claimed that 'incipient' prostitutes could be sectioned into categories of 'occasional' or 'persistently' promiscuous and 'occasional or temporary' prostitute, and lastly, the 'chronic or habitual' prostitute.[15]

It was within this context of the public condemnation of casual relationships, illicit sex and extramarital relationships that Edith Thompson was hanged on 9 January 1923 for allegedly colluding with her lover in the murder of her husband Percy. The case attracted massive media coverage with much voyeuristic and prurient commentary. People queued from 4 a.m. to attend the trial, and a frenzied mob was said to have gathered outside her home in Ilford. Many people believed that her true crime was being an unfaithful wife and revelling in her own sensuality. The tragedy left four people dead, as the hangman subsequently committed suicide. For some reason part of the Home Office file on the case is closed until 2022.[16]

In parallel, and weaving in and out of all this confusion of ideas, were the feminist campaigns for an equal moral standard and the social purity/vigilance crusade for a more broadly based legislative onslaught against immorality. The National Vigilance Association (NVA) and the Association of Moral and Social Hygiene (AMSH)[17] are usually cited as the most influential in these respects, but although the role of the NVA in campaigning for legislative and moral reform has been recognised by historians,[18] the AMSH's long-term resistance to what it believed to be unjust and discriminatory law has received less attention. It is my objective to address this discrepancy.

Thus in 1916 the AMSH launched a campaign against what it chose to call the 'solicitation laws'[19] and backed up its arguments with a national survey of police attitudes towards prostitutes and street soliciting.[20] This was followed, a few years later, by the draft 'Public Places (Order) Bill' of 1923.[21] The aim of this Bill was to repeal all statutory references to the 'common prostitute' loitering, wandering, soliciting or importuning in public places and to replace them with a simple non-discriminatory provision applying to 'any person'. Section 1 of the Bill provided that: 'Every person who, in any public place, wilfully causes annoyance to any person by words or behaviour offensive to public order or decency, shall be liable on summary conviction to a penalty not exceeding forty shillings for every such offence.' No person was to be taken into custody for such an offence 'except upon complaint of the person aggrieved', as distinct from the usual practice of relying upon police testimony that the person 'appeared' to be annoyed. This addressed a long-standing grievance of

the AMSH as the majority of prosecutions were based solely upon police testimony, and, as James Morton reveals, most of this evidence was fabricated.[22]
Accordingly the Bill was introduced (on behalf of the AMSH) into the House
of Commons in 1925 by Viscountess Astor, and to the House of Lords in 1926
by Lord Balfour of Burleigh.[23] This Bill was, in fact, one of a number of
attempts from 1885 onwards to amend the solicitation laws.[24]

The burden of the AMSH argument had been that women were being
prosecuted for soliciting men when in truth it was men who solicited women.
In this respect its case was strengthened as a result of a number of legal chal-
lenges known as the 'Hyde Park Cases'.[25] On one such occasion a well-known
public figure, Sir Almeric Fitzroy, Clerk to the Privy Council, was arrested and
charged with 'wilfully interfering with and annoying persons using Hyde
Park'. It was reported in *The Times* that two policemen had observed Sir
Almeric attempting to engage in conversation with a series of young women
who appeared to resent his attentions.[26] The police claimed that he had
resorted to 'extreme violence' both in the park and at the police station when
he attempted to resist arrest and prosecution.

Sir Almeric was subsequently convicted of the offence and fined £5 plus
£10 costs, but the conviction was quashed on appeal on the ground that one
of the women, Mrs Turner, was a 'notorious prostitute', even though Sir
Almeric had admitted to two out of four of the cases that were said to have
been proven. Sir Almeric declared that he had gone to the park for a period
of rest and meditation and complained that although he was not a wealthy
man he had been obliged to 'spend hundreds of pounds in order to find out
the history of Mrs Turner's character'. The chairman of the London Sessions
in November 1922 was reported to have observed: 'Unless some person has
made a complaint, a conviction under that section ought to be impossible. It
is not the law of the land that one person may not speak to another without
being formally introduced. I go further and say a man may speak to a woman
without being charged with an offence.'[27] Consequently, Alison Neilans (the
Secretary of the AMSH) wrote to the Bishop of Kingston commenting that
the public had been quite content to allow the arrest of women on the evidence
of the police, but made a terrible fuss if they arrested men of any importance.
She suggested that this type of incident was the result of demands that men
and women should be treated equally, but that there was deep public antipathy towards the prosecution of men on charges of indecency, especially, she
believed, when the prosecution was based upon uncorroborated evidence.[28]

A number of similar incidents occurred during 1928,[29] the most high
profile of which was that of the ex-MP and well-known author on social
issues, Sir Leo Chiozza Money. Sir Leo (aged 57) and Miss Irene Savidge (aged
22) were charged on 23 April 1928 'with being concerned together in behaving in a manner reasonably likely to offend public decency at Hyde Park, contrary to Regulation 24 of the General Regulations for Hyde Park'.[30] As with
Sir Almeric, Sir Leo struggled all the way to the police station complaining, 'I
am not the usual "riff-raff", I am a man of substance. For God's sake let me

go!'[31] The police responded to his threats by withdrawing Miss Savidge from her place of employment and interviewing her for five hours without the benefit of a female chaperone. On returning home the young lady was said to have fainted. The case was then referred to the Director of Public Prosecutions and escalated into a major scandal. [32] There were two judicial inquiries into the conduct of the police which were accompanied by parliamentary debate and massive press coverage. The effective immunity from prosecution of men who were prostitutes' clients, which both the Fitzroy and Chiozza Money cases exposed, continues to this day.

A further embarrassment for the Metropolitan Police was provided in 1928, when Sergeant Goddard's involvement with night-club and brothel owners was revealed.[33] The consequences of these cases were two temporary slumps in the number of solicitation charges in the Metropolitan Police district, declining from 2,187 in 1922 to 590 in 1923, and from 2,224 in 1928 to 646 in 1929.[34]

By 1924 the AMSH had decided that the public had become sufficiently aware of the injustices perpetrated upon prostitutes for it to be worth petitioning the Home Office for the appointment of a committee of inquiry. It therefore proceeded to organise a deputation of 42 societies to lobby the Home Secretary.[35] However, the impact of this strategy had already been weakened through the activities of a number of vigilance, refuge and reformatory organisations that had been campaigning for a strengthening of the solicitation laws.[36] In 1917 a deputation of these societies had appeared before the Home Secretary urging him to extend the operation of the law to provide for the compulsory detention of girls under 18 for up to three years if they had been convicted as 'common prostitutes'.[37] In 1924 this group of organisations appealed independently to the Home Office for the appointment of a departmental committee.

It was against this background of conflicting demands and police dissatisfaction with the shortcomings of the legislation that the Street Offences Committee 1928[38] was appointed under the chairmanship of Hugh Macmillan, KC.[39] The terms of reference were: to consider 'offences against the criminal law in connection with prostitution and solicitation for immoral purposes[40] in streets and public places and other offences against decency and good order'.[41]

Macmillan obviously disliked the assignment as his sole cause for self-congratulation was that he managed to obtain the signatures of all the members of the committee for the final report, although eight out of the 15 made reservations. This particular committee was to be the first of a series of twentieth-century government-appointed committees and, when looked at in retrospect, it was the most liberal in its recommendations. Nevertheless the report was filled with ambiguities and contradictions, or with what Carol Smart has referred to as 'circularity of logic'.[42] It was claimed in the report that the law was only dealing with the way in which the individual woman conducted herself in public and not with her private morality (although this statement was contradicted by the presence of over thirty references to morality in the report). Furthermore the phrase 'immoral purpose' was not included within the statutes being considered. Even so, the argument that the law was 'not concerned with morality' was to remain the basic rationalisation for not incriminating the prostitute's client, since his brief involvement in the transaction was not considered to be the cause of annoyance. The committee recommended that there should be two new offences, both of which were to be gender-neutral and which would not include the stigmatising term 'common prostitute'. First it was proposed to make it an offence for any person to importune a person of the opposite sex for immoral purposes in a street or public place (which contradicted the statement on private morality). Second, it would have made it an offence for any person to frequent any street or public place for the purpose of prostitution or solicitation so as to constitute a nuisance. For this second offence the evidence of more than one annoyed person would be required.[43]

On the surface it would appear that these proposed offences would have gone quite a long way towards meeting the demands of the AMSH. Most significantly they would have addressed its objection to the creation of a specific class of women who were held solely responsible for an offence involving both sexes. However, the AMSH condemned them as 'utterly unsatisfactory' claiming that they were contrary to the fundamental principles of 'justice' and 'equality' between men and women for which the Society had stood since the 1870s.[44] Thus, in regard to the first offence, the AMSH criticised the inclusion of the words 'immoral purpose', stating that it was contrary to British law to make the 'purpose' of an act an offence, when sexual intercourse, if achieved, was not an offence. Moreover, it insisted that immorality had *never* been an offence. In addition it argued that the vague definition of an 'immoral purpose' would be incapable of satisfactory proof and, in the absence of the offended citizen, such evidence would still rest upon the word of a policeman who would be required to testify to the nature of the offensiveness. In effect this would still amount to the woman concerned being labelled as a 'common prostitute' on moral grounds.[45] This nexus of arguments continued to inform the AMSH (and later the Josephine Butler Society's) analysis of prostitution law reform for the rest of the century.[46] When looked at with the benefit of hindsight, it would appear that the AMSH lost a significant opportunity in 1928 for supporting a reform that moved in a liberalising direction.

THE POLICE

During the early part of the twentieth century the police had been the focus of a considerable amount of criticism and public dissatisfaction, leading to accusations of blackmail, corruption and rough handling of suspects. In addition to the criticisms levied at the police by the AMSH, concerning the inappropriate and discriminatory treatment of prostitutes, there were other allegations accusing police officers of accepting favours or bribes, instead of carrying out their duties.[47] These problems were addressed in 1908 by the Royal Commission upon the Duties of the Metropolitan Police and again in 1929 by the Royal Commission on Police Powers and Procedures.[48]

Being conscious of these issues the Street Offences Committee defined the duties of the police towards prostitutes in the Street Offences Report (1928), while being careful to give the force its wholehearted support. With reference to the regulation of street prostitution it stated that:

> In Scotland it is necessary to have two witnesses or one witness with corroborative facts and circumstances. While we in no way impugn the credibility of evidence of the police, we regard it as desirable that wherever possible corroboration should be found from members of the public and where this is not possible we commend the practice which obtains in one town of confronting the accused at the time of arrest with the person alleged to have been importuned and reporting to the Court what then passed in the presence of the accused.[49]

When the Royal Commission on Police Powers and Procedures reported in 1929 it argued that street offences were the subject of laws that did not command the general support of the public, for a considerable section of the population regarded them as an unwarranted interference in the lives of private citizens, or as penalizing conduct that was not the business of the state. Therefore the police found themselves in a particularly difficult position with regard to these offences. When they enforced the law rigorously officers claimed that they were blamed for their harshness, but when they were lenient they were criticised for collusion and corrupt dealings. Consequently they stated that the public were unwilling to cooperate in assisting with the enforcement of the law by providing the police with the necessary evidence, which they had a duty to furnish. The commission concluded that the law itself was defective as it was believed by witnesses to be out of harmony with public opinion. As the report observed, 'The fact that the police are called upon to enforce such laws inevitably impairs their good relations with the public and, further, the sense of antagonism thus aroused tends to hamper the police in their general duties of suppressing and detecting crime.'[50]

The commission welcomed the 1928 Macmillan Street Offences Committee's suggestion that the law ought to be reformulated so that the offence constituted would be a matter no longer of annoyance but of 'molestation by offensive words and behaviour' on the ground that 'the proof of annoyance had taken on an indirect and perfunctory nature, which was not calculated to foster in the mind of a policeman a proper sense of the completeness of proof required in a criminal trial'.[51] These issues were not resolved, as the recommendations of the Street Offences Committee did not lead to government action. Nor did they appear to have much impact upon policing practice during the 1930s and 1940s as convictions for soliciting offences for England and Wales fluctuated between one and two thousand per year until after the Second World War, when they rose steadily year upon year to over ten thousand in 1952 and 1953. At the time, these figures were portrayed by politicians and the press as a national disgrace, although, as already mentioned, the number of prosecutions and convictions for solicitation had fluctuated over the half-century, and those of the 1950s were much the same as between 1906 and 1915.[52]

THE WOLFENDEN COMMITTEE

In 1954 the Home Secretary, Sir David Maxwell Fyfe, appointed the second departmental committee of the twentieth century to be charged with investigating the issue of street offences and to make recommendations for legislative reform. It became known by the name of its chairman, John Wolfenden. It appears that the familiar pressures created by street soliciting were amplified during the 1950s by sensational media reporting about prostitution in London and by allegations concerning organised foreign gangs of exploiters. This added a sense of urgency to the Wolfenden recommendations in 1957, which were to drop the need to provide evidence that a citizen was annoyed and to increase penalties. The report resulted in the enactment of these proposals in the Street Offences Act 1959,[53] a measure that was pressed through parliament by the use of the whip. In contrast the Sexual Offences Act 1956[54] (containing sections on brothel-keeping and the protection of women and girls from sexual abuse) was passed through without comment while the Wolfenden Committee was sitting, and regardless of their relevance to the committee's discussions. The significance of the 1956 Act, as far as Wolfenden was concerned, was that it supplied a 'loophole' in the form of owner-occupied or tenant-occupied flats into which the street prostitute was encouraged to move. In this situation a woman was able to operate legally and without being labelled as a 'common prostitute', but only by herself and in isolated circumstances. It is my contention that the two Acts cannot be looked at separately as they work against each other in ways which increase the vulnerability of an already disadvantaged section of the community. And this state of vulnerability is achieved through a policy of deterrence which criminalises prostitution-related activities, leaving women prey to exploitation and violence, either in isolated flats or in shadowy back-streets.

Consequently, I am arguing that the Wolfenden recommendations were used to strengthen the impact of a law which incorporated the 'common prostitute' as a member of a legally defined group of women and placed a judicial stamp of approval on the type of social stigmatisation set out above. This enabled legislators to formulate normally unacceptable measures (including a presupposition of guilt, arrest without warrant on police evidence alone and the prostitutes' caution) in order to ensure prosecution. These measures were rejected in the late 1960s, following an attempt at reform, by a majority of politicians in the House of Lords when it was suggested that the same principles should be applied to the all-inclusive category of 'any person'. In addition I argue that despite the initial success of the 1959 Act, in sweeping women off the streets and into call-girl flats, the policy resulted in a substantial increase in all forms of prostitution, which aggravated the problems for the police and the welfare agencies.

There are also a number of unavoidable subsidiary arguments that grow out of the debate, the most contentious of which is the continuing discussion about morals. The Wolfenden Committee used as the rationale for its argument the proposition that the law was not about morals but about the protection of the public from what was harmful and injurious. On the other hand it was perfectly clear that senior judges, politicians, the media and a large proportion of the public believed that the law *was* concerned with morals, particularly when it dealt with prostitution. Yet they still embraced the Wolfenden solution. This contradiction was encapsulated by the third government committee appointed to address the issues (the Vagrancy and Street Offences Working Party 1976), which supported the status quo by claiming that 'the conduct with which the law seeks to deal is conduct which people find offensive precisely because it is committed by prostitutes in pursuing their calling'.[55]

Further contradictions are created by the officially supported argument that prostitution is a trade or a profession which women willingly adopt as a way of life.[56] But while the law acts in ways that withdraw civil rights from prostitutes[57] and makes it almost impossible to practise the occupation legally, there is little appreciation amongst policy-makers of the need to protect the women from the violent and exploitative punter. I maintain, therefore, that the regulation of a legal trade, which prostitution is, should provide protection as well as controls.

Much of the ambiguity that arises out of English law originates from the fact that prostitution is not in itself an offence, although the air of criminality that surrounds it leaves many people believing otherwise. This misunderstanding is fostered by references to 'convicted prostitutes', the creation of 'vice squads' and the collation of 'statistics related to prostitution offences'. Yet the Wolfenden Committee founded its recommendations on the basis that the law was about public order and about protecting the innocent from exploitation, and not about morals.

The final thread to weave its way through this work is the issue of children who become prostitutes. Concern over the sexual exploitation of children was the driving force behind the protective legislation of 1885–1922, which was consolidated in 1956. These anxieties were set aside in favour of pushing prostitution out of sight and, as a result, young girls became increasingly vulnerable to charges of loitering or soliciting and exposed to sexual abuse and exploitation by older men. But although it cannot be disputed that the Street Offences Act 1959 was effective in its aim of clearing the streets the problems that it generated prompted a fourth review of the law, this time by the Criminal Law Revision Committee (CLRC) 1980–86. The recommendations of this committee led to the criminalisation of kerb-crawling, and, to some extent, of the solicitation of women by men. The resulting Sexual Offences Act 1985[58] increased the complexity of the law and, while appearing to introduce an element of equality of treatment, it heightened the vulnerability of prostitutes by increasing the necessary speed of kerb-side transactions. This leaves the street-worker with insufficient time to judge the intentions of a potentially violent punter.

This book is primarily about the history and development of parliamentary legislation and policy as they applied to female prostitution in England and Wales during the twentieth century. The first two chapters, which address the historical, philosophical and legislative backgrounds to prostitution, lean heavily upon secondary sources. However, the remainder of the work makes use of primary sources. Part II concentrates upon the deliberations of the Wolfenden Committee as revealed through Home Office papers, while the final two sections deal with the aftermath of the legislation, the discourse over morals, and the attempts to amend the 1959 Act. As a social scientist with a varied background I have not approached the subject of prostitution from a narrow legalistic angle but from a broader historical and sociological perspective, for the purely legal angle has been covered adequately by other scholars.[59]

More particularly the work focuses on the legislation imposed upon female prostitutes by a predominantly male legislature, largely because this is the topic that interests me and because the law has assumed that a 'common prostitute' is a woman,[60] as was confirmed in the Wolfenden Report, where it was stated that: 'It would take us beyond our terms of reference to investigate in detail the prevalence of prostitution or the reasons which lead women to adopt this manner of life.'[61] This assumption was upheld more recently in *DPP* v. *Bull* (1994)[62] when a charge was brought against Andrew John Bull for 'loitering for the purpose of prostitution' contrary to section 1(1) of the Street Offences Act 1959. The magistrate dismissed the action on the ground that there was no case to answer. It proceeded to the Divisional Court where Lord Justice Mann and Mr Justice Laws upheld the judgment. In summing up Lord Justice Mann stated that, 'the term "common prostitute" is ordinarily regarded as applying to a woman . . . in my judgment and with the confirmation of the Wolfenden Committee report the legislation is neither ambiguous, obscure nor productive of absurdity'.[63] Plainly, the mischief that the Act was intended to remedy was a mischief created by women.

I have also approached my subject from a liberal rather than from a radical feminist angle, as I believe that the law is of central importance to women, both in reflecting change and in other circumstances resisting regressive reforms. My approach to the subject has been aptly summed up by Smart, who, at the end of a chapter on the attitudes of magistrates towards prostitutes, wrote:

> Working in any area of law reform raises the possibility of perpetuating the cause of the problem by ameliorating its symptoms. But we have to realise that working for reforms is not always an attempt to ameliorate a static situation, but is frequently an attempt to stop a situation from deteriorating further. In this respect there is little option for feminists but

to confront the law, even though working on specific campaigns around prostitution sustains the very distinction between prostitute women and non-prostitute women which is so divisive. Arguably a major priority must be to remove the legal category of common prostitute, which, as we have seen, lends support to conventional wisdom about divisions between moral classes of women. If the law ceased to be able to define the issues around which the women's movement should organise, it would be far easier to concentrate on the issues that unite rather than those that have always successfully divided women.[64]

Finally, I would like to remind the reader that this book is a historical narrative, and therefore I have used the words 'prostitute' and 'prostitution' within their historical context as these are the words used in legal texts and documents. One of my aims has been to make a distinction between the word prostitute and the term 'common prostitute' as incorporated within statute in order to create a distinct and recognisable group of women who may be prosecuted for loitering or soliciting. That is not to say that I am unaware of the stigma attached to the designation of prostitute. Indeed, most of the terminology is offensive in one way or another. However, by the end of the twentieth century new terms had been adopted in order to overcome the stigmatisation associated with prostitution. These include 'sex work', 'sex worker' and 'sex industry', and consequently they appear in the final chapter.

NOTES

1. Leader, 1 July 1885, 'The Foreign Element of the Great Social Evil', *William Acton Scrap Book*, The Women's Library, London (hereafter WL).
2. *Vigilance Record*, July 1899, p. 7. Canon Scott Holland (1847–1918), Canon of Truro in 1882 and St Paul's in 1884; Regius Professor and Canon of Christ Church 1910.
3. See Chapter 2 for an account of the Magdalene movement.
4. The Penal Reform League became the Howard League for Penal Reform in 1921.
5. Penal Reform League, 'Prostitution: Its Nature and Cure', London (1912), pp. 11–12.
6. See F. S. Bullock, 'White Slave Traffic', New Scotland Yard, 12 June 1913, (PRO) MEPO, 2/1312, p. 4. Bullock was the Central Authority in the UK who was responsible for collecting information on trafficking and overseeing the implementation of the International Convention on the Suppression of the White Slave Traffic, signed in Paris, 4 May 1910.
7. Ibid.
8. A. F. Tredgold, 'Mental Deficiency in Relation to Venereal Disease', National Council for Combating Venereal Disease, London (1918), pp. 7–8. A. F. Tredgold was the medical expert who gave evidence to the Royal Commission on the Care and Control of the Feeble Minded 1908.
9. London County Council Medical Officer of Health, 'Common Lodging-Houses and Kindred Institutions', London County Council (1927), pp. 12–13.
10. In this context the word 'vicious' was used to imply debauchery.
11. League of Nations (LN), Advisory Commission for the Protection and Welfare of Children and Young People, 'Minutes of the Ninth Session', 9 April 1930 [C. 246. M. 121], pp. 91–2.
12. LN Advisory Committee on Social Questions, 'Prevention of Prostitution, A Study of Measures Adopted or Under Consideration Particularly with Regard to Minors' (1943) [C.26. M. 26.], pp. 42–63.
13. The Institute for the Scientific Treatment of Delinquency was founded in 1932 and based at

the London School of Economics. Areas of study included criminology, juvenile delinquency, social and behavioural disorders, mental health, psychology, social work and probation work. The official organ of the institute was the *British Journal of Delinquency.*

14. Edward Glover, 'The Psycho-Pathology of Prostitution', London (1945), p. 6.

15. LN, 'Prevention of Prostitution', pp. 52–3.

16. Jill Dawson (2000), *Fred and Edie*, Hodder and Stoughton, London, p. 275.

17. The Association of Moral and Social Hygiene (AMSH) was created out of the Ladies'
National Association and the British Branch of the Abolitionist Federation, both of which
were established to fight the state regulation of prostitution in the 1870s.

18. Edward. J. Bristow (1977), *Vice and Vigilance*, Gill and Macmillan, Rowman and Littlefield,
Dublin; Frank Mort, (1987), *Dangerous Sexualities: Medico-moral Politics in England since
1830*, Routledge and Kegan Paul, London; Lucy Bland (1995), *Banishing the Beast: English
Feminism and Sexual Morality, 1883–1995*, Penguin Books, London.

19. *Shield*, September 1929. 'Solicitation laws' included all legislation, including local acts and
by-laws, which referred to the 'common prostitute' loitering and/or soliciting in public places.

20. Details of this campaign, and the responses of the different police forces can be found in
3/AMS Box 314, WL.

21. A copy of the Public Places (Order) Bill can be found amongst the evidence submitted by the
AMSH to the Wolfenden Committee. See (PRO) HO. 345/8.

22. See James Morton (1998), *Bent Coppers*, Warner Books, London, p. 257.

23. Nancy Witcher Langhorne Astor, succeeded her husband William Waldorf, 1st Viscount
Astor (1848–1919), MP for Plymouth (1919). She was the first woman to sit in the House of
Commons. Lord Balfour of Burleigh, 11th Baron. Representative Peer for Scotland 1923–63;
Chairman of Medical Research Council 1936–1948; Director Lloyds Bank 1945–63;
President of the AMSH 1949.

24. For a history of these measures see 'Report of the Street Offences Committee 1928' (hereafter referred to as Cmd. 3231), paras. 22–34.

25. This sort of case could be pursued under a number of Acts which were outside the main legislation, including: a) Parks Regulation Act 1872: First Schedule, para. 16, 'No person shall
wilfully interfere with or annoy any other person using or enjoying a park'; b) Metropolitan
Police Act 1839, sub-section 13: 'Every person who shall use any threatening abusive or insulting words or behaviour with intent to provoke a breach of the peace or whereby a breach of
the peace may be occasioned.' c) Hyde Park General Regulation Acts, 1872 and 1926.

26. *The Times*, 9 and 16 October 1922, appearance and conviction of Sir Almeric Fitzroy in
Marlborough Street Police Court, *The Times*, 10 and 11 November, appeal upheld.

27. AMSH, 'Prostitution and Solicitation', reprint of Annual Report 1924–5, p. 7, 3/AMS, Box
314, WL.

28. Alison Nielans to the Bishop of Kingston, 5 May 1925, 3/JBS/2, Box 134, WL.

29. See *The Times*, 23 May 1928, for the case of Miss O'Malley, who was charged on police evidence with soliciting. She was able to produce medical evidence that she was *virgo intacta* and
the case was dismissed. The magistrate (Mr Graham-Campbell) stopped the case and commented that he had to be satisfied that the defendant was a common prostitute. H. W.
Wilberforce, the Deputy Chairman: London Sessions (28 April 1928), upbraided the police,
stating that it was essential to provide evidence that a woman was a 'common prostitute' and
that it was the duty of the police to make every effort to obtain corroborative evidence. Yet
another case involved a Major Bell Murray, who was acquitted of a charge of being drunk
and annoying women. For a comment on both cases see Alison Nielans' letter to the Bishop
and Members of the House of Commons, 5 May 1925, 3/JBS/2, Box 134, WL.

30. *The Times*, 2 May 1928.

31. Ibid. The case was covered extensively between 25 April and 12 June 1928. See also Morton,
Bent Coppers, pp. 69–71.

32. *The Times*, 18 May 1928, accusations against the police of giving false evidence.

33. See Clive Emsley (1991), *The English Police: A Political and Social History*, Harvester
Wheatsheaf, New York, pp. 135–6.

34. Criminal Statistics of the Metropolitan Police. Annual Total Charges for Street Solicitation
in the Metropolitan Police District 1920–53.

35. *Shield*, September 1929; A. Henderson, Labour Home Secretary, 22 January 1924–
4 November 1924.

36. *Shield*, September 1929. The NVA, the Church of England and refuge and reformatory
workers lobbied for an extension of the solicitation laws.

37. This coincided with a Criminal Law Amendment Bill, which had similar provisions (discussed in Chapter 11).

38. Cmd. 3231, appointed on the 14 October 1927. The AMSH had misgivings over the appointment of a number of committee members whom it considered unlikely to be 'impartial', including Sir Chartres Biron, Chief Magistrate for the Metropolis, Sir Leonard Dunning, an Inspector of Constabulary and Lady Joynson-Hicks, wife of the Home Secretary.

39. For the life of Lord Hugh Macmillan see: Lord Macmillan (1953), *A Man of Law's Tale*, Macmillan, London. Macmillan took silk in 1912 and became Lord Advocate in 1930. He is perhaps best remembered for his part in the celebrated negligence case, the 'Snail in the Ginger Beer Bottle', *Donoghue* v. *Stevenson* [1932] A.C. 562; 1932 S.C. (H.L.), in which his casting vote affirmed the duty of the manufacturer to take care that his product was not injurious to the health of the consumer.

40. The term 'immoral purpose' is used ubiquitously within government texts and references, but is rarely used within statutes, thus it reflects the perceptions of government officials and contributes towards the confusion which envelopes both official and unofficial discussions.

41. Cmd. 3231, p. 4.

42. Carol Smart (1995), *Law, Crime and Sexuality: Essays in Feminism*, Sage Publications, London, p. 64.

43. Cmd. 3231, pp. 28–9. The proposed offences would still have applied to women as it was agreed that soliciting between men was covered by the Vagrancy Act 1898.'Importuning' was to be defined as offensive words or behaviour. 'Offensive words' presumably meant soliciting and 'molesting' meant handling. 'Nuisance' in the second offence would require evidence of annoyance from the person concerned.

44. The fight against the double standard of morality was a central issue for many feminist groups during the early part of the twentieth century.

45. *Shield*, September 1929, pp. 223–38.

46. Problems were to arise during the late 1960s, when the Society supported the inclusion of the term 'immoral purpose' in Lord Chorley's Bill to amend the Street Offences Act 1959.

47. See James Timwell, 'The Royal Commission on the Metropolitan Police: The Truth About the Enquiry', published by The Police and Public Vigilance Society (undated, probably 1910).

48. Royal Commission Upon the Duties of the Metropolitan Police 1908, Cd. 4260–3; Royal Commission on Police Powers and Procedures 1929, Cmd. 3297.

49. Cmd. 3231, para. 56.

50. Cmd. 3297, 196–204.

51. Ibid.

52. During this earlier period the number of prosecutions for soliciting offences were higher, averaging around 10,500 and the convictions were lower, averaging around 9,000. See Report of the Committee on Homosexual Offences and Prostitution (1957), Cmd. 247, Official Statistics, Appendix 11, p. 143 (hereafter Cmnd. 247).

53. Street Offences Act 1959 [7 & 8 Eliz. 2. c. 57].

54. Sexual Offences Act 1956 [4 & 5 Eliz. 2. c. 69].

55. Working Party on Vagrancy and Street Offences Working Party (1974), para. 234.

56. Ibid., para. 234, 'it can equally be contended that there is no reason why prostitution should not be subject to legal regulation as are other trades'.

57. The right to a fair trial, lack of family life, restrictions on movement, restricted access to welfare services, taking children into care, etc. Moreover, although a prostitute is also obliged to pay tax if the Inland Revenue catches up with her, she may not register as a business.

58. Sexual Offences Act 1985 [Eliz. 2. c. 44].

59. Abraham A. Scion (1977), *Prostitution and the Law*, Faber and Faber, London; Peter Rook and Robert Ward (1993), *Sexual Offences*, Sweet and Maxwell, London.

60. The Sexual Offences Act 1967 section 5 (1) creates an offence of knowingly living wholly or in part on the earnings of another man. Section 6 provided for offences which are in line with sections 33 to 35 of the Sexual Offences Act 1956 and refer to brothels. It is, therefore, acknowledged that a man may be a prostitute, but not a 'common prostitute'.

61. Cmnd. 247, para. 223.

62. *DPP* v. *Bull* (1994), 4 All. E.R. 411.

63. Ibid.

64. Smart, *Law, Crime and Sexuality*, p. 67.

PART I

The Regulation of Prostitution: Society and Law

CHAPTER 1

Technologies of Power

What is a woman but an enemy of friendship, an unavoidable punishment, a necessary evil, a natural temptation, a desirable affliction, a
constantly flowing source of tears, a wicked work of nature covered
with a shining varnish? (St Chrysostom, 347–407)

Within the grand catalogue of criminal offences, the asking for a reward by a
young woman in return for a sexual service must surely rate as a trivial misdemeanour.[1] Yet across the centuries and within many cultures, the female
prostitute has been a focus of anxiety for those who wish to regulate society.
The study of the prostitute and prostitution engages a variety of disciplines,
including theology, medicine, politics, law, social policy, sociology, history, literature, art, and the generalised social observation of human frailty, of which
most of us are guilty. Experts and social commentators have catalogued, analysed, pathologised, legislated and fantasised, while the well-meaning have
rescued, redeemed, protected and punished. Many anxious observers have
looked for causes, and have sought a cure for a presumed malady afflicting
women whose behaviour is often seen as a barometer of social ills.

This chapter looks at some of the ways in which female prostitution has
been rationalised by social thinkers, theologians and medics, and examines the
biblical roots of stigmatisation. It illustrates the ways in which various groups
and individuals have sought to define the prostitute's behaviour as different
from normal womanly conduct (for example, sinful, pathological, or danger-
ously contagious), and in so doing, confirm her diminished status and justify
the need for regulation and control.

THE THEOLOGY OF CONTROLLING BODIES

During the nineteenth century the state apparatus for controlling deviance
developed in a variety of ways. Among the techniques listed by Stanley Cohen[2]
are the centralised and rationalised bureaucratic apparatus, the classification
of deviant groups into different types and categories, their separation into

purpose-built institutions, and the decline of punishments involving physical pain in favour of influencing the mind of the individual. This transformation, so elegantly described by Michel Foucault,[3] is said to have taken place at the end of the eighteenth century and at the beginning of the nineteenth. In contrast to this approach, I would suggest that the control of women through a process of classification, segregation and reformation preceded the development of the prison and the asylum by many centuries and had similar objectives. The incarceration of both 'troublesome' and 'compliant' women in institutions including convents, municipal brothels, reformatories, penitentiaries, Magdalene and Lock hospitals was an established practice well before the nineteenth century. The convent (and the reformatory) served a variety of functions apart from the purely religious or penitential as, for many women, they were places of refuge or retirement free from the perils of repeated pregnancy and of controlling male company.[4]

During the Middle Ages the penitentiary was more common on the continent of Europe than in Britain, and it expanded in importance when the reclamation of prostitutes developed into something of a crusade. Justification for the reformatory focused upon assumptions about the intrinsic sinfulness of women that were supported by Judaeo-Christian theology. Salvation was to be achieved through penitence, and it was to this end that convents under the patronage of Mary Magdalene were established and began to proliferate under the sponsorship of a succession of popes.[5]

The appeal of Mary Magdalene to the early Fathers of the Catholic Church is conveyed by Benedicta Ward,[6] who interprets the theological reasoning that underpinned the movement. She found that Mary Magdalene was a composite character, created out of several women named 'Mary' mentioned in the New Testament, and claimed that, 'The Middle Ages both contracted her person and expanded her history . . . Out of several women they made one, and then examined the possibilities open to this composite person.' The potency of the legend was such that it was impossible to think of her as anything other than what the myth had made her. Ward writes that:

> Mary Magdalene has always been one of the most popular of saints, perhaps because of the extremes of her career from prostitute to hermit, from sin to sanctity, from grief to glory. She has been seen from the earliest times in scripture and in liturgy as the one woman who, with the mother of Jesus, shared with the apostles the rare and essential distinction of having been with the Lord. She has been called the 'apostle to the apostles', the 'friend' and even the beloved of Christ, a sinful woman who loved greatly and was forgiven much.[7]

Although her name became synonymous with prostitute, her status as such is not confirmed in the Gospels. She was described variously as a woman out of whom Jesus had cast several devils, a woman of the city who was a sinner and a woman who loved much. The story of Mary Magdalene is of central importance to the Christian message. Her strength lies in the provision of an icon for the redemption of original sin (and therefore redemption of women), which complements the purity of the Virgin Mary, whose sanctity and chastity the majority of women cannot hope to emulate. The two Marys are described by Marina Warner[8] as 'a diptych of Christian patriarchy's idea of woman', the two female figures being seen in the opposing sexual terms of virgin and whore. She argues that Magdalene, like Eve, was brought into existence by the powerful undertow of misogyny in Christianity which associated women with the dangers and degradation of the flesh. The purity of the Virgin made Mary Magdalene an essential contrast: she became the new 'Eve' and represented the first signs of the possibility for a reversal of the fall of Adam, which had separated man from the love of God. Mary Magdalene's role in discovering the empty tomb and proclaiming the resurrection became critical to the story of the New Testament, because it extended the possibility of redemption to women. In the words of St Gregory the Great, 'Lo, the guilt of the human race is cut off whence it proceeded. For in paradise a woman gave death to man; now from the tomb a woman announces life to men and tells the words of the Life-giver, just as a woman (Eve) told the words of the death-bearing serpent.'[9]

And of Peter Chrysolougus:

> On this latter day, a woman runs to grace who earlier ran to guilt. In the evening she seeks Christ who in the morning knew she had lost Adam. 'Then cometh Mary and the other Mary to the sepulchre'. Matthew (28. 1). She who had taken perfidy from paradise hastens to take faith from the sepulchre; she hastens to snatch life from death who has snatched death from life.[10]

The theological significance of Mary Magdalene stretches far beyond her presumed promiscuity, and she became synonymous with the image of unfaithful Israel that is found in the imagery of sin throughout the scriptures. Ward considers this mystery:

> Mary Magdalene takes to herself the image of unfaithful Israel, so graphically described by the prophets as a prostitute in relation to God. This image was transferred by the New Testament writers to the whole of humanity in the new covenant and therefore each soul in sin can be described as a prostitute. Just as the sin of Eve was described as lust because that image best describes the disobedience of the fall, so the sins of Mary of Magdella were seen as prostitution; that is, unfaithfulness to the love which is the name of God.[11]

The view of the prostitute as the embodiment of sin was encapsulated by St Paul in his letter to the Corinthians (1 C 6: 15–17) in which he equates sex with spirituality.[12]

> Know ye not that your bodies are members of Christ? Shall I then take the members of Christ and make *them* the members of a harlot? God

forbid. What? know ye not he who is joined to a harlot is one body? For two, saith he, shall be one flesh. But he that is joined to the Lord is one spirit.

St Paul laid down the foundations of the belief that celibacy was superior to marriage, thereby increasing the significance of women's responsibility for sexual incontinence and making sex with a harlot inadmissible. He also bequeathed to the world a view of womanhood which was elaborated upon by later theologians, including St Augustine and St Thomas Aquinas,[13] largely to the detriment of women. The dogma of original sin has remained at the heart of the doctrinal contradictions that, according to Karen Armstrong,[14] are an invention of Christianity that has been used by the Church to condemn any natural human enjoyment of sex.[15]

> Every flicker of desire is an experience of essential sin and a reminder of our sinful nature. Augustine bequeathed to the West a terror of sin as a raging and ungovernable force. And there at the heart of each formulation of the doctrine is the woman, Eve, the 'cause of all the misery, all that burden of guilt and evil, all that human wallowing in sin. Sin, sex and women are bound together in an unholy trinity.[16]

The power of the Catholic Church meant that theological teaching was translated into dogma, and from dogma into policy and action. However, the contradictions presented by the potency of the sexual drive, the sanctity of marriage and the fear of damnation made the institution of prostitution inevitable. It became the 'lesser' or the 'necessary' evil permitted in order to safeguard more cherished institutions and to prevent men from committing graver sins. Justifications multiplied. 'If you eliminate prostitutes from society,' declared St Augustine, 'you disrupt everything with lust.'[17]

Jacques Rossiaud[18] describes the situation in the south-east region of France in the medieval period. The municipal brothel was seen to fulfil a dual function of servicing the needs of young unmarried men and of protecting the virtue of wives and daughters. 'No-one went to the brothel furtively. For young men whoring was a way of life . . . and proof of physiological normality.'[19] Prostitution developed into an organised and institutionalised way of life. A similar situation in Reformation Augsburg is described by Lyndal Roper,[20] who shifts the fulcrum of the debate from the sinfulness of women to the proprietary rights of men. At the beginning of the Reformation, the municipal brothel was seen as a civic resource, with complimentary visits being awarded to visiting dignitaries. The municipal women were subject to regular inspection and distinguished from other women by the clothes they wore, although they retained some dignity and status within the town and a right to participate in a variety of religious ceremonies.

From the viewpoint of the authorities the municipal brothel offered many advantages. It provided a means of regulating prostitution, limited the spread of disease, helped to maintain social order by keeping the sexual excesses of its citizens in check and raised a considerable amount of revenue. In addition, men were given access to a variety of women while the ideology of monogamy remained intact. When the Nürnberg Council found that some of its municipal women were giving preferential treatment to favoured clients, it ordered the practice to be stopped. Prostitutes were not allowed to develop disruptive practices that would imperil the distinction between the respectable women (wives and daughters) and the common woman who was owned by all. In Augsburg, as in other places, prostitution presented authorities with many problems as it placed in the public sphere an area of life that usually belonged to the private. Where regulation has existed, clandestine prostitution was harshly punished and the whores' claim to sexual autonomy was destroyed through enforced commonality.

Roper argues that if prostitution is a transaction it needs to be placed within the context of other exchanges taking place in a given society. In medieval Augsburg a seduced virgin could claim not only for child-bed and child support, but for the loss of her 'honour'. The woman's 'honour' was a material asset that could be sold, and it was separate from the woman herself. Similarly, in England a man could sue his wife's lover for 'criminal conversation', or the loss of *his property* in her domestic and reproductive services. In Augsburg the wife's virginity was also sold, which was acknowledged by a traditional gift given to the bride the morning after the wedding. She then gained a new honour as wife, which was tied to her continued fidelity. Roper writes that, 'in prostitution the woman is classed as "dishonourable" because she has severed the link between money and fidelity to one man . . . but the bond between money and sexual ownership remains, for she is owned by all men'.[21]

The theme of male ownership is a potent one. Phyllis Trible[22] elaborates on the Hebrew scriptures in which the wombs of women belong to God. Sarah is betrayed by her husband Abraham who, pretending that she is his sister, permits King Abimelech to take her into his harem. God punishes Abraham by closing every womb of the house of Abimelech, but with the liberation of Sarah divine blessing comes to the other females: 'Yahweh, who has closed wombs in judgment for sin, opens them for fertility.' Man made in the image of God assumes this ownership. Abraham may give away the womb of his sister but not the womb of his wife, which remains a sacred possession, a covenant with God, to be reserved for his own seed.

Eve, formed from the rib of Adam, was not granted the privilege of personhood. In adultery or prostitution the woman assumes possession of her own person: she no longer belongs to the man, therefore the sin remains with her.[23] The theme of male ownership is brought out sharply through the story in Judges 19: 1–30. It begins with a declaration of love when the unnamed Master goes after a woman who has already left him. He 'speaks to her heart' and persuades her to accompany him on a journey, but on finding himself in alien territory he protects himself from an angry mob by giving them his concubine. They rape and abuse the Master's concubine throughout the night and leave her clinging to his host's doorstep in the morning. On returning home

with the woman strapped to his donkey, he expresses his anger and humiliation by dismembering her body, making twelve portions which he distributes
throughout all the tribes of Israel.[24] Proprietorial attitudes towards women
rest on such texts.

Change came for Augsburg with the Reformation and the city brothel was
closed in 1532, 14 years before the Southwark stews in London were closed by
Henry VIII.[25] As Protestantism began to flourish in England, the ambivalent
attitudes of the Catholic Church gave way to a harsher ethic. The fallen
woman became an agent of the Devil and the licensed brothel became the
mark of a godless society.[26] Prostitution was seen as a product of papistry and
became, increasingly, a secular concern. Olwen Hufton writes that, in
Protestant regions, most of the evidence comes from the law courts. 'We see
the prostitute through the prism of the judge and the prosecuting authorities.
She emerges as a criminal.'[27] The licensed brothel disappeared on the
Continent during the seventeenth century and prostitution became increasingly subjected to secular control. As the responsibility for regulating prostitution shifted from the Church to the state and police regulation, the emphasis
moved away from the maintenance of social harmony to the reduction of
syphilis, especially within the military.

Prostitution in Britain developed differently from on the Continent; there
was no shortage of 'strumpets', but also no municipal brothel nor Magdalene
convents to house them. By the middle of the eighteenth century, the unruly privately owned brothel became a feature of urban life that was troublesome to the
authorities. Concern mounted over the twin issues of illegitimacy and prostitution. The brothers John and Henry Fielding[28] proposed a variety of measures
to deal with them, including a laundry that was to be set up to provide work for
orphaned girls. Others had more coercive objectives, for example Saunders
Welch, the High Constable of Holborn, who suggested that a hospital should
be erected to house prostitutes until they repented.[29] In 1758 a Magdalene
Home was established in St George's Field through the auspices of a London
silk merchant, Robert Bingley. It was intended as a retreat for the purposes of
reform, but became a popular attraction due to the sermons delivered in its
public chapel by the charismatic preacher Dr William Dodd. Eric Trudgill[30]
argues that although the constitution of the Magdalene Home was genuinely
humane, a mawkish sentimentality developed which, far from softening hearts,
had the opposite effect. 'The sermons and poems of Dodd, still more the series
of novelettish penitent histories allegedly, but most improbably, written by the
inmates of the Home, helped to foster a species of self-indulgent, complacent
philanthropy moved more by maudlin fiction than magdalen fact.'[31]

THE NINETEENTH-CENTURY MAGDALENE MOVEMENT

The moral climate of Britain changed in the aftermath of the French
Revolution and official attitudes towards the prostitute hardened. The rise of

the Evangelical movement was a reaction to the laxity of the eighteenth-century Enlightenment culture. Trudgill writes of the transformation of the public's image of the prostitute. She was 'no longer the daughter of wretchedness nor the elegant penitent, but a recalcitrant sinner to be won to repentance with severity and discipline'.[32] Protestant theology meant that the mind of the fornicator was concentrated upon the consequences of sin, as he lacked the redemptive balm of the confessional.

Over the years the Magdalene movement expanded and diversified, giving way to a far more coercive and oppressive philosophy that was driven by a quest for retribution as well as for repentance. The Evangelicals became increasingly involved in rescue work and by the time of the accession of Queen Victoria in 1837, the Religious Tract Society had issued five hundred million tracts on the subject.[33] The Society for the Suppression of Vice, founded in 1802,[34] busied itself with the prosecution of obscene publications, Sunday trading, the closing of bawdy houses and with lobbying for changes in the law. Michael Mason[35] finds that the Vice Society was 'unique amongst all Evangelically derived bodies in tackling moral questions by means of law', aiming to bring the power of the police and courts to bear upon moral transgression. In the late 1880s the National Vigilance Association (NVA)[36] incorporated the Vice Society and employed similar tactics. It cooperated with the police and pursued prosecutions in an effort to close down brothels and drive prostitutes off the streets. Repressive operations became a feature of the nineteenth-century moral missionary movement in which middle-class women took a prominent part.

During the 1850s, prostitution became a matter of considerable public concern and new ways were devised for encouraging women to enter penitentiaries. The Midnight Meeting movement launched in 1849 by John Blackmore and Theophilus Smith offered tea and sermons to prostitutes.[37] These meetings served as recruiting grounds for penitents who were then redirected into asylums. Middle-class women became increasingly involved in various forms of missionary work. They proselytised, raised funds and sat on 'Ladies' Committees' appointed to oversee the running of homes. As the inmates were generally working-class, the system served to strengthen, rather than break down, class barriers.

The growth of rescue work and the setting up of asylums, penitentiaries and reformatories continued throughout the nineteenth century until all religious groups were involved. Mason estimates that by 1860 there were 2,500 places available in English asylums, and Bristow[38] suggests that by 1900 there were over three hundred homes and refuges caring for about six thousand women annually. To this figure has to be added the inestimable number of women who were targeted through non-institutional channels. Ultimately a very large number of 'unfortunate' women found their way into the various organizations established for their moral reformation. Underpinning the philosophy of the movement was an intention to retrain women for 'useful' work in the community, although most commentators point out[39] that they were frequently sent back into the occupations in which they had experienced their downfall, namely domestic service. Servants were in a particularly vulnerable position. Many of them were very young, lived far from home and earned only a few pounds per year, plus board, lodging and uniform. If a girl was mistreated, sexually abused or became pregnant, she might lose her 'character' and find great difficulty in obtaining alternative employment. For women who found themselves in this position, or who worked in the sweated trades, or who eked out a living through seasonal work, prostitution could provide a much needed alternative source of income.

At the inception of the British Magdalene movement, it was believed that the penitentiary would provide a more appropriate and humane way of dealing with 'wayward' women than placing them in prisons or poor houses, although there is little doubt that many institutions were prisons in all but name. The essence of the movement was its voluntary nature, yet some buildings were surrounded by high walls to prevent escape. Many young women rebelled and tried to abscond but, having nowhere to go, were frequently picked up by the police and returned to the home. Managements generally worked in partnership with the municipal authorities, although they were less accountable for organisational procedures than a state institution. In addition, the need to raise funds meant that the inmates were frequently exploited in an effort to undercut the local laundry trade. Redemption might sometimes involve a variety of coercive measures, including shaven heads, institutional uniforms, bread and water diets, restricted visiting, supervised correspondence, solitary confinement and even flogging.[40] In addition to these privations, the women would be subjected to religious indoctrination, leaving the 'successfully reformed' obsessed with a morbid sense of sin.

The diversity of controls and the developing trend towards repressive legislation have been demonstrated by Linda Mahood[41] in her study of the reformatory movement in nineteenth-century Scotland. Her work is interesting in the context of this study as the Glasgow system of police regulation became the blueprint for the Street Offences Act 1959. Mahood discovered a high degree of cooperation between local state representatives and philanthropic organisations, endeavouring to force middle-class standards of sexual and vocational propriety on working-class women.[42] These women were scrutinised, stigmatised and targeted through the legislation aimed at 'cleaning up the streets'. She claims that the classification of 'prostitute' was, like that of the 'homosexual', a created category invented by moral reformers who wished to impose an 'alien' interpretation on the activities of working-class women. The label was applied gratuitously to classify women whose mode of dress, behaviour and physical appearances were not acceptable. She concluded that the definition of who was or was not a prostitute was deeply political.

The presence of unaccompanied young women on the streets was acutely unsettling for middle-class Victorian society, with its carefully guarded and chaperoned daughters. When seemingly unruly females collected in numbers, mistrust was amplified. This 'fear' was played upon much later by the Wolfenden

Committee and was to become one of the main points used to rationalise its recommendations.[43] The increasing numbers of independent working women became a cause of concern and was especially resented when they showed signs of financial freedom and personal autonomy. Independent young women were simultaneously criticised for 'immodesty', 'unwomanly' behaviour, 'vanity' and 'love of finery' as their behaviour suggested that they were not acquiring the necessary skills for their true vocation as wives and mothers.

This section has provided only a brief overview, but it highlights a number of important markers which are relevant to this study. At the beginning of the nineteenth century, moralists had tended to refer to all promiscuous women as prostitutes. The single mother was viewed as an immoral character and was often sent to the workhouse to prevent the child from becoming a charge upon the parish. Prostitution and vagrancy presented the only rational choice left open to such marginalised women. As a social category the stigmatising label of 'prostitute' was fluid; it provided a means of socially controlling both the virtuous and the deviant woman since the prostitute became an outcast and despised member of the community. The evolution of the nineteenth century brought the development of a police force and new forms of containment, which provided the framework through which the state and moralists could increasingly use the law as a means for imposing moral strictures upon working-class communities. The use of law required stricter definitions of terms with the result that the flexible moralising definitions contended with the fixed and legal. As the key terms of 'prostitute', 'prostitution' and 'brothel' were never statutorily determined, freedom was retained within the developing legal framework for personal interpretations, leading to ambiguity and contradiction.

REPRESENTATION

'Women have no history,' declared Virginia Woolf in 1929. 'The history of England is the history of the male line.'[44] Over fifty years later Dale Spender railed against the patriarchal society that had silenced women's voices. 'Men have enclosed the events of their lives, written them down, passed them on and constructed a visible, active and glorious line of male descent'.[45] Spender argued that in a male-dominated society, the 'experts' were men, denying women the reassurance of female authority. While knowledge was constructed by men, the significance of women was seen only in relation to men's experience. The majority of women gained significance and approbation through marriage, as wives, mothers and daughters. Alternatively they might be condemned or eroticised as participants in clandestine relationships outside the home.

Historically women have been represented in ways that reflect the fears and fantasies of men, reinforcing the political agenda of the time. The icon of woman ranges from the impossible perfection of the 'good wife . . . more precious than jewels'[46] to the passionless purity of the Virgin Mary, and conversely, through every possible shade of misogyny, ridicule, malice and hatred. Historical accounts of prostitution[47] have shown that the female prostitute has not always fallen within the later category. Roper's work on Augsburg shows that the position she holds in a given society and the level of acceptance have varied over time and within different cultures. The modern view of the prostitute and of prostitution have been coloured by Victorian social attitudes with its complex and contradictory responses to sexuality. It was during this period that the increasing pressures of industrialisation, the rise of the medical expert, the demographic imbalance and the ideology of a woman's place intensified concern over prostitution as a social issue. It became known as the 'great social evil'. The Victorian representation of women in polarised versions of good and evil became particularly divisive, with the depraved or 'fallen' woman of the streets being counterbalanced by the 'angel in the house' who protected the family from the harsh world of capitalism.[48] The 'pure woman', wrote Trudgill, was an outlet for quasi-religious emotion. She represented a 'symbolic confirmation of true Christian faith, and a foretaste of heavenly love and peace'.[49] The working-class woman was excluded from this paradise, so that the social construction of marriage and prostitution became mechanisms that reinforced class differences and separated women from each other.

The celebrated Victorian venereologist William Acton aptly portrayed these assumptions and cast women into alternative roles of 'pure' and 'fallen'. In doing so he conflated modesty with a lack of sensuality, writing:

> The majority of women (happily for them) are not very much troubled with sexual feelings of any kind . . . as a general rule a modest women seldom desires any sexual gratification for herself . . . The married woman has no wish to be treated on the footing of a mistress.[50]

Mason writes that, as far as he knows, this comment is without parallel within the sexual literature of the day. Yet within a year of publication it had crossed the Atlantic, and Dr William Sanger (1858) was confidently stating that 'the forces of desire can neither be denied nor disputed, but still in the bosom of most females that force exists in a slumbering state until aroused by some outside influence'.[51]

In contrast to the gentle image of the middle-class wife, the working-class woman with her muscular arms and red hands was seen as both sexually responsive and available to men.[52] The 'angel in the house' belonged to the private sphere, identified with property and with the accumulation of wealth, whereas the working woman belonged to the public sphere, which was a male province symbolised by common ownership and service. Acton perceived the prostitute in these terms, arguing inconsistently that whilst regulation was a necessary precaution to protect the armed forces from venereal disease, most prostitutes were healthy and vigorous with excellent constitutions. In 1868 he gave evidence to the Select Committee of the House of Lords during which he repudiated the Victorian image of the 'fallen woman' and maintained that prostitution was a temporary stage in a woman's life. He claimed that it was generally followed by an advantageous marriage, or by business enterprise, using the proceeds of her earnings.[53] Acton regarded prostitution as inevitable and ineradicable, believing that the best course of action was amelioration. He therefore promoted the Continental system of regulation, which included regular medical inspection and registration. In his evidence to the committee, Acton pursued his image of the robust woman, declaring that the vaginal inspection, for which a speculum was used, was performed with accuracy and great dispatch, the average time occupied being three minutes.[54] Not surprisingly many prostitutes felt otherwise, finding the procedure, which the feminists termed 'instrumental rape', both painful and disgusting.[55]

Frances Finnegan observed that although the Lords accepted Acton's evidence, he himself based his opinions on the theories of the French physician, Alex Parent-Duchatelet.[56] In his writings, Parent-Duchatelet reflected the Augustinian tradition of prostitution as a necessary evil contributing, 'like drains and refuge dumps', to the maintenance of social harmony and safeguarding respectable marriages. This notion gained acceptance during the Victorian period and was articulated through uninhibited expressions of the double standard, including those of the respected historian W. E. H. Lecky, whose notorious remark in his *History of European Morals* (1869) declared that although the prostitute was the symbol of degradation and sinfulness, she was ultimately the most efficient guardian of morals. 'But for her, the unchallenged purity of countless happy homes would be polluted.'[57] The rise of the medical expert, coupled with the high level of venereal infection in the armed forces, had a profound effect upon the way in which the prostitute was understood. She was represented as a 'reservoir of pollution', an 'emissary of death' and a threat to both the physical and spiritual health of the nation. Fear of the prostitute was resolved through measures of control, and it was to this end that regulation became established in many parts of the world.

Parent-Duchatelet is described by Alain Corbin[58] as the most prestigious theoretician and apostle of regulationism. His monograph, *De la prostitution dans la ville de Paris*, published in 1836, focused upon prostitution as a problem in public health, to be controlled and regulated by an enlightened government. Through his writings the prostitute was pathologised and seen as an active carrier of contagion, which legitimated coercive interference. He believed that the temporary nature of the prostitute's career posed a particular threat to society. They 'come back into society . . . they surround us . . . they gain access to our homes'. He maintained that it was necessary to know 'who' the prostitutes were in order to protect society from moral, social and sanitary contagion. He portrayed her as idle, improvident and dirty and believed that confinement or prison was a necessary counterbalance required to impose discipline. Corbin observes that Parent-Duchatelet's portrait of the child-like, pleasure-loving whore inspired many novelists and was subsequently repeated so often in literature that it distorted the vision of later researchers.[59]

In her study of Victorian prostitutes in York, Finnegan comes to a less colourful conclusion. Unlike the robust women of Acton's testimony, her research indicated that the majority of women involved in prostitution were uneducated, poor and unhealthy. Many of them were homeless or living in insanitary slums and frequently reduced to a state of utter destitution through alcoholism, disease and repeated imprisonment. She comments that, throughout the Victorian period, women consistently outnumbered men and many were obliged to compete for the limited employment opportunities which were mostly in domestic service.

Once outside the protective nucleus of the family, the unattached woman was perceived a problem, and political concern developed over the numbers of 'surplus' women. One of the most favoured solutions was emigration to the colonies where it was hoped that they might fulfil their true vocation as wives and mothers, whilst propagating Christian values and respect for the Motherland. The journalist William Greg addressed this problem in the *National Review*,[60] where he pointed out that many single women came from the middle classes and were not naturally suited to pioneering agriculture. He spoilt his argument with a degree of spitefulness, by referring to the 'old maids' who were 'too proud to sink, too sensitive or refined to toil, or too spoiled to purchase love at the expense of luxury'.[61] Greg was dismayed by the thought that any woman should be compelled to lead an incomplete and independent existence, rather than 'completing, sweetening and embellishing the existence of others'.

Greg was a commentator who made broad assumptions about women, reflecting the accepted opinion that, in addition to achieving true fulfilment through marriage, they had a 'positive duty' to serve men and to procreate. Many middle-class spinsters proved to be more spirited than Greg was prepared to give them credit for, and it was through their active discontent that the feminist movement was born. In his article on prostitution in the *Westminster Review*[62] he argued that lust was not the cause of women's fall into prostitution and claimed that female desire did not exist until intercourse had been experienced. He believed that the position of the prostitute would be greatly improved if she had a legally recognised role to fulfil. Greg was a regulationist who used the threat of disease as a way of rationalising coercive measures. His suggestions included building more lower-class housing, placing existing lodging houses under police surveillance, subjecting all prostitutes to regular medical inspection and removing the diseased to hospital. He played upon the generally held Victorian view of the prostitute as an impoverished and diseased outcast, describing her life as a litany of horrors and chiding middle-class women for their callous indifference.[63] Although their arguments were conflicting, both Greg and Acton sought to rationalise the need for regulation by identifying prostitutes as a specific group of women outside the common stream and in need of control.

In addition to the idea of genteel Victorian womanhood was the medically supported theory that regular intercourse was an essential part of men's private health. Writers such as August Debay (1802–90) promoted regular marital intercourse as a more appropriate and moral way of avoiding the hazards of infection.[64] Therefore a woman who had no sexual appetite was still expected to submit to her husband's needs. This was a line supported by Acton, who considered that withdrawal of conjugal rights for fear of pregnancy represented a mental disorder.

The woman's narrative is conspicuously absent from these 'expert' pronouncements, which mould the inclinations and desires of women to satisfy the needs of men. In the immediate term, the evidence of men such as Acton helped to influence legal, medical and social policies, even though their ideas were based upon assumptions and on a very partial understanding of women's desires. In the long term, it influenced a view of history that became accepted by future generations, making it difficult for people to bypass the myths and stereotypes that obscured reality. Roy Porter and Lesley Hall[65] elaborate some of the problems encountered by historians of sexual attitudes:

> Such traditional histories implicitly assumed the male voice . . . Feminists have exposed the male fantasy embedded in such views. They have shown that within patriarchy, sexuality has always been posited upon gendered divisions, and that because males have commanded political, military, economic and cultural power, it has been men who have specified sexual roles and sexual division of labour. This has resulted in all manner of male-constructed fantasies about the nature of the opposite sex – virgin, vamp, whore, the frigid, the femme fragile and femme fatale, and so forth: many blatantly contradictory, and mostly victim blaming.

Mason faced this difficulty when researching his study of Victorian sexual attitudes. He regretted that contemporary records were written by men and that the evidence used to illustrate women's sexual responses derived from men's utterances. He hoped that these facts would not distort his interpretation of women's role.

The outcome of bias has been that the dominant discourses of the time conceptualised women in ways that, we assume, had no grounding in reality, but which served only to perpetuate their subordinate role. At the same time, the limitations imposed by religious ideology and by its construction of women in fantasised roles (Madonna, angel in the house, whore, witch, and so on), made it easy for people to locate the prostitute as separate and detached from ordinary people, someone for whom special measures of control and regulation were necessary and appropriate. Middle-class men had constructed an ideology within which their sexual needs were overpowering and irresistible, though at the same time creating a family structure that required decorum and gentility. Prostitution was a counterbalance but it represented a health risk. The need for regulation was constructed and rationalised around class and gender difference, which separated the independent working-class whore from the 'normal' woman who conformed to the expectations of the culture. The defamation of the prostitute's character helped to rationalise these choices.

EDUCATION: THE MANIPULATION OF MINDS

The inability or unwillingness of some women to conform to the accepted patterns of feminine behaviour created problems for those wedded to conformity. For writers such as Acton and Greg, there was no satisfactory alternative to marriage and they were unwilling to confront the political implications of a demographic imbalance that left one in three women single and one in four who would never marry.[66] Many of these largely forgotten Victorian spinsters fought hard for equal educational opportunities, university entrance and access to the professions, which would provide them with alternatives to marriage.[67] Unfortunately they were obliged to battle against the established conviction that women's intellect was inferior to men's and that study was damaging to their reproductive health. There was also the suggestion that education was a form of selfish self-indulgence when it circumscribed procreation. The educational reformer and economist Dr W. B. Hodgson (1864) defensively remarked that it was unnecessary to 'maintain the absolute identity of the male and female constitutions' in order to make good the claim for a wide extension of female education.[68] Traditionally the education of girls was intended to provide upper- and middle-class women with feminine accomplishments befitting them for the marriage market, whereas the working-class girl, if she received any education at all, was expected to acquire household skills that would fit her for domestic service.[69] These attitudes were supported by many women. As one mother quoted by Ray Strachey in 1928 remarked, 'You can't send a girl into the drawing-room repeating the multiplication table.' So why should she trouble to learn it?[70]

Although it is often stated that 'knowledge is power', education is not always the receipt of knowledge. Ivan Illich[71] observed that the pupil is schooled 'to confuse teaching with learning, grade advancement with education, a diploma with competence and fluency with the ability to say something new'. Education can be, and frequently is, a form of indoctrination intended to mould the minds of pupils and to transmit a specific set of moral and social values. Spender argues that no body of knowledge can be seen as politically neutral in a world founded upon structural and gendered inequalities. She maintains that women's historical exclusion from the production of cultural forms, including legitimate language, has prevented the transmission of women's meanings of the world.[72] 'In crude terms', language had been made by men and used for their own purposes.[73]

Spender's views may seem extreme, but her work has been influential. She must be partly responsible for the more careful evaluation of words and phrases that has become known as 'political correctness'. Certainly, many of the sexist and racist comments that are quoted in this volume would be found unacceptable by the start of the twenty-first century. From a legal point of view definition is critical, as the meaning of words is integral to the process of law through which legal precedent is created. For example, the use of the term 'common prostitute' to categorise a group of women, many of whom are merely 'poor' and 'working-class', has been central to women's complaint against the law on prostitution for well over a century, but it has remained firmly in place. Once again, women's voices have been silenced or ignored.

SCIENCE

During the nineteenth century the blossoming of science[74] bestowed the expert with a new and impressive authority. In the latter part of the century, Cesare Lombroso and William Ferrero reflected the Victorian obsessions for measurement and cataloguing to forge a connection between natural physiological variations in females and an in-born predisposition towards criminality or prostitution. Although Lombroso's work on men has become less respected, his work *The Female Offender* (1895)[75] has been remarkable for the durability of its thesis that crime among women is related to their physiology and biological destiny.[76] Downes and Rock explain, somewhat wearily, that the defects of criminological positivism need to be exposed again, because in the view of some women theorists (Smart, 1997 and Heidensohn, 1987) it remains a living body of thought, setting an agenda that is still operative.[77]

As a result of their experiments, Lombroso and Ferrero concluded that the lower incidence of recorded crime among women was due to their more primitive nature. Some surprise was expressed at the attractiveness of many prostitutes, but it was argued that as they aged, degenerative criminal features became more apparent. They assumed that prostitution represented the female corollary to criminality in men. In other words, prostitution was not merely a form of deviance, let alone the rational choice of normal women, but the female equivalent of male criminality, which would therefore justify punishment.[78] The Introduction (by Frank J. Pirone) to the 1956 edition of *The Female Offender* describes Lombroso as one of the 'giants of nineteenth-century psychiatrists and physiologists' who had a 'psychological and sociological impact upon the culture of his time'. Among the female offenders whom he observed were two children, one of 12 and the other of 9. The first was said to be the 'complete type of criminal' and the second the 'prostitute'. Both children exhibited criminal behaviour. The younger manifested criminal symptoms by throwing her dolls in the gutter and lifting her skirts up in the street. The 12-year-old had been subjected to a chloridectomy at the age of 11[79] but continued to practise onanism. It is regrettable that over a hundred years later it should still be necessary to deconstruct theories based on such disturbing assumptions and doubtful methodology.

Perhaps the most serious aspect of Lombroso's work, in terms of its eventual consequences, was the notion that criminality and immorality could be seen as diagnosable hereditary characteristics, revealing the 'born offender' for whom there was no cure. His subjects were placed into many sub-divisions, including the 'epileptic delinquent' and the 'morally insane', the latter being a hopelessly incurable recidivist who was best confined for life in a mental asylum. These questionable categories[80] became common currency in academic circles and influenced social policy. For example, in 1918 the medical expert A. F. Tredgold developed Lombroso's theories, arguing that a mixture of hereditary disorders, infectious diseases and circumstantial conditions (epilepsy, alcoholism and tuberculosis) were related to feeble-mindedness, criminality and prostitution. Tredgold gave evidence to the Royal Commission on the Care and Control of the Feeble Minded (1908), and the influence of his ideas can be detected in the Mental Deficiency Act 1913,[81] which led in some instances to the incarceration of promiscuous and/or pregnant young women in mental hospitals.[82] They also gave rise to serious discussion of eugenic measures including sterilisation and the segregation of patients to prevent breeding.

Sir Cyril Burt advocated this last solution for the female adolescent delinquent, claiming that:

> In secret, many of these loose and languid precocities become 'tempters of the opposite sex, purveyors of disease, and spreaders of vicious knowledge amongst their friends and casual acquaintances; and with extreme cases of this kind, if only to protect society, segregation must be advocated, even perhaps at the risk of discomfort and of neurotic development in the individual . . . Moreover, since the condition is sometimes hereditary, the girl's home frequently contains other examples of the same oversexed constitution. For her, therefore, the home may be the last place in which she can be left with security.[83]

Anxiety over these issues gave rise in 1932 to the appointment by the government of a departmental committee:

> To examine and report on the information already available regarding the hereditary transmission and other causes of mental disorder and deficiency; to consider the value of sterilisation as a preventative measure, having regard to its physical, psychological and social effects and to the experience of legislation in other countries permitting it; and to suggest what further enquiries might usefully be undertaken in this connection.[84]

Fortunately for the prospective patients, this particular committee produced a well-balanced and cautious report, which did not recommend compulsory sterilisation. However the discussion of eugenics that it contains highlights the dangerous consequences that may flow from the speculations of people like Lombroso when they are accepted as valid. Lombroso's work legitimated the view of prostitution as pathological, suggesting that women who turned to the practice suffered from a medical condition that might be hereditary. This confirmed the theory of difference that has persisted for many decades and is still incorporated in the law. There is also the long-term influence that an accepted body of work may have on future generations of theorists, which may guarantee its survival as an analytical tool.[85] Finally he conflated prostitution with criminality, a connection that persists in many people's minds, even though prostitution is not in itself a criminal offence.[86]

The gravity of these types of link should not be underestimated. Similar connections were exposed by Jacob Bronowski [87] when he traced the relationships between the Blumenbach skull collection, housed in the University of Göttingen, and the crematorium at Auschwitz where his compatriots were reduced to ashes. Bronowski writes:

> Early in the 1800s Johann Friedrich Blumenbach had put together a collection of skulls that he got from distinguished gentlemen with whom he corresponded throughout Europe. There is no suggestion in Blumenbach's work that the skulls were to support a racist division of humanity, although he did use anatomical measurements to classify the families of man. All the same, from the time of Blumenbach's death in 1840 the collection was added to and added to and became a core of racist, pan-Germanic theory, which was officially sanctioned by the Nationalist Socialist Party when it came into power . . . And that was not done by gas. It was done by arrogance. It was done by dogma. It was done by ignorance. When people believe they have absolute knowledge, with no test in reality, this is how they behave. This is what men do when they aspire to the knowledge of gods.

NOTES

1. This is the legal definition of prostitution deriving from case law, in *R. v. de Munck* (1918), which refers to acts of lewdness and will be covered below. The social and cultural understanding of the prostitute and prostitution frequently crosses the boundaries of adultery and promiscuity or any form of sexual behaviour outside marriage. Broader and varying interpretations of the definitions of prostitute and prostitution become apparent as the thesis unfolds and are still evident in the contemporary use of words such as 'slag'. This ambivalence is reflected in the fact that there has never been any statutory definition of these terms.
2. Stanley Cohen (1985), *Visions of Social Control: Punishment and Classification*, Polity Press, Cambridge, pp. 13–14.
3. Michel Foucault (1979), *Discipline and Punish: The Birth of the Prison*, Penguin Books, London.
4. See Susan Haskins (1993), *Mary Magdalene: Myth and Metaphor*, HarperCollins, London.
5. See Vern Bullough and Bonnie Bullough (1987), *Women and Prostitution: A Social History*, Prometheus Books, New York, Ch.7.
6. Benedicta Ward [S.L.G.] (1987), *Harlots of the Desert*, Cistercian Publications, Kalamazoo, Ch. 2.
7. Ibid., p. 10.
8. Marina Warner (1976), *Alone of All Her Sex: The Myth and Cult of the Virgin Mary*, Picador, Pan Books, London, Ch. 12.
9. Ward, *Harlots of the Desert*, p. 14.
10. Ibid.
11. Ibid., pp. 14–15.
12. Reay Tannahill (1980), *Sex in History*, Hamish Hamilton, London, p. 139.
13. St Augustine of Hippo (354–430) and St Thomas Aquinas (1225–74).
14. Karen Armstrong (1986), *The Gospel According to Women*, HarperCollins, London, Ch. 1.
15. This theme has been brilliantly developed by Uta Ranke-Heinemann (1990), *Eunuchs for the Kingdom of Heaven: The Catholic Church and Sexuality*, Penguin Books, Harmondsworth.

16. Armstrong, *The Gospel According to Women*, p. 32.
17. Saint Augustine, *De Ordine* II, IV. 12 PL XXXII, col. 1000. Quoted in Tannahill, *Sex in History*, p. 26.
18. Jacques Rossiaud (1988), *Medieval Prostitution*, Basil Blackwell, Oxford.
19. Ibid., p. 39.
20. Lyndal Roper (1991), *The Holy Household: Women and Morals in Reformation Augsburg*, Clarendon Press, Oxford, Ch. 3.
21. Ibid., p. 128.
22. Phyllis Trible (1978), *God and the Rhetoric of Sexuality*, SCM Press, London, pp. 24–5.
23. This is reflected in the English law on prostitution, in that the client is not culpable, but is tempted by the woman and merely accepts an offer.
24. See Phyllis Trible (1984), *Texts of Terror: Literary-Feminist Readings of Biblical Narrative*, Fortress Press, Philadelphia, Ch. 2.
25. See, for example, Edward J. Burford (1976), *Bawds and Lodgings: A History of the London Bankside Brothels, c.100–1675*, Peter Owen, London, p. 9. The Bankside whorehouses or 'stews' were a feature of London life from Roman times. In 1161 Henry II signed an ordinance officially regulating and licensing these brothels. They were closed down in 1546 by Henry VIII.
26. Olwen Hufton (1995), *The Prospect Before Her: A History of Women in Western Europe*, HarperCollins, London, Ch. 8.
27. Ibid., p. 306.
28. Henry Fielding (1707–54), English novelist and playwright. Called to the Bar in 1740; campaigned against legal corruption; helped his half-brother Sir John Fielding (1721–80) to found the Bow Street Runners as a fledgling detective force.
29. Bullough and Bullough, *Women and Prostitution*, p. 186.
30. Eric Trudgill (1976), *Madonnas and Magdalens: The Origins and Development of Victorian Sexual Attitudes*, Heinemann, London, Ch. 11. Dodd was disgraced in 1774 and subsequently executed for forgery.
31. Ibid., p. 279.
32. Ibid., p. 281.
33. Ibid., p. 282.
34. The Society for the Suppression of Vice (SSV) was founded in 1802, with a mission to purify Britain. See E. J. Bristow, *Vice and Vigilance*, p. 157.
35. Michael Mason (1994), *The Making of Victorian Sexual Attitudes*, Oxford University Press, p. 70.
36. The National Vigilance Association (NVA) was formed after the passage of the Criminal Law Amendment Act 1885 (see Chapter 2). It incorporated the SSV.
37. Mason, *The Making of Victorian Sexual Attitudes*, p. 92.
38. E. J. Bristow, *Vice and Vigilance*, Gill and Macmillan, Rowman and Littlefield, Dublin, p. 3 and Ch. 2.
39. Hufton, *The Prospect Before Her*; Frances Finnegan (1979), *Poverty and Prostitution: A Study of Victorian Prostitutes in York*, Cambridge University Press; Linda Mahood (1990), *The Magdalenes: Prostitution in the Nineteenth Century*, Routledge, London.
40. Bristow, *Vice and Vigilance*, describes the conditions in operation in the Church Penitentiary Association's Highgate Penitentiary, the country's largest, which were recorded by the Bishop of London. 'Inmates were sweated in the laundry, fed mainly on bread and butter, flogged and subjected to "black hole" punishments in the coal cellar. Exercise was ruled out because an earlier chaplain believed it stirred up the passions.'
41. Mahood, *The Magdalenes*.
42. Ibid., p. 117.
43. See Cmnd. 247, para. 232. The quotation of a statement made by the Metropolitan Police in 1881, 'At half-past twelve at night a calculation was made a short time ago that there were 500 prostitutes between Piccadilly Circus and Waterloo Place.' (See Chapter 3.)
44. Woolf, L. (1966), *Collected Essays by Virginia Woolf*, Vol. II, Hogarth Press, London (p. 141), quoted in Dale Spender (1983), *There's Always Been a Women's Movement this Century*, Pandora, London, p. 1.
45. Ibid.
46. Proverbs, 31.
47. See, for example, Fernando Henriques (1962), *Prostitution and Society: A Survey* and (1963), *Prostitution in the New World*, MacGibbon & Kee, London; Bullough and Bullough, *Women*

and Prostitution; Nicki Roberts (1992), *Whores in History: Prostitution in Western History,* HarperCollins, London.
48. See also Edward Shorter (1977), *The Making of the Modern Family*, Fontana/Collins, London, Ch. 7.
49. Trudgill, *Madonnas and Magdalens*, p. 28.
50. William Acton (1857), 'Functions and Disorder', quoted in Finnegan, *Poverty and Prostitution*, p. 1.
51. Dr William Sanger (1858), quoted in Erna Olafson Helerstein, Leslie Parker Hume and Karen M. Offen (1981), *Victorian Women*, Harvester Press, New York, pp. 415–16.
52. For a development of this theme, see Leonore Davidoff (1983), 'Class and Gender in Victorian England', in J. L. Newton, M. R. Ryan and J. R. Walkowitz (eds), *Sex and Class in Women's History*, Routledge & Kegan Paul, London.
53. See Finnegan, *Poverty and Prostitution*, p. 2. and Peter Fryer's 'Introduction' to the new edition of William Acton (first published 1857), *Prostitution*, London (1968).
54. For references and discussion of these points see, Finnegan, *Poverty and Prostitution*, Ch. 1; William Acton (1968) [1887] *Prostitution*, ed. Peter Fryer, MacGibbon and Kee, London, passim; Keith Nield (ed.), (1973), *Prostitution in the Victorian Age*, Greg International Publishers, Farnborough.
55. See, for example, Joanna Trollope (1994), *Britannia's Daughters: Women of the British Empire*, Pimlico, London (complaint of a registered prostitute published in a reforming pamphlet), p. 171.
56. Dr Alex Parent-Duchatelet (1836), *De la prostitution dans la ville de Paris*, J. B. Baillière, Paris.
57. This is a much quoted comment, and can be found in Bristow (1977), *Vice and Vigilance*, p. 53.
58. Alain Corbin (1990), *Women for Hire* (trans. Alan Sheridan), Harvard University Press, Cambridge, MA.
59. Ibid., pp. 1–4.
60. *National Review*, April 1862.
61. W. G. Greg, 'Why are Women Redundant?', *National Review* 14 (1862): 436–40. Quoted in Patricia Hollis (1979), *Women in Public, 1850–1900*, George Allen & Unwin, London, p. 38. See also Sheila Jeffreys (1985), *The Spinster and her Enemies: Feminism and Sexuality, 1880–1930*, Pandora Press, London, pp. 86–7; Mary Poovey (1989), *Uneven Developments: The Ideological Work of Gender in Mid-Victorian England*, Virago, London, Ch. 1.
62. W. G. Greg, 'Prostitution', *Westminster Review*, 53 (1850): 238–68.
63. See M. Poovey (1990), 'Speaking of the Body', in M. Jacobus, E. F. Keller and S. Shuttleworth (eds), *Body Politics: Women and the Discourse of Science*, Routledge, London, Ch. 2.
64. See E. Olafson Hellerstein, L. Parker Hume and K. M. Offen, *Victorian Women*, Harvester Press, New York, p. 175.
65. Roy Porter and Leslie Hall (1995), *The Facts of Life: The Creation of Sexual Knowledge in Britain, 1650–1950*, Yale University Press, Newhaven and London, p. 9.
66. See S. Jeffreys, *The Idea of Prostitution*, Spinifex, Melbourne.
67. For example, the pioneers of women's further education, Miss Beale, Miss Buss, Miss Clough and Emily Davis. The opening up of higher education for women was in its initial stages aimed at improving the educational standards of governesses through the work of the Governesses' Benevolent Institution under the leadership of the educational reformer, F. D. Maurice. See Olive Banks (1964), *Feminism and Family Planning*, Liverpool University Press, p. 36; Josephine Kamm (1965), *Hope Deferred: Girls' Education in English History*, Methuen, London and (1966), *Rapiers and Battleaxes: The Women's Movement and its Aftermath*, George Allen and Unwin, London.
68. W. B. Hodgson, 'On the Education of Girls', a lecture delivered on 11 June 1864 (published in 1869), pp. 4–5, quoted in J. Kamm, *Rapiers and Battleaxes: The Women's Movement and its Aftermath*, George Allen and Unwin, London, p. 191.
69. Ibid., Ch. 8.
70. Ray Strachey (1928), *The Cause: A Short History of the Women's Movement in Great Britain*, G. Bell & Sons (repr. 1987, 1988 & 1989, Virago, London), p. 125.
71. Ivan Illich (1971), *Deschooling Society*, Penguin, London, p. 9.
72. Dale Spender (1981), *Man Made Language*, Routledge & Kegan Paul, London. Although Spender acknowledges that some women writers have broken through the barrier of male restrictions and been heard, she argues that the claim that women have succeeded in the male

literary world is based upon four or five women writers: the Brontes, Jane Austen, George Elliot and Virginia Woolf, with 'Jane' and '*George*' predominating, p. 205. See also Elaine Showalter (1977), *A Literature of their Own: British Women Novelists from Bronte to Lessing*, Princeton University Press.

73. Spender, *Man Made Language*, p. 52.
74. General reading of official texts from the first half of the twentieth century (Royal Commissions, League of Nations Documents, etc.), demonstrate the enormous effect that men such as Linnaeus, Mendel, Darwin and Freud had on the thinking of the period. Classification, genetics, natural selection and psychiatry became intermingled in ways that, at their best, were confusing, and at worst, sinister and dangerous.
75. Cesare Lombroso and William Ferrero (1959 edition), *The Female Offender*, Peter Owen, London (first published 1895).
76. See, for example, Alison Morris (1987), *Women, Crime and Criminal Justice*, Basil Blackwell, Oxford, Ch. 3. Morris claims that biological determinism is not a matter of history, but that it continues to dominate theory and practice.
77. David Downes and Paul Rock (1989), *Understanding Deviance: A Guide to the Sociology of Crime and Rule Breaking*, Clarendon Press, Oxford, p. 276; Carol Smart (1977), *Women, Crime and Criminology: A Feminist Critique*, Sage, London; Francis Heidensohn (1985), *Women and Crime*, Macmillan, London.
78. Lombroso and Ferrero, *The Female Offender*, Ch. 7.
79. Ibid., p. 99. 'Chloridectomy' is the spelling used in the book. For a discussion of clitoridectomy (surgical removal of the clitoris as a cure for insanity) see Elaine Showalter (1995), *The Female Malady: Women, Madness and English Culture, 1830–1980*, Virago, London, pp. 75–8.
80. Lombroso's sub-divisions included a variety of hereditary conditions and racial characteristics as well as behavioural responses to social and environmental circumstances such as tattooing or suicide. The women of dark-skinned races were 'savage', exhibiting primordial characteristics. They were 'difficult to recognise for women, so huge are their jaws and so hard and coarse their features'. The venal women were frequently obese. The white-skinned criminal, who was characterised by asymmetric heavy features, was a reversion to the primitive state.
81. Mental Deficiency Act 1913 [3 & 4 Geo. 5. c. 28].
82. One such case was revealed on BBC Radio 4, 28 February 2000, concerning a woman named Edna Martin from Manchester. The court sent her to an approved school in 1933, after her grandfather handed her over to the police for having intercourse with a man. She ran away six times and was eventually placed in the Blackburn asylum, where she was subjected to punishments including beatings, confinement to a padded cell and wearing a strait-jacket. She was eventually transferred to Reading with the help of her brother and allowed out in 1959 after making strenuous efforts to conform to the accepted standards of good behaviour and normality. See also Paula Bartley (2000), *Prostitution, Prevention and Reform in England, 1860–1914*, Routledge, London, Chs 5 and 6; Royal Commission on the Care and Control of the Feeble Minded 1908.
83. Sir Cyril Burt (1952), *The Young Delinquent*, University of London Press, p. 244. (9th edn).
84. Report of the Departmental Committee on Sterilisation (1933), Cmd. 4485.
85. See Havelock Ellis (1890), *The Criminal*, London, in which Ellis wrote that, 'It is a remarkable fact that prostitutes exhibit the physical and psychic signs associated usually with criminality in a more marked degree than criminal women', p. 221. See also Otto Pollack (1950), *The Criminality of Women*, New York; S. and E. Glueck (1934), *Five Hundred Delinquent Women*, New York. S. and E. Glueck divided prostitutes into voluntary and compulsive categories, compelled by their own psychoneurotic needs (p. 91); H. Benjamin and R. Masters (1964), *Prostitution and Morality: A Definitive Report on Prostitution in Contemporary Society and an Analysis of the Causes and Effects of Suppressing of Prostitution*, Souvenir Press, London.
86. This was brought home to me at a personal level when the editor of the *Police Review* queried this particular point.
87. Jacob Bronowski (1974), *The Ascent of Man*, British Broadcasting Corporation, p. 374.

CHAPTER 2

The Legislative Background

This chapter provides a largely descriptive account of the evolution of secular legislation pertaining to prostitution between 1824 and 1950, with a brief reference to the earlier development of the law on vagrancy. It demonstrates the increasing complexity of the law in this area as different factions fought for the legal means to establish public order and provide protection for women and children from sexual abuse. Mary Poovey has argued that the British law on prostitution is contradictory in that it views women both as passive and in need of protection and as an aggressive force requiring control.[1] The following account demonstrates that, although the different Acts have had conflicting aims, the protective aspect of the law was not extended to the prostitute but was intended to protect the chaste white woman from sexual exploitation. This has been achieved by maintaining that the 'common prostitute' was a member of a separate and identifiable group of women who were different from the normal.

In addition, it is shown that attempts to limit the spread of venereal disease in the twentieth century became more complicated as the flaws in the state system for regulation were made apparent.

Traditionally, the disciplining of sexual incontinence was within the province of the Church. This was achieved through the ecclesiastical (or 'bawdy') courts,[2] which were concerned with a variety of moral infractions, including marital infidelity, fornication, incest, homosexuality, brothel-keeping and prostitution. From the sixteenth century onwards, the power of these courts declined and prostitution became a matter of secular concern. The primary historical link between prostitution and the state was with the control of vagrancy, and therefore, by association, with unemployment, poverty and crime.

During the sixteenth century, a raft of Tudor legislation was enacted to deal with the increasing number of vagrants caused by the break-up of monastic estates and with the displacement of peasants due to the enclosures and inflation.[3] In an effort to deal with these problems Parliament in the reign of Henry VIII and Elizabeth I passed a succession of Vagrancy Acts[4] compelling the wandering poor to return to their place of settlement. Since provision for the poor was based upon compulsory local rates, the pregnant woman and the single mother were especially disliked.

The unattached woman was always vulnerable. Elizabeth Melling records a number of instances when the pregnant woman or single mother was mistreated in an attempt to evict her from the parish. The respectable but unmarried woman fared little better, as some counties denied her parish relief with the intention of forcing her into work. Ivy Pinchbeck[5] has argued that this practice was responsible for the pauperisation of domestic service. Vagrancy, or 'wandering abroad', was to some extent forced upon the unattached women and prostitution was sometimes the only means of survival. Consequently, the prostitute was subsumed within the general definition of vagrant or 'able-bodied' poor, and viewed as a potential cause of disorder.[6] In this way a disparate set of personal circumstances became conflated and subjected to social scrutiny and moral judgements.

A variety of punishments were inflicted upon both the vagrant and the prostitute. Under Henry VIII's Act of 1530–31, the vagrant (man, woman or child) was to be taken to the nearest market town, tied naked to the end of a cart and beaten with whips throughout the town. Prostitutes were also subjected to cruel and sadistic penalties including whipping, branding, head-shaving, standing in the pillory or cage, having their noses split open, or being plunged into stinking water.[7]

Government concern over the level of vagrancy resurfaced during the early part of the nineteenth century, when the numbers of rootless and unemployed people increased. This was partly due to the demographic movements accompanying industrial development. In 1806 the eminent London magistrate Patrick Colquhoun estimated that out of England's ten million inhabitants, there were ninety thousand vagrants.[8] The Vagrants Act of 1824[9] was passed to deal with a situation seen by the government as a threat to social stability and the prostitute was again incorporated within the general category of vagrant. The 1824 Act was resented by the poor for its 'sus' law provisions under which an individual found 'wandering abroad' became a suspected person who could be required to give a good account of himself or herself.[10] If a woman was apprehended in a public street or highway, behaving in 'a riotous or indecent manner'(drunk and disorderly, fighting, soliciting, and so on), she was deemed to be an 'idle and disorderly person' and liable for a penalty of one month's imprisonment with hard labour. Further offences attracted a longer term.

The 1824 Act is the first occasion on which the term 'common prostitute' was used to distinguish a group of women as separate and identifiable legal subjects. The use of the word 'common' is generally seen as pejorative, especially as it has a variety of different meanings, ranging from 'frequent' to 'vulgar'. The most likely explanation for the use of the term is that the 'common woman' was 'available to all', or common to all men; a state that is only marginally removed from that of public property.[11]

The nineteenth-century increase in vagrancy was accompanied by a steep rise in the number of criminal convictions. Lionel Rose claims that between 1806 and 1826 criminal commitments quadrupled, although the population increased by less than a half. The solution was not to be found in the eighteenth-century penal code, which was responsible for around two hundred offences attracting the death penalty.[12] This brutal system frequently resulted in juries being unwilling to enforce the law, and through 'pious perjury' many people remained unpunished. Between 1823 and 1826 the Home Secretary, Sir Robert Peel, instituted a series of reforms intended to deal with the situation. They including the formation of the 'New Police' aimed at administering and taming the disorder of the city, feared by the middle classes for its insanitary conditions and impoverished inhabitants. Police Acts were passed in 1839[13] and 1847,[14] containing sections applying to the policing of prostitution, very similar to those in the 1824 Vagrants Act and referring to the 'common prostitute' as a specific category of person. The Metropolitan Police Act 1839 and the Town Police Clauses Act 1847 provided for the arrest of common prostitutes who solicited in a public place to the annoyance of its inhabitants or passengers. Both imposed a fine of two pounds, but the latter allowed for a short term of imprisonment. The continued spread of uniformed police and the development of local government led to the proliferation of local Acts and by-laws containing similar provisions. These multifarious Acts, which sought to limit and regulate street prostitution, became known to their opponents as 'solicitation laws'.

The new police represented a major incursion into the lives of working people and were initially greatly resented, especially when they appeared to be acting as arbiters of morality.[15] A correspondent to the *Morning Post* complained in 1858,

> It is reported that the police are now to be particularly diligent in clearing the streets of prostitutes, driving them away and arresting them if troublesome. Such a proceeding harshly carried out by the ordinary police will be an unwarrantable and unmanly wrong done to the wretched women unless some place be at once provided for their reception, or to afford them a chance of reformation. Public morality is now outraged. But by such blind coercive measures as the wholesale arrest of prostitutes, or at once driving them from their haunts, public safety will be endangered. Without means of living or opportunity of gaining a livelihood either honestly or immorally, they must either starve or thieve. Earnestly as we advocate the adoption of effective means for the repression and control of prostitution we protest in the name of human justice against making a raid on these wretched women and casting them wholesale into prison without offering them any other alternative than starvation.[16]

This anonymous correspondent's observations are interesting, as the police were apparently responding to an influx of tourists from Berlin to London. The article demonstrates where police loyalties lay and their lack of concern for the fate of the women. It also suggests that the requirement to prove

annoyance was ignored. From the point of view of policing, vagrants, prostitutes and thieves represented the low life of the city. Many impoverished single
women merged into the capital's fragile economy, surviving on laundry work,
petty theft and seasonal migration to the countryside. Police surveillance of
prostitution legitimated official infiltration into working-class communities,
making general surveillance easier.[17] A century and a half later, police tactics
remain very similar.[18] A further intrusion was the Industrial Schools
Amendment Act 1880,[19] which enabled the police to withdraw children from
places deemed to be brothels and send them to industrial schools for training.
Walkowitz refers to this as 'blackmail', as it prevented poor people taking in
prostitutes as lodgers, on pain of losing their children.[20]

As the social and geographical distance between rich and poor increased,
intrusive methods of policing became more acceptable to the middle classes,
and ultimately to the 'newly respectable' working classes.[21] The moralisation
of the poor became a middle-class crusade that legitimated coercive measures,
just as the reformation of prostitutes legitimated a variety of asylums and
penitentiaries. In the long run, the new police failed to stamp out prostitution,
change drinking habits or limit popular festivals, so that the first Metropolitan
Police Commissioner (Richard Mayne) advocated that these activities be
licensed rather than abolished through criminal sanctions.[22]

THE CONTAGIOUS DISEASES ACTS

Commissioner Mayne's logic was perhaps acceptable to some sections of the
ruling classes, who were anxious to limit the reproductive excess of the
'residuum' for fear that uncontrolled reproduction would threaten middle-
class prosperity.[23] The idea that the administration and regulation of sexuality were an acceptable and rational objective found expression in the
Contagious Diseases Acts (CDAs) of the 1860s.[24]

This area of Victorian legislation has already been well researched and
analysed, most notably by Judith Walkowitz (1980) in her ground-breaking
book *Prostitution in Victorian Society*. Nevertheless a short résumé is necessary if a complete picture is to be presented. There were a number of factors
that probably made the CDAs inevitable, the most pressing of which was
Britain's responsibility for the cost of maintaining the armed forces required
to police the Empire, when so many men were debilitated by syphilis and by
other forms of venereal disease.[25] As the ordinary serviceman was not allowed
to marry (unless the commanding officer's permission was given), access to
prostitutes was considered to be a necessity, and regulation seemed the
obvious solution. This system was already well established on the continent of
Europe. Numerous governmental, medical and military committees and conferences on the subject of venereal infection added to the sense of urgency.[26]
Moreover, Britain was criticised by the European authorities for its lax regime,
which was said to threaten the integrity of the continent.[27]

In 1859 a Royal Commission was appointed to inquire into the sanitary state of the army in India.[28] Its two-volume report, running to two thousand pages, was published in 1863. In 1862 the Admiralty appointed a committee to enquire into the state of disease amongst the naval forces and to look into the working of regulation in foreign ports. This report was never published. A medical committee was appointed in 1864 by the Admiralty and War Office to report on the pathology and treatment of venereal disease in the armed forces. A further select committee of the House of Commons was appointed in 1864; its report, published in 1866, came out in favour of regulation. In conjunction with these reports, the writings of Acton and Greg were influential on government policy. Finally, proprietorial attitudes towards poor women and the establishment of the new police made administration of the CDAs an operational possibility.

There were three Contagious Diseases Acts: 1864, 1866 and 1869. The Act of 1866 repealed the Act of 1864 but re-enacted and tightened up its provisions, while the 1869 Act extended its provisions to 18 military stations and garrison towns in England and Ireland. They provided for the surgical examination of women suspected of prostitution and their detention in Lock hospitals for up to three months if they were found to be infected with a venereal disease. Certified hospitals were obliged to provide religious instruction. Provision was made for a woman to sign a voluntary submission, but if she refused she was liable for up to three months in prison, with hard labour. The Acts were administered by plain-clothes policemen drawn from the Metropolitan Police. Given the vagueness of the term 'common prostitute', any poor woman was liable to arrest.

PROTECTIVE LEGISLATION
(THE REPEAL MOVEMENT AND ITS CONSEQUENCES)

The work of Josephine Butler and the campaign for the repeal of the Contagious Diseases Acts has been well documented and does not need to be repeated. But it is worth looking at the arguments that were used to oppose the Acts because they remain valid and still apply to the current legislation and to the various arguments used for reform.

On the moral front it was argued that the Acts embodied the state's recognition and encouragement of vice as a necessary evil. Women were cured of disease but new customers invariably infected them. A double standard of morals was invoked, which excused and encouraged incontinence in men while condemning it in women. Furthermore the tolerated brothel provided a front for more serious evils, including the violation of children and the traffic in persons. On the humanitarian front, the implementation of the Acts was regarded as a degrading violation of the person, while registration meant that women were confirmed in their role as prostitutes instead of being provided with alternative employment. Constitutionally, the Acts represented a withdrawal of personal liberty by giving arbitrary powers of classification and arrest to the police, which frequently encouraged corruption. A provision for compulsory incarceration for five days before examination, contained in the final Act of 1869, denied the women their fundamental right of habeas corpus.[29] The women whom the police chose to accuse of prostitution were placed in an impossible position, as refusal to comply with the requirement to submit to a vaginal inspection led to a prison sentence whereas coopera- tion resulted in certification. Incidentally, some women who prostituted themselves willingly referred to themselves as the 'Queen's Women'.

Public response to the Acts was not immediate. However, a number of prominent people (most notably Florence Nightingale and Harriet Martineau) became aware of their existence and began to draw attention to what was happening. A meeting was called on 5 October 1869, which gave rise to the National Association for the Repeal of the CDAs, followed by the establish- ment of the Ladies' National Association, headed by Josephine Butler.[30] Nearly seventeen years of campaigning followed, leading to the suspension of the Acts in 1883 and repeal in 1886.[31] Working men in the north of England adopted the cause because they saw the Acts as a threat to the moral integrity of their wives and daughters, although this was not the aspect of the debate that moved the hearts of the general public and which eventually led to repeal. In this respect, Paul McHugh lists a variety of factors including the failure of the Acts to achieve what was claimed for them, a change in society's attitudes towards morality, the strength of the Liberal coalition against the Acts (all of the Nonconformist bodies, the National Liberal Federation and the Trades Union Congress), the persistence of the agitators and political expediency. Although McHugh seems to suggest that the Acts were effective in decreasing the incidence of infection,[32] the women were only as safe as their last customer and clandestine prostitution continued unabated. There was also the escalat- ing cost of the exercise to take into consideration, along with the uncongenial nature of the work for medical practitioners.

Home Office commitment to a policy of regulation was demonstrated fol- lowing the Report of the Royal Commission on the Administration of the Contagious Diseases Acts (1871). The commission, to which both Josephine Butler and John Stuart Mill gave evidence, did not recommend the repeal of the Acts, but advised the government to discontinue compulsory examination and the imprisonment of women in Lock hospitals. The Home Secretary, H. A. Bruce, responded by announcing a new scheme to replace the Acts.[33] He proposed that 'in deference to public opinion' the existing Acts should be repealed and the Vagrancy and other Acts be used to greater affect. He also proposed that special medical wards should be attached to every gaol in the country in order to provide for the medical examination of women who were suspected of being unchaste, leading to an extended detention of nine months to effect a cure. The scheme was to apply to the whole of the country. Josephine Butler denounced it as 'nothing but an arrangement for catching, examining, cleansing and returning to the streets women for the safe enjoyment of men'.[34] Her outburst was understandable, since Bruce's scheme would have constituted a national extension of the principles behind the CD Acts.

The eventual repeal of the Acts came about not so much as a result of the campaign, but in response to the investigative journalism of W. T. Stead, whose salacious articles in the *Pall Mall Gazette* were filled with lurid details of the violation of virgins and the trafficking of children from England to brothels on the continent. These articles gave rise to intense public anxiety over what generally became known as the White Slave Trade.[35] The moral panic that followed was reflected in parliament and the press, and caused many Church-based organisations to embark upon a prolonged crusade. Campaigners included the Young Women's Christian Association, the Mothers' Union, the National Council of Women Workers and a coalition of women's groups which became known as the Traveller's Aid Society. According to Stefan Petrow,[36] public anxiety over the issue, combined with the findings and recommendations of the Select Committee on the Protection of Young Girls 1881 (that street soliciting should be made an offence regardless of annoyance), led to increased police pressure upon street walkers and a countervailing reaction from critics who accused them of the indiscriminate arrests of prostitutes, of blackmail and of corruption. Proactive police tactics that had driven women off the streets resulted in an increase of prostitutes frequenting pleasure palaces and music halls and in a corresponding vigilance drive to effect the closure of assorted places of popular entertainment.[37] A series of Criminal Law Amendment Bills were presented to parliament between 1883 and 1885, but heightened controversy over these issues, combined with strong opposition to a clause making solicitation without annoyance illegal, delayed the passage of the final Bill.[38] The Home Secretary, R. A. Cross, finally decided to delete the clause,[39] which secured the Bill's enactment.

THE CRIMINAL LAW AMENDMENT ACT 1885[40]

Apart from the repeal of the CDAs the main triumph of the repeal campaign was the enactment of the Criminal Law Amendment Act 1885, which was responsible for raising the age of consent to sexual intercourse from 13 to 16.[41] The motivating concern of the Act's sponsors was the protection of innocent white women and children from abduction, transportation and detention for the purpose of prostitution in foreign brothels. The Act provided for the suppression of brothels by making the landlord, tenant, lessee or occupier liable to prosecution if s/he knowingly harboured prostitutes or allowed any part of the property to be used for the purpose of prostitution. In addition to these measures, section 11 (the Labouchère amendment) provided for the criminalisation of homosexual acts between consenting men in private, which was to be the cause of much misery for some and rejoicing for others.[42] The 1885 Act turned out to be a very partial measure. It failed to cover incest, it contained a three-months statute of limitation and it incorporated a provision that enabled a man to avoid prosecution by swearing that he believed the girl in question was over the age of 16 at the time of the offence. The protective nature of the Act was soon to be tested in court. One such case was reported in the first edition of the National Vigilance Association's journal, the *Vigilance Record*, in February 1887. It involved the prosecution of a man for the procurement of a woman who had been induced to travel to England on the promise of employment. The magistrate concluded that since the woman was 27 and had already lived an immoral life abroad the charge was not sustainable.[43]

The passage of the Act was followed by the formation of the National Vigilance Association (NVA) which aimed at enforcing its provisions. The view that the NVA and various related social purity organisations[44] succeeded in reducing prostitution by suppressing brothels and cooperating with the police authorities has recently been challenged by Paula Bartley.[45] She argues that the evidence is inconclusive, since although many brothels were closed, prostitution continued to flourish and the police were not always wiling to cooperate with the social purists. One of the tragic consequences to follow from the closure of brothels was an increase in the number of prostitutes to be found soliciting in the back streets of London, some of whom became the victims of Jack the Ripper and Dr Thomas Neill Cream.[46] What is certain is that by 1898 the CLA Act appeared to be sufficiently ineffective for an extension of the 1824 Vagrants Act[47] to be proposed in order to suppress the prostitute's tout or bully, by means of making 'living on the earnings of prostitution' a punishable offence. According to Walkowitz,[48] the unsatisfactory situation was a direct result of the administration of the 1885 Act, as prostitutes had been forced out of the small lodging houses they had traditionally inhabited and into the hands of pimps and bullies, thereby increasing third-party control of the trade. There had also been an xenophobic reaction, as the pimp was invariably thought to be a foreigner, in view of an increase in immigration from Eastern Europe.[49]

The 1898 Act empowered the police to search property in which it was suspected that prostitutes and their pimps resided. The onus of proof that a man was not living on the earnings of a prostitute was placed on the accused and the convicted man could be sentenced to flogging as a rogue or a vagabond under the terms of the 1824 Vagrants Act. As the prostitute's pimp was generally despised and believed to be foreign, little consideration was given to the coercive nature of the legislation and the Bill passed rapidly through both Houses with little debate.

THE INTERNATIONAL DIMENSION, 1885–1949

The panic over 'white slavery', the passage of the 1885 Act and the formation of the NVA represent a watershed which had international repercussions. By 1898 William Coote,[50] the secretary and leading light of the NVA, had become dissatisfied with the association's lack of progress and with the inadequacy of legislative means for combating the white slave traffic. The prosecution of traffickers posed too many problems as it required the cooperation of different governments and the creation of national and international legislation to deal with a single offender. Coote realised that if the NVA were to have any real impact, something more ambitious would have to be attempted. Inspiration, he claimed, came to him in a 'vision' in which he was 'commanded by God' to embark upon a missionary tour of the capitals of Europe and to describe the horrors of the white slave trade to foreign dignitaries and government officials.[51] His initial aim was the formation of national committees, followed by a series of international conferences focusing upon the need for legislation. These committees were to be the lynch-pin of a new organisation, providing the enthusiasm and the volunteers required to implement policies. It was hoped that public pressure would force reluctant governments into changing their penal codes and put an end to immorality. Coote was a skilled diplomat and his commitment to the cause and his personal appeal to the various heads of state paved the way for future developments. The first International Congress organised by the NVA was held in London during June 1899. The conference agenda set out a number of key objectives. First there was the need for agreement over the exact nature of the crime which they wished to prosecute,[52] and second, the need for recommendations for coordinating the international legislation which would be required to pursue and extradite offenders. On the voluntary side there was the proposal for a parallel organisation to deal with trafficking from an international point of view and to give support to the administration of international legislation. Information would be pooled and collated and used to pressurise governments into coordinating schemes for the protection of women and girls travelling under suspicious circumstances. It was for this purpose that the NVA launched the International Bureau for the Suppression of the White Slave Traffic (IB), which was, in reality, only an extension of its own administration.

The London Congress of 1899 marked a turning point during which political fortunes changed and a significant proportion of the public became sufficiently disturbed by reports of the white slave traffic to lobby for intergovernmental action.[53] The NVA/IB was fortunate in finding enthusiastic supporters amongst influential politicians abroad, most significantly the French regulationist Senator Berenger.[54] This development created an unholy alliance between abolitionists and regulationists, adding a new dimension of contradictory reasoning to the wider issue of prostitution. The only area of agreement was the need to prevent trafficking. The NVA capitalised upon the interest generated by the conference and sought ways of involving more governments. To this end, and with the help of the Foreign Secretary, Lord Salisbury, the *Transactions of the International Congress on the White Slave Trade* were bound together in a single volume and distributed by the Foreign Office to European heads of state and to the President of the United States of America.[55] It is a measure of Coote's political influence, and of the concern that the issue of trafficking had aroused, that he was able to persuade the Foreign Office to comply with his wishes.

Despite the differences between the abolitionist and regulationist points of view, the NVA decided that this was a propitious moment to launch a 'National Purity Crusade', harnessing the combined energies of the 'Church, the Press and the Platform,'[56] and to inform the public of 'the existence of the mischief which stalks abroad, slaying the young moral life of the cities'.[57] The crusade was accompanied by a propaganda campaign proclaiming the need for 'more drastic legislation to deal with the hydra-headed monster of vice'.[58] Coached by officials from London, the local committees organised drawing-room meetings[59] and public lectures in order to spread the message to a wider public. Links were also established with the Jewish Association for the Protection of Girls, which had similar objectives and a headquarters in London. In conjunction with these developments, the NVA/IB organized a series of preliminary conferences and a congress in alternate years.[60] The first took place in Amsterdam during 1900, followed by Frankfurt in 1902.

By the turn of the century the international work of the NVA had become highly organised and it established a formidable propaganda machine. Its definition of the white slave trade was, moreover, accepted by many people as incontestable fact. Trafficking was presented by a variety of organisations as the widespread practice of abduction, defilement and transportation of virgin white women in order to replenish worn-out stocks in foreign brothels.[61] Corbin argues that far from being a new phenomenon the 'white slave traffic' was merely an extension of a widespread system of trading in women that had been practised in regulationist states, involving traffickers who ensured a constant supply of prostitutes for the many brothels in Europe.[62]

It was generally believed that one of the most routine methods of persuading young women to travel abroad was that of spurious offers of employment. Therefore ways of controlling employment agencies and of preventing young girls from embarking on theatrical tours preoccupied the NVA. Success in the United Kingdom came with the enactment in 1913 of an Act aimed at prohibiting or restricting young people from being taken out of the UK for the purpose of singing, playing, performing or being exhibited for profit, or by requiring a licence issued by a magistrate before embarkation.[63] The matter had already been addressed at a more local level through the London County Council (General Powers) Act (which addressed the NVA's concern over disreputable employment agencies), making the LCC the authority responsible for licensing and controlling employment agencies in the County of London.[64] Protection had already been extended to children through the Children Act 1908,[65] which prohibited them from residing in or frequenting a brothel. The NVA then turned its attention to the problem of massage parlours. The Bill for registration and inspection of these establishments was passed by parliament on 21 October, 1915 and came into operation on 1 February, 1916.[66]

The issue of trafficking was closely interwoven with government concern over immigration, which culminated in a series of Aliens Acts and orders between 1905 and 1920.[67] The 1905 Act empowered officials to board boats and conduct medical inspections of passengers, rejecting those deemed to be undesirable. This of course included women suspected of being prostitutes and their companions. In addition aliens who committed offences attracting more than a fine could be expelled and known foreign prostitutes repatriated.

THE INTERNATIONAL AGREEMENT

The first official governmental conference was arranged with the help of Senator Berenger through the invitation of the French government and was held in Paris in 1902. Corbin identifies this event as the moment when a large section of the French public was aroused by the popular press and the issue of 'white slavery' became as notorious in France as it had been in England.[68] It was also a point of no return when trafficking became the subject of international treaty and political manoeuvring. Consequently, the resolutions passed at the first congress in 1899 were transformed into the articles of an international agreement[69] under which State signatories set out to coordinate measures that would protect young women from the speculative attentions of men who regarded them as merchandise. The Protocol Final was signed on 25 July 1902 and the International Agreement signed after the succeeding international conference in 1904. The agreement covered a number of essential points including the supervision of ports and railway stations. However, female protection was accompanied by a corresponding loss of freedom for travellers, as the preservation of their virtue was to be accomplished through careful surveillance by an army of voluntary workers at ports and railway stations, on the lookout for lost or suspicious-looking individuals.[70]

In England the NVA led a deputation to the Home Secretary, asking for the privilege to fulfil this duty on behalf of the UK, arguing that lady workers would be more suitable than police constables.[71] The UK-based International Guild of Service to Women, inaugurated in 1903[72] for the purpose of extending care and protection to women, was to be pressed into service. This offer of help was accepted by the Home Office and a surveillance and intelligence network established, connecting port police with railway and steamboat agents.[73] The distinction between the voluntary and official agents became increasingly blurred as the IB passed on coded information to agents of the various national committees throughout Europe.[74] Diplomatic or consular officials were then informed of the arrival of suspected traffickers in order to alert the local authorities and facilitate the arrest of the victim and accomplices. The women involved in these surveillance duties wore special badges to signify their office and their willingness to be of service to female travellers.[75] Wherever possible declarations were to be obtained from foreign prostitutes in order to establish their identity and discover who had caused them to leave their country of origin. It was assumed by the authorities that they had travelled under duress and arrangements were made for their anticipated 'voluntary' repatriation. When a woman was destitute, the cost of repatriation was to be shared by the countries involved.[76]

Contracting states were charged with the duty of establishing a central authority in order to collect and disseminate information relative to the procuring of women or girls for immoral purposes abroad. These authorities were then expected to keep in contact with the other national authorities and to assist in gathering, collating and disseminating information regarding the traffic. In Great Britain this duty was assigned to F. S. Bullock, Assistant Commissioner of the Metropolitan Police. In contrast to the emotional reactions of many campaigners, Bullock had a pragmatic approach to the problems created by prostitution and to the effectiveness of the legislation. By 1913 he felt able to state that there was 'no reason to believe that there was any organised system of trafficking in women'.[77] In 1910 he became one of three UK representatives to attend the international conference held in Paris,[78] which culminated in an International Convention for the Suppression of the White Slave Traffic.[79]

THE FIRST INTERNATIONAL CONVENTION

The 1910 Convention was important for a number of reasons. First it included a legal definition of the crime of trafficking,[80] placing it among those offences that qualified for extradition. Second, contracting governments agreed to enact the necessary domestic legislation required to punish offenders and to communicate the details to other countries, using the French government as intermediary. The most significant section was to be found in the Final Protocol: 'The case of detention, against her will, of a woman or girl in a brothel could not, in spite of its gravity, be dealt with in the present Convention, seeing that it is governed exclusively by internal legislation.'[81] This left contracting parties free to continue with their individual systems for regulating institutionalised prostitution, which greatly limited the effectiveness of the convention and suggested that signing was a matter of political expediency.

There was therefore a fundamental split between the aspirations of the philanthropists who wished to eliminate vice, and what individual governments were willing or able to deliver within the confines of their own legislation. Despite these limitations, William Coote continued to travel around the world on his mission to establish national committees and enjoyed many glittering receptions laid on by European heads of state[82] and, as with the *Transactions*, the record of his mission, *A Vision and its Fulfilment*,[83] was distributed by the Foreign Office to all the kings and queens and heads of state in Europe and to the President of the United States of America.

THE LEAGUE OF NATIONS[84]

Second and Third International Conventions

The importance of the movement did not die away with the First World War, as the issue of trafficking was kept alive by the International Bureau.

Following the war, the League of Nations made a commitment to honour the terms of previous international agreements and to give high priority to the needs of women and children.[85] Article 23(c) of the Covenant of the League of Nations (1919) stated: 'The members of the League of Nations will entrust the League with the general supervision over the execution of agreements with regard to the traffic in women and children.'[86]

A new Convention on the Traffic in Women and Children was adopted in 1921,[87] raising the age of legal protection to 21 and dropping the term 'white slave traffic'.[88] Yet there is little evidence to show that this redefinition was followed by a more enlightened approach towards racial and imperial questions, which would have recognised the issue of trafficking in women of a different colour. The contradictions that underpinned the movement before 1921 continued to create tensions in the post-war period, as it was discovered that most of the 'traffic' consisted of journeys undertaken by women who were over the age of legal protection and who had already practised prostitution in their own country.[89] It was therefore difficult to isolate the question of trafficking from the various forms of commercialised vice,[90] emphasising the gulf between the aspirations of philanthropists and those of administrators.

Blurring of boundaries continued, and during the Seventh International Congress it was resolved that the definition of the offence of 'trafficking' should remain intact even if the victims did not leave their country of origin or place of habitual residence. Likewise, the age limit should be removed from the relevant articles of the conventions.[91] These impractical suggestions, which would have identified all movements of prostitutes as trafficking, were incorporated in the League of Nations Second International Convention of 1933.[92] This convention extended protection to *all women*, regardless of their age or their willingness to prostitute themselves. Long after the League of Nations had collapsed and after the Second World War, the United Nations drew up a final convention in 1949,[93] which incorporated provisions similar to those of 1933. Britain failed to ratify either of the last two instruments, as the UK government considered that their terms of reference had been drawn too widely, as they broadened the definition of procurement and lacked any reference to gain. This point was eventually addressed by the Criminal Law Revision Committee in 1982, which commented that 'The enforcement of an offence going as wide as the Convention appears to require would, we believe, be uneven and largely ineffective.'[94]

PROTECTIVE LEGISLATION, 1900–22

Following the Vagrancy Act 1898 three more statutes grew out of the 'social purity' and feminist campaigns to protect women and children from sexual abuse and trafficking.[95] These were the Punishment of Incest Act 1908, the Criminal Law Amendment (White Slave Traffic) Act 1912, and the Criminal Law Amendment Act 1922, which were later consolidated into the Sexual

Offences Act 1956.[96] The Campaign for the Repeal of the CDAs and the development of a politically active feminist movement had initiated the deployment of tactics aimed at securing a variety of legislative changes.[97] The social purists, including those associated with the NVA, stressed the role of the law in the moral education of the community,[98] whereas feminists saw legislative reform as a means of achieving political equality through the franchise and protecting women and children from sexual abuse by men. Mid-Victorian feminists had identified the law as the ultimate embodiment of male power, but despite the contradiction, many came to believe that legislative reforms, which gave equality to women, would provide a solution.[99]

The issues of trafficking and the protection of women from sexual exploitation became areas of intense concern for women's groups. Both national and international organizations[100] appointed sub-committees that dealt specifically with prostitution and morals. For example, the Women's Suffrage Alliance had an Equal Moral Standard Commission and the National Council of Women (NCW) appointed a series of sub-committees, most of which had some relationship to the subject of prostitution. NCW sub-committees included emigration and immigration (prevention of trafficking), housing and sanitation (slum conditions, which encouraged incest), temperance (alcoholism, which led to immoral behaviour), prevention and protection (meaning prostitution) and patrolling (meaning the fight for the acceptance of women police officers). It was argued that women officers were the key to patrolling public places and controlling street prostitution, while at the same time keeping an eye open for traffickers and for young women in moral danger. Teresa Billington-Greig was one of the few prominent feminists who spoke out against the White Slave Traffic Bill, complaining of an 'epidemic of terrible rumours' that 'strained credulity'. These included tales of drugged handkerchiefs and hypodermic syringes. She conducted her own inquiry and found no one who could verify a single story.[101] The success of the Bill was partly due to Coote's campaign for international laws, which fed into areas of xenophobic and eugenic prejudice. This had the additional effect of increasing the level of support for domestic legislation against 'white slave trafficking' as London was considered to be a clearing house for the international trade, despite the lack of confirmation from the Metropolitan Police that there was any evidence of the existence of trafficking.

The CLA Act 1912 and the CLA Act 1922 were specifically aimed at dealing with gaps identified by the critics of the CLA Act 1885. The CLA Act 1912 amended the CLA Act 1885, the Vagrancy Act 1898 and the Immoral Traffic (Scotland) Act 1902. It increased police powers, widened the terms of reference under which an offence was committed and increased penalties. Section 5(1–4) tightened up the provisions concerning brothels, making it an offence for the tenant, lessee or occupier of premises knowingly to permit any part of the premises to be used as a brothel. A landlord or lessor who failed to evict such a person was guilty of 'aiding and abetting' the commission of an offence. The consequence of these provisions were that the police increased the surveillance of single women, making it more difficult for them to find lodgings, and in some cases landladies found themselves in prison.[102] Thus under the provisions of this Act a constable was empowered to arrest without warrant any person whom he had good cause to suspect of procuring or attempting to procure a girl or woman under 21 to be a common prostitute. The court was authorized to sentence a man convicted of this offence to be privately whipped, the severity of which was to be determined by the court. Among the amendments to the previous Acts was the substitution of the wording in section one of the Vagrancy Act 1898 ('and has no visible means of subsistence'), to read 'or is proved to have exercised control, direction, or influence over the movements of a prostitute in such a manner as to show that he is aiding, abetting, or compelling her prostitution'. This prevented a man from claiming as his defence that he had other 'legitimate' means of subsistence and was merely cohabiting with a woman who was a prostitute. Section 7(4) extended the offence to females who exercised control, direction or influence over a common prostitute for the purpose of gain.

The passage of the Act was influenced by a blend of prurient moralising and genuine concern for women's safety. But although it did not make prostitution in itself a criminal offence it reinforced the branding of women as 'common prostitutes' and portrayed them as victims who were under the control of wicked men, rather than as free agents. It was a portrayal of women that Teresa Billington-Greig abhorred. The broadening of offences also drew into the net any male person who associated with a prostitute, and whose assumed influence over her warranted fines of up to £100 and/or two years' imprisonment with hard labour with whipping for repeat offences.

That the Bill came before Parliament at all was due to the dogged persistence of those who had helped to draft and promote it, principally W. A. Coote. But it was also assisted by an emotional response to the death of William Stead on the *Titanic*, and by the creation of a 'Pass the Bill Committee', which promoted the measure as a fitting tribute to his memory. The harshness of the legislation could only rest upon the belief that prostitution was a permanent rather than a temporary occupation and that the unrepentant prostitute did not deserve the protection extended to the chaste woman. The trafficker, or pimp, was demonised as a foreigner (most likely Jewish) who made his living through the prostitution of women. This placed the willing prostitute in an impossible position because although her prostitution was not an offence, she was still tainted with criminality.

As a result of the 1912 Act the type of women whom Josephine Butler had portrayed as the exploited victims of a heartless state were transformed into the accessories to a serious crime: that of facilitating the exploitation of their own person. The Bill had been controversial, and subjected to prolonged debate in parliament. The principal advocate, Arthur Lee MP, insisted that it was aimed 'only at those sinister creatures who batten upon commercialised vice, and who make a profitable business out of kidnapping, decoying, ruining, and subsequently turning into prostitutes unwilling girls'.[103]

Even so, no real consideration was given to the needs of the entrapped women, while legal powers enabling the police to act as arbiters of public morals were increased. Not surprisingly, feminists reported that the Act was proving to have a detrimental effect on such women. Sylvia Pankhurst observed that the Act, which had been passed 'ostensibly' to protect women, was being used almost exclusively to punish them by hounding them out of accommodation.[104]

The urge to protect and control survived the First World War, and campaigners were still anxious to strengthen legal measures for the protection of women. The 'Pass the Bill Committee' was transformed into the Criminal Law Amendment Committee, which aspired to protect girls up to the age of 21 from seduction and sexual abuse.[105] The Bishop of London was responsible for promoting a further Criminal Law Amendment Bill in 1914,[106] which proposed: (1) raising from 13 to 16 the age at which the consent of a young person of either sex was a defence to a lesser charge of indecent assault; (2) raising from 16 to 18 the age at which a woman could consent to unlawful carnal intercourse (outside the bonds of marriage); (3) extending to 12 months the time within which proceedings could be taken against persons who had unlawful carnal intercourse with girls of or above the age of 13 and under the age of 18 (which at the time was limited to six months); (4) taking away the defence allowed to a person charged with the defilement of girls between 13 and 18, and abduction of girls under 18, that the defendant had reasonable cause to believe that the girl was over the age of 16 or 18, as the case may be. The Bill foundered, but new Bills were presented to the House in February and March 1917, and in 1918 and 1921.[107] A similar blend of protective and offensive measures was combined. In addition they sought variously to curb the spread of venereal disease, to extend the powers of the Indecent Advertisements Act 1889, and to give the courts power to order the detention of a girl under the age of 18 in an approved institution if she had been convicted of loitering or soliciting for the purpose of prostitution (under any of the multifarious Acts which made this an offence), or if the court had reason to believe that her mode of life made such detention expedient. Given the powers that were already contained in the Mental Deficiency Act 1913, this would have made it possible to detain any supposedly 'promiscuous' woman under 18 in an institution. The final Bill of 1921 was enacted in 1922 and was directed mainly towards protective measures. It removed the defence of 'reasonable cause to believe' (except in the case of a first offence by a man under 24), it removed the defence that a child under 16 had consented to indecent assault, it extended to nine months the period during which a victim of rape could lodge a complaint and it increased penalties for brothel-keeping. These offences were perceived as measures for the protection of children and young women, but the civil rights implications became more apparent when the sexual mores of young people changed (or became less regulated) during the latter half of the century.

THE THREAD OF REGULATION, 1864–1968

Walkowitz's generally accepted view that the CDAs created an 'outcast' group has attracted some criticism. Petrow, for example, has found many references where pity rather than contempt was extended to the prostitute. If moral censure had been the only cause for condemnation, pity might have prevailed, but the fear of disease has often overridden other considerations, leaving the authorities willing to legitimate the less tolerant aspects of public opinion. The labelling of women as 'common prostitutes' was critical, as a simple means of identification had to be found. For without classification, the grey area between promiscuity and prostitution would have rendered the legislation too imprecise, pressure from the moralists would have increased and the objections concerning civil liberties made more difficult to evade. The responsibility for identification was usually given to the police, for whom it was convenient to assert that there was a professional class of women involved. Even so, the confidence with which this labelling could be done began to unravel during the First World War, when it became clear that some women had a liking for soldiers regardless of whether money was exchanged. This was made clear in the *Shield* in 1917, when the Association of Moral and Social Hygiene (AMSH) protested against the coercive clauses included in the CLA Bill of that year. In response, a letter from an anonymous reader of *The Times* was quoted, in which the correspondent fulminated against the sexual 'freelance' woman who prostituted her body, 'not for money, not as a trade, but because she wants to do so'. It had apparently become just as important to deal with the immoral 'non-prostitute', whom the correspondent accused of infecting four times as many men as the professional woman infected. 'At present,' he complained, 'they stalk through the land, vampires upon the nation's health, distributing and perpetuating amongst our young manhood diseases which institute a national calamity.'[108]

Venereal disease, like prostitution, was a metaphor for physical and moral decay and was thought by many to threaten the institutions of social order and racial progress.[109] However, the level of concern was as acute for women as it was for men, as many suffered the unexpected consequence of infection by their husbands and consequently passed on congenital disabilities to their offspring. Some women attempted to shift the responsibility for infection on to men, and many concluded that spinsterhood and chastity were preferable to marriage. Christabel Pankhurst coined the unrealistic slogan, 'Votes For Women and Chastity for Men'.[110] She assumed that once women's suffrage had been achieved, economic equality would follow and prostitution would become unnecessary.

Following the repeal of the CDAs, the medical profession finally admitted that the attempt at the regulation of prostitution had failed. The Acts had not addressed the problem of infection in men or reached the women working outside the system. The gradual realisation that venereal disease was prevalent amongst the general population caused it to be redefined as a civilian rather than a military problem, and a greater emphasis was placed upon voluntary methods of control and healthy living.[111] Despite this evolution of thought the level of infection continued to cause concern. A Royal Commission was set up in 1913[112] and reported in 1916, by which time the country was at war so that the corresponding rise in the cases of venereal disease amongst the troops revived the focus upon VD as a military problem. The various military commanders adopted different approaches according to their inclinations. Some, such as Lord Kitchener,[113] had encouraged the men to preserve their strength for the sake of the nation, while others thought that illicit sex was a necessary adjunct to the dangers of combat[114] and therefore that prophylactic provision ought to be made available.

The government responded to the outbreak of war with the Defence of the Realm Act 1914 (DORA) and in view of the rise in infections, Regulation 13A, which authorised the deportation of prostitutes from the vicinity of military camps, was added in April 1916. As a result the military authorities in Cardiff banned women from public houses between 7 a.m. and 6 p.m., and five women were arrested and given a 60-day sentence of imprisonment.[115] In a similar vein, policewomen in Grantham were asked to help keep women, children and girls at home, only to discover that the troops were being entertained privately.[116] The government later admitted that Regulation 13A had proved to be ineffectual. Men moved out of town if they wanted to visit a prostitute, while women moved from one district to another or denied that they were prostitutes. The so-called 'good-time girl' and the 'amateur prostitute' remained unaffected and became the new bogies. In the wake of the failure of the 1917–18 Bills, the government introduced the notorious Regulation 40D,[117] which prohibited any women who suffered from a communicable disease from having sexual intercourse with a member of His Majesty's Forces. A woman charged with such an offence had the 'right' to be remanded for a period (not less than a week) for the purpose of medical examination, to establish whether or not she was suffering from such a disease (syphilis, gonorrhoea or soft chancre).[118] The possibility that the woman had contracted one of the aforesaid diseases from her own boyfriend or husband was ignored by the authorities.

The evidence shows that the temptation to embark upon coercive measures was never far from the surface and the justifications were usually on 'moral' grounds, which were more liberally applied to disadvantaged members of the community. In 1909 the Royal Commission on the Poor Laws had recommended that public assistance authorities should have the power to detain paupers suffering from venereal infections if, on medical inspection, they were considered to be a danger to others. When the Royal Commission on Venereal Disease reported in 1916, it subscribed to this policy, and although it recommended a voluntary system, it recognised that heightened public awareness of the social costs of disease might lead to the acceptance of more coercive measures.[119] Following the report the government established a free and confidential system for dealing with infection. However, the commission's conclusions, that the number of people infected with syphilis was not likely to fall below 10 per cent of the population in big cities and that the percentage affected by gonorrhoea would greatly exceed this proportion, left the moralists fully prepared to campaign for more restrictive measures, if only in respect to the 'irresponsible' element. These feelings manifested themselves in some quarters through a backlash against prophylactic methods of control, perceived, like the regulation of prostitution, to represent the state's endorsement of promiscuity. The Medical Women's Federation (MWF) issued a manifesto on the subject, stating:

> We desire to point out that in the case of women either prophylaxes or early preventative treatment would be used as preventative of conception. The complete carrying out of such a system must include the distribution of packets and the placing of posters drawing attention to the system in public lavatories and other suitable places. Whether or not safety could be obtained, promiscuous intercourse would be looked upon as free from risk and infection and to a great extent free from risk of conception and as recognised and protected by the State and Health Authorities, who would become in the eyes of the ignorant the consenting party to their action. We believe that by no such method can the problem of venereal disease be met, and that a phase of society would be produced as vicious and degenerate as any of which history has record. *Safety from infection would not be attained, while moral degradation and sex excesses would rot the very foundations of society.*[120] (original italics)

Although this statement fed into concerns over the falling birth rate and disapproval of contraception, the point being made by the MWF is a familiar one. It was argued that encouraging promiscuity by making illicit intercourse safe would in the long run increase the incidence of disease while prophylactic measures only provided a partial remedy. According to the MWF and like-minded organisations, the answer was not safe sex but higher moral standards. However, as Roger Davidson has shown, endorsement of coercive methods led along a downwards path as some practitioners showed a willingness to adopt eugenic principles involving 'controls on marriage and conception and the enforced treatment of pregnant women known to be infected'.[121]

In 1917[122] there was a separate Act aimed at controlling the treatment by unqualified practitioners of venereal disease and at the control and supply of remedies. However, DORA, together with its regulations, was abandoned in stages after the First World War was over. Predictably, similar tactics were deployed again during the Second World War, when the rate of venereal infection rose substantially. Defence Regulation 33B[123] was introduced in November 1942 in an attempt to limit the spread among the general population. The regulation required venereal disease specialists to pass on information concerning the sexual partners of patients to the local medical officer of health. If the same contact was named twice, he or she would have a notice served upon them, requiring them to submit to examination and treatment. A clearance certificate would be issued when the patient was judged to be free of the disease. Any person who refused to comply with the regulation risked three months' imprisonment or a £100 fine although the informer, who might also be infected, was free and anonymous. The AMSH denounced the regulation, claiming that when a sharp rise in syphilis infection had occurred in 1932, the government had not thought it necessary to bring in panic measures.[124] The British Medical Association, on the other hand, supported it on the ground that no one should be free to 'run around' spreading infection. Others were more critical. *Time and Tide*[125] maintained that there was nothing to be said for regulation, medically, morally, or legally. In particular it deplored the creation by law of an 'informer' and of a new class of 'suspected person' against whom exceptional measures could be taken, complaining: 'This is Nazi to the very core.' It was hoped that the government would have the sense to withdraw it.

However, instead of withdrawing the regulation, the Ministry of Health issued Circular 2896 in 1943, empowering and encouraging local authorities to follow up alleged contacts after only one notification. Informers were encouraged to describe alleged contacts, and health visitors embarked upon tours of public houses and dance halls in an effort to track them down and persuade them to submit to examination. Regulation 33B was annulled in December 1947 but the principle was not so lightly relinquished. On 5 January 1948, Circular 5/48, entitled '"Expiry of Defence Regulation 33B": Suggested methods of continuing to trace sources of infection', was distributed to county councils and county borough councils. The Ministry of Health recognised the usefulness of the discontinued regulation and was anxious to encourage authorities to continue the practice of tracing contacts, notwithstanding the expiry of the wartime regulation. The leaflet went on to suggest a web of deceit, encouraging patients to divulge confidential information about their contacts and to suggest issuing them with a card that would later be presented to the clinic, so that the informant and contact could be linked. The name of the informant would not be given to the health visitor who interviewed the contact, so that awkward questions could be circumvented.[126]

Although the controversy declined in importance after the war, it never entirely went away. A new upsurge in the incidence of disease during the 1960s brought attempts to enact similar measures. A Private Members' Bill was presented to the House of Commons in 1962 by Richard Marsh MP[127] that would have provided for the restoration of provisions formerly contained in Defence Regulation 33B, which would have empowered local authorities to require anyone who had been named twice to report for examination. He was particularly concerned about high-risk groups such as prostitutes.[128] A final attempt was made by Sir Myer Galpern in 1969,[129] which would have provided for a penalty of £20 or two months' imprisonment on first conviction and a fine of £50 and two months' imprisonment for a second conviction. The JBS urged Sir Myer Galpern to reconsider his proposals, on the ground that Regulation

33B had failed to reduce the incidence of venereal disease. It was also claimed that Regulation 33B had discouraged people who suspected that they might be infected from seeking medical help and had undermined the patient–doctor relationship. Moreover, since the complainants remained anonymous, the regulation was an infringement of British justice and a violation of human rights, because it deprived the named contact of the legal protection against deformation of character that was afforded to all other persons.[130]

Support for either Bill was insufficient to secure an Act, but what fails by regular means sometimes succeeds by stealth. In 1962 the *Daily Herald*[131] featured the story of a Mrs Allegranza, a 'Ban the Bomb' protester, who had been committed to Holloway Prison for 18 weeks. Mrs Allegranza alleged that she had been subjected to a compulsory vaginal examination, which she had found distressing. A question was asked in the House and the Minister of State for the Home Office, R. A. Butler, denied that VD tests were compulsory, stating that this one had been carried out with the patient's consent.[132] However, a statement made by Miss Oonagh Lahr suggests otherwise, as she and a number of 'Ban the Bomb' protesters had been subjected to the same treatment. She was particularly upset to find that pregnant women were subjected to intrusive inspections, which on occasion had been the cause of miscarriage.[133]

The Ministry of Health had not dropped the matter either, although it maintained a lower profile. In 1968 a new (Statutory Instrument) regulation, The National Health Service (Control of Venereal Disease) Regulations 1968, was issued along with a memorandum.[134] The memorandum provided detailed instructions on the methods to be adopted for tracing contacts and for transferring this information between various health authorities, while maintaining patient confidentiality. It was judged that these procedures held out the greatest prospect for effective preventative action, given the worrying increase in cases of syphilis and gonorrhoea. The screening of special groups, including prostitutes of both sexes, was felt to be of particular importance as a means of controlling the sources of acquired infection. It had been found that speedy contact tracing was the method most likely to produce satisfactory results, and that bringing promiscuous females under treatment contributed a disproportionately high degree of success to the control of infection.

In pursuance of this policy special 'contact tracers' were to be employed by local health authorities. A detailed form, which would provide a personal description of the contact and would state whether or not the patient had been solicited, was to be filled in by the medical officer (hospital doctor or GP) when interviewing a patient, and a fee paid to him. Armed with these details the contact tracer was then expected to visit likely venues, try to identify the 'culprit' and 'if possible' transport him/her immediately to the nearest clinic, at whatever time of day or night that might be. It was also suggested that individual health authorities should set up a central office so as to enable contract tracers to pool information and correlate descriptions. The contact tracer was to remain immune from accusation of slander.

It was claimed in the memorandum that these complex procedures were the most important single preventative measure that could be taken in an attempt to control the disease, especially as it might enable the medical authorities to make contact with promiscuous groups. And although the memorandum continually underlined the importance of patient confidentiality, the same emphasis was not extended to the contact. In the case of casual contacts it was suggested that consideration should be given to the use of a more active tracing system in which identifying details concerning the contacts were diligently sought. Such details, if conscientiously pursued, would inevitably have provided a database that included prostitutes and allegedly promiscuous females. Whether such a list, once compiled, would remain confidential is a matter for speculation. In view of the fact that the 1968 regulation revoked and modified the confidentiality procedures incorporated in the regulation of 1948, so as to enable the information to be exchanged between medical practitioners and their employees (hospital doctors and GPs),[135] it seems quite feasible that other departments of authority might feel that they ought to be given access to the material.

These 'official' attempts to limit the spread of venereal disease demonstrate the consequences of allowing stereotyped views of women as 'good or bad' to influence policy. In this instance there seems to have been a sincere acceptance within the Ministry of Health and some medical circles that women were the core of the problem, and that if only prostitutes and promiscuous women could be identified the spread of infection would be curbed. This comfortable assumption must have been undermined with the onset of the AIDS epidemic in the 1980s, when the complexity of some people's sexual lives became apparent.

NOTES

1. Mary Poovey (1989), *Uneven Developments: The Ideological Work of Gender in Mid-Victorian England*, Virago, London, p. 53.
2. This is a fascinating area in itself; see Christopher Hill (1964), *Society and Puritanism in Pre-Revolutionary England*, Secker and Warburg, London, Ch. 8; E. J. Bristow (1977), *Vice and Vigilance*, Gill and Macmillan, Rowman and Littlefield, Dublin, pp. 12–13; John Addy (1989), *Sin and Society*, Routledge, London.
3. Elizabeth Melling (1964), *Kentish Sources*, Kent County Council.
4. 22 Hen. VIII. (1530–1) c. 12; 27 Hen. VIII. (1535–6) c. 25; 1 Ed. VI. (1547) c. 3; 3 & 4 Ed. VI. (1549–50) c. 16; 5 & 6 Ed. VI. (1551–2) c. 2; 5 Eliz. (1562–3) c. 3; 14 Eliz. (1572) c. 5; 18 Eliz. (1575–6) c. 3; 39 Eliz. (1597–8) c. 3; 43 Eliz. (1601) c. 2. Quoted in Melling.
5. Ivy Pinchbeck (1977), *Women Workers in the Industrial Revolution, 1750–1850*, Frank Cass, London, p. 80 (first published 1930).
6. General disorder could be dealt with through the Justices of the Peace Act [34 Ed. 3. A. D. 1360–1], which provided for the restraint and imprisonment of persons 'not of good fame' suspected or thought likely to cause a breach of the peace, and for their binding over on surety of good behaviour. The Disorderly Houses Act 1751 [25 Geo. 2. c. 36] provided for the prosecution of keepers of bawdy houses (i.e. brothels) or disorderly houses.
7. Edward J. Burford and S. Shulman (1994), *Of Bridles and Burnings*, Robert Hale, London, p. 79.
8. Lionel Rose (1988), *Rogues and Vagabonds: Vagrant Underworld in Britain 1815–1985*, Routledge, London, p. 3.
9. The Vagrants Act 1824 [5 Geo. 4. c. 83]. Section 3 provided that: 'every common prostitute wandering in the public streets or public highway, or in any place of public resort, and

behaving in a riotous or indecent manner; . . . Shall be deemed an idle and disorderly person . . . and it shall be lawful for any justice of the peace to commit such offender (being therefore convicted before him by his own view or by the confession of such offender, or by the evidence on oath of one or more credible witnesses), to the house of correction, there to be kept to hard labour for any time not exceeding one calendar month.' Further offences would lead to imprisonment for three months under further definitions of 'a rogue and a vagabond', and as an 'incorrigible rogue'.

10. Section 8 of the Act empowered a constable to apprehend any person charged as an idle and disorderly person etc., take their goods and possessions, and convey them to the Justice of the Peace, who could order the searching of their goods and their person who was also empowered to order the sale of such goods and possessions to pay costs.

11. One explanation, given to me by a QC, is that the common prostitute, like the barrister and the taxi-driver, is obliged through common law to make herself available indiscriminately to all who can afford to hire her. This explanation raises many questions. For example, a common calling (trade or profession), carries with it both privileges and duties. The barrister has undergone a lengthy training and the taxi-driver a shorter one, and they are both restrained and protected by rules and regulations. The statement that prostitution is a trade or profession is used by the sex worker to demand respect and by the legislator to justify regulation. The legality of prostitution also means that it can be taxed, although a prostitute is not allowed to register her enterprise as a business.

12. See Douglas Hay (1977), 'Property, Authority and the Criminal Law', in Douglas Hay et al., *Albion's Fatal Tree, Crime and Society in Eighteenth-Century England*, Penguin Books, London, p. 62.

13. Metropolitan Police Act 1839 [2 & 3 Vic. c. 47]. Section 54 provided that:

   (1)   every person shall be liable to a penalty of not more than forty shillings, who within the limits of the Metropolitan Police District, shall in any thoroughfare or public place commit any of the following offences; that is to say,

   (11) Every common prostitute or street walker loitering or being in any thoroughfare or public place for the purpose of prostitution. Or solicitation to the annoyance of the inhabitants or passengers:

   (13) Every person who shall use any threatening abusive or insulting words or behaviour with intent to provoke a breach of the peace or whereby a breach of the peace may be occasioned: And it shall be lawful for any constable belonging to the Metropolitan Police force to take into custody, without warrant, any person who shall commit such offence within view of any such constable.

14. Town Police Clauses Act 1847 [10 & 11 Vic. c. 89]. This Act made similar provisions, substituting the word 'importuning' for 'soliciting' in section 28 (repealed by the Street Offences Act 1959), and: '35. Every person keeping a house, shop, room, or other place of public resort, within the limits of the special Act for the sale or consumption of refreshments of any kind who knowingly suffers common prostitutes or reputed thieves to assemble at and continue in his premises shall, for every such offence, be liable to a penalty not exceeding £20.'

15. See Robert D. Storch (1986), 'The Plague of Blue Locusts: Police Reform and Popular Resistance in Northern England, 1840–57', reprinted in M. Fitzgerald, G. McLennan and J. Pawson, *Crime & Society*, Routledge, London, p. 86.

16. *Morning Post*, 1 February 1858. William Acton Scrapbook, WL.

17. See Judith R. Walkowitz (1980), *Prostitution and Victorian Society*, Cambridge University Press, p. 192.

18. See, for example, the research project conducted on behalf of the feminist organisation Rights of Women (ROW), during the 1980s: S. Mavolwane, S. Miller and J. Watson (1989), 'Policing Prostitution', Rights of Women, 52–54 Featherstone Street, London. The report begins by describing the monitoring of police responses to prostitution in the King's Cross area of London between 1982 and 1985. Following on from this project a separate survey was conducted centred on the areas of Balham, Paddington and Bayswater. The research team recorded that it had found evidence of the increasing criminalisation of black people, a disregard of civil liberties and codes of practice, the police giving advice that prostitutes were not entitled to consult a solicitor over a loitering offence, failure to give a prostitute's caution or a formal legal caution on arrest, arrest of prostitutes on a rota basis (including when they were not working) in order to maintain police control of the streets, and a failure

to provide an effective strategy to ensure women's safety. With reference to the Street Offences Act 1959, the authors comment that, 'The construction of this particular piece of legislation, whereby a woman is already proved guilty before she enters the court, is exceptional in British legal history', p. 39.

19. Industrial Schools (Amendment) Act 1880 [17 & 18 Vict. c. 14–16]. This Act was passed as a result of the work of the social purity campaigner Ellice Jane Hopkins.

20. Walkowitz (1980), *Prostitution and Victorian Society*, Chs 11, 12, p. 311 n. 84. See also P. Bartley (2000) *Prostitution Prevention and Reform in England, 1860–1914*, Routledge, London, pp. 84–5. The removal of children by the social services, on the ground that a prostitute is a bad mother, remains a constant fear for many prostitutes.

21. See Clive Emsley (1991), *The English Police: A Political and Social History*, Harvester Wheatsheaf, New York, p. 75.

22. Steve Uglow (1988), *Policing Liberal Society*, Oxford University Press, p. 27.

23. The work of Thomas Malthus on the relationship between the rate of population increase, poverty and starvation must have been influential in this respect. See Thomas Robert Malthus, *First Essay on Population 1798*, reprinted by Macmillan Co., London, 1926. For a discussion of Malthus in terms of his influence upon sexual mores, see Roy Porter and Lesley Hall (1995), *The Facts of Life: The Creation of Sexual Knowledge in Britain, 1650–1950*, Yale University Press, New Haven, CT, pp. 127–8.

24. Contagious Diseases Act 1864 [27 & 28 Victoria c. 85]; Contagious Diseases Act 1866 [29 & 30 Victoria c. 34, 35]; Contagious Diseases Act 1869 [32 & 33 Victoria c. 96].

25. By 1864, 33 per cent of the home-based troops had been hospitalised on account of venereal disease.

26. International Medical Congress, Paris 1867; International Medical Congress, Florence 1870; International Medical Congress, Vienna 1873; International Medical Congress, Brussels 1875. See Sheldon Amos (1877), *A Comparative Survey of Laws in Force for the Prohibition, Regulation and Licensing of Vice in England and Other Countries*, Stevens & Co., London, pp. 1–2. See also Benjamin Scott (1894), *A State of Iniquity: Its Rise, Extension and Overthrow*, reprinted 1968, Augustus M. Kelly, New York; Henry J. Wilson (1907), 'A Rough Record of events and incidences connected with the Repeal of the Contagious Diseases Acts, 1864–6–9 in the United Kingdom, and of the movement against state regulation of Vice, in India and the Colonies, *1858–1906* Parker Brothers, Sheffield.

27. Amos, *A Comparative Survey*, p. 2. During the 1875 Congress M. Vleminkx (of Brussels) expressed the opinion that the free range of prostitution in England constituted a danger to the Continent. 'Hygiene ought to be international'. . . involving the 'joint action of all nations'.

28. Royal Commission appointed May 1859, to enquire into the 'Sanitary State of the Army in India'. Chairman Lord Herbert succeeded by Lord Stanley on his resignation. Reporting in 1863, it suggested that more constructive means for the occupation of leisure hours should be adopted.

29. See Alan Ramsay Skelley (1977), *The Victorian Army at Home: The Recruitment and Terms and Conditions of the British Regular, 1859–1899*, Croom Helm, London, pp. 55–7; Edward M. Spiers (1980), *The Army and Society, 1815–1914*, Longman, London, p. 162.

30. Josephine Butler was portrayed as a saint by her early biographers, e.g. L. Hay-Cooper (1921), *Josephine Butler and her Work for Social Purity*, London Society for Promoting Christian Knowledge, or as the heroine of the repeal campaign. For an alternative view see Bertrand O. Taithe, 'From Danger to Scandal, Debating Sexuality in Victorian England: The Contagious Diseases Acts (1864–1869) and the Morbid Imagery of Victorian Society', PhD thesis, University of Manchester (1992). Taithe argues that most of the action took place in the North of England and that Josephine Butler was not as influential as she has been made out to be, but was used as a political front by male-dominated societies.

31. A good account of these incidents can be found in Paul McHugh (1980), *Prostitution and Victorian Social Reform*, Croom Helm, London and Trevor Fisher (1995) *Scandal: The Sexual Politics of Late Victorian England*, Alan Sutton Publishing, Stroud.

32. This is a debatable point as the incidence of disease declined for a number of reasons, including higher standards of sanitation, provision of recreational facilities and better medical care. See, for example, Spiers, *The Army and Society*, pp. 143–5.

33. 'Bruce's Bill' was introduced to the House on 13 February 1872. It was entitled 'A Bill for the prevention of certain Contagious Diseases and for the better Protection of Women'.

34. Accounts of this incident are to be found in A. S. G. Butler (1953), *Portrait of Josephine*

Butler, Faber and Faber, London, Ch. 5; E. Moberly Bell (1963), *Josephine Butler: Flame of Fire*, Constable, London, pp. 97–8 and 210.

35. There are innumerable accounts of these events. See, for example, Charles Terrot (1959), *The Maiden Tribute: A Study of the White Slave Traffic of the Nineteenth Century*, Frederick Muller, London; Glen Petrie (1971), *A Singular Iniquity: The Campaigns of Josephine Butler*, New York.
36. Stefan Petrow (1994), *Policing Morals: The Metropolitan Police and the Home Office 1870–1914*, Clarendon Press, Oxford, Ch. 5.
37. See, for example, L. Bland (1995), *Banishing the Beast: English Feminism and Sexual Morality, 1883–1995*, Penguin Books, London, pp. 105–8.
38. A helpful account can be found in T. Fisher (1995), *Scandal: The Sexual Politics of Late Victorian England*, Alan Sutton Publishing, Stroud, pp. 19–29.
39. Ibid., p. 133.
40. Criminal Law Amendment Act 1885 [48 & 49 Vict. c. 69].
41. See Ann Stafford (1964), *The Age of Consent*, Hodder and Stoughton, London.
42. See Fisher, *Scandal*.
43. *Vigilance Record*, 15 February 1887.
44. For example, the London Council for the Promotion of Public Morality and the Birmingham and Midland Counties' Vigilance Association and many others.
45. Bartley, *Prostitution Prevention*, Ch. 7.
46. See Judith R. Walkowitz (1992), *City of Dreadful Delight: Narratives of Sexual Danger in Late Victorian London*, Virago, London, Ch. 7; Colin Wilson and Robin Odell (1987), *Jack the Ripper: Summing up and Verdict*, Bantam Press; Angus McLaren (1993), *A Prescription for Murder: The Victorian Serial Killings of Dr. Thomas Neill Cream*, University of Chicago Press.
47. Vagrancy Act 1898 [61 & 62 Vict. c. 38 & 39]:

    (1) Every male person who –
        (a) knowingly lives wholly or in part on the earnings of prostitution: or
        (b) in any public place persistently solicits or importunes for immoral purposes, shall be deemed a rogue or a vagabond within the meaning of the Vagrants Act 1824.
    (2) If it is made to appear to a court of summary jurisdiction by information on oath that there is reason to suspect that any house or any part of a house is used by a female for purposes of prostitution, and that any male person residing in or frequenting the house is living wholly or in part on the earnings of the prostitute, the court may issue a warrant authorising any constable to enter and search the house and to arrest the male person.
    (3) Where a male person is proved to live or to be habitually in the company of a prostitute and has no visible means of substance, he shall, unless he can satisfy the court to the contrary, be deemed to be living on the earnings of prostitution.

48. Judith R. Walkowitz (1983), 'Male Vice and Female Virtue: Feminism and the Politics of Prostitution in Nineteenth Century Britain', in Ann Sinitow, Christine Stansell and Sharon Thompson (eds), *Desire: The Politics of Sexuality*, Virago, London, p. 51.
49. Bristow, *Vice and Vigilance*, p. 170, comments on the mass influx of foreign immigrants from Eastern Europe during the 1900s, a number of whom were pimps and bullies and established trafficking connections between London and South America. This contributed to the climate of opinion in which the Aliens Act of 1905 was passed.
50. William Alexander Coote died in 1919, having devoted himself for over thirty years to the cause of social purity. His obituary in the *Vigilance Record*, November 1919, describes him as having 'a fire about him; a quiet flame, but it was always burning'. He was said to be a man of deep faith and limitless patience, who was devoted to moral protection and legal reform. He was awarded the Légion d'Honneur, but despite his close relationships with the British Foreign Office and extensive (self-appointed) diplomatic engagements, he was not awarded any official recognition in his own country. This is probably because, although his powers of persuasion were recognised, his moralising zeal was not really appreciated. Even so, his tenacity and diplomatic skills seem to have been the driving force behind the creation of the international movement.
51. William A. Coote (1916), *Romance of Philanthropy*, NVA publication, pp. 177–83, also W. A. Coote (1910), *A Vision and its Fulfilment*, NVA publication, passim.

52. *Vigilance Record*, July 1899. The congress resolved that the offence of trafficking consisted of 'the procuring of women or girls by violence, fraud, abuse of authority, or any other method of constraint to give themselves to debauchery'.
53. An examination of the archival records of societies such as the YWCA and the GFS (amongst others), demonstrates the intensity of the concern that had been generated by the type of propaganda issued by the NVA and reported generally at the time.
54. Berenger was a liberal Catholic who became the life and soul of the French vigilance movement. He was the founder of the Society for the Revival of Public Morality and organiser of the French National Committee. He made the struggle against the white slave trade his main political aim. See A. Corbin, *Women for Hire: Prostitution and Sexuality in France after 1850*, trans. A. Sheridan, Harvard University Press, Cambridge, MA, pp. 258, 278.
55. Twenty-four papers delivered by delegates at the 1899 London Congress. See *Vigilance Record*, October 1900.
56. *Vigilance Record*, May 1902.
57. Ibid.
58. Coote, *Romance of Philanthropy*, p. 211.
59. *Vigilance Record*, October 1902. This appeal had an unabashed class bias.
60. Amsterdam (1890); Frankfurt (1902); Zurich (1904); Paris (1906); Madrid (1910); London (1913); Warsaw (1930); Berlin (1933); Paris (1937); London (1949); Brussels (1958); Geneva (1965).
61. Ample evidence can be found of the level of anxiety that was generated by the issue of 'white slavery' in the 'Traveller's Aid Society' archives, WL; the 'Young Women's Christian Association' archives, Modern Record Office, University of Warwick; and the 'Girls Friendly Society', 25 Queen's Gate, London.
62. Corbin, *Women for Hire*, pp. 280–2.
63. Children (Employment Abroad) Act 1913 [3 & 4 Geo. 5. c. 7].
64. Coote, *Romance of Philanthropy*, pp. 126–31. The NVA was particularly concerned with theatrical and music-hall agencies, which placed young women in what it considered to be very vulnerable situations.
65. Children Act 1908 [8 Edw. 7. c. 67.]
66. Coote, *Romance of Philanthropy*, p. 132.
67. Aliens Act 1905 [5 Edw. 7. c. 13]; Aliens Restriction Act 1914 and 1919 [4 & 5 Geo. 5. c. 12, and 9 & 10 Geo. 5. c. 92]; Aliens Order 1920, No. 448. Section 8 of this order provided for a central register of aliens under the direction of the Secretary of State. The chief officer of each police district was to be the registration officer for his district.
68. Corbin, *Women for Hire*, pp. 289–98.
69. International Agreement for the Suppression of the White Slave Traffic, signed in Paris on 18 May 1904, ratified in Paris, 18 January1905 by Great Britain, Germany, Denmark, Spain, France, Italy, Russia, Sweden, Norway, Switzerland, Belgium, Netherlands, and Portugal. Treaty Series No. 24. HMSO [Cd. 2689].
70. Article 2 of the International Agreement 1904 stated: 'Each of the Governments undertakes to have a watch kept, especially in railway stations, ports of embarkation, and *en route*, for persons in charge of women and girls destined for an immoral life. With this object instructions shall be given to the officials and all other qualified persons to obtain, within legal limits, all information likely to lead to the detection of criminal traffic.' Article 3 stated: 'The Governments also undertake, within legal limits, and as far as can be done, to entrust temporarily, and with a view to their eventual repatriation, the victims of criminal traffic when destitute, to public or private charitable institutions, or to private individuals offering the necessary security.' In the UK this work was undertaken by middle-class volunteers belonging to various groups, mainly the Traveller's Aid Society (which was a coalition of different societies), the NVA, the International Bureau and the Jewish Society for the Protection of Girls and Women.
71. Coote, *Romance of Philanthropy*, p. 199.
72. Undated pamphlet issued by the International Bureau for the Suppression of the White Slave Traffic, NVA/IB, Box 193,WL.
73. Ibid.
74. Ibid.
75. Ibid.
76. Repatriation was a core policy, but was to involve the help of voluntary organisations, which were expected to care for the woman while arrangements were made for her return home. If

a woman had no financial means the cost of transporting her to the frontier would be met by the country in which she was resident and the remainder by the country of origin. As this policy does not seem to have been very successful, governments found other ways of limiting prostitution, including immigration controls and repression of commercialised vice. Traffickers also found ways of circumventing regulations, including moving on to a different country or returning to the country from which the woman had been expelled, via a different border. See Bascom Johnson (1928), 'The Attitudes of Governments Towards Foreign Prostitutes', *Journal of Social Hygiene*, Vol. XIV, No. 3, March, pp. 129–38. By 1930 the issue had become contentious, with the International Bureau recommending compulsory repatriation and the punishment of women who returned to the country from which they had been expelled. See 'Repatriation of Prostitutes: A Memorandum on the Proposals of the International Bureau', International Bureau (1931), IB/Box 193, WL. The AMSH protested, stating that: 'The defence of society against the traffic in women is not the same thing as the protection of society against prostitutes.' See 'The Compulsory Repatriation of Prostitutes', AMSH (1931), 3/AMS Box 102, WL.

77. F. S. Bullock, 'White Slave Traffic', New Scotland Yard, 12 June 1913, (PRO) MEPO, 2/1312, p. 4. Bullock based his statement on the basis of consultations with chief constables from many of the major towns in England. See also text of 'The Fifth International Congress, 1913', NVA publication, WL.

78. 'Correspondence respecting the International Conferences on Obscene Publications and the White Slave Traffic. Held in Paris, April and May 1910.' Presented to Parliament by Command of His Majesty (HMSO, 1912).

79. 'International Convention for the Suppression of the White Slave Traffic', signed in Paris May 1910. Signed by Austria and Hungary, Great Britain, France, Belgium, Brazil, Denmark, Spain, Italy, The Netherlands, Portugal, Russia, Sweden. Treaty Series 1912. No. 20. [Cd. 6336].

80. The criminal offence of trafficking was finally defined as the procuring and leading away of an under-age girl for immoral purposes, and/or the procuring and leading away, by fraud or force, of a woman of full age, for immoral purposes abroad. Contracting states agreed to take steps to adapt their legislation in ways that would enable them to prosecute offenders.

81. International Convention for the Suppression of the White Slave Traffic, signed Paris May 1910. 'Final Protocol', para. D. 'The case of detention, against her will, of a woman or girl in a brothel could not, in spite of its gravity, be dealt with in the present Convention, seeing that it is covered exclusively by internal legislation.'

82. For example, in 1910 delegates at the Madrid Congress attended a reception given by HRH the Infanta Isabella. Coote described the occasion: 'The Scene was a brilliant one, several members of the royal family being present, together with various Government Ministers, the Papal Nuncio, the Archbishop of Seville. The beautiful rooms, splendidly illuminated, and enriched with costly pictures and valuable porcelain' (*Vigilance Record*, November 1910).

83. Ibid.

84. See also Sheila Jeffreys (1997), *The Idea of Prostitution*, Spinifex Press, North Melbourne, Australia, Ch. 1.

85. An International Labour Conference of the League of Nations was held in Washington in October 1919, during which a commitment was made to respect the dignity of women and children. See 'League of Nations records on the International Conference on Traffic in Women and Children', Geneva 1921 [C. 484. M. 339] p. 9.

86. See 'A Century of Cooperation', I.B. booklet 1955, NVA archives, WL.

87. 'League of Nations Convention on the Traffic in Women and Children', Geneva, 18 October 1921 [A. 125 (1) 1921. IV].

88. Edward J. Bristow (1982), *Prostitution and Prejudice: The Jewish Fight against White Slavery, 1870–1939*, Clarendon Press, Oxford. The use of the word 'white' is described as a 'Eurocentric misnomer', since the largest role in trafficking was played by the Chinese and Japanese, p. 2.

89. League of Nations, Geneva (1927), 'Report of the Special Body of Experts on Traffic in Women and Children, Part I [C 52. M. 52. 1927] p. 43. The body was set up in March 1923, as a result of an initiative by Miss Grace Abbott. Miss Abbott was the first American representative to the League of Nations Advisory Committee on the Traffic in Women and Children. The purpose of the project was to ascertain the extent of the traffic in women and children for the purpose of prostitution. The Body of Experts submitted its report to the

Council of the League of Nations in 1927. It did not make specific recommendations, but suggested that third-party profiteering was the cause of the problem, and expressed the hope that an increasing number of countries would move towards the abolitionist policy of suppressing the tolerated brothel. It also made vague comments about the need for higher moral standards. See also Bristow, *Prostitution and Prejudice*, p. 39.

90. Ibid., p. 9.
91. *Vigilance Record*, June–July 1927, p. 55.
92. 'International Convention for the Suppression of the Traffic of Women of Full Age, 1933.' A copy of this Convention may be found in the International Bureau publication, 'Introductory note on the legislative development of the International Conventions against the traffic in Women and Children, 1943', p. 3. NVA archives, WL.
93. 'United Nations Convention for the Suppression of the Traffic in Persons and the Exploitation of the Prostitution of Others, 1949.'
94. Criminal Law Revision Committee, 'Working Paper on Offences Relating to Prostitution and Allied Offences' (1982). The CLRC also pointed out that Article 1 of the United Nations Convention 1949 required the punishment of any person who procures the prostitution of another person, as opposed to previous conventions that made it an offence to procure a woman to become a prostitute, para 5.10.
95. A large number of organizations were involved in campaigning for legislative reform, in particular the NVA, the AMSH and their associate members. The following list were members of the NVA National Committee of Great Britain: Young Women's Christian Association (YWCA); YWCA (International Union); London Diocesan Council for Preventative, Rescue and Penitentiary Work; Church Army; Salvation Army; Jewish Association (Gentlemen) for the Care and Protection of Girls; Jewish Association (Ladies) for the Care and Protection of Girls; National Council of Evangelical Free Churches; National Union of Women Workers (NUWW); International Catholic Society for Befriending Young Girls; Metropolitan Association for Befriending Young Servants; West London Mission; Traveller's Aid Society; London Council for the Protection of Morality; Girls' Friendly Society; Society for the Rescue of Young Women and Children. Many of these societies also supported the AMSH but others supported only the AMSH. Amongst these were the Ladies National Association; the Social Purity Alliance; the White Cross League; the Penal Reform League; the Mothers' Union; the International Alliance of Women. Many feminist organisations, primarily concerned with the franchise, were also involved with the campaign for legal reform. This can be demonstrated by the large number of references to the subject in the three main militant papers *Votes for Women*, the organ of the Women's Social and Political Union (WSPU); the *Suffragette* and the *Vote*, which was the organ of the Women's Freedom League (WFL).There were many feminist organisations involved, including the National Union of Women's Suffrage Societies; the Conservative and Unionist Women's Societies; the Church League for Women's Suffrage. Many women belonged to a number of different societies and worked for a variety of 'women's' causes on a non-party political basis. See J. Walkowitz, *Prostitution and Victorian Society*, pp. 126–7.
96. Incest Act 1908 [8 Edw. 7. c. 45]; Criminal Law Amendment Act 1912 [2 & 3 Geo. 5. c. 56]; Criminal Law Amendment Act 1922 [12 & 13 Geo. 5. c. 56]; Sexual Offences Act 1956 [4 & 5 Eliz. 2. c. 69].
97. See, for example, Constance Rover (1969), *Women's Suffrage and Party Politics in Britain, 1866–1914*, Routledge & Kegan Paul, London; Cheryl Law (1997) *Suffrage and Power: The Women's Movement, 1918–1928*, I.B.Tauris Publishers, London. The campaign for the vote was the principal feminist cause, but the 'equal moral standard' came a close second. There were many other causes, including equal pay, family planning and peace. Tactics could range from the usual methods of lobbying politicians to the more militant strategies adopted by some feminists, such as stone-throwing and arson.
98. F. Mort, pp. 103–6. *Dangerous Sexualities: Medico-Moral Politics in England since 1830*, Routledge and Kegan Paul, London.
99. See, for example, Christabel Pankhurst (1913), *The Great Scourge And How To End It*, London, Lincoln's Inn House, Kingsway. There is also a useful collection of period pieces in Sheila Jeffreys (ed.) (1987), *The Sexuality Debates*, Routledge & Kegan Paul, London. See also Susan Kingsley Kent (1989), *Sex and Suffrage in Britain, 1860–1914*, Routledge, London, Ch. 5. The terms 'feminist' and 'social purist' should not be seen as definitive, as there was a great deal of overlap and no agreement as to who was qualified to belong to which group.

100. For example, the National Union of Women Workers (NUWW), founded in1847, which became the National Council of Women (NCW) in 1919, and the International Women's Suffrage Alliance, founded in 1904, which became the International Alliance of Women (IAW) in 1926. The IAW coordinates women's concerns and works as a non-governmental organisation, seeking to improve the status of women through the United Nations and the International Labour Organization. Both organisations are still flourishing. For the history of the IAW see Arnold Whittick (1979), *Woman into Citizen*, London; Leila J. Rupp (1997), *Worlds of Women: The Making of an International Women's Movement*, Princeton University Press, Princeton, NJ.

101. Teresa Billington-Greig was a former member of the Women's Social and Political Union and the Women's Freedom League. Quoted in Bland, *Banishing the Beast*, p. 299.

102. See Bland, *Banishing the Beast*, pp. 301–3.

103. P.D. 5th Ser. Vol. XXXIX, col. 574, 10 June 1912.

104. Quoted by Walkowitz, 'Male Vice and Female Virtue', p. 56.

105. See S. Jeffreys (1985), *The Spinster and her Enemies: Feminism and Sexuality, 1880–1930*, Pandora, London, Ch. 4.

106. Criminal Law Amendment Bill 1914 [4 Geo. 5]

107. CLA Bill, 15 February 1917, 'A Bill to make further provision with respect to the punishment of sexual offences and the prevention of indecent advertisements; and matters connected therewith', presented by Secretary Sir George Cave supported by Mr Solicitor General and Mr Hayes Fisher; CLA Bill, 29 March 1917, 'A Bill to make further provision with respect to the punishment of sexual offences and the prevention of indecent advertisements; and matters connected therewith', presented by Secretary Sir George Cave supported by Mr Solicitor General and Mr Hayes Fisher. These bills were by no means identical. Among other things the Bill of 15 February contained a provision for the imprisonment of women convicted of soliciting, and the Bill of 29 March included powers to detain young girls. Sexual Offences Bill, 11 April 1918, 'An Act to make further provision with respect to the Punishment of Sexual Offences and the treatment of Venereal Disease and the Prevention of Indecent Advertisements', and matters connected therewith, presented by the Earl Beauchamp. A further bill modelled on a submission by the AMSH was presented in 1921. This was defeated after a clause criminalising lesbianism was added during the third reading.

108. *Shield*, December 1917, p. 383.

109. Roger Davidson (1994), 'Venereal Disease, Sexual Morality, and Public Health in Interwar Scotland', *Journal of the History of Sexuality*, 1994, Vol. 5, No. 2, pp. 267–93.

110. Pankhurst, *The Great Scourge And How to End It*, p. 37.

111. See L. Bland (1985) '"Cleansing the Portals of Life": The Venereal Disease Campaign in the Early Twentieth Century' in M. Langan and B. Schwarz (eds), *Crisis in the British State, 1880–1930*, London.

112. Final Report of the Royal Commission on Venereal Disease (1916), Cd. 8189 XVI.

113. Lord Kitchener (of Khartoum and of Broome), 1850–1916. Chief of Staff and Commander-in-Chief in South Africa 1900–02; Commander-in-Chief, India, 1902–09; Consul-General in Egypt 1911; Field Marshal and Secretary for War 7 August 1914; recruited the 'Kitchener armies' for the First World War, died when HMS *Hampshire* was mined off Orkney on 5 June 1916.

114. See Helen Ware (1969), 'The Recruitment, Regulation and Control of Prostitution in Britain from the Middle of the Nineteenth Century to the Present Day' (1969), unpublished PhD thesis, University of London, Vol. 2.

115. Ibid.

116. Gail Braybon (1987), *Women Workers in the First World War*, Croom Helm, London.

117. Defence of the Realm (Consolidated) Regulations (1914) (13): 'The competent naval or military authority may by order require every person within any area specified in the order to remain within doors between such hours as may be specified in the order, and in such cases if any person within that area is or remains out between such hours without a permit in writing from the competent naval or military authority or some person duly authorised by him, he shall be guilty of an offence against these regulations.' Regulation 40D. (1918): 'No woman who is suffering from venereal disease in a communicable form shall have sexual intercourse with any member of His Majesty's Forces or solicit or invite any member of His Majesty's Forces to have sexual intercourse with her.' 'If any woman acts in contravention of this regulation she shall be guilty of a summary offence against these Regulations.' 'A

woman charged with an offence under this Regulation shall, if she so requires, be remanded for a period (not less than a week) for the purpose of such medical examination as may be requisite for ascertaining whether she is suffering from such a disease as aforesaid.' 'The defendant shall be informed of her right to be remanded as aforesaid and that she may be examined by her own Doctor or by the Medical Officer of the Prison.' 'In this regulation the expression "venereal disease" means syphilis, gonorrhoea, or soft chancre.'

118. *London Gazette*, 26 March 1918. Report and wording of Regulation 40D and 40C, pp. 3751–2 Defence of the Realm Act, 3/AMS Box 311, WL.
119. See Roger Davidson, ' "A Scourge to be Firmly Gripped": The Campaign for VD Controls in Inter-war Scotland', *Social History of Medicine*, 6 February 1993, pp. 213–35.
120. Paragraph from the 'Medical Women's Federation Manifesto', as quoted in an occasional paper, published by the AMSH, September 1920.
121. Roger Davidson (1993) ' "A Scourge to be Firmly Gripped": The Campaign for VD Controls in Inter-War Scotland', *Social History of Medicine*, Vol. 6, February, pp. 213–35.
122. Venereal Diseases Act 1917 [7 & 8 Geo. 5. c. 23].
123. Defence Regulation 33B, Statutory Rules and Orders, 1942, Volume 11, Emergency Powers (Defence), HMSO. Defence (General) Regulations (Amendments : Nov. 5) 1942 No. 2277 (Compulsory treatment of venereal disease), p. 89.
124. 'Defence Regulation 33B', memorandum issued by the AMSH, revised edition, 1946.
125. *Time and Tide*, 24 November 1942.
126. Ibid.
127. 'Control of Venereal Disease'. A Bill. To provide for the compulsory examination and treatment of persons suspected of suffering from venereal disease by the restoration of provisions formerly contained in Defence Regulation 33B. 3 July 1962 [10 & 11 Eliz. 2].
128. P.D. 5th Ser. Vol. 662, cols. 291–4, 3 July 1962.
129. Control of Venereal Disease Bill (1968), Sir Myer Galpern.
130. Margaret Schwarz (secretary to the AMSH) to Sir Myer Galpern, 25 February 1969.
131. *Daily Herald*, 29 August 1962.
132. PD, 5th Ser. Vol. 650, col. 182, 7 December 1961.
133. Copy of statement sent by Miss Oonagh Lahr to the JBS, Anthony Greenwood MP, Richard Marsh MP and the National Council for Civil Liberties, 1962. Miss Lahr had spent 18 months in Holloway. She stated that although the VD test was meant to be optional, this was never made clear to her by the nurses and doctors. She did not sue for assault. JBS collection, 3/JBS/2, WL.
134. S. I. 1968, No. 1624. National Health Service, England and Wales. 'The National Health Service (Venereal Diseases) Regulation 1968', signed by Kenneth Robinson, Minister of Health, 14 October 1968 [M.H. 806]. National Health Service, 'Control of Venereal Disease', memorandum distributed to Regional Hospital Boards, Hospital Management Committees and Boards of Governors. Ministry of Health, Alexander Fleming House, London [HM(68)84]. Section 3 states: 'Every Regional Hospital Board and every Board of Governors of a teaching hospital shall take all necessary steps to secure that any information obtained by officers of the Board with respect to persons examined or treated for venereal disease in a hospital for the administration of which the Board is responsible shall be treated as confidential except for the purpose of communicating to a medical practitioner, or to a person employed under the direction of a medical practitioner in connection with the treatment of persons suffering from such disease or the prevention of the spread thereof, and for the purpose of such treatment or prevention.'
135. The difficulty experienced by medical practitioners in making contact with the patient's source of infection was set out by Richard Marsh during the Second Reading debate in the House of Commons, 3 July 1962, col. 292–3. The new regulation was an attempt to overcome these obstacles.

PART II

The Wolfenden Committee:
Regulating Prostitution in the 1950s

CHAPTER THREE

The Origins of the Report

O mother
    What shall I cry?
        We demand a committee, a representative committee,
        A committee of investigation.
            T. S. Eliot, 'Coriolan' (1931)

The Street Offences Committee was appointed in 1927 in response to public pressure, coming from both liberal and conservative factions,[1] but against a backdrop of criticism of the police.[2] A broadly similar situation pertained in the early 1950s, when a renewed perception of moral crisis led to demands being made in parliament and by some Church authorities for the appointment of a royal commission to inquire into the state of the law. On this occasion public antipathy towards the police had declined, convictions for loitering or soliciting were rising steeply and the popular press enjoyed amplifying the sense of crisis. The Home Office had rejected Hugh Macmillan's proposals as impractical,[3] but as the women's organisations were continuing their campaign for an equal application of the law, it was thought (by the Home Secretary, David Maxwell Fyfe) that a 'satisfactory', though 'highly controversial', reform of the legislation could be achieved only with the support of a strong and independent committee or commission.[4]

THE ORIGINS OF THE REPORT IN THE 1950s

The 1950s were a time of post-war consolidation and steady economic growth. Many of the women who had previously supplanted men in factory and field became resigned to a world of domestic reconstruction. The increase in employment opportunities was generally in low-paid, part-time, segregated work, which was represented as providing 'pin-money' with which to buy the new labour-saving devices, or unnecessary luxuries. Men were still perceived as the bread-winners and women as the home-makers. Concurrently, some middle-class occupations continued to impose a marriage bar on women until the 1970s. The Crowther Report in 1959 and the Newsom Report in 1963 emphasised the importance of educating girls for their future roles as house-wives and mothers.[5] At the same time the idealisation of domesticity and home-craft by the ubiquitous weekly women's magazine was such that they were elevated to the status of a gratifying career. Full employment and rising prosperity heralded a new consumer society and a decade of conservatism. In courting the women's vote, government walked a political tightrope by main-taining preferential treatment for men through taxes and employment and by encouraging women with manageable family commitments to return to employment in the national interest. Yet society stood on the threshold of a liberal era that was to be characterised by student protest,[6] the CND, second-wave feminism and liberalising legislation.[7] For despite the generalised pres-sures to identify with home-making, the Second World War had introduced liberalising changes for women from which there was no turning back.[8]

In 1951 the AMSH achieved a small triumph. A memorandum was com-posed proposing that prostitutes should be given the same legal protection from procuration as the so-called 'innocent women'. The Bill was introduced into the House of Commons under the Ten-Minute Rule on 13 December 1950 by Mrs Barbara Castle and became the Criminal Law Amendment Act on 22 June 1951.[9] This Act was more important than it might at first appear, as most of the trafficking in persons fell outside the remit of international con-ventions, since it consisted of a trade in working prostitutes. The Labour Government Home Secretary, James Chuter Ede, was supportive of the CLA Bill, but declared himself to be anxious about the possibilities of blackmail and was therefore more cautious with regard to reforming the solicitation laws[10]. However, this extension of protection for women was supported by all political parties and favourably received by the quality press,[11] which sug-gested that the Act removed a blot from British legislation. Curiously, the enactment of this Bill coincided with the adoption by the General Assembly of the United Nations of the Convention for the Suppression of the Traffic in Persons and the Exploitation of the Prostitution of Others 1949, which the British government did not sign, on the ground that it did not give colonial governments the right to refuse to adopt the convention if they so wished.[12] Although the UN convention was welcomed in some quarters, renewed feel-ings of antagonism towards prostitutes and prostitution emerged at the begin-ning of the decade and were being reflected by the newspapers.

THE MEDIA

Some feminists have speculated as to the reasons for the hardening of atti-tudes during the 1950s. Smart,[13] for example, claims to have identified two moral panics. The first wave, which came at the beginning of the decade before the Wolfenden Committee was set up, focused upon the impression of deprav-ity given to tourists visiting London for the coronation.[14] The second preceded the enactment of the committee's recommendations and reflected xenophobic anxieties over the immigration of foreign gangsters and pimps. Certainly post-war British society compensated for domestic boredom by returning to more regular peacetime preoccupations with sexual titillation and scandal.

Mort[15] paints a contrasting picture, providing a glimpse into a newly evolving world and writing of London as presenting 'a sense of continual rest-lessness . . . a sort of shifting gear as a post-war generation started to get into its stride'. This intriguing mixture of myth and reality was played upon by the media of the time and must have contrasted sharply with official expectations of marital fidelity and well ordered productive lives.

Regardless of the motivations, the discourse over prostitution continued unabated in the popular press. During 1949 the *Sunday Pictorial* wrote a series of articles describing, in exaggerated language, the conduct of foreign gangs 'sucking rich fortunes from the moral sewers of the West End'. Yet it also castigated the 'degenerate' rich nationals who were 'allegedly' living debauched lives in Chelsea.[16] In 1951 the Paddington Moral Reform Council produced a memorandum urging the government to appoint a departmental committee to enquire into the problems of prostitution in London and to make recommendations for tightening up the solicitation laws. Its recommended penalty for a first offence by a prostitute was £50, with powers to imprison for up to fourteen days.[17] The Council's recipe for 'moral reform' implied that harsher measures for controlling women were necessary. *Time and Tide* was critical of the Reform Council's punitive attitude, pointing out that prostitution was not a crime and that the law already rested upon an injustice, namely, the use of the stigmatising term 'common prostitute'.[18] Despite the pressures, Chuter Ede was not convinced of the need for another departmental committee, although this did not deter others from writing in a similar vein. In 1955, the *Empire News* reported Chief Inspector Fabian[19] of Scotland Yard's suggestion that 'for a third offence' a girl should be classed as a persistent offender and sent for corrective training in order to learn a trade suitable to her abilities. This was to be followed by a three-year probationary period after release.

The *People* had commissioned its own 'special investigation' into 'vice gangs in the capital' and used its findings to issue a direct challenge to the Home Secretary. Reference was made to 'vast earnings' and 'incredible fortunes' (£1 million in ten years) made out of organised evil.[20] *Reynolds News* warned of an invasion of 7,000 'good-time girls' planning to make London their 'Mecca' in coronation year.[21] This prediction was supported by the *News of the World*, whose correspondent reported on the 'easy pickings' to be wrested from the thousands of foreigners visiting London.[22] In media parlance the vice barons and the prostitutes were invariably foreign, but when English girls were involved the problem was generally considered to be the irresistible temptation of American servicemen.[23] The locations where organised vice was said to be 'rampant' were Soho, Paddington, Marylebone, Chelsea, Bond Street, Piccadilly, Bayswater, Notting Hill and Finchley. Outside London, other major cities were mentioned, including Manchester,

Liverpool and Birmingham, although most convictions for street offences took place in London.

The popular press appealed to the least commendable qualities in its readers, invoking greed and envy, strengthened by salaciousness, prurience and xenophobia. Post-war antipathy towards immigrants mirrored earlier anxieties concerning the flow of Jewish aliens. In this connection, Colin Holmes has commented upon the sexual hostility that was common among receiving societies, which was noticeably heightened when the immigrant group was male-dominated.[24]

LOCAL AUTHORITIES

There were, in addition, the more prosaic anxieties over rents, property values and 'law and order', concerns which were loudly articulated by the local authority officers of Paddington and Westminster. Paddington, in particular, was a focus of discontent, as it was discovered that the Ecclesiastical Commissioners were extensive ground landlords. The properties under question had been divided up into individual apartments that were occupied by single women who were allegedly working as prostitutes. Speaking on behalf of the council, Alderman Walter Goss (Labour) urged the government to introduce legislation 'immediately' in order 'to deal with the law on prostitution, soliciting and the use of premises by prostitutes'.[25] He demanded the eviction of women from flats and an end to soliciting on the streets, a recipe that would lead, inevitably, to the only possible solution: the legalised brothel.

This situation seems to have been a long-running one, since a special committee had been appointed a decade earlier in order to investigate matters relating to the Paddington Estate and its connection with the Ecclesiastical Commissioners. A report on the situation had been presented to the London Diocesan Conference in 1944. The *Shield* had concluded that what was required was new legislation in order to prevent the letting of premises to individual women for the purpose of prostitution and the education of the public to support it.[26] It appears that the AMSH's approach to prostitutes was, however, somewhat ambivalent, since pressure to limit the impact of prostitution in one area generally increased it in another. This conundrum was to be the essence of the problem facing Wolfenden.

OFFICIAL STATISTICS

As noted earlier, the official statistics for prosecutions and convictions of street offences had fluctuated over the half-century and could be used to fuel anxiety. There had been a overall decline in the number of prosecutions and convictions for England and Wales between 1912 and 1929. They varied between one and three thousand for the following decade and declined again during the war.

During the post-war period there was a steady rise, reaching 10,319 prosecutions and 10,291 convictions in 1952, and reaching 11,916 and 11,878 by 1955[27] while the Wolfenden Committee was sitting. The statistics for the Metropolitan area, of 9,683 charges in 1952 (a difference of only 636 from the figure for England and Wales), demonstrates that most of the prosecutions for 1952 took place in London. It has been suggested that the post-war rise in convictions was part of a police campaign to amplify the problem and pressurise the government into dropping the requirement to prove annoyance.[28] It must also have been a response to increasing demands, coming from the media and the public, to reduce the visibility of street prostitution.[29] However, in his evidence to the Wolfenden Committee, PC Scarborough of the Metropolitan Police maintained that the rise in apprehensions was due to an increase in manpower (almost doubling in C Division) since 1947. He explained that 'the young man who came in 1947 now has more experience and is doing the job as he should'.[30]

Perhaps the more significant figures are to be found in the differences between the prosecutions and convictions for England and Wales of 10,837 prosecutions and 9,632 convictions in 1906 and 11,916 prosecutions and 11,878 convictions in 1955.[31] Disregarding the fluctuations, this shows a rise of little over a thousand in nearly fifty years. One might conclude that during the 1950s the problem (such as it was) was a localised Metropolitan concern that could have been dealt with by the Metropolitan Police.

Nevertheless, as the Wolfenden Report indicated, the number of convictions was not a reliable reflection of the total number of women on the streets, as many of them were repeat offenders: 'We have, in short, no reliable evidence whether the number of prostitutes plying their trade in the streets of London has changed significantly in recent years. What has probably happened is that they have shifted the scene of their activities to other and more residential areas and thereby have given grounds for complaint from those ordinary citizens who live in these areas.'[32] In a similar way, it poured doubt upon the notion that the police had been operating a 'rota' system, for although some women were arrested many times others had been apprehended only occasionally. Of the 808 prostitutes involved in 6,829 arrests in 1953, 181 had been arrested once and one had been arrested 27 times, with no regular pattern between the two extremes,[33] indicating that although the ratio was a significant factor, the figures provided only a rough indication of what had actually happened.

This uncertainty was reflected by the philanthropists Seebohm Rowntree and G. R. Lavers,[34] who in 1951 with the assistance of the Metropolitan Police and a journalist estimated that there were around 10,000 prostitutes in London (2,000 of whom worked in the West End) and an absolute maximum of 60–70,000 in the whole of Britain. They did not attempt to break down these figures in any meaningful way, so the reader is left to assume that they referred to street prostitutes. Rowntree and Lavers argued that although the total number of prostitutes was quite small, the evil that they gave rise to could be demonstrated by the number of men who used their services. They speculated that there were around 250,000 transactions per week in London alone. As with so many other observers of the social scene, the 'evil' was associated with the supply rather than the demand.

In view of this heightened concern, a research worker, Mrs Rosalind Wilkinson, was appointed by the British Social Biology Council (BSBC) in 1949 to investigate the 'problem' of prostitution in London. She found that there were many women who operated spasmodically and managed to avoid arrest for soliciting. They came in late at night, picked up a serviceman and took him home, while remaining for only five minutes on the street to complete the financial transaction. When writing of activities in Piccadilly Circus, she surmised that, 'Those who put in such occasional, brief appearances in this district probably far outnumber those who stand, night after night, taking a series of short-time clients, and who are arrested.' Consequently, she believed that the official figures underestimated the actual numbers.

The picture that Mrs Wilkinson painted of London life supported Wolfenden's contention that statistics were an unreliable guide. For example, 655 prostitutes in Soho and Mayfair had given rise to 3,000 separate arrests, whereas in the Victoria area, many women had been arrested up to eight times during 1949. She concluded that Hyde Park, Victoria and Paddington were the main areas for both soliciting and police activity, whereas in Stepney a number of girls from borstals and approved schools often solicited without ever being arrested.[35]

The British Social Biology Council, which commissioned the survey, was another organisation with aims that were quite clearly of a moral nature and there was more than a hint of eugenics in its declared principles, which associated personal responsibility with population problems and vice. The Council wanted to preserve and strengthen the family as the basic social unit, reduce promiscuity, eliminate commercial vice and diminish the incidence of venereal disease. This was to be achieved through the dissemination of biological knowledge. Sir Julian Huxley was the BSBC's Vice-President and Sir Hugh Linstead MP was listed as being its 'Honorary Parliamentary Adviser'.[36] The Council had identified prostitution and street soliciting as urgent social problems and was sufficiently concerned by the threat they posed to the moral order to have a sub-committee deal specifically with the problem. Like the Paddington Moral Reform Council, the BSBC had a very explicit agenda and was intent upon influencing government policy and forcing changes in the legislation. The publication of its book, *Women of the Streets: A Sociological Study of the Common Prostitute*, was conveniently timed for 1955.

To sum up, there were obviously a number of different competing discourses taking place within society during the decade preceding the setting up of the Wolfenden Committee. They ranged from the uncompromising stance taken by Alderman Goss, who wanted the elimination of street prostitution and prostitutes' flats from his borough, to the protective measures enacted in the CLA Act 1951. For Goss and his associates, prostitution in itself was not the problem; it could be tolerated so long as it was organised and controlled, which meant the creation of regulated brothels. He was, understandably, defending his constituents' expectations of reliable property values and the right to a peaceful life. Similarly, the anxieties about American servicemen were related to the overlapping subject of promiscuity rather than to prostitution. Young British women were asserting their independence and escaping some of the social controls that had previously restricted their freedom. Envy and apprehension were linked to the general dislike of what was viewed as 'Americanisation' and the deterioration of British society.[37] But in both cases (promiscuity and prostitution), the essence of the offensiveness was to be found in the independent behaviour of the women involved.[38]

In addition, the inflow of post-war immigrants had stirred up social pressures that led to xenophobic excesses and apprehension. The Marylebone magistrate Frank Powell fuelled the flames of this resentment when he warned the public against a flood of 'coloured' men moving into Britain in order to live on the immoral earnings of women.[39] Exaggeration and wild rumour brought the inevitable appeals for a return to flogging[40] and coincided with a surge of British nationalism, which was reinforced by two major events. In 1951 the triumphal Festival of Britain attracted five and a half million foreign visitors and the prestigious trade links that went with it. This event was followed, in 1953, by the coronation of Queen Elizabeth II and the arrival of numerous dignitaries. It can hardly be surprising that the newly elected Conservative government resolved to rid London of its growing reputation among foreign visitors as the vice capital of the world.

THE HOME OFFICE MEMORANDUM

By 1951 the Home Office had already determined to do something to resolve the situation. A senior Home Office official, Philip Allen, was sent to the United States in order to investigate the regulation of prostitution in American cities, where, despite its illegality, a flourishing call-girl system operated. Allen reported back to the Home Office and an expurgated version of this report was eventually distributed to the committee.[41] Although the 'problem' was largely confined to London, the Home Secretary, Sir David Maxwell Fyfe, considered it necessary to pursue a course of action that would result in reforming the 'undeniably ineffective' solicitation laws. In February 1954 he issued a Cabinet memorandum expressing his concern regarding prostitution and proposed a number of remedies. The dilemma he outlined in his introduction revealed that the activities of prostitutes in the streets of London had attracted a great deal of attention in the press and from leaders of the churches. Demands had been made in parliament for more effective measures to be put in place to check the 'evil', and for a royal commission to enquire into the situation and make suggestions for reforming the existing law. The Home Secretary thought it right to raise with his colleagues the question of appointing a commission of enquiry.[42]

A second, parallel, issue posed legal difficulties. This was the demand coming from local authorities for effective action to be taken against people who let single flats, often at exorbitant rents, to women who used them for the purpose of habitual prostitution. Maxwell Fyfe noted this problem, but failed to explain how soliciting might be checked without compromising any solution to the letting of flats. However, he did outline a course of legislative action for the reform of the solicitation laws, which bore a remarkable similarity to the final recommendations of the Wolfenden Report.[43] The essence of this reform was the amendment of the law so as to make soliciting or importuning 'for the purpose of prostitution' an offence in itself, without the necessity to prove annoyance. This would be supported by increased fines and progressive penalties for successive offences and imprisonment for repeat offenders, without the option of a fine. These recommendations were in direct contrast to the reforms advocated by the AMSH and its supporters, which had emphasised the importance of corroborative evidence and equality between the sexes.

Maxwell Fyfe realised that the objection to these proposals would be that they would drive the traffic underground, increase the likelihood of women being exploited for financial gain and lead to the growth of a 'call-girl' system. The enquiries that Philip Allen had made in the United States led him to believe that these fears were unfounded and that the 'call-girl' system would have the advantage of removing a public scandal from the streets and preventing vulnerable young men from being exposed to obvious temptation. He speculated that this amendment would be highly controversial and strongly opposed by the women's organisations. 'I believe, therefore, that legislation on these lines could not be introduced without the support of a strong independent commission or committee.'[44] The Wolfenden Committee was to spend the next three years coming 'independently' to the desired conclusion.

The Home Office memorandum clarifies a number of aspects of the Wolfenden Report which remained confused until the official documents became available for public viewing. In particular, it reveals that 'prostitution' rather than homosexuality was the first concern of the Home Secretary, and was not, as some observers have suggested, 'tagged on as an afterthought'.[45] Prostitution was, in Maxwell Fyfe's view, 'the more urgent and obvious problem'.[46]

Homosexuality and prostitution were separate and unrelated issues, which were lumped together by Home Office officials as if they were undifferentiated forms of deviance. It appears that there had been a substantial post-war increase in the number of homosexual offences (four- to five-fold over pre-war figures) and some high-profile cases that had attracted public attention.[47] But although Maxwell Fyfe was not in favour of legislative reform, he feared that the Home Office might become subject to criticism if a committee were set up only to consider the issue of prostitution. His perception of a 'homosexual' was of a person who suffered from a pathological condition, which might be 'treated' in one of the newly developed institutions for mentally abnormal offenders.[48] He did not feel that any change in the law governing homosexuality was necessary, only that public anxiety over the issue ought to be addressed and that it would be expedient to cover both subjects under the single banner in order to educate the public. [49] As with the prostitute, detention was considered desirable so that medical tests and treatment could be imposed upon the prisoner while his corrupting influence was withdrawn from the public domain.

As I have shown, statistics were not the most reliable way of measuring an assumed increase in the numbers of prostitutes on the streets. In any case this was not Maxwell Fyfe's main concern. The 'problem' that had upset him was not the quantities of streetwalkers but their 'visibility'. Similarly the police were not deterred by the letter of the law from arresting women, nor were the magistrates inhibited from convicting them, although there were obvious benefits to be gained from regularising the law in this respect. Therefore we have to look for other reasons for setting up the committee. In this respect a great deal of pressure had come from the press and conservative bodies such as the Church and moral welfare organisations, added to which was Maxwell Fyfe's personal obsession with the dilemma. And as Allen's report and Maxwell Fyfe's memorandum showed, what was required from the 'independent' committee was not so much a recommendation for ways of speeding up the 'merry-go-round' of arrest, conviction, fine and return to the streets, but something more subtle: a law that would effectively banish women from the streets altogether. And he seems to have had no great awareness of the possible consequences of this policy.

NOTES

1. On the one hand, a number of refuge and vigilance groups had pressed the Home Office for new restrictions on the movements of young women and for harsher penalties for street soliciting. On the other hand, some women's organisations had campaigned for the abandonment of the term 'common prostitute' and for an equal application of the law between men and women. In addition they had criticised the police for ignoring the statutory requirement to prove annoyance in cases of street soliciting.
2. In view of these critisms the Street Offences Committee quoted from the orders laid down for the guidance of the Edinburgh police, that: 'considerable forbearance should be shown by constables in dealing with these unfortunate women, many of whom are greatly to be pitied . . . arrests should only be made as disagreeable necessities reluctantly performed because a warning has been disregarded.' Cmd. 3231, para. 55.
3. That is, to substitute the term 'any person' for 'common prostitute' and make two separate offences covering molestation and soliciting.
4. See 'Sexual Offences' (1954), 'Secret' Cabinet Memorandum by the Secretary of State for Home Department, C. (54) 60.
5. Elizabeth Wilson (1977), *Women and the Welfare State*, Tavistock Publications, London, p. 82; Celia Briar (1997) *Working For Women? Gendered Work And Welfare Policies in Twentieth Century Britain*, UCL Press, London, Ch. 6.
6. The first rumblings of youthful discontent, accompanied by middle-class disapproval, were to be found in the emergence of the 'Teddy Boy' of the mid-1950s. The CND also provided an area of protest that involved a wider spectrum of the population.
7. Foremost among these was the enactment of the Wolfenden Committee's recommendation on the decriminalisation of homosexual acts between consenting adults. Sexual Offences Act 1967 [14 Eliz. 2. c. 60.]
8. A good example of this was the unwillingness of women to return to domestic employment and the subsequent demise of the female servant class.

9. Criminal Law Amendment Act 1951 [14 & 15 Geo. c. 36.]
10. Chuter Ede to Mrs Barbara Castle, 25 September, 1950, 3/AMSH, Box 65, WL.
11. *The Times*, 14 December 1950, 'Legal Protection For Women'; *Time and Tide*, 14 April 1951; *Rostrum*, 1951; *New Statesman and Nation*, 27 January 1951.
12. *Reynolds News*, 6 May 1950. See also A. W. Brian Simpson (2001), *Human Rights: The End of Empire*, Oxford University Press, Oxford.
13. C. Smart (1981), 'Law and the Control of Women's Sexuality: The Case of the 1950s', in B. Hutter and G. Williams (eds), *Controlling Women: The Normal and the Deviant*, Croom Helm, London, pp. 45–53.
14. The Coronation of Queen Elizabeth II, 2 June 1953.
15. F. Mort (1999), 'Mapping Sexual London: The Wolfenden Committee on Homosexual Offences and Prostitution 1954–57', *New Formations*, No. 37 Spring, p. 92. Mort writes mostly with reference to the homosexual scene.
16. *Sunday Pictorial*, 23 January 1949, 'Vice: Another Frank National Inquiry'; *Sunday Pictorial*, 30 January 1949, 'The "Smart Set" With Gutter Morals'.
17. *Time and Tide*, 14 April 1951.
18. Ibid.
19. Commander Robert Fabian was said to be Britain's best-known and most popular police-man during the late 1940s and 1950s. See Patrick Higgins (1996), *Heterosexual Dictatorship: Male Homosexuality in Post-War Britain*, Fourth Estate, London, pp. 227 and 259. On retire-ment he worked for the Kelmsley Press, a group that owned a large number of newspapers, including the *Empire News*. Fabian did much to improve the public image of the British policeman and the Metropolitan police as crime-fighters. See also Robert Fabian (1950), *Fabian of the Yard: An Intimate Record by Ex-Superintendent Robert Fabian*, The Naldrett Press, London.
20. *People*, 1 July 1951, 'One Gang Made Million In Ten Years'.
21. *Reynolds News*, 2 November 1952, 'Trade Routes of Shame'.
22. *News of the World*, 20 November 1953, The Dangerous Missions of Detective Heather, 'How The Yard Broke Up the Call-Girl Racket'.
23. *Lynn News & Advertiser*, 1 May 1953.
24. Colin Holmes (1979), *Anti-Semitism in British Society, 1876–1939*, Edward Arnold, London.
25. *Daily Mirror*, 24 February 1953. Alderman Walter Goss (Paddington).
26. *Shield*, October 1944.
27. Cmnd. 247, Appendix 11, Statistics Relating to Prostitution Offences (a) England and Wales, p. 143.
28. Ware 'The Recruitment, Regulation and Control of prostitution in Britain from the Middle of the Nineteenth Century to the Present Day', PhD thesis, University of London.
29. Smart, 'Law and the Control of Women's Sexuality', p. 50. Jeffrey Weeks (1989), *Sex, Politics and Society: The Regulation of Sexuality Since 1800*, Longman, London, p. 240. Weeks observed that increasing police zeal in prosecuting offenders (both homosexuals and prosti-tutes) coincided with the appointment of Sir Theobald Mathew (an ardent Roman Catholic) as Director of Public Prosecutions in 1944, and Sir John Nott-Bower as the new Metropolitan Police Commissioner in 1953, under the aegis of the fervently anti-homosex-ual and moralistic Home Secretary, Sir David Maxwell Fyfe, pp. 239–40.
30. PRO. HO. 345/12. ch/5.
31. Cmnd. 247, p. 143.
32. Ibid., para. 232.
33. Ibid., para. 271.
34. B. Seebohm Rowntree and G. R. Lavers (1951), *English Life and Leisure. A Social Study*, Longmans, Green and Co., London, pp. 208–11.
35. British Social Biology Council (1955), C. H. Rolph (ed.), *Women of the Streets*, Martin Secker and Warburg, London, Ch. 3. p. 45, 'Prostitute Population'.
36. Sir Julian Sorell Huxley (1887–75), Professor of Zoology, King's College, London (1925–27); Fullerian Professor at Royal Institute (1926–29); Secretary to Zoological Society of London (1935–42); first Director of UNESCO (1946–48). Writer on science, biology, ethics and humanism. Formulated pragmatic ethical theory of 'evolutionary humanism'. Sir Hugh Linstead MP was a member of the Wolfenden Committee.
37. See, for example, John Costello (1985), *Love Sex and War: Changing Values, 1939–45*, Collins, London; David Reynolds (1995), *Rich Relations: The American Occupation of Britain, 1942–1945*, HarperCollins, London.

38. This point was made by Kellow Chesney, with reference to William Acton's concern over the spread of venereal infection, writing, 'For this reason he was by no means an enemy of brothel keepers . . . every brothel keeper had an interest in keeping down venereal disease amongst her lodgers . . . he obviously considered the growing independence of prostitutes a social misfortune.' Kellow Chesney (1970), *The Victorian Underworld*, Penguin Books, Harmondsworth, p. 442.
39. *Westminster and Pimlico News*, 23 October 1953, 'Magistrate Warns Coloured Men'.
40. *Evening Standard*, 10 December 1952, article by H. Montgomery Hyde MP. *Kensington Post*, 14 February 1959, 'Plea for Return of Flogging'.
41. PRO. HO. 345/2. W. Conwy Roberts to Wolfenden 21 September 1954, 'Do you think that there is any useful purpose to be served by Allen's circulating to the Committee a report of the visit which he and Cole paid to the States, i.e. an expurgated version . . . It will require vetting on one or two parts but that should not take long.' Wolfenden to Roberts 22 September 1954, 'I think that it would be a good idea that members of the Committee should see an expurgated edition of Allen's report of his visit to the States if only to remind the Committee that problem is also part of their job.' It seems that prostitution was seen as secondary from the outset.
42. PRO. CAB. 129/66. C. (54) 60.
43. Cmnd. 247, pp. 116–17.
44. PRO. CAB. 129/66.
45. Smart, 'Law and the Control of Women's Sexuality', p. 50.
46. PRO. CAB. 128/27. 20 (4).
47. For example, Lord Montagu of Beaulieu was tried for homosexual offences during 1953 and 1954. The trials received high press coverage. Sir John Gielgud was arrested for persistently importuning on 21 October 1953. He pleaded guilty and was fined £10. Ian Harvey, the Conservative MP for Harrow, resigned his parliamentary seat in 1958, after being caught with a Guardsman in Hyde Park in the early hours of the morning. When a former Labour Party chairman, George Brinham, was murdered by a youth of 16, the youth was acquitted of murder on the grounds that he had been provoked by Brinham's homosexual advances. This is in strong contrast to the attitudes of judges (during the period in question) towards the case of women who kill violent partners. See Ann Jones (1991), *Women Who Kill*, Victor Gollancz, London. The fact that Edith Thompson's husband (discussed above) had been violent towards her did not work in her favour.
48. PRO. CAB. 129/66. C.60.
49. Higgins, *Heterosexual Dictatorship*, p. 5.

CHAPTER FOUR

Preliminary Organisation

When the idea for a royal commission was first proposed it did not meet with the approval of the Prime Minister, Winston Churchill, nor with that of all of the Cabinet. Nevertheless Maxwell Fyfe appears to have been determined to pursue the matter,[1] and in the end the more manageable solution of a departmental committee was substituted. The committee, chaired by John Wolfenden, was appointed on 24 August 1954 and was composed of 15 members.[2] In order to create what was considered to be an appropriate balance, it included both Scottish and English members, two MPs, three doctors, three lawyers, three academics, churchmen of different denominations, a peer, a secretary from the Home Office, Conwy Roberts (who became the committee's secretary), and an assistant secretary from the Scottish Home Department, E. J. Freeman.

There were only three women despite the fact that the committee had been appointed primarily to consider the most appropriate method of abolishing street prostitution. But although there is no reason to suppose that a body of women would have been any more sympathetic towards the needs of prostitutes than a group of men, the gender imbalance was a failing that meant that the interest and concern stimulated by the discussion of homosexuality took precedence over prostitution. Two of the women (Mrs Kathleen Lovibond and Lady Stopford) rarely spoke, but they did eventually find sufficient spirit to make an official reservation over the issue of the committee's recommendation to fix maximum penalties for living on the earnings of prostitution. This imbalance was an important factor in the bias towards criminalising women and exonerating men and was strengthened by the many stereotypical assumptions about the nature of women that influenced the committee's judgement.

The committee met on 62 days, over half of which were devoted to the oral examination of witnesses. The whole process took three years and much of the time was taken up with the composition of the report. The committee's terms of reference were to consider:

(a) 'the law and practice relating to homosexual offences and the treatment of persons convicted of such offences by the courts; and

(b) the law and practice relating to offences against the criminal law in connection with prostitution and solicitation for immoral purposes, and to report what changes, if any, were desirable.'

The implications of the difference between the wording of these two remits were important. Homosexual connection between men was already a criminal offence and therefore the possibility of recommending a relaxation was open to the committee. Prostitution, on the other hand, was not in itself a criminal offence (although many associated activities were),[3] so the decriminalisation of 'prostitution' was not an issue. This meant that, as the law stood in 1954, a man who importuned another man for homosexual purposes was inciting him to commit an illegal act, whereas a woman who solicited a man for the purposes of prostitution was not. Moreover, solicitation without causing annoyance was perfectly legal. Not surprisingly, the AMSH was indignant that the two subjects had been lumped together as if they were the same, believing that it would cloud the issues and divert the committee's attention from the problems of prostitution.[4]

The use of the words 'treatment . . . by the courts' in connection with homosexuality was also significant and to some extent ominous because, like Maxwell Fyfe, many of the witnesses assumed that homosexuals were suffering from a pathological condition that might be treated and perhaps cured, either in or out of prison, and a recommendation to this effect might be made by the judge. This terminology placed a question mark over the validity of the legislation that oppressed homosexuals. Conversely there was no suggestion within the remit of a pathological or contagious condition in connection with prostitution. There was also no mention of 'treatment', of 'causes', or of amelioration of the circumstances that led to it, although the British Medical Association was convinced that prostitutes suffered from mental illness. Nevertheless the concept of a female personality disorder seemed to influence the thinking of the committee, and a suggestion for research into the aetiology of prostitution was eventually included in the final recommendations. However, the 'treatment' of homosexuals in the wider public arena was open for discussion and, in particular, the efficacy of a legal system that put men into prison when their offence was of a moral nature and committed in private.

Perhaps even more confusing was the inclusion of the term 'immoral purpose' in the second half of the remit, as there was no reference to 'immorality' within the legislation applying to women, and the report made it quite clear that 'women' had been the subject of this part of the inquiry. If proof of immorality were to be applied to women it could be made only by reference to the evidence of the person to whom the 'immoral' proposal had been made, although this was the type of evidence that the Home Office wanted to dispense with in order to make prosecution simpler. Moreover, if the term were to be applied to women, the woman who failed in her immoral purpose was the one who was likely to be prosecuted, whereas the woman who succeeded would be likely to go free.[5]

The account of the current legislation, as set out in the final report,[6] made it clear that the term 'immoral purpose' applied to men, as the list of current offences pertaining to prostitution included section 32 of the Sexual Offences Act 1956 and the Immoral Traffic (Scotland) Act 1902,[7] both of which made it an offence for a male person to solicit or importune for 'immoral purposes', although male importuning did not feature as a matter of any concern for the committee in its discussion of prostitution. There was no doubt that women's public display of sexual availability was the problem that had to be addressed, and that the 'immorality' that this display symbolised had to be eradicated.

The conflation of homosexuality and prostitution as problems of sexual deviance diminished the clarity with which the issues were perceived, for although the homosexual was thought of in male terms there was no specific group of people within the community who were easily recognisably 'homosexual' and the stigma of immorality was not automatically applied to them. The issue of men soliciting men was incorporated in the discussion on homosexuality and in a more lenient manner. Part II of the report, dealing with homosexuality, stated that, 'for the most part, those convicted of importuning are in no sense male prostitutes; they are simply homosexuals seeking a partner for subsequent homosexual behaviour'.[8] The committee concluded that the severe penalties imposed for this offence provided the disincentive that prevented male soliciting from becoming a comparable nuisance to that of females, thus rationalising its proposal for steeper penalties for women. This was not the only disparity, as the Procurator Fiscal from Glasgow observed, for the 'homosexual offence' provided a much broader and more fluid definition. In contrast, when it came to the prostitute on the street everybody knew who and what they were talking about.[9]

This 'recognition' of the prostitute as a specific category of person was to become fundamental to the discussion because, as the committee was to discover, the legislation depended for its effectiveness upon the belief that there was an identifiable class of women who could be conveniently labelled. The reality was that the terms of reference for offences connected with prostitution were more limited than those concerning homosexuality, indicating that the Home Office had a definite outcome in mind. So despite the inclusion of the words 'immoral purpose', it became very convenient for the committee to see its role in narrow terms, to confine its discussions on soliciting to women and to argue that the law was not concerned with private morals. The final recommendations were thus to be constructed around the need to protect the ordinary decent citizen from what was harmful and injurious, or offended his sense of decency, as if these parameters were somehow outside the realms of moral judgement. The argument consequently turned on the issue of what ought or ought not to be permissible for men and women within the public or the private realm, reflecting the maintenance of white heterosexual male power within the private sphere of the home, where the law rarely penetrated.[10]

The limitations of the remit with regard to prostitution were enormously useful to the committee as they absolved it from any commitment actively to explore the wider social issues or to base its findings upon scientifically assessed data, leaving it at liberty to rely upon the 'opinions' of 'experts' who peddled their own certainties.[11] The committee was therefore free to dismiss arguments and grey areas as 'outside its terms of reference' or alternatively to discuss issues at length without letting them influence the final outcome. Nor was it necessary to define the meaning of key terms such as 'prostitution', or what was meant by 'illegal sexual intercourse' or even seek to define 'who' could legitimately be described as a 'prostitute'. The only thing that needed to be clarified was 'the role of the law', which was crystallised by the constantly repeated pejorative metaphor of 'cleaning up the streets'. The changes in the criminal law which the Home Office had in mind (abandoning the proof of annoyance, escalating fines and imprisonment for repeat offences) were not intended to be liberalising, and any relaxation that the committee might have recommended in connection with prostitution would, it must be assumed, have been ignored. Wolfenden knew this from the outset. Homosexuality, on the other hand, had been included as a counterbalance and the potential for imaginative and innovative proposals was greater.

THE FIRST PHASE: CLOSED SESSIONS

John Wolfenden was supported throughout the proceedings by the Home Office official, W. C. Conwy Roberts, who acted as secretary and personal mentor.[12] Roberts developed a very close association with Wolfenden, and it is obvious from the correspondence between them that he remained firmly focused upon the Home Office objectives and appeared to be the guiding force steering the committee towards the desired end.[13] It was during the first meeting in the autumn of 1954 that the committee arrived at the unanimous, but contentious, decision that proceedings should be conducted in private.[14] The reason given for this ruling was the nature of the subject matter, which was felt to be so delicate and embarrassing that witnesses would be inhibited by a public hearing. It was also considered necessary to ensure that the various witnesses would feel able to express their opinions freely, without the threat of selective reporting and sensational amplification by the press, which, it was feared, would influence public opinion.[15] This fear had some credibility in the light of the pre-committee coverage of salacious material by some sections of the press. And neither the press nor the public were credited with the capacity for impartiality for which the committee members had been chosen.[16] Basically they wanted to conduct their proceedings in private and without the stress of public controversy, which would have lessened the impact of the final report.

The AMSH and similarly minded bodies were seriously alarmed by this development. A number of organisations wrote to John Wolfenden urging him to ensure an open debate, even if it was only in connection with prostitution, arguing *inter alia* that the publication of evidence would be invaluable to social workers.[17] Roberts and Wolfenden detected a 'plot' hatched by the women's organisations, assuming that they were in league with each other.[18] It was suggested that these organisations wanted open meetings merely to check up on each other's evidence, enabling them to take political action counteracting the effect of anything with which they disagreed.[19] Wolfenden was grateful to Roberts for assisting him in 'seeing through the tortuous maze of the minds of these worthy ladies'.[20]

Battle lines were drawn in the sand of Roberts' imagination. The AMSH, it seems, had made 'sinister references' to the possibility of 'taking matters further' through the medium of letters to the press or parliamentary questions.[21] And it was thought best not to 'burden' the various societies with too much information, but rather to produce an uninformative standard letter which could be distributed to all complainants.[22] Roberts determined that only people considered to be of 'real standing' would be given a full reply. This created a further problem for Wolfenden, as Lord Balfour of Burleigh (President of the AMSH) wrote to him directly, and therefore had to be given a civil answer. The less deferential Roberts dismissed His Lordship as a 'stooge'.[23] 'By providing reasons for our decision,' wrote Roberts, 'are we not providing these good people with material for the manufacture of further bullets . . . are they not likely to seize upon each of our reasons and criticize it individually?'[24] Wolfenden replied, 'It is always safer to give no reasons, and if they are going to start up an agitation the less ammunition we give them the better.'[25] Nevertheless the extent of the protest had been sufficient to provoke Roberts into seeking the backing of the Home Secretary for the committee's decision.[26]

THE SECOND PHASE: WHO SHALL WE INVITE TO THE PARTY?

One of the first tasks the committee had to undertake was to determine which of the various public bodies, private organisations and individual members of the public should be invited to give evidence. It was obvious that many were interested, but Roberts was anxious to avoid members of the 'lunatic fringe' who would inevitably apply, and with whom 'it would be quite pointless to trouble' the committee,[27] although quite what qualified a body for lunatic status is not clear. Gender imbalance was an unconsidered though central aspect of the process of selection. The preliminary list of suggested contributors was almost entirely male, and represented the extended arm of the state and other aspects of social authoritarian control. Roberts was emphatic upon this point: 'It is clearly desirable that the Committee should be acquainted as fully as possible with the law and practice as they stand, and the difficulties to which they give rise, and this can best be achieved by hearing the experts first.' The suggested experts included the Chief Commissioner of Police, the Chief Metropolitan Magistrate and the Lord Chief Justice. They would be followed by representatives of the probation services, prison officers, police organisations, the Bar Council, the Law Society, welfare officers, borough councils and local authorities, Church Commissioners, the British Medical Association, the Institute for the Study of Delinquency, the Association of Boys Clubs, the Headmasters' and Headmistresses' Associations, the Howard League, and an assortment of medical bodies specialising in mental health.[28]

The predominantly male committee, which was familiar with the competitive spirit of the public school system, assumed that members of the establishment would have the required knowledge. But Dame Rachel Crowdy was one professional authority whom Roberts studiously ignored. Crowdy had been honoured for her work as Principal Commandant of the Volunteer Aid Detachment during the First World War and had subsequently become the secretary to the League of Nations Advisory Committee on Trafficking in Women and Children. Her knowledge of the subject matter was probably unrivalled throughout the country. In September 1954, Crowdy wrote to Wolfenden advising him to read the abstracts of Government Reports on the System of Licensed Houses and the relevant documents that would explain why the majority of countries had abolished them.[29] Wolfenden replied in 'politely non-committal terms'[30] and passed the letter over to Roberts.

Roberts had drawn up a Home Office memorandum[31] for distribution to the committee, but had deliberately refrained from dragging in the international conventions,[32] as he considered the subject matter to be stale and of little relevance to the 'real problems with which the committee were faced'.[33] He had informed Wolfenden that he had the misfortune to be present in New York when the (United Nations) Convention had been discussed. As usual, Wolfenden left the matter in Roberts' hands,[34] who felt that the Committee had quite enough to do considering the law as it was, without delving too far into why the legislation had been enacted in the first place.[35]

However, Rachel Crowdy's position had been supported by the Labour MP Barbara Castle, who in 1953 wrote to the *Daily Herald*[36] suggesting that victimising the prostitute would not end prostitution: 'We would do much better to study the League of Nations Report 1943 on the "Prevention of Prostitution".'[37] This was a document that emphasised the responsibilities of the individual and which looked forward to an improvement in social services and a sexually responsible society in which the incidence of prostitution would be greatly reduced.

The AMSH and the other women's organisations were conspicuously absent from the initial list of suggested contributors, but they were not slow in putting themselves forward. Miss Chave Collisson, the Secretary of the AMSH,[38] wrote to Wolfenden requesting that representatives from 16 supporting societies could be allowed to send observers or alternatively to submit a written memorandum.[39] Roberts assumed that this was yet another attempt on behalf of the women's organisations to get something approaching a public hearing.[40] The argument put forward on this occasion had been that the arrangement would be advantageous to 'both sides'. This was thought by Roberts to be either an 'impertinence' or a 'threat'. Wolfenden reacted irritably,

'These people really are the limit; why should we be subjected to a mass meeting?'[41] By 22 June, Roberts had the arrangements organised to his own satisfaction and with a view to 'oiling the wheels' he had agreed with Miss Collisson that the AMSH and its supporting societies should be allowed to bring a total of seven people on the tacit understanding that only three or four would be allowed to speak. To Roberts this solution appeared to be very satis-factory: 'All the people will be members or officers of the Association and will attend as such, but by this means, two of the more vociferous clamourers for a place in the sun can be included and, we may hope, silenced. These two people represent the Salvation Army and Roman Catholic interests and as the team originally proposed included a representative of the Church of England Moral Welfare Council perhaps we should be wise to accept this offer.'[42] Wolfenden replied in like terms and congratulated Roberts for his skill in oiling the wheels, reducing the numbers of women speaking to three and contriving to keep most of them silent.[43]

Such sexist comments may not have seemed as out of order in the 1950s as they would do half a century later, since equally derogatory remarks can be found in respected literature of the time. For example, the social survey pro-duced by Rowntree and Lavers, *English Life and Leisure*, was peppered with personal criticisms of the individuals whom they had interviewed. One woman was described as 'thin and rather acid with a tongue capable of lashing her husband', while her 'wounded look' was 'pure histrionics'. A second was 'very pukka Memsahib', and her 'tongue had a barb to it and much of her gossip was malicious'. She was not the sort of woman to be suspected of pro-miscuity, as she probably never stopped talking for long enough to enable a man to make an improper advance. A third woman was 'an awful gossip, this being her one joy in life', and when she started talking she became intolerable, while the tedious prattle of a fourth did her husband a great deal of harm.[44] These unkind observations were reserved mostly for the women and must have been considered acceptable by both authors and publisher, despite the fact that the individuals involved would probably have recognised themselves from the descriptions of their lifestyles. It seems that in the imagination of many men, women were regarded as caricatures, to be either despised or ignored. Quite apart from the misogyny that *English Life and Leisure* contains, it is worth noting that a personalised assessment of other people's lives was accepted as valid social research data.

Wolfenden and Roberts were in tune with this sort of stereotyped portrayal of the opposite sex. They appeared to view independent groups of 'women' as if they were homogeneous and tiresome entities, which they were at liberty to condense into as small a sample as possible. Roberts noted that the commit-tee was not obliged to give hearings to more than three or four advocates of any one point of view,[45] and the women's organisations obviously fell into this category. His view was extraordinarily blinkered, considering the stream of male 'authority figures' who were destined to pass before the committee, many of them peddling the same unimaginative and coercive solutions for cleaning up the streets. Yet despite (or rather because of) the accumulated knowledge of 80 years of campaigning, this group of educated and qualified women were not regarded as an asset, let alone 'experts', but were furtively reduced to a comic turn.

PREPARING TO GIVE EVIDENCE (THE AMSH)

During November 1954 the AMSH convened a private conference in order to rally its supporters, discuss principles, and prepare itself for lobbying the oncoming committee. The 'Solicitation Laws' were reviewed and the Public Places (Order) Bill re-examined. The AMSH used this opportunity to coordinate strategies and prepare the evidence that it would submit to the committee. In preparation for the conference, it published an orange leaflet entitled 'Points For Consideration'. The leaflet began with the rather confusing assertion that witnesses who gave factual evidence to the Street Offences Committee 1928 'were led through cross-examination to the deep waters of the principles behind their facts, and into the social and legal implications of those principles'. It went on to say that 'the intervention of the law into matters of sexual morality must be limited to defined principles'.[46] These perplexing statements were to be its downfall as far as the Wolfenden Committee was concerned.

The 'defined principles' to which the AMSH referred were both feminist and moral in nature and derived from the principles of the Abolitionist Federation, formulated by Josephine Butler during the 1870s. In brief they rejected repressive measures that discriminated against a specific class of person (the common prostitute) on the basis of morals (i.e. through the regulation of prostitution), and denounced the propagation of a double moral standard. They supported the notion that prostitution was a matter of conscience rather than of criminal law, but advocated the punishment of any public provocation to debauchery (procuration),[47] providing there was no re-establishment of a *police des moeurs*. At the core of its concern was the rejection of any legislation within the sphere of sexual morals that failed to recognise the autonomy and the responsibility of the individual, which the AMSH declared was 'the basis of morality'.[48] The AMSH analysis was somewhat confusing, but the solution it favoured was the creation of offences that impacted equally upon men and women who caused annoyance to each other and did not pick out and condemn the 'common prostitute' on the basis of a moral judgement.

In submitting evidence to the committee the AMSH made the same mistake as many other societies by spreading itself too widely. It prepared page after page of unnecessary background material, including the history of the Association's involvement in campaigning, the significance of the legislation to sexual morality, a survey of laws concerning prostitution, the sad story of Micheline Pierre (a trafficked woman) and the fateful 'orange leaflet'. This document was picked out of the collection by Roberts and passed on to Wolfenden, who reacted with astonishment: 'The more I read this remarkable orange document the more ridiculous it seems to me to be.' He concluded that the evidence of 'tendentious bilge' that it supplied made valueless anything else that the Association had to say: 'It just shows how the ordinary plain citizen like me needs to have his eyes opened.'[49] He was horrified to think that organisations all over the country were being whipped up into a frenzy of activity by such 'rubbish'. From this point onwards, there was little chance of the AMSH being taken seriously. What Wolfenden was to call the 'Old Women's Society'[50] was both comical and irrelevant.

Martin Pugh writes of the period (1945–59) between the end of the war and the beginning of the women's movement as 'The Nadir of British Feminism'.[51] Looking at the century as a whole this is probably correct, but the movement had by no means vanished. There were many feminists who adhered to the old values and continued the fight from within a host of different affiliations, including the Women's Citizens Association and the National Council of Women (NCW) and even the Townswomen's Guild.[52] These organisations were very largely concerned with developing citizenship and social responsibility among women. Nevertheless, for Wolfenden and the committee, the arguments around the double standard were inconsequential. They were dismissed by Roberts as outdated and trivial, an attitude that can be demonstrated by one of his earlier letters warning Wolfenden to be prepared for the imminent onslaught of women's societies clamouring for an open hearing. At the end of the list of societies he adds, '(not to mention the Suffrage Fellowship et al !)'[53] For Roberts witticism and ridicule were inseparable. He was a man in a hurry who had a goal in mind and was not concerned with intellectual arguments. The historical significance of the relationship between the suffrage movement and the fight for an equal moral standard passed him by, as they were outside his field of knowledge or interest, and as far as his mission was concerned, inconsequential.

Over the three-year period during which the committee sat, a great deal of time was devoted to listening to oral presentations. This seems to have been an intrinsically wasteful process, as many of the groups and individuals had already submitted written texts that were available for the committee to read in advance. These documents became the basis for discussion and cross-examination. The historian Patrick Higgins argues that the proceedings were a charade that was set up in order to placate the different individuals and factions, fooling them into believing that their opinions were being listened to in Whitehall.[54] Although this is a cynical view, it can be given credence through the type of condescending comments made by Roberts and Wolfenden, with their mirthful reference to 'yet another billet doux from the women of England'[55] who were 'looking for a place in the sun'. In fact there is little evidence to show that the committee was influenced by any of the contributors or by their assorted prejudices, but it undoubtedly proceeded from a position of ignorance to something approaching irritable disintegration!

THE THIRD STAGE: THE LEARNING CURVE

There is a certain logic in the system favoured by the British of appointing a group of high-status, intelligent and respected professional people to make an unbiased appraisal of a contentious problem, but it is important that they are properly briefed. This should enable them to look with clarity and without prejudice at the questions involved and make recommendations for change if they are needed. With homosexuality a process of intellectual inquiry and exploration did take place, but with prostitution no such journey was thought to be necessary and it was not required within the terms of reference. Wolfenden made this quite clear from the start, stating that the prostitution side of the review did not involve matters of principle as it did with homosexuality, but involved searching for practical measures to ameliorate a situation that could not be radically altered.[56] Prostitutes were not considered to be women with problems, as they *were* the problem. On the other hand the possibility for research into the reasons 'why' men used the services of prostitutes was dismissed as 'impractical'.[57] This meant that the imbalance between the amount of attention paid to homosexuality and that paid to prostitution, as separate legal concerns, was extended to the quantity and quality of attention given to the constituent elements of the problem of prostitution.

One of Roberts' first tasks after the committee had been appointed was to produce a memorandum for the benefit of the members, which stated: 'For some years past, successive Home Secretaries have been pressed in Parliament, in the Press, by leaders of Local Authorities, leaders of the Church and civil organisations, to introduce measures more effective than the present law.'[58] The memorandum went on to note that it was not so much the conduct of individual prostitutes on the streets that caused annoyance to passengers and passers-by as the gathering together of large numbers of prostitutes who annoyed passengers at large. The difficulty arose from the fact that the law had to deal with the individual, and in this instance the individual was not actually doing anything that could be described as annoying. Therefore, it was finding a method for preventing women from gathering together in groups that became the problem. This involved finding a simple formula for convicting the individual and providing a penalty that would create an effective deterrent so as to pre-empt this possibility.[59] The 1928 Street Offences Committee had failed to come up with an acceptable solution. Roberts was determined that the Wolfenden Committee should do better.

Alongside the Home Office memorandum, the committee were able to study the report made by Philip Allen of the trip to America made by himself and Commander Cole of the Metropolitan Police, which, although expurgated, was still confidential. This manuscript revealed some interesting details of policy and practice in America as well as transatlantic attitudes towards sexual morality and prostitution. Judging by the committee's final report Allen seems to have significantly influenced its thinking, if only because his narrative suggested that the Americans had solved the problem. The report,

'Prostitution in the USA', [60]commented on what was described as a 'short visit' during which the pair visited New York, Chicago, Los Angeles, Baltimore, Philadelphia, San Francisco and Washington. Allen was impressed by the fact that in all of these cities it was unusual to see a prostitute openly soliciting. Those who were soliciting were said to frequent 'low-class areas', and as their activities were very discreet they could not be said to 'constitute a public nuisance'. He did not consider to what extent his visit might have been stage-managed.

Across most of America prostitution was a criminal offence, and in some states fornication and adultery were also criminalised. This, Allen surmised, indicated the high moral tone adopted by the legislatures, but it did not lead him to question some of the practices adopted by the authorities, which included telephone tapping and the use of *agents provocateurs* to entrap unwary practitioners. The method used to achieve a prosecution involved a plainclothes policeman who, on being solicited, would return with the woman to her apartment, agree the terms of the transaction and then wait until she had undressed before arresting her. Not surprisingly, the New York Chief Magistrate thought that these practices constituted distasteful work likely to have a corrupting influence on the police. He concluded that streetwalking ought not to come under the criminal code but be part of health and welfare law, which would enable the women to receive psychiatric treatment. As in the UK, the procurer was seldom charged with an offence because it was said 'rather conveniently' to be difficult to obtain supporting evidence. When a woman was apprehended with her customer, his culpability would be overlooked on condition that he gave evidence against the woman.[61]

The level of sentencing was also steeper than in the UK. In Chicago the fact that a woman was a known prostitute was used in evidence against her and an offence of 'loitering to the discomfort of a passer-by' could attract a penalty of $100. A woman convicted of 'unlawful intercourse' could be sentenced to up to one year's imprisonment. Although the term 'unlawful intercourse' included adultery, this was rarely prosecuted, the critical factor being the exchange of money for sex. A similar set of ordinances applied in California.[62]

The general invisibility of prostitute women led to a particular pattern of events when a man wanted to avail himself of her services. The visitor would either make enquiries of his taxi-driver or consult the bell-hop in his hotel, who would then contact a 'call-house', which acted as the intermediary that recruited the woman and arranged the assignation. The police generally turned a blind eye to this sort of procedure, so long as it did not develop into a large-scale racket. The main disadvantage from their point of view was that (unlike in the UK) they did not have the high level of intelligence and personal knowledge of the whereabouts and activities of individual prostitutes that they would liked to have possessed. This deficiency was increased by the apparent absence of brothels, which had been superseded by the call-house, which the police had found difficult to infiltrate.[63] The main outlet for prostitution was therefore the call-girl system, which, in comparison with 'the free-for-all' on the streets of London, recommended itself to the committee as a very attractive alternative.

The Americans also pursued an oppressive policy towards venereal infection, which was not very different from the Contagious Diseases Acts. In some cities, including New York and San Francisco, women's courts had been established that tried, among other things, what were referred to as 'moral offences'. In San Francisco the Director of Public Health was empowered to detain any person arrested for a sex offence and subject her to a medical examination. The procedure followed was that when a woman was arrested for a prostitution offence she would be quarantined for 48 hours in a cell in the building where the women's court was housed. If she was found to be infected she would then be transferred to a cell reserved for medical treatment in the county jail, and discharged only when she was officially cured. If the examination proved negative the court dealt with the woman in the ordinary way and as a result she still ended up in the county jail.[64] It did not seem to occur to the members of the Wolfenden Committee to question the ethics of any of the above procedures, and as the document was confidential it was not open to the scrutiny of organisations such as the AMSH or the National Council of Women, which one may assume, would have been severely critical of this approach.

There is little doubt that members of the committee were deeply influenced by Allen's Report and that it was exactly what Maxwell Fyfe and Roberts wanted them to hear. The reasoning behind the American approach had been underlined by Dr Richard Koch, a lecturer at the University of California, Berkeley, who had been in charge of the Venereal Diseases Division of the San Francisco Department of Public Health. He estimated that 15 per cent of all men would 'indulge in immoral practices' and find a prostitute, however difficult it was made for them, whereas another 15 per cent would never do so however easy it might be. The remaining 70 per cent were vulnerable to temptation if it was put in their way.[65] Therefore the law enforcement agencies worked on the theory that prostitution could best be limited by making it as difficult as possible to find a woman. Unlike the British, the Americans were quite clear about where they stood on the issue of morality, as prostitution was defined as a criminal offence for which both men and women could be indicted and they were not therefore led into the maze of contradiction and dissembling in which Wolfenden was to become involved.

THE FOURTH PHASE: DEFINING THE PROBLEM
(PREPARATORY BRIEFINGS)

In addition to the above sources of information Wolfenden himself wrote a background paper presenting the problems in clear and concise terms.[66] His essay was probably the most balanced and logical document to be produced during the three-year sitting. Wolfenden appreciated that the committee was faced with, and expected to find solutions for, two different problems that were opposite in nature and could not be easily reconciled with each other. First there were the women who 'flaunted' themselves on the streets 'pestering passers-by', and second there were the women who could not be evicted from flats because the legislation was inadequate.

The burden of Wolfenden's argument was that it was the function of the law not to impose a code of morals, but to protect the public, especially the young, from what was offensive and injurious. Therefore the law ought not to be concerned with prostitution *per se*, in so far as it was a matter of private consensual behaviour. He reasoned that if a substantial body of people found certain forms of conduct repugnant, they ought to be made difficult to perform. The fact that the public found the women's behaviour *morally* repugnant did not get in the way of his basic argument. It appeared that women who congregated, paraded, solicited or importuned gave offence to a substantial number of 'respectable' citizens and therefore constituted a public nuisance that could legitimately be dealt with through legislation. The current law was inadequate for dealing with this problem, and the penalties for 'soliciting to the annoyance' of a passer-by no longer acted as a deterrent. Wolfenden concluded that it was necessary to pinpoint the sort of activity that they wished to inhibit, which was 'the insulting behaviour of women who congregated in groups to the annoyance of the general public'.[67]

It had also been demonstrated by the police that the 'annoyance' given to any specific person (which represented a subjective state of mind) could rarely be proved, and that the individual in question would most likely be unwilling to give evidence in court. The pressure to dispense with this requirement had been a persistent request of the law enforcement agencies, and it was probably inevitable that the committee would recommend that proof of annoyance should be dropped. However, Wolfenden rather surprisingly, proceeded to argue the case for the feminists:

> Further, there seems to be little point in retaining the words 'common prostitute', defined by reference to the commission of some other offence and making liable to specific penalties a category of persons so ill defined. If what is objected to is soliciting or importuning, the simplest thing to do is to say so, without reference in the law to subjective states of mind or to categorisation on an emotive basis. The offence would then be defined as 'persistently soliciting' *tout court*, or, if the addition is desirable on other grounds 'persistently soliciting persons of either sex'. The word 'persistently' would safeguard an innocent inquirer, and would require proof of three or four approaches to a passer by.[68]

This solution acknowledged three of the main objections presented by the women's movement, as it removed the stigmatising label of common prostitute, it was gender-neutral, and proof of annoyance was replaced by proof of persistence. Thus presumably something more than police evidence would have been necessary for a prosecution to be successful.

Two possibilities presented themselves as logical alternatives for a solution to the overall problem. The first involved the abolition of the requirement to prove annoyance, coupled with the imposition of a system of substantially increased and graduated fines, culminating in a prison sentence for the persistent offender. This would involve balancing the severity of the deterrent effect of the penalty against the likelihood of an increase in 'not guilty' pleas. A careful balance had to be achieved in order to avoid the disadvantage of an increase in the amount of time and money that the police and the courts would be required to devote to the issue. The alternative approach, still aimed at preserving public decency, was the legalisation and regulation of controlled brothels. The prostitutes could then be 'driven off the streets' and the whole affair conducted more 'respectably' behind closed doors.[69] This would have the added advantage of removing temptation from the view of susceptible young men. Wolfenden appreciated some of the drawbacks inherent in this second proposal, as the penalties for soliciting would still have to be increased if the women were to be removed, and the general public might not find licensed brothels an acceptable solution. He realised that it was undesirable to allow third parties to profit from the running of licensed houses and speculated that this objection might apply to the 'call-girl' flats, which would undoubtedly increase in number if the streets were cleared of prostitutes.

Wolfenden finished his paper with a request for clarification on a number of points, including why some continental countries had tried and abandoned licensed houses, what measures could be taken to reduce the nuisance effect of the 'one-girl' flat and to what extent the problems of the West End were replicated in provincial cities.[70]

Roberts' reception of this analysis revealed the extent to which he intended to steer the thinking of the members of the committee towards the solution originally set out by Maxwell Fyfe. On 15 February 1955 he wrote to Wolfenden expressing his concern:

> When I read the paper first I was very attracted by it. It leads logically to nice tidy conclusions of the sort to which the Committee are gradually being drawn. But on closer analysis it conceals some of the vital and controversial issues on which previous efforts – including the Street Offences Committee – have come unstuck.[71]

Roberts was unhappy about the possible consequences of circulating Wolfenden's paper 'in its present form and at the present time' as he felt that the committee might be disposed to do something along those lines. He argued that the definition of the offence was crucial and considered that the simplified description of 'persistent soliciting' would be insufficient as the essence of the problem was not solicitation but 'hanging around'. 'If the penalties were increased courts would tend to look fairly closely at the facts and to prove solicitation it would have to be established that men were actually approached'. The prostitutes would then avoid apprehension by waiting for the men to approach them. Roberts' alternative definition was therefore formulated as '*loitering* or *being* in any thoroughfare or public place *for the purpose of* prostitution or solicitation to the annoyance etc.'[72]

In an effort to clarify his mind, Roberts translated Wolfenden's paper into a series of questions, which he returned with the request that they should not be considered 'as anything more than an *aide mémoire*' aimed at assisting them in their discussions. For example, what was the function of the law? What would be the impact of increasing penalties on police, courts and prostitutes? If the women were driven off the streets, would there be a decrease in demand, or more call-girl flats and an increase in exploitation? What ought to be done about brothels, licensed houses and the thorny problem of premises used for habitual prostitution by individual women? [73]

Despite these elaborate preparations the Committee proceeded to flounder once it began to operate. It was obviously dealing with a hugely complex set of issues, yet it was constrained by its limited remit and by a profound ignorance of the historical roots of the legislation. This latter deficiency became apparent as the witnesses filed through the committee room.

NOTES

1. PRO. CAB. 127/20 (4).
2. Sir John Wolfenden (Chairman) 1906–85: born in Halifax, Yorkshire; Fellow and tutor in philosophy at Magdalen College, Oxford (1929–34); headmaster of Uppingham (1934–44) and Shrewsbury (1944–50); Vice-Chancellor of Reading University from 1950. He was made a life peer in 1974.

   Mr James Adair, OBE; Scottish solicitor with extensive experience of criminal prosecutions; former Procurator Fiscal of Glasgow. Adair was an elder of the Church of Scotland and implacably opposed to any liberalising of the law on homosexuality. He contributed a six-page reservation to the final report.

   Mrs Mary G. Cohen, OBE: Vice-President, Scottish Association of Mixed Clubs and Girls' Clubs; Vice-President, City of Glasgow Girl Guides; took active interest in Girls Training Corps. Mrs Cohen was by far the most lively of the women members.

   Desmond Curran: Senior Consultant Psychiatrist at St George's Hospital, Tooting; Civilian Consultant in Psychological Medicine to the Royal Navy; member of Standing Advisory Committee on Mental Health to the Central Health Service Council; joint author of *Psychological Medicine* (4th edn, 1954).

   The Revd. Canon V. A. Demant, Regius Professor of Moral and Pastoral Theology at the University of Oxford and Canon of Christ Church, Oxford.

   The Hon. Mr Justice Diplock, QC: Recorder of Oxford; appointed to the High Court as a judge in 1956, after which he reduced his commitment to the committee.

   Sir Hugh Linstead, OBE: Conservative MP for Putney, 1942–66; pharmaceutical chemist and barrister.

   The Marquis of Lothian: Junior Minister at the Foreign Office. One of the gentler spirits, who did not appear to be convinced that there was a large-scale problem.

   Mrs Kathleen Lovibond, CBE JP: Chairman of Uxbridge Juvenile Courts; magistrate for 20 years; served on many public bodies, including hospital management committees.

   Mr Victor Mischon, DL: solicitor and Labour leader of the London County Council during 1954.

   Revd. R. F. V. Scott: Scottish Presbyterian minister; St Andrew's Church, Dundee; Barony Church, Glasgow; St Columba's, Pont Street from 1938; resigned from committee in 1956 when he was made Moderator of the Church of Scotland.

   Mr Goronwy Rees: Principal of the University College, Wales, Aberystwyth; resigned from Committee after the publication of indiscreet articles (see text).

Lady Stopford: doctor and magistrate; wife of the Vice-Chancellor of Manchester University.

Mr William T. Wells, MP, QC: member of Lord Chancellor's Committee on Practice and Procedure of Supreme Court, 1947–53; member of Magistrates' Court Rules Committee. Labour MP for Walsall, 1945–74.

Dr Joseph Whitby, MD London, MRCP, DPM, DPH: a busy GP in North London, with special interest in psychiatry.

Secretary: Mr W. C. Roberts (Home Office).

Assistant Secretary: Mr E. J. Freeman (Scottish Home Dept).

3. These offences were taken for granted, and the possibility of decriminalising any of them was not considered.

4. *Shield*, December 1954, p. 8.

5. Ibid.

6. Cmnd. 247, paras. 234–48.

7. Immoral Traffic (Scotland) Act 1902 [2 Edw. 7. c. 11]

8. Cmnd. 247, para. 120.

9. PRO. HO. 345/16/59. Mr James Robertson, Procurator Fiscal, on behalf of the Magistrates of the Corporation of Glasgow. This issue of recognition and knowing who they are was equally clouded, as can be seen by the many references to the 'amateur prostitute' to be found in the literature of the 1920s–1940s. The 'upstart prostitute' was often the promiscuous girl who confused officials by offering something for nothing, usually to the soldiers.

10. During the period in question the social control of women within the home was still maintained through the unequal distribution of wealth, conjugal rights, expectations of housewifely duties and the unwillingness of the police to interfere in domestic disputes, etc. See for example Michèle Barrett and Mary McIntosh (1987), *The Anti-social Family*, Thetford Press, Thetford; Faith Robertson Elliot (1986), *The Family: Change or Continuity?*, Macmillan, London.

11. As shown in my introduction, the 'expert' was afforded great respect: he/she was usually seen as an impartial and responsible person. Patrick Higgins comments that: 'In British culture at the time professionals rarely challenged one another, and those outside the professional group usually adopted a suitably deferential attitude to the pontifications of the "expert".' P. Higgins, *Heterosexual Dictatorship: Male Homosexuality in Post-War Britain*, Fourth Estate, London, p. 18.

12. Roberts and Wolfenden seemed to be in constant touch with each other. Higgins comments that Roberts and Wolfenden developed a close working relationship, with Wolfenden acting as Roberts' protector. My impression is that Roberts made every effort to ensure that the Home Office expectations of the committee were fulfilled.

13. PRO. HO. 345/2. Wolfenden to Roberts, 28 August 1954, 'I want you to realise from the start that we shall depend very much upon you and your colleagues. And you must not hesitate to instruct me on any point.'

14. PRO. HO. 345/2. Roberts, 1 November 1954. Rough draft of letter to the Secretary of State: 'From the number of letters received by the Chairman it is apparent that the women's organisations are combining to bring pressure on the Committee to hold its meetings in public, at least as far as prostitution is concerned.' These refer to organisations coming under the ambit of the Status of Women Committee, which was an umbrella group that helped to coordinate the activities of 17 national affiliated organisations.

15. Ibid. 'However well intentioned the press might be . . . an injudicious selection could easily bias public opinion.'

16. PRO. HO. 345/2. Roberts to Wolfenden, October 1954. 'Evidence would not be reported fairly by the press and therefore would not be balanced . . . An open meeting would give rise to controversy.'

17. PRO. HO. 345/2. Roberts, 1 November 1954. 'It is also urged that public interest demands publication of the evidence, which would, it is claimed, be invaluable to social workers.'

18. PRO. HO. 345/2. Wolfenden to Roberts, 25 October 1954. 'It looks as if some of these well-meaning societies have been putting their heads together.'

19. PRO. HO. 345/2. Roberts to Wolfenden, 26 October 1954. 'I would not like to guarantee that these worthy ladies have in mind their own evidence. I think it is more likely that they want meetings open so that they can send observers to hear what other witnesses are saying. This would enable them to organise pressure groups to counteract the possible effect of evidence with which they did not agree. This is quite legitimate politics, but would not tend to help the Committee in its difficult task.'

20. PRO. HO. 345/2. Wolfenden to Roberts, 27 October 1954.
21. Ibid. 'As you noted there is a sinister reference to "in the first instance" . . . which means parliamentary questions . . . but no need to worry.'
22. PRO. HO. 345/2. Wolfenden to Roberts, 1 November 1954. 'Have replied to the Methodists with what has now become a standard letter . . . They are a nuisance.'
23. PRO. HO. 345/2. Roberts to Wolfenden, 15 November 1954. 'I think that there is no doubt that he is writing as the agent or stooge of AMSH. Firing bullets made by Chave Collisson.'
24. Ibid.
25. PRO. HO. 345/2. Wolfenden to Roberts, 18 November, 1954.
26. PRO. HO. 345/2. Roberts, 1 November, 1954. 'While, therefore, the decision is one for the Committee itself, I think that the members would feel fortified in adhering to the original decision if they could be assured that this decision commended itself to the Secretary of State.'
27. PRO. HO. 345/2, Roberts to Wolfenden, 27 August 1954. 'Procedures for dealing with applicants. The Committee might be asked to empower the Chairman to decide which of the bodies and persons applying to give evidence should be invited to do so and in what form. There will inevitably be a lunatic fringe with which it would be quite pointless to trouble the Committee and you could then decide to throw them out.'
28. Cmnd. 247, final list of contributors, pp. 152–3.
29. PRO. HO. 345/2. Dame Rachel Crowdy to Wolfenden, 20 September 1954.
30. PRO. HO. 345/2. Wolfenden to Roberts, 22 September 1954.
31. PRO. HO. 345/7. Home Office Memorandum.
32. See Chapter 2 for international conventions.
33. PRO. HO. 345/2. Roberts to Wolfenden, 23 September 1954.
34. PRO. HO. 345/2. Wolfenden to Roberts, 28 September 1954. 'I am perfectly prepared to leave it to you to decide if the League of Nations papers are of any use.'
35. PRO. HO. 345/2. Roberts to Wolfenden, 23 September 1954.
36. *Daily Herald*, 21 November 1953.
37. League of Nations Advisory Committee on Social Questions, Geneva (1943), 'Prevention of Prostitution', [C. 26. M. 26. 1943. IV.]
38. Chave Collisson, 1897–1982. Chave was born in Texas and graduated in Australia, the United States and London. She was a prominent member of a number of societies, including the AMSH, the Abolitionist Federation, the International Alliance of Women and the British Commonwealth League. Chave was a dedicated reformer and inspirational speaker and campaigner. Her fight to oppose the Street Offences Act 1959 exhausted her and she retired as Secretary to the JBS in 1960. The Chave Collisson Educational Trust awards grants to projects intended to promote the status of women in developing countries.
39. PRO. HO. 345/2. Chave Collisson to Wolfenden, 9 May 1955.
40. PRO. HO. 345/2. Roberts to Wolfenden, 10 May 1955.
41. PRO. HO. 345/2. Wolfenden to Roberts, 11 May 1955.
42. PRO. HO. 345/2. Roberts to Wolfenden, 22 June 1955.
43. PRO. HO. 345/2. Wolfenden to Roberts, 23 June 1995.
44. S. B. Rowntree and G. R. Lavers, 'The Case Histories of 200 Persons Over The Age Of Twenty', in S. B. Rowntree and G. R. Lavers (1951), *English Life and Leisure*, Longman, London, pp. 1–120. Intended as a scientific study but contains much personal and insulting commentary that is purely the opinion of the authors.
45. PRO. HO. 345/2. Roberts to Wolfenden, 10 May 1955.
46. PRO. HO. 345/2. AMSH. 'Orange document' leaflet setting out remit for Conference on 4 November 1954.
47. The phrase 'public provocation to debauchery' would have included all statutory offences concerning the trafficking of women, but it is possible that it might have included men soliciting women and broader concerns such as pornography.
48. PRO. HO. 345/8. Written evidence submitted to the departmental committee, 1955, p. 8 of main document and separate leaflet on principles.
49. PRO. HO. 345/2. Wolfenden to Roberts, 22 November 1954.
50. PRO. HO. 345/16/59. 'The old women's societies', Wolfenden to Glasgow Burgh Magistrates.
51. Martin Pugh (1992), *Women and the Women's Movement in Britain, 1914–1959*, Macmillan, London, Ch. 10.
52. Even societies that were viewed as generally conservative, such as the Town's Women's Guild or the Women's Institute, created a space for women in which they could be themselves and

pursue political ideas that were 'women-centred' and not necessarily in line with their husbands' views.

53. PRO. HO. 345/ 2. Roberts to Wolfenden, 26 October 1954.
54. Higgins, *Heterosexual Dictatorship*, p. 16.
55. PRO. HO. 345/2. Roberts to Wolfenden, 9 December 1954.
56. PRO. HO. 345/6. Summary of record of general exchange of views at the 14th meeting.
57. PRO. HO. 345/6. 'Minutes of Meeting, 16 May 1955.'
58. PRO. HO. 345/7/1. Home Office Memorandum.
59. Gathering in numbers has always been seen as a greater political threat than the isolated individual, as for example a workers' strike, a protest meeting or a march of disaffected citizens.
60. PRO. HO. 345/6. 'Prostitution in the USA', note by Allen.
61. Ibid.
62. Ibid.
63. Ibid.
64. Ibid.
65. Ibid.
66. PRO. HO. 345/3. Wolfenden's paper for circulation to the committee, 1955.
67. Ibid.
68. Ibid.
69. Ibid.
70. Ibid.
71. PRO. HO. 345/3. Roberts to Wolfenden, 25 February 1955.
72. Ibid.
73. PRO. HO. 345/4. Set of 13 questions to aid discussion.

CHAPTER FIVE

Listening to the Experts

The witnesses, as they filed past the committee, did little to clarify the dilemma that confronted Wolfenden. They displayed a wide spectrum of views that merely emphasised the intractable nature of prostitution and revealed that there was no consensus of opinion or solid support for new draconian measures. Wolfenden was obviously aware of the illogicality of some aspects of the legal situation, but although he claimed to rebuff the moral arguments, he concluded that the operational difficulties that would be presented by dropping the pejorative label of 'common prostitute' would be insuperable.

For some of the witnesses the state-regulated brothel offered the obvious solution and the committee was bound to consider this option. Consequently, Sir Hugh Linstead was sent to France to investigate the reasons that had prompted the French government to close down the *maisons de tolérance* (brothels) immediately after the war. Of course the members ought to have been better informed in the first place, as Britain had led the world in the fight to protect women from trafficking for the purpose of prostitution. But the inevitable outcome of Roberts' engineering was that the debate focused upon 'prostitutes' as a public nuisance, without being balanced by an awareness of the parallel dangers of trafficking and the sexual abuse of women which had motivated the protective legislation that parliament consolidated in 1956.

THE FIFTH STAGE: ASSESSING THE EVIDENCE

Rented property and brothels

In 1955 the suppression of brothels was still covered by the Criminal Law Amendment Act 1885. The Act had provided the authorities with extensive powers enabling them to deal with landlords or tenants who allowed their properties to be used for the purpose of prostitution.[1] In addition the Vagrancy Act 1898 had given the police the authority to search property when they had reason to suspect that a man was 'knowingly' living wholly or in part on the earnings of prostitution. Wolfenden considered that to be an illogicality, as the law was 'intended to run someone in for knowingly permitting something to take place which is in itself not an offence'[*sic*].[2] The Vagrancy Act introduced a further anomaly since it required a man to prove that he was not living on a woman's earnings, thus reversing the principle of being innocent until found guilty.[3] But these draconian measures were not sufficient to satisfy the respectable burghers of London. Paddington, Westminster and Mayfair City Councils wanted to put an end to the legal distinction between the one-woman flat and the two-women apartment, as only the latter could legally be described as a brothel, leaving the solitary 'call-girl' immune to prosecution.

The origin of this problem arose partly from the lack of a statutory definition of the key terms of 'prostitute', 'prostitution' and 'brothel', therefore the accepted definitions derived from precedent. In the case of the word 'brothel', the precedent was *Winter* v. *Woolfe* (1930)[4] which defined a brothel as a place resorted to by persons of the opposite sex for the purpose of illicit intercourse (outside the bonds of marriage).[5] The proposition that a house used by one woman for the purpose of prostitution was a brothel had been rejected in 1895 (*Singleton* v. *Ellison*). This ruling was supported in 1916 (*Mattison* v. *Johnson*) and again in 1955 (*Strath* v. *Foxon*).[6]

The matter was settled in the Central Criminal Court on 9 February 1956[7] in the case of *R.* v. *Silver, Pullinger and others*, when Judge Maud directed the jury to return a verdict of 'not guilty' against nine men who had been indicted under the Vagrancy Act 1898 with knowingly living wholly or in part on the earnings of prostitution. The nine men involved were engaged, either as landlords or agents, in letting individual flats to individual prostitutes in the full knowledge that the women intended to use the premises for the purpose of prostitution. Maud J. pointed out that section 13(2) of the CLA Act 1885 referred not to the lessor or landlord, but to the tenant, lessee or occupier. The landlord or lessor was committing an offence only if, under section 13(3), he or she knowingly let the premises for use as a brothel. It was not within the ambit of the law to prosecute the lessor or landlord who let premises for the purpose of habitual prostitution to one prostitute only, since in common law it required two women to work in a premises before it could be designated as a brothel.[8]

The complexity of the prostitution debate, and the intractable nature of the problems can be demonstrated through the controversy surrounding apartments and brothels. Maud J. was in no doubt whatsoever that the matter of the one-girl flat was a moral one, and that the government ought to legislate to prevent the mischief involved. On delivering his judgment, he described the whole episode as 'utterly, completely and disgustingly immoral . . . It may be that the problem is so grave that Parliament must do something about it.'[9]

When Paddington, Mayfair and Westminster City Councils appeared before the committee they had similar objectives. They wanted the women out of the flats *and* off the streets, because they believed that the two were linked together. They also wanted draconian measures introduced to enforce these opposing goals. Westminster City Council admitted that its real aim was to get rid of prostitution altogether, but at the same time it was constrained by the need to preserve individual liberty. But since the council had found that

measures (such as eviction) aimed at getting rid of prostitution were impractical, and not within the ambit of the law, it was obliged to attack the evil
of prostitution through 'annoyance' and the prosecution of facilitators.[10]
Paddington Council approached the same problem from a different angle.
Councillor P. Dyas stated: 'Ours is a particular problem and it is one that we
do not propose to tackle as a moral issue; that is best left to another tribunal.'
He then proceeded to adopt a moral platform. Solicitation, he complained,
'was carried out in the public gaze, offending decent citizens'. The women
'hang around and annoy people by the very sight of them'. They 'mingled
with decent women, making coarse jokes . . . the evidence of what they have
been doing is strewn around'. All of it disgusted him. However, he and his colleague, Alderman Goss, were 'heartily in favour of the licensed brothel . . .
which was the proper way to control the problem . . . our main aim is to drive
them off the streets because of public indecency.' Consequently the two councillors were in favour of medical supervision and police control. In fact
Councillor Goss had experienced the pleasurable and relaxing 'benefits' of the
brothel system during the First World War. 'You could get a drink there and
a little music'.[11]

Faced with the contradictions of the Westminister City Council's position,
Mrs Cohen questioned its representative, Alderman Sir Arthur Howard. 'Do
you think it is possible to stop prostitution, because that is what you are trying
to do, are you not? You are going to make it practically impossible. Do you
think you are trying to do the impossible?'[12]

The alderman's answer was a classic illustration of why legislating for
human sexual behaviour was so beset with problems, which were never likely
to be resolved:

> You assume that prostitution is defined, and that takes us back to the
> problem we all have to face. There is a persistent inclination in human
> beings, of both sexes, to indulge in sexual intercourse, despite what laws
> and Churches have done that persists, and we did not see that there was
> any prospect of creating any law which would be operable, which would
> make it a crime. Even if we did think it was possible to create legislation
> of that sort, we do not believe human nature would change so much that
> the practice of extra-marital intercourse would slowly disappear.

It was at this juncture that the committee ought to have paused in order to
embark upon a serious and informed debate over the feasibility of returning
to some form of state-regulated prostitution, which was what the city councillors and many others had been suggesting. It could then have adapted legislative precedents or have rejected regulation on the basis of reasoning that
pertained to the liberties of the women confined in such establishments. It
failed to do either because it lacked the necessary historical knowledge,
including that of the campaign to repeal the Contagious Diseases Acts, that
of the twentieth-century feminist campaign for additional protective measures, and that of the parallel work of the League of Nations. It appeared that

no one had bothered to read the background information provided by the AMSH, and Roberts had intentionally withheld the many publications of the League of Nations and the UN, believing that they would be a distraction. Thus the committee's main reason for rejecting brothels had little to do with the rights of women; it was that the brothel was not considered to be acceptable to the general public.

As mentioned above, in an effort to clarify the situation, Sir Hugh Linstead travelled to France to investigate the reasons for the closure of the *maisons de tolérance*. Although his report concentrated very largely upon the medical aspects of regulation, it made some important observations about the inadvisability of brothel-keeping. Sir Hugh discovered that the French Ministry of the Interior did not want to return to the system of regulating prostitutes and of placing them under the control of the police authorities. It had found that the owners of brothels had exploited the women who were placed at their mercy. It also found that reforms requiring the closure of brothels, passed in April 1946, had improved the situation in small towns where the private practice of prostitution was difficult, but had made little difference to the bigger ones where systems of control were more difficult to enforce. In the meantime, brothel-keeping had become clandestine and prices had increased. Moreover, the houses did not provide any useful segregation of prostitutes from the rest of the community as at least half of the inmates continued to work on the streets. A doctor from the Ministry of Health informed Sir Hugh that he supported the closure of brothels as he had observed a dramatic reduction in the instance of venereal disease, which had dropped from 40 per 100,000 in 1946 to four per 100,000 in 1954.

As part of a drive against street soliciting the French legislature had introduced harsher penalties. Fines had been greatly increased, with the option of imprisonment from six months to five years. The courts had rebelled against these heavy sentences and were unwilling to enforce them, which led to a new drive to have them reduced in order to obtain a conviction.[13]

In her polemical account of prostitution, the radical feminist Kathleen Barry[14] described her visit to the *maisons d'abattage*[15] in the North African quarter of Paris during 1978. The 'closed prostitution houses' then masquerading as 'hotels' were illegal, but still tolerated and policed. As she and her companion began their walk through the narrow streets, they were suddenly struck by a crowd of approximately three hundred men, jostling excitedly, body to body, against the closed gates of the hotel. It was 6.00 p.m. on Easter Saturday evening, and the crowds grew larger as the night progressed. In every house six or seven women were expected to serve 80–120 men per night. The customer paid 30 francs at the door, was given a towel and was allowed to spend six minutes with a woman.

The more measured account of the *maisons de tolérance*, by Alain Corbin, elaborates upon the wider programme of controls, which included the discipline enforced by the *dames de maisons* and the use of hospitals and the prisons. Corbin confronts the sinister reasoning behind the system, which addressed some of the concerns of Alderman Howard. A class of women were deployed in order to keep men pure, by channelling their extra-marital sexuality, in the hope of preventing the spread of 'unnatural' practices.[16] This had been part of military theory from time immemorial. Moreover, governments, churches and municipalities had reaped vast profits from the brothel system.

The historical significance of the law on brothels seems to have escaped the committee, as the initial aim of the CLA Act 1885 had been to prevent trafficking. Brothels were made illegal because the investigations of William Stead and others had revealed that they acted as a cover for the violation of children and the sexual slavery of women.[17] This had been confirmed by the League of Nations Special Body of Experts in 1927,[18] which concluded that the tolerated brothel created the engine of trafficking in humans for the purpose of prostitution. Wolfenden did not have the background historical knowledge of the great crusades to abolish trafficking, and therefore failed to understand the passionate concern of the feminists on this, as on many other issues, stating that '. . . the intensity of the women's organisations is difficult to understand unless it were generated by the injustice of the male partner in heterosexual prostitution going unpunished'.[19]

Equally important in feminist terms, as well as fundamental to Wolfenden's final argument, was the implication behind Alderman Howard's comment on the importance of preserving individual liberty. The Wolfenden Report became famous because it was seen as a defining statement of the liberal philosophy, in which the private life of the citizen was accepted as unproblematic and the private and the public world could be distinguished, informing both legal policy and practice.[20] Councillor Goss reaffirmed this position in his unselfconscious support of the double standard. It was not the thought of the sexual encounter in comfortable sensual surroundings that disgusted him, but the mingling of the public and the private world, the flaunting of public women in the gaze of respectable wives, daughters and impressionable sons. The sexual availability of public women was taken for granted (despite much discussion of morals), while the public display that threatened the private world of intimate relations, 'male' social control and sexual property was not.[21]

The street: police, welfare and administration

When the women from the NCW appeared before the committee, they were invited to introduced themselves in the usual manner. Mrs Lefroy was a lawyer and a magistrate and was also a past President of the NCW. Mrs Bligh was Secretary of the Moral Welfare Committee, and Lady Nunburnholme was the British Honorary Vice-President of the International Council of Women and Chairwoman of the Council's International Affairs Committee. 'Splendid,' intoned Wolfenden. One suspects that they were not going to be taken seriously, as Roberts and Wolfenden were still busy looking for clues as to 'how these ladies get to work'.[22] In contrast when the Commissioner of the

Metropolitan Police, Sir John Nott-Bower, presented himself, he established an instant rapport with the men on the committee. They felt comfortable in each other's presence.

However, Nott-Bower's testimony[23] was not all that Wolfenden might have expected. He looked at the policing of prostitution from a practical and administrative point of view and required legislation that would make the tasks of arrest and prosecution easier, without increasing the investment in man-power and resources. This was the rationale behind the drive to dispense with the requirement to prove annoyance, which had, in Hugh Macmillan's words, been the enactment of a 'dead letter'.[24] Nott-Bower foresaw many dangers and disadvantages in pushing women off the streets and into flats and he agreed with the possibility mentioned in the Home Office memorandum that both the number of 'call-girls' and the openings for their exploitation would increase:

> I think from our point of view, and even more from the point of view of the general public, it would be a very great pity to introduce a large class of people who had a financial interest in prostitution, which they have not now. It is our experience now that some prostitutes leave their profession and they are quite free to do so whenever they like – but, of course- the more people you get who are financially interested in their activities the less free they would become to chuck their profession if they wished to do so. I think that is one of the evils that might arise if you bring into existence a fairly large class of people with a financial interest in prostitution who do not exist today.[25]

Rather surprisingly, Nott-Bower appeared to share some common ground with the women's movement insofar as he did not think of the customer as blameless: 'The prostitute only exists because of the demand of men and there is no reason to believe that demand would be substantially decreased if she were driven off the streets.' He viewed with some apprehension the appearance, between the prostitute and the client, of a new class of intermediary who would have, to a greater or lesser degree, a financial interest in vice. He also foresaw an increase in brothels, flat-farmers, one-girl flats and soliciting from windows, arguing that driving the trade underground would not remove the demand. If the men could not find what they required on the streets, then supply would have to be satisfied in other ways and the organisation of prostitution would pass into the hands of exploiters. This meant that the position of the ponce would be strengthened and the taxi driver, hotel porter and café tout would be drawn into the trade.[26]

A further anxiety would be presented by the difficulty of establishing that the woman was a 'common prostitute', and he feared that the consequences of a single mistake might do irreparable harm to the good name of the police. If the evidence needed to establish the woman's status as a prostitute no longer required the testimony of an aggrieved person, then two policemen would be needed for observation instead of one. In the Commissioner's considered opinion the task of the police would be made more difficult by the proposed reforms, but they would still be held responsible if the administration was unsatisfactory.[27]

Wolfenden's suspicions that statistics were not a reliable guide were confirmed when Nott-Bower agreed with PC Scarborough that there had been an increase in police activity, rather than an increase in the number of prostitutes. He related the rise in the number of arrests to the addition of a special 'rowdyism' patrol in 1951, which had been operating in C Division. About 80 per cent of arrests had been due to the activities of this patrol. Bayswater Road, Hyde Park, Pimlico and the West End were seen as trouble spots and the police had responded to complaints from the public in these areas. As suspected, a form of rota system did exist, with an average pattern of one arrest per fortnight for a regular working prostitute. Nott-Bower considered the system to be a pretty futile exercise, as some women were arrested, put on bail and rearrested on the same night. Like Wolfenden, he was anxious to 'clean up the streets' but not to do so at the expense of cluttering up the courts. The magistrates became 'fed up' and the courts did not like being overburdened with prosecutions which dislocated their routine.[28]

Hyde Park, he explained, was a separate issue, as it had its own set of regulations, which had been introduced in 1950. Clause 59 of the Hyde Park Regulations concerned 'Behaving in a manner reasonably likely to offend against public decency'. The problems of Hyde Park were related not only to fornication but, more seriously in the mind of the Commissioner, to the homosexual activities that took place in the 'world famous' urinals. The Commissioner possessed a 'detailed classification and geography'[29] of the trouble-spots of the metropolis, which were plotted out on maps with red lines around the geographical areas of maximum sexual activity. He assured the committee that although the problem of soliciting for the purpose of prostitution was 'the crux of the matter', it was a major problem only in the central area of London, 'the West End being by far the worst'.[30]

Nott-Bower's position was supported by the Chief Metropolitan Magistrate, Sir Lawrence Dunn, who argued that the situation had not worsened during recent years and that the women were concentrated in sufficient numbers to be a real problem only in the West End. While the provision for proving annoyance remained in place there would be no point in increasing penalties, because cases would be contested and a higher standard of evidence required. He believed that prison sentences would be futile. 'What will be the result?' he asked. Men's appetites would not be removed.

> If women are debarred from seeking their custom in the street it will make the acquisition of a flat and a telephone essential. Supply must be satisfied by the brothel and the call-girl and will pass into the hands of those able to organise them. Knowing as I do the virtual impossibility of obtaining evidence to convict a ponce in the present state of affairs this opens up a most unpleasant vista. The women will be completely in the

hands of their men (or women). Opportunities for corruption, or attempted corruption by police, publicans, club proprietors and house agents would immediately increase . . . I must earnestly recommend that before any decision is taken to drive the women off the streets, there should be a most exhaustive examination of all the implications; certainly the work of the police will be made infinitely more difficult.[31]

The Director of Public Prosecutions, Sir Theobald Mathew, appeared as an individual witness, but maintained that he had no knowledge of prostitution.[32] This was presumably because prostitutes rarely pleaded 'not guilty'. The Scottish Procurator Fiscal, James Robertson, considered that 'if they appealed to the High Court, every conviction would be dismissed; much more would have to be proved than just the fact that the woman was a common prostitute'.[33] Lady Nunburnholme maintained that prostitutes pleaded guilty out of convenience, because it was not usually to their advantage to do otherwise. When attending Bow Street Magistrates Court as an observer she found that 23 cases out of 24 had been dealt with in 19 minutes. The twenty-fourth concerned an 18-year-old girl who had left home after a quarrel. She had been remanded in Holloway Prison for two weeks and after pleading 'not guilty', she was put on probation for two years. Lady Nunburnholme insisted that the girl had received no previous warnings and there was no evidence of guilt, yet she had been labelled as a 'common prostitute'.[34] Although such stories may be apocryphal, they were given some credence by Sir Lawrence Dunn, who quoted figures that he had extracted with some difficulty from the Home Office. He found that 550 women had appeared on 2,250 charges at Bow Street Magistrates Court during a three-year period. He was puzzled that 'for some reason the women themselves acquiesce by pleading guilty', but countered this comment by stating that if they did not, they found themselves in a very difficult position.[35] He hoped that any reform of the law that the committee or parliament contemplated would be an improvement on the current position.

Dunn and Nott-Bower were not the only establishment figures to voice their anxiety. Miss J. H.Clark and Miss M. M. Brown from the Association of Headmasters, Headmistresses and Matrons of Approved Schools found that girls who absconded and ran away virtually disappeared. Some were never found. They testified that the girls did not need to solicit because they hitched lifts from lorry drivers and exchanged sex for transport, living promiscuously for up to twelve months at a time. When they were found they had no money on them.[36] Miss H. L. Long, Director of the Social After-Care Association (Women's & Girls Division), was equally troubled. She submitted a memorandum in which she noted that approximately 90 per cent of girls who went to borstal or prison in the age group of 17–21 had been promiscuous in return for goods and services. This was a matter of clothes, meals, cigarettes and accommodation. 'The fact that so many girls can live in this fashion for months before being picked up indicates that they rarely need to accost or solicit men, but find a ready market for their services.' Miss Long suggested that more should be done to protect young girls from drifting into this sort of life, and recommended that the age at which 'care and protection' cases came before the courts should be raised. She attributed the deterioration in behaviour to changes in moral outlook and believed that the churches, the schools and the media had a duty to help combat these problems.[37] Presumably that would be achieved through moral education and religious indoctrination.

Looking back at the above account, it would appear that the women's movement was not alone in its critique of the existing legislation or the proposed changes. Although the various local authorities were unanimous and unyielding in their condemnation of prostitutes, other witnesses were more cautious and balanced in their judgements. The police were anxious to have legislation that would be effective and operable, but not at the expense of storing up new problems that would be costly and difficult to administer. It appeared that the police had an unwritten contract with many of the women, and could therefore make it difficult for them if they wished to. Prostitutes often had their own favourite pitches and the police liked to have the advantage of knowing who the women were and where they could expect to find them. In this way they believed that they could maintain a tenuous form of discipline and control over the street scene. There was also the perception that crime and prostitution went together. Hence knowing who the women were and maintaining a reasonably friendly relationship with them could yield dividends. In fact they actually preferred the prostitutes to be on the streets, not hidden away in flats and massage parlours[38] where they were out of sight, independent, or under the control of more dangerous, invisible forces.

There were other indications of deficiencies which ought to have been addressed. For example, Mrs Wilkinson had discovered through her research that rootless and unemployed young girls who drifted anonymously into the metropolis had already been failed by the welfare and support services. These organisations included unsympathetic employees in labour exchanges, National Assistance Board officers whose judgmental attitudes greatly reduced the women's chances of finding work, mental health authorities that inappropriately interned and institutionalised young women who were not mentally ill, the probationary services, police and welfare workers and religious institutions that appeared to be strangers to the virtue of compassion.[39]

These were questions that the Home Office could and should have addressed. What, for example, had happened to the children who had disappeared from remand homes, approved schools and borstals? Was detention in an approved school a suitable way of dealing with a sexually active young woman? Was the Children and Young Persons Act 1933[40] being satisfactorily implemented? Was there an adequate and efficient support system (either official or voluntary) available for young women who found themselves in this situation? The broader sociological aspects of the problems were outside the committee's remit and, although they were highlighted, they did not give rise to any great concern, nor were they looked at as an alternative means of ameliorating the situation. The problem of violence against women was never considered by the committee, nor was the need to educate young men.

These were social and feminist issues that in the climate of the 1950s women found difficult to pursue in the face of interrogation. For example, the two lawyers, Adair and Wells, cross-examined Miss Mackenzie, JP and confused her when she attempted to argue for equality of treatment. They underlined the fact that when a woman was seen by two policemen importuning citizens she had to go to court. 'But the man is not under surveillance,' she countered, 'and he should be.' 'The man does not belong to a class,' replied Adair.[41] Miss Mackenzie contended that in her experience men solicited women, yet they did not have the label of immorality attached to them. 'Men are a perfect menace,' she complained. 'A man stood beside me for a quarter of an hour and I was out walking my dog. The law should be equal, it is a matter of supply and demand.' 'You have missed the point,' she was told. 'Men come out of Glasgow Central Station and are accosted by women, is it right? They are not looking for prostitutes. What would you do?'[42] She had no simple legal alternatives to suggest because she viewed the problems in a wider social context.

Chave Collisson had pursued a similar line when asked by Wolfenden if she had ever been annoyed? 'Not at my age,' she replied, 'but my sister was continually solicited and I continually had stories poured into my ear.' There was never a single case in which I could call to a policeman for help. Why this terrible fuss about men?' Wolfenden evaded the issue by concentrating on the details of drafting the legislation in ways which protected the innocent woman. Unfortunately for the female witnesses the broader issue of harassment by men provided no leverage, as the matter of *women's safety* was not within the remit and could conveniently be ignored.

The moral imperative

Wolfenden found himself caught up in a web of contradictions from the very beginning, as most of the witnesses insisted upon addressing the subject through the distorting prism of morality. In his biographical memoir, *Turning Points*,[43] he discusses the importance of the committee's remit which, he insisted, confined the team to recommending changes to the 'law and practice' relating to criminal offences. 'We were not there to write a sociological treatise or a handbook of moral theology or a textbook for medical students.' He used the remit as a form of protection, claiming that it excluded the moral debate and allowed him to maintain that the offence of 'loitering or soliciting' revolved around nuisance. Yet his first initiative, after reading the various written submissions, was to invite the Lord Chief Justice, Lord Goddard,[44] to address the committee on the relationship between law and morality. Lord Goddard became the committee's first witness and despite his reputation for being 'harsh', 'uncompromising' and even 'brutal', Wolfenden found him 'gentle, generous and in every way helpful'.[45] Lord Goddard was a man of high status and in Wolfenden's eyes an 'expert', both of which were high on his list of priorities. He obviously gained immense personal satisfaction from interviewing the Lord Chief Justice and consequently showed him great deference: 'Lord Goddard is not to be held responsible for any of the views which the Committee ultimately expressed. But he did get us off to a splendid start in the important exercise of clearing our minds, taking our bearings, setting our course, getting ourselves into context, whatever you like to call it; and I am abidingly grateful to him.'[46] Nevertheless, Lord Goddard lived up to his reputation. He was anxious to bring back whipping for male importuners and regretted that 'it can no longer be given for that most detestable of offences – living on a woman's earnings'.[47]

The moral debate created further confusion because it fell into two camps. On the one side there were those who asserted that matters of personal morality were not the business of the law, and on the other those who maintained that morality and law had identical functions and that the legitimacy of law was established through the enforcement of moral standards. The latter argument was divisive as the traditional moralists supported the 'woman-blaming'[48] Judea-Christian doctrine, while organisations such as the AMSH championed the Christian ethics of monogamous relationships within marriage, but attacked the double standard.

And in addition, moral grounds were used to strengthen the argument for justifying the harsh penalties that some of the witnesses and members of the committee wished to inflict. In support of this reform witnesses maintained that decent citizens were outraged by the flagrant nature of the prostitutes' display, that clean-living young men were being tempted and corrupted and that older men might have their careers ruined by false accusations. Consequently, and largely to protect the men, it was argued that fines and imprisonment might dissuade young women from entering prostitution.

The committee was not impressed by the arguments promoted by the women's movement, including upholding the unity of the moral law[49] (which meant the responsibility of every individual for their own actions), the sanctity of the human person and an equal moral standard. When confronted by Dowager Lady Nunburnholme and Mrs M. F. Bligh of the NCW, Wolfenden maintained that as a headmaster he was also a moralist and believed in an equal moral standard between men and women. But on being faced with the suggestion that 'the time had come to investigate the client', he insisted, 'the client is indulging in a private vice but the prostitute is openly inciting to a particular course of behaviour and I do not see anything unjust in the law taking cognisance of that and penalising it accordingly'.

During the same interview, he and Adair supported this hypothesis with the evidence of their own investigations in the West End of London. The women they had observed were 'beautifully dressed' and went around 'in gangs'; they followed the life because they earned 'big money' and 'they liked it'. But for the men it was different, as it was more difficult for them to be chaste.[50] Like George Orwell's animals, some were more equal than others.[51]

The notion that prostitutes belonged to a particular 'class' of women was reinforced through the publication of the BSBC's *Women of the Streets*. This book was one of the few sociological studies of prostitutes and prostitution that the committee had at its disposal, and considering the lack of prostitute witnesses, or of any rigorous Home Office research project, it would have been to the committee's advantage to have given it more careful attention. Among other things the book contained short biographical details of 48 women with whom Mrs Wilkinson had become familiar, and included many telling descriptions of the sad circumstances of their lives. Some of the commentary had both 'moral' and political implications. For example, one religious body ran a hostel for girls, which a young woman was said to have entered 'voluntarily'. The administrators of this institution later expressed satisfaction when the girl was imprisoned, because she had refused to respond to their influence. Similarly a Roman Catholic approved school requested that its name should be kept out of court proceedings, and 'showed no interest in the girl' involved.[52]

Yet both witnesses and members of the committee continually returned to the usefulness of placing young women in care and to the redemptive possibilities of bringing prostitutes into contact with moral welfare workers and court missionaries. Harsher penalties were justified on this basis. Roberts dismissed the book in his usual fashion; it was 'a money spinner rather than a serious piece of work'. However, in the final report Wolfenden chose to quote, out of context and unacknowledged, an observation made by Mrs Wilkinson that had been published in *Women of the Streets:*

> Our impression is that the great majority of prostitutes are women whose physiological makeup is such that they choose this life because they find in it a style of living which is to them easier, freer and more profitable than would be provided by any other occupation. As one of our witnesses put it: 'Prostitution is a way of life consciously chosen because it suits a woman's personality in particular circumstances.'[53]

This particular phrase was to be used ubiquitously in order to give expression to the nature of the problem and to reinforce the idea that the legislature was dealing with a specific group of women who were identifiable by their deviant personality traits. But it is interesting in that it also points to a transitional period in ideological thinking, since in a post-feminist world this remark could be translated as a rational choice on the part of the women rather than evidence of deviance.

THE MEDICAL MODEL

In her seminal work, *Prostitution and Victorian Society*, Judith Walkowitz[54] describes 'the making of an outcast group'. Through her research she found that the Contagious Diseases Acts had worked in such a way that prostitutes were both professionalised and marginalised, separating them from the working-class community to which they naturally belonged. There was, of course, nothing new in this process. There had always been a desire to isolate and separate the prostitute from the rest of society in order to create and maintain a recognisable and manageable group with an inferior status. This might be done by confining the women to special temples, harems, brothels or municipal districts, or banishing them outside the city wall. Prostitutes were usually subjected to special rules, made to wear distinguishing clothing, or had disfiguring punishments inflicted upon them. Before they could redeem themselves and re-enter respectable society, there was a period of purification that was voluntarily undertaken, involving a process of repentance and redemption. A sexual service was maintained for the advantage of men, but it was the women who were suspected of harbouring disease and made to shoulder the guilt associated with illicit intercourse.

This sequence of events is very similar to those portrayed by Bryan S. Turner[55] when describing the place of sickness in the creation of 'culturally patterned disorders'. Through this process deviance becomes legitimised and institutionalised as an available social pattern. Turner argues that 'sickness is related to marginality and exclusion from mundane activity, despite the fact that these exclusions are themselves ritualised and institutional. The cure for such behaviour involves social rituals designed to reintegrate the individual into the social group and reaffirm conventional membership by the expurgation of the offending sickness.'[56] In the 'necessary but evil' school of thought, prostitution is accepted as inevitable, but the need to label and classify it is ever present. The process of labelling and exclusion was continually at work during the presentations of evidence and deliberations of the committee, and nowhere was it so obvious as when it related to medical issues. With both prostitution and homosexuality there was a recurrent tendency to see them as forms of illness and deviance. This increased the legitimacy of the idea that prostitutes constituted a special group of people.

There were three doctors on the committee, Joseph Whitby, Desmond Curran and Lady Stopford. Whitby was a London GP with psychiatric experience and Curran a consultant psychiatrist at St George's Hospital, Tooting. Both of the men identified with their professional role, but one would not have known that Lady Stopford was a doctor without being supplied with that additional information. Patrick Higgins writes that Whitby and Curran regarded themselves as 'experts'. Certainly the idea of sending young women to remand centres for social reports, medical diagnosis, psychiatric assessments, grading and 'treatment' appealed to them. Curran suggested that the Criminal Justice Act 1948[57] should be implemented for young prostitutes and that regional psychiatric and observation centres be established.[58] At the same time they were always ready to jump to the defence of men (as Adair had done during his exchange with Miss Mackenzie), arguing that they were not soliciting or looking for prostitutes. This was a recurrent theme.

The British Medical Association (BMA) submitted a lengthy analysis of both homosexuality and prostitution,[59] although it is not clear on what basis it came to its conclusions, apart from relying upon speculation and opinion. Under the heading 'Causes', it listed the multiplicity of life experiences that propelled a young woman towards the selection of prostitution as a means of making a living. In the opinion of the BMA, the average prostitute was the product of an unsatisfactory home and inadequate parenting. She had been subjected to either too much or too little discipline and deprived of parental love and security. On reaching adolescence she had developed into a lazy, self-indulgent young woman with a taste for glamour and a desire for easy money. This desire for glamour persisted into adulthood and was associated with emotional immaturity and a failure to accept reality. During childhood she had rebelled against authority, frequently truanting from school and becoming involved in minor incidences of delinquency. She sometimes exhibited a small degree of mental deficiency or mental subnormality, which was associated with both intellectual inferiority and social inadequacy. Despite all these drawbacks, the BMA believed that the prostitute had contributed to a decrease in the prevalence of venereal disease by generally insisting that her customers used a contraceptive sheath.

However, this catalogue of misery was compounded by the qualification that it was the opinion of the BMA that 'in most cases of habitual prostitution there is an innate deviation of temperament which amounts to a perversion of the normal female sexual impulse'.[60] The client on the other hand was 'very often an unaccompanied male who had taken alcohol and who has probably no intention of seeking a sexual partner until solicited'.

Having painted this picture of childhood deprivation and of general social inadequacy, the BMA proceeded to recommend a considerable increase in fines and imprisonment in order to drive young prostitutes off the streets, where their presence was both corrupting and degrading. Despite this it went on to suggest a wide range of social and welfare changes, some of which were moderately liberal. However, the emphasis was on detention, supervision and training in various state institutions. It was argued that girls would benefit from the formative experience of a disciplined ordered life, supervised hard work and restriction of liberty. It seems that the BMA had given the committee what it wanted to hear, as words such as 'imprisonment' or 'increased fines' were always highlighted by heavily pencilled underlining.[61]

Doctors from the Davidson Clinic, Edinburgh, confirmed the BMA's prognosis. Dr Winifred Rutherford had been flattered by the simpering praise of one 'old lag' who came periodically for treatment. He reported a remarkable change in his behaviour after consultations with the lady doctor. 'I am quite different after a few hours with you. I begin to watch the girls. I begin to watch their heels, their ankles, their skirts.' But the prostitutes were different. Dr Kreamer confirmed that they rarely presented themselves. 'They are usually unsuitable people, because they seem to be such unintelligent people, dull or psychopathic.'[62]

Perhaps the most depressing and destructive pronouncement came from the Paddington Green Hospital: 'There is in fact a type of ill child who is ready to be seduced or assaulted.'[63]

Among the Wolfenden Committee papers there is yet another indication that disadvantaged young women might be sectioned and put away. This consists of a 'confidential' report on the implications of the Royal Commission on the Law Relating to Mental Illness, which concluded:

> It will be seen that under the Committee's proposals, compulsory admission to hospital for psychopathic patients over the age of twenty-one would only be permissible when they have committed a criminal offence which would also make them liable to imprisonment . . . If the Committee on Homosexuality and Prostitution recommended major changes in the law which at present makes certain forms of sexual behaviour criminal offences, it might under the Royal Commission's proposed system affect the number of such patients who would be compelled to accept medical treatment.[64]

The committee knew that proposals for the imprisonment of prostitutes might result in more women being sent to mental hospitals for the treatment of 'imaginary or real' psychopathic disorders. The Mental Deficiency Act 1913[65] had been used in this way and was the cause of much misery. It divided the mentally ill into idiots, imbeciles, feeble-minded persons and moral imbeciles. Many young women were confined to institutions for the mentally ill as a result of the provisions of this Act. They were sent there by their parents, merely because they had been unfortunate enough to become pregnant.

The BSCB's *Women of the Streets* gave one detailed example of a child prostitute who had suffered in consequence of this system. Nancy was a pretty and cheerful little girl who had been certified as mentally deficient when a child and had later run away from her parents. After being arrested by the police for soliciting she was confined in a mental institution, from which she absconded. She was then taken to a closed institution, where she received no letters or visits from either family or friends for over a nine-month period. After experiencing more problems with the staff, Nancy was placed in a low-grade ward as a punishment. Mrs Wilkinson seems to have been her only support. Not surprisingly, the girl became very unhappy and her mental health deteriorated.[66]

The period of incarceration in such cases was considered to be a matter of clinical judgement and some women have remained in such institutions all their adult lives. It seems obvious that the evidence should have alerted the committee to some of the dangers inherent in institutionalising young women, yet various members were constantly recommending an extension of the period during which a girl could be placed under a 'care and protection' order. Protection of young women 'for their own good' became an extended form of punishment with no fixed boundaries, and was another example of the way in which notions of morality were woven into law, even though this was denied. And those involved in the administrative process knew that the future could be bleak. For example, Mr Langmuir, a Scottish magistrate, tried to deflect women by warning them of their fate: 'I try to give them a picture of themselves in the years to come, as wretched old hags.' This was accompanied by a succession of medical examinations.[67] No such apocalyptical fate awaited the client.

NOTES

1. Criminal Law Amendment Act 1885, Section 13, provided that:
   Any person who

   (1) keeps or manages or assists in the management of a brothel, or
   (2) being the tenant, lessee, or occupier [person in charge] of any premises, knowingly permits such premises or any part thereof to be used as a brothel or for the purpose of habitual prostitution, or
   (3) being the lessor or landlord of any premises, or the agent of such lessor or land-lord, lets the same or any part thereof with the knowledge that such premises or some part thereof are or is to be used as a brothel, or is wilfully a party to the continued use of such premises or any part thereof as a brothel, shall on summary conviction in manner provided by the Summary Jurisdiction Acts be liable –

   (1) to a penalty nor exceeding twenty pounds, or in the discretion of the court, to imprisonment for any term not exceeding three months, with or without [hard labour].
   (2) on a second or subsequent conviction to a penalty not exceeding forty pounds, or, in the discretion of the court, to imprisonment for any term not exceeding four months, with or without hard labour.

2. PRO. HO. 345/12 /12.
3. Vagrancy Act 1898, section 1(3), 'Where a male person is proved to live with or be habitually in the company of a prostitute and has no visible means of substance, he shall, unless he can satisfy the court to the contrary, be deemed to be knowingly living on the earnings of prostitution.'
4. *Winter* v. *Woolfe* (1930) 1 KB 549.
5. The phrase 'unlawful sexual intercourse' has been held for the purpose of the Sexual Offences Act 1956 to mean 'illicit' intercourse, that is, intercourse outside the bonds of marriage, *Chapman* (1959) QB 100 (1958) 3 All ER 143, CCA (s. 19 (1)); *R* v. *Jones* (1973) Crim LR 710, CA (s. 17 (1)).
6. *Singleton* v. *Ellison* (1895) 1 QB 607; supported by *Mattison* v. *Johnson* (1961) 85 LJKB 714; *Strath* v. *Foxon* (1955) 2 QB 294.
7. PRO. HO. 345/3. Judge Maud, Central Criminal Court, London, 9 February 1956. Judgment delivered in the case of *R.* v. *Silver, Pullinger and seven others.*
8. Ibid.
9. Ibid.
10. PRO. HO. 345/12/16.
11. PRO. HO. 345/12/12.
12. PRO. HO. 345/12/16.
13. PRO. HO. 345/2. Notes of discussion in Paris on Tuesday, 18 January 1955, between Sir Hugh Linstead and representatives of the Ministry of Public Health, the Police, and the Ministry of the Interior.
14. Kathleen Barry (1995), *The Prostitution of Sexuality*, New York University Press, pp. 193–4 and (1979), *Female Sexual Slavery*, Prentice Hall, NJ. Barry was one of the first of the second-wave feminists to write about prostitution. She took an uncompromising view of prostitution as abusive in all circumstances.
15. *Maison d'abattage*, literally translated as 'house of slaughter'. This was the title given to small prostitution hotels in Paris.
16. A. Corbin, *Women for Hire: Prostitution and Sexuality in France after 1850*, trans A. Sheridan, Harvard University Press, Cambridge, MA.
17. For a contemporary account see B. Scott (1890), *A State of Iniquity: Its Rise, Extension and*

Overthrow, Kegan Paul, Trench, Trubner, London; T. Fisher (1995); *Scandal: The Sexual Politics of Late Victorian England*, Alan Sutton, Stroud, and (1997), *Prostitution and the Victorians*, Alan Sutton Publishing, Stroud.

18. League of Nations (1927) 'Report of the Special Body of Experts on Traffic in Women and Children' [C52.M.52.1927].
19. PRO. HO. 345/6. Notes of general discussion, 21 February 1955.
20. Katherine O'Donovan (1985), *Sexual Divisions in Law*,Weidenfeld and Nicolson, London.
21. There is a considerable amount of feminist literature that enlarges upon this theme. For example, O'Donovan has argued that the idea of privacy has been used to preclude some forms of intervention, leaving women without protection from domestic violence, marital rape and exploited labour within the home (p. 181); S. Uglow, (1988), *Policing Liberal Society, Oxford University Press*, Oxford; Adrienne Rich, 'Compulsory Heterosexuality and Lesbian Existence', *Signs*, Vol. 5 (1980), No. 4, pp. 631–60. Rich argues that heterosexuality is a political institution that perpetuates male dominance. Maggie O'Neill (1996), 'Researching Prostitution and Violence: Towards a Feminist Praxis' in Marianne Hester, Liz Kelly and Jill Radford (eds), *Women, Violence and Male Power*, Open University Press, Buckingham. O'Neill maintains that violence is endemic within prostitution and that a certain level of violence is seen as 'acceptable' by social control agencies, such as the police.
22. PRO. HO. 345/2. Roberts to Wolfenden, 5 November 1954.
23. PRO. HO. 345/7/6.
24. Report of the Street Offences Committee,1928, para. 35, p. 17.
25. PRO. HO. 345/12/5.
26. PRO. HO. 345/7/6.
27. PRO. HO. 345/7/6. Sir John Nott-Bower, Chief Commissioner Metropolitan Police.
28. Ibid.
29. F. Mort, 'Mapping Sexual London: The Wolfenden Committee on Homosexual Offences and Prostitution, 1954–57', *New Formations*, No. 37. Spring 1999, pp. 92–113.
30. PRO. HO. 345/7/6.
31. PRO. 345/7/5.
32. PRO. HO. 345/7/7.
33. PRO. HO. 345/16/59. Mr James Robertson B.L., Procurator-Fiscal of Police, Glasgow.
34. PRO. HO. 345/13/27. Interview with NCW.
35. PRO. HO. 345/7/5.
36. PRO. 345/15/49. Association of Headmasters, Headmistresses and Matrons of Approved Schools.
37. PRO. HO. 345/9/82.
38. London massage houses had become a matter of concern for the NVA from the beginning of the twentieth century. Members of the association made systematic visitations and discovered 'startling evidence of a scandalous nature'. Efforts were then made to ensure that they were inspected and registered by the London County Council. This was achieved in 1916. A. Coote (1916), *Romance of Philanthropy*, NVA publication, pp. 131–2.
39. British Social Biology Council (1955), Ch. 6. *Women of the Streets* was edited by Bill Hewitt, alias C. H. Rolph, an ex-Chief Inspector of the City of London Police who gave up his position in order to take up journalism. Hewitt became chairman of both the Homosexual Law Reform Society and the Albany Trust. (See Antony Grey (1992), *Quest for Justice: Towards Homosexual Emancipation*, Sinclair-Stevenson, London, p. 37.) It is difficult to tell how much influence Hewitt had over the contents of the book, but it was likely to be considerable. *Women of the Streets* also contains some useful statistics in its Appendix.
40. Children and Young Persons Act 1933 [23 & 24 Geo. 5. c.12]
41. This was a disingenuous remark on the part of Adair, who would have known very well that men did look for prostitutes.
42. PRO. HO. 345/16/58.
43. Lord J. Wolfenden (1976), *Turning Points: The Memories of Lord Wolfenden*, Bodley Head, London, pp. 135–6.
44. Rayner Goddard, Baron (1877–1971); called to the Bar in 1899; appointed High Court judge in the King's Bench Division in 1932; Lord Justice of Appeal and Privy Councillor in 1938; life peer in 1944; Lord of Appeal in Ordinary in 1944; Lord Chief Justice from 1946 to 1958. Goddard was a firm believer in both capital punishment and flogging. He is remembered for his part in the Old Bailey trial of Christopher Craig and Derek Bentley for the murder of PC Sidney George Miles. The 19-year-old Bentley was hanged. For a biography see Fenton

Bresler (1977), *Lord Goddard: A Biography of Rayner Goddard, Lord Chief Justice of England*, Harrap, London.

45. Wolfenden, *Turning Points*.
46. Ibid.
47. PRO. HO. 345/7/12.
48. There is a great deal of feminist theology that expands upon this point, written mostly by women, but sometimes by men. See, for example, Kevin Harris (1984), *Sex, Ideology and Religion: The Representation of Women in the Bible*, Barnes & Noble Books, New Jersey. Harris uses biblical text to illustrate the representation of women as property, as sub-human beings, as silly prattlers and naggers, as cowardly temptresses and betrayers, as the source and cause of evil, and so on.
49. The 'unity of the moral law' was an important concept for the AMSH, as it referred to the moral responsibility of the individual, which, it maintained, formed the basis of morality. It applied to all aspects of life, not only to sexual morality. See Alison Neilans (1939), 'The Unity of the Moral Law', *Scottish Women's Temperance News* 1941, and republished as a pamphlet: Box. 3/AMS, 'Miscellaneous, 1940–59', WL.
50. PRO. HO. 345/13/27. Interview with the NCW, 13 July 1955.
51. George Orwell (1975), *Animal Farm*, Penguin, Harmondsworth.
52. British Social Biology Council.
53. Cmnd. 247, para. 233.
54. J. R. Walkowitz (1980), *Prostitution and Victorian Society*, Cambridge University Press, Cambridge, Ch. 10.
55. Bryan S. Turner (1987), *Medical Power and Social Knowledge,* Sage, London.
56. Ibid., p. 52.
57. Criminal Justice Act 1948 [11 & 12 Geo. 6. c. 58]. This Act provided a range of possible options for detention and treatment of young offenders. Section 4 provided for the treatment of offenders suffering from mental conditions, in hospitals or nursing homes, either as a voluntary patient under section one of the Mental Treatment Act 1930, or as a residential patients in institutions or places approved of for the purpose of section one of the CJ Act 1948. It would seem that Curran was pursuing the idea that prostitutes were suffering from a treatable mental condition.
58. PRO. HO. 345/4. Committee notes and correspondence.
59. PRO. HO. 345/9/95. Memorandum submitted by the BMA.
60. Ibid.
61. Ibid.
62. PRO. HO. 345/16/62.
63. PRO. HO. 345/7.
64. PRO. HO. 345/5/39/C. Confidential report on proposed recommendations by the Royal Commission on the Law Relating to Mental Illness and Mental Deficiency, chaired by Lord Percy Newman, reported 1957. This led to the Mental Health Act 1959 [7 & 8 Eliz. 2. c. 72].
65. Mental Deficiency Act 1913, Section 2(1) provided that:

    > A person who is a defective may be dealt with under this Act by being sent or placed in an institution for defectives or placed under guardianship –
    > (a) at the instance of his parent or guardian, if he is an idiot or imbecile, or at the instance of his parent if, though not an idiot or imbecile, he is under the age of twenty-one; or
    > (iv) is in receipt of poor relief at the time of giving birth to an illegitimate child or when pregnant of such a child.

66. British Social Biology Council, BSBC, pp. 101–3. Mrs Wilkinson considered that the position of women certified under the Mental Health Act who were living as prostitutes was unsatisfactory, leading to a deteriorating situation rather than providing support.
67. PRO. HO. 345/16/59.

CHAPTER SIX

Formulating an Offence

The nebulous and confusing definition of 'who' could be defined as a prostitute and what was meant by prostitution was the central riddle confronting the committee. This problem proved to be especially perplexing because it involved transforming images that crossed boundaries of fantasy, religious conviction and outright prejudice into something that was clearly definable from a legal standpoint. And most crucially, the solution that they arrived at would have to avoid the embarrassment of implicating any woman who was considered to be 'innocent' and who might otherwise challenge the basis upon which the labelling rested.

SO WHO, OR WHAT, WAS A PROSTITUTE?

It seems reasonable to assume that with so much evidence to draw upon the matter might have been settled. But it was not. The media had presented a clearly defined picture of a painted foreign woman, usually French, sometimes German, who was accompanied by a black pimp. She earned vast sums of money and returned home with the proceeds. She was unmistakably recognisable as 'foreign' and 'bad'. But this was not the individual who haunted the imagination of people such as Alderman Arthur Howard, who was more concerned about the spread of promiscuity and who would have liked to follow in the footsteps of the American states that had made fornication and adultery into criminal offences. Nor was it the rebellious child who disappeared without trace into the shadowy world of long-distance lorry drivers. Mrs Cohen, a committee member whose philanthropic work was with the Girl Guides, was also concerned about expressions of youthful sexuality and the undefinably grey areas of recognition. 'Is it not beginning', she asked, 'to get a little difficult now to distinguish a prostitute from an ordinary person?' It had, in fact, become increasingly difficult from the First World War onwards to pick out a recognisable group of women who could be labelled as professional, as the number of promiscuous young women seemed to have increased and the so-called 'amateur prostitute' became an added cause for anxiety.[1] The Second World War lessened the grip of parental authority still further, youthful sexuality was more openly displayed and the older generation was more anxious to suppress it. Logic was missing from the argument, however. But '*why*', asked the Howard League, 'pick out the prostitute strolling along and not the lovers on the grass'?[2]

For law to be acceptable, it requires legitimacy as well as effectiveness. The obvious confusion of thought did not inspire confidence. How could anyone be sure? Nott-Bower was fearful lest one wrongful arrest of an 'innocent' woman should irreparably damage the reputation of the police. But as there was no statutory definition of prostitute, prostitution or brothel, the judiciary had to rely upon precedent. When the definition of a 'prostitute' was queried, it was said that the courts had a reliable 'working formula'. This formula came from the case of *The King* v. *de Munck* (1918)[3] in which a woman was charged with attempting to procure her own daughter, Kathleen, to be a common prostitute.[4]

Kathleen de Munck was a girl of 14 who had been encouraged by her mother to solicit men in the West End and entertain them alone in a room fitted out as a bedroom. Although money was exchanged it was proved that the girl remained a virgin. The Court of Criminal Appeal was asked to determine the meaning of the word 'prostitute' and what was meant by prostitution. Darling J. stated, 'We are of the opinion that prostitution is proved if it be shown that a woman offers her body commonly for lewdness for payment in return.' The meaning of the term 'lewdness' was not defined, but it did not require an act of sexual intercourse.[5]

A number of anomalies arose out of this case. The prostitute in question was not a woman but a child just beyond puberty and entitled to protection. Although the mother's behaviour was deplorable, the girl's future security was not going to be achieved by labelling her as a common prostitute. But still more troubling, the ruling greatly widened the meaning of the term 'prostitution', which had been commonly understood to refer to acts of sexual intercourse, hence the age-old concern over sexually transmitted diseases. Consequently, the activities of a great many employees in a variety of entertainment venues would increasingly be looked upon with suspicion, drawing into the net of recrimination those women who worked in saunas, massage parlours, and so on. At the same time the protective aims of the CLA Act 1885,[6] and of the later Children Acts, were being undermined through the ubiquitous use of the disparaging term 'common prostitute' in the offensive side of the law. One of the consequences was that, in cases of under-age girls loitering or soliciting, it was implied that the child was at fault rather than the man who had sexually abused her.[7]

A similar pattern of events can be seen in respect to the definition of a brothel. In *Winter* v. *Woolfe* (1930)[8] the respondent, Eileen Allen Woolfe, owner of a cottage at Fen Ditton, Cambridge, was accused of knowingly allowing her property to be used for the purpose of habitual prostitution between 24 November 1929 and 2 February 1930. The defendant held tea dances on Sunday afternoons that were frequented by Cambridge undergraduates and girls said to be of the 'working-class type'. Some of the women involved were already known to the police in Cambridge, although it was not proved that they were prostitutes or that money had exchanged hands.[9] Police surveillance established evidence that 'acts of lewdness and impropriety on the part of men and women had taken place between 7 and 11 p.m. at the premises on several occasions between the dates charged. There was evidence of actual sexual intercourse between a man and a woman on November 24, on December 8, 1929 (twice) and on February 2, 1930 (in a motorcar on land adjoining the premises).'[10] The case was dismissed by the justices. But on appeal it was stated by Avory, J., that in his opinion the word 'brothel' in the CLA Act 1885 had been given too restricted a meaning by the courts (although it had been given no statutory meaning within the Act). The court ruled that it was not necessary for the Crown to prove that the women concerned were prostitutes or that they had received money. Swift J. agreed. He was satisfied that the respondent was unlawfully and knowingly permitting the premises to be used by persons of the opposite sex for the purpose of illicit sexual intercourse. The premises were therefore declared to be a brothel within the meaning of the 1885 CLA Act.[11]

The judges' thinking took much the same course as Alderman Howard's. They did not like the thought of promiscuous working-class women (known to the police as morally undesirable characters) having intercourse with Cambridge undergraduates, and no doubt they thought that they ought to put a stop to it. It was argued that the premises were being run as a 'disorderly' or 'bawdy house' (although liquor was not for sale) and it did not matter that there was no nuisance involved because such places could often be very 'discreet'.[12] Therefore, the mischief that they wanted to guard against was that of unmarried young people of different social classes having intercourse together.[13] Moreover, it was shown that fornication had taken place not on the premises, but in a motor-car on land adjoining the property. This case represented the type of skewed thinking that the AMSH complained of, since it was coloured not only by class prejudice and moral assumption, but by an element of moral policing.[14]

These were the legal parameters within which the committee was obliged to work. But the prostitute was much more than a legal subject: she was a fertile source of wry humour and submerged fantasy, as well as an emblem for corruption and disease. The committee traded in these conflicting and contradictory images, alternately portraying the women as feeble-minded, inadequate and polluting, or as expensively dressed, sophisticated whores. The mode of representation and the suggested remedy would vary according to which case the member wished to argue; whether withdrawing women for observation and 'treatment', or sanitizing the public place by driving women off the streets. To add to this catalogue of insult a variety of dehumanising analogies were made. Adair, for example, spoke of the women as if they were insects swarming menacingly around the military camps, where they ensnared innocent and nicely brought up servicemen.[15] But perhaps the most damaging of all the misconceptions was the publicised comment of Mrs Wilkinson when she claimed that violence against prostitutes need not be taken so seriously as violence against other women: 'A beating is of far less significance to the girl herself than others who hear about it imagine, and the girl is usually prepared to encourage their misplaced sympathy. The girls are not beaten up for failing to go out, but usually after some domestic incident in which they have given the equivalent of what they have received.'[16] On occasions these stereotyped beliefs were challenged, as when Wolfenden and Adair asked the women of the NCW if there was not any real temptation for young men. Mrs Bligh answered, 'There is an assumption that men have sexual needs which have to be satisfied immediately and that chastity and fidelity are much more difficult for men.'[17]

> Wolfenden: I get the impression from what I hear that a large number of these ladies, beautifully dressed as they are, are in fact engaged in the occupation because they like it, and that it is not really, at any rate in all cases, necessary to go back into case histories – what happened when they were twelve – and certainly not about economic stress, in these days especially. They seem to follow this particular calling, in a good many cases, because they like it and because they find it is a comparatively easy way of making a good deal of money and being able to live and dress, and doubtless eat and drink – at standards at which they would not be able to reach if they behaved as honest women.
> Lady Nunburnholme: I entirely agree but I think that indolence more than liking for the life is the predominant motive.
> Wolfenden: Very likely, but I am only trying to suggest, with great diffidence and a good deal of rashness, that it seems to me that there are a great many women who in fact for one reason or another, like this way of spending their time and at any rate, if they are indolent have not been able to think of another one, and have enjoyed being there, and will be there however much we deplore it either on grounds of sex inequality or moral consideration, or what not and however much we think the world would be a better place without them.[18]

Prostitutes, Wolfenden presumed, constituted a group of women who enjoyed the life and the money it provided and the most that could be done was to ameliorate the worst effects of their activities. This justified his belief that encouraging the women to set up independently was an acceptable solution, which would at least protect the vulnerable citizen from what was 'offensive and injurious'. Yet it was obvious, even from the few data available, that this fatalistic fantasy picture was not the reality. For example, the headmistresses and social workers who had first-hand experience of the women and girls had shown that many of the prostitutes were very young women who had come out of hostels, approved schools and borstals. To have recommended changes that offered better care and wider opportunities for these girls would have been a more profitable way forward.

One of the most significant omissions from the representations was the total lack of evidence from women who were, or had been, prostitutes. The Society of Labour Lawyers wanted to remedy this imbalance by bringing some prostitutes before the committee, but it was considered that it would be a bad idea to introduce 'sponsored women'.[19] Presumably the committee felt that the witnesses might be specially chosen with the intention of swaying the members in a particular direction. Wolfenden's memoir gives a slightly different story, claiming that an (unnamed) group of highly respectable lawyers had arranged 'for a party of girls from the street to come and expound their point of view'. Wolfenden writes, 'my colleagues were looking forward with naughty expectation to my conduct of this particular interview, and were more than usually fertile in their suggestions about questions which might be asked'.[20]

It seems that the committee members were unable to suppress their own erotic fantasies about the women whom they regarded with such contempt and planned to suppress with prison sentences. Their minds were diverted by the thought of the 'cross-grained creatures with no sensibility and nothing fallen about them'.[21] Wolfenden records that the prostitutes cancelled their interview when they found that they had to enter the Home Office building, thus depriving the committee of a first-hand experience.[22] At a later date a rather different interpretation was put upon events. Lady Vickers remarked that Wolfenden had told her that he could not get any prostitutes to give evidence so the writing of the report 'was all done by hearsay'.[23] In the light of the general unwillingness to look more deeply into motivations and causes, it seems unlikely that anyone apart from the Society of Labour Lawyers had tried to fill the gap.

In 1959 a book entitled *Street Walker* was published anonymously. It is purported to be the true story of the life of a prostitute, but one suspects it is fiction as the heroine ends up by walking across the sands into the sunset. The book contains a working knowledge of many of the aspects of a prostitute's life, including fear, violence, misery and betrayal. Wolfenden is quoted on the front cover remarking, 'One of the difficulties we had while the Departmental Committee was sitting was to get a first-hand account of the life and attitude of the prostitute herself. I only wish this book had been available then.'[24]

At the time a great many people assumed it was genuine. The AMSH, for example, reprinted a review of *Street Walker* by Lena Jeger MP, first published in the *Tribune*,[25] in which she writes:

> What do you mean, Sir John? Are you suggesting that if members of your Committee had read this book it would have made any difference to them . . . It was all too obvious that the Wolfenden Committee had no first-hand knowledge of prostitutes. It would have been more credible had it had the modesty to confess failure and ignorance, and lack of time.[26]

Time was not the problem. It had been spent on doing other things.

SIXTH STAGE: FRAMING AN OFFENCE

In 1928, Hugh Macmillan had argued that one of the main reasons for the street offences review was the fragmented state of the law. This was not put forward as an important consideration in 1954. The need to construct an effective offence was the prime purpose of the committee and the justification for this objective was exemplified by the minimalist remit of 'cleaning up the streets'. The discussion on how to reframe the legislation so that it should be effective ran like a constant thread throughout the proceedings.

To recap the Home Office concerns, the current legislation:

* was ineffectual in preventing soliciting;
* relied upon the subjective evidence of an annoyed citizen who invariably declined to appear in court;
* resulted in prosecutions on the basis of uncorroborated evidence of a policeman;
* led to women being picked upon on the basis of a police 'rota' system; and
* was supported by derisively inadequate penalties.

Requirements for a new offence were:

* a penalty that would embody the essence of the problem, which, in Roberts' terms, was that of 'hanging around' for the purpose of prostitution;
* to ensure conviction of women who were prostitutes and not endanger the 'innocent' woman;
* a balanced deterrent with penalties sufficiently severe to discourage street soliciting without leading to appeals against conviction;
* an offence that did not overburden the courts;
* penalties which the courts would be willing to impose; and
* a procedure that was cost-effective in police terms.

In private the committee rejected the contentious and nebulous arguments surrounding moral values because they did not lend themselves to any workable conclusion, although the committee had assured the NCW and the AMSH that morals were important.[27] It decided instead to attack the problem of street offences through the original concept of 'annoyance' or 'nuisance', but at the same time to abandon the requirement to prove that any given individual had been annoyed. This course of action was rationalised on the basis that it was the case not that one individual annoyed another, but that a collection of individuals annoyed a community. It therefore became necessary to attack one circumstance (the prosecution of a woman who was not causing annoyance to anyone) in order to prevent a potential nuisance from developing.

This analysis presented the committee with a very specific problem, which was how to frame an offence that would successfully remove the prostitute from the street without the prosecutor being obliged to provide evidence that anybody had been inconvenienced. The key was to demonstrate that the loitering was 'for the purpose of prostitution', which would be based upon the assumption that the annoyance caused by prostitution was greater than other forms of annoyance and therefore the annoyance could be taken for granted and did not require proof. This inevitably led the committee back to considering the use of the term 'common prostitute' used in the current legislation.

The evidence shows that Wolfenden was not entirely comfortable with the retention of this term. He stated that he 'could not quite accept with equanimity the assumption that a certain act when performed by most people was not an offence, but became one when committed by a common prostitute'.[28] The women's societies had argued that the term 'common prostitute' was not defined by statute and that she ought not be the subject of specific legislation while the male client was not implicated.

They maintained that the use of the term 'common prostitute':

• introduced to the court an individual assumed to be of low moral character;
• provided a presumption of guilt;
• guaranteed that her evidence would be thought worthless;
• branded the woman as a convicted prostitute;
• made reformation more difficult; and that
• the power to define *who* was a prostitute should not be in the hands of the police.

Women also complained that when men importuned them, nothing was done about it.

The first five main points had been listed in the Home Office memorandum that had been distributed to the delegates when the committee was formed, so the members were familiar with these arguments from the beginning. On 25 and 26 July 1956, the committee met with the Commissioner of Police and the Chief Metropolitan Magistrate in order discuss the possibilities of defining the offence of solicitation by reference to the habitualness or persistence of the offender.[29] The minutes of the meeting record that:

> The Chief Magistrate pointed out that to impart the element of habitualness or persistence of the offender, thus avoiding the necessity of charging the woman as a 'common prostitute', would require something other than the evidence required under the present formula. The words 'common prostitute' were useful because they supplied evidence that the woman, if she could rightly be so called, was addicted to a particular form of behaviour – without these words it would be more difficult to infer that the woman was loitering etc., for the 'purpose of prostitution'; the court would probably require some sort of overt act – e.g. actual and definite approaches to men. The Commissioner of Police agreed, and felt that to remove the words 'common prostitute' would make the task of the police almost impossible. It would be necessary to watch the prostitutes as they now watched male importuners, and to employ plain-clothes men and women in the detection of soliciting

offences – a course to which he would have strong objection. The detection of a case of male importuning called for the employment of two men for half an hour; the same prolonged observation would be necessary in the case of women.[30]

These interviews took place while the draft report was under way, and it seems to have provided the defining justification for the final recommendations. It was an argument not only for retaining a label that provided a presumption of guilt but also for a less exacting level of justice for women than for men.

The committee archives contain a number of undated drafts of the final report, which include some discussion of the final conclusions. Among these papers there are responses to the objections set out above. It was argued that:

- the courts did not find the lack of statutory definition a drawback because they had a satisfactory working formula;
- it had not been proved that any injustice flowed from the fact that a woman was introduced to the court as a 'common prostitute';
- no evidence had been submitted to the committee that would suggest that prostitutes felt aggrieved by this label;
- prostitution was a 'trade' like any other trade and therefore could be justly subjected to regulation;
- there was no evidence to suggest that the label interfered with any attempts at reclamation;
- retention of the label was an integral part of the law, as it prevented a woman from resuming her anti-social behaviour in the event of its being lifted; and
- if she refrained from returning to prostitution, there was no problem.[31]

This was the most extraordinarily complacent set of statements. First, the 'working formula' was based not upon any verifiable fact but upon the use of yet another non-statutory definition, that of 'lewdness' in exchange for reward. Yet there had been no evidence to show that 'lewd' acts had occurred between Kathleen de Munck and the men she had entertained, nor was there any clarification of what constituted lewdness. All that was known was that the girl and her mother had solicited in the West End and that money had been exchanged. The rest was conjecture. Second, there *was* evidence of injustice as the committee had been told that women were processed through Bow Street Magistrates Court at the rate of three a minute, which was hardly enough time to challenge the evidence.[32] The prosecution of these women was based upon police evidence and rarely supported by the required corroboration of an annoyed citizen. As Alderman Russell from Westminster City Council said, the police 'had nothing to prove'![33] Yet this unsatisfactory situation was one of the main reasons for setting up the review in the first place, since the police were open to public criticism for flouting the law when they provided only perfunctory evidence of annoyance. Third, no prostitutes had been interviewed by the committee or had submitted written evidence, or been given the opportunity of objecting to how they were treated by the police, the courts or the probationary services.[34] Fourth, if prostitution was 'a trade like any other trade', that gave it a certain measure of legitimacy, and it should therefore have had the same protections as those accorded to any other trade. Instead the women were targeted by local authorities and police who made their lives perilous. Finally, there had been no attempt to discover to what extent the label of 'common prostitute' inhibited a woman when she tried to obtain alternative employment.

On the vexed question of equality the committee argued that, 'we should agree that from the moral point of view there may be little or nothing to choose between the prostitute and her customer. But . . . it is not the duty of the law to concern itself with morality as such. If it were the law's intention to punish prostitution *per se*, on the ground that it is immoral conduct, then it would be right that it should provide for the punishment of the man as well as the woman. But that is not the function of the law.'[35]

Once again the statement seems to be disingenuous. At an earlier session, for example, Wolfenden had remarked, 'We must take care not to make ourselves vulnerable to those who agree that women must not be excessively penalised when their male customers were not guiltless.'[36] Clearly, this question of equality remained a problematic consideration until the end. And yet again, while the compilation of the report was in progress, Wolfenden queried whether there were any other arguments from the women's organisations that the committee should take care to counter. Mrs Cohen answered:

> their main plank was equality of moral standards between the sexes; the Report could stress that its concern was with the law and not with moral standards. Any objection that driving prostitutes off the streets would make life unbearably hard for them, and incidentally draw upon unjust distinctions between 1 and 2 girl flats, could be answered by pointing out that the streets were the ultimate of degradation and that being a prostitute in a brothel was not aiding and abetting its management.[37]

But the representatives of the women's movement and a number of other witnesses had drawn the committee's attention to the broader social issue of women's safety, pointing out that there was no need for any woman to solicit, as the majority were pestered and importuned by men, and that some lorry drivers were only too willing to pick up girls under the age of consent and demand sexual services as payment for the cost of the journey. On this issue, as on others, the committee revealed its masculine bias and a regrettable lack of historical knowledge. Expenditure proved to be another constraint that influenced policy. Thus, following the interviews with the Chief Constable and the Chief Magistrate, it was argued on the basis of cost that it would not be possible to adopt the recommendations that had been set out in the Public Places (Order) Bill, which had advocated the gender-neutral phrase, 'Every person who in any public place habitually or persistently loiters or importunes etc.' It was maintained that 'the problem of prostitution is, in the terms of numbers of people involved, far greater than that of the male importuner and, for that matter, far more of a public nuisance'.[38]

The committee had undoubtedly failed to understand the full meaning of the double standard of morality, as interpreted by early feminists,[39] which was not merely a complaint that men did not have to account for their actions. It had also been argued that while many men abused and exploited women and children with impunity, they expected female members of their own families to observe high standards of sexual propriety. The feminists wanted *men* to behave decently and women to be protected from those who would not. This was the reasoning behind the great crusade for protective legislation that had taken place at the beginning of the century. It was also the rationale behind the 'unity of the moral law', signifying that 'morality' applied to all human actions and not just to sexual matters.[40] It was easy for the committee to ignore such notions as there was no generally understood concept of sexual harassment during the 1950s and no legislation that was used to guard against it. This meant that there was little prospect of balancing out the committee's representation of beleaguered men with a feminist analysis of violence and abuse against women, or with the idea of prostitution as part of a continuum of male violence, which was to become part of mainstream feminist theory during the 1990s.[41]

PENALTIES

The committee gradually worked its way towards a solution, the essence of which was to be substantially harsher penalties, which were to take the form of much steeper fines and up to three months' imprisonment for repeat offenders. 'The only thing', insisted Mr Langmuir (Glasgow Corporation magistrate), 'that will disturb their quiet serenity is imprisonment.'[42] In a post-war period when working-class women had refused to return to domestic service, it was particularly irksome for some people to observe prostitutes 'apparently' earning large sums of money and living (as Wolfenden had suggested) in a manner that was above their status. The Clerkenwell magistrate, Frank Powell, believed that it was necessary to be 'cruel to be kind'. 'Never mind if they do it because of the child; we have driven them out of Clerkenwell into Bow Street.'[43] For a number of witnesses prison was the only deterrent but, as usual, the more pragmatic voice of the police advised greater caution. Police Constable Anderson stated that prison would not help, as they would be just the same when they came out, and it would increase the burden on the prisons.[44] The writer T. E. Jones, Barrister-at-Law, whose book *Prostitution and the Law* (1951)[45] must have been available to the committee, had argued that prison would push prostitution underground and idleness would have a hardening effect.

Contradictory views were typical of much of the testimony, but the pressure for stiffer penalties uncovered another uncomfortable truth highlighted by Dr Whitby. If the law was to be directed not at the public annoyance caused by prostitutes frequenting in numbers, but at the occasional acts of loitering for a purpose, then the proposed penalties were quite disproportionate to the individual acts themselves.[46] This reasoning should also have been applied to the ubiquitous use of the words 'innocent', 'guilty' and 'dishonest'. For if the law was directed towards the relatively harmless acts of individuals, then of what, in the mind of the accuser, was the individual woman guilty? Was she guilty of aspiring to (and enjoying) a standard of living that was above her station and not facing up to reality? Was she guilty of sexual misconduct that, though not illegal, was disapproved of on moral grounds? Or was she guilty only of 'hanging around' for a purpose that was legal? If this was the case, what elements made it dishonest, let alone immoral? Of course there was nothing new about accusations of high earnings and flamboyant dress: they had frequently been made a century earlier. But during the 1950s, following the austerities of the war, flamboyant display seemed particularly inappropriate for women. In addition there was undoubtedly an element of jealousy mixed up with the feelings of disgust at the women's behaviour.

The anxieties associated with adopting penalties that included prison sentences included:

- an increase in 'not guilty' pleas;
- overloading the prisons; and
- an increase in bribery and corruption.

On the positive side it was considered beneficial that the women might have medical care and would be put in closer touch with welfare and probationary services. But, as Miss Chave Collisson graphically put it,

> Are the people who come here . . . proposing that they should be sentenced to higher fines? . . . the more you fine a woman the more she is going to work to pay the fine. Are we going to sentence them to imprisonment? Are we thinking of individual women or of the effect on others, because a prostitute who is put in prison, when she comes out, is certain to go straight back to her profession. You cannot in the atmosphere of a prison with a number of other prostitutes there, enforce compulsory reformation on a person; it must be voluntary, so we must make an impact on the prostitutes themselves. Once you have driven them off the streets they will go into the brothels. If you do not have them on the streets, they will be somewhere else. You do not eliminate them, you do not make them any better, you do not make them give it up. You merely say that the men who want them cannot find them on the streets but will still find them in a brothel.[47]

Wolfenden's official argument in the face of this problem, remained the same: '. . . we must be careful to remember' that to reduce the amount of prostitution 'is not the primary concern of the law'.[48] It was, as he repeatedly said, a matter of 'cleaning up the streets'.

CAUTIONING

The proposed abandonment of the need to prove annoyance created a further difficulty, one that had been anxiously expressed by Nott-Bower during his interview. The mistaken arrest of an 'innocent' woman who was merely waiting for a husband or friend would bring the police and the law into disrepute. Therefore the system of police cautioning and registration of prostitutes that had been adopted in Glasgow and Edinburgh recommended itself to the committee, as it had succeeded in reducing the amount of street prostitution in these cities without any attendant difficulties. The Scottish system was explained to the committee by Mr W. Hunter and Mr J. Robertson of the Association of Chief Police Constables, from Edinburgh, where police in plain clothes were employed in order to observe women. Once they were satisfied that the woman in question was importuning for the purpose of prostitution, she would be cautioned in the street. She would then have her name placed upon a police register and a report would be sent to the court missionary. On the third occasion she would be taken to the police station for a formal cautioning and on the fourth she would be taken to court. The problem of prostitution in Edinburgh was said not to be so great, and call girls were not thought to be a problem. But the behaviour of young people had to be carefully scrutinised as they were in the habit of collecting around the coffee stalls in the centre of the city.[49] This indicated that recognising *who* was a prostitute was not, after all, as simple as had been suggested. It also gave some support to the view of the American sexologist, Alfred Kinsey, who had argued that the traditional form of prostitution would decline, because an ever-increasing number of non-prostitute women were having intercourse with lovers or fiancés.[50]

PRESSURES

The process of arriving at an acceptable formula was not as smooth as Wolfenden suggested in his biography. To begin with there were considerable differences between the attitudes of some of the committee members. Sir Hugh Linstead, for example, was a liberal-minded man who suggested extending the powers of local authorities to help and house women who wished to give up prostitution. Lord Lothian proved to be more sceptical, believing that apart from the West End of London the problem was very small, whereas Dr Curran, Dr Whitby and James Adair were hardliners. The two doctors showed their colours: they were anxious to have young prostitutes remanded in custody for medical and psychiatric tests, but seemed unconcerned about the activities of the men who used them. They preferred a strategy that removed them from the path of temptation. Adair was equally emphatic and viewed the possibility of an expanding off-street trade with equanimity.[51] Of the three women only Mrs Cohen made a substantial contribution to the debate, injecting an otherwise scarce element of humanitarian concern for the women whose lives would be affected by their recommendations. She questioned the retention of the criminal charge upon police registers, pointing out that in Scotland it was removed after three years, giving the women a fresh start. She thought that £25 was too steep a fine when compared to fines for other sorts of street offences, and pressed for imprisonment and heavier fines for male assaults against children. All three women took the problem of children and exploitation more seriously than the men.

When it became obvious that nothing would be recommended to curb the expansion of third-party exploitation the three women issued a joint statement setting out their reservations. They argued that, as the proposed new measures might give rise to the creation of a new class of middlemen (Nott-Bower's point), a maximum of two years' imprisonment was a quite inadequate penalty for living on the earnings of prostitution, and should be increased to five. Their reservation became part of the final report.[52]

It appears that in the absence of any solid research or prostitutes' evidence the members of the committee were just as susceptible to the allure of unsubstantiated fantasies as the expert witnesses, the general public or the press. When the committee discussed the framing of an offence it strained not so much to provide justice for the accused prostitute, but to prevent itself from being made vulnerable to the women's arguments concerning the double standard of morality and to provide an efficient solution to the problem of street soliciting that was cost effective in terms of police resources. Similarly, the argument put forward by the committee for the retention of the term 'common prostitute' was that it was needed in order to ensure an effective offence that would not leave 'innocent' women vulnerable to humiliating accusations. This concern for the innocent woman did not take into account the widening of the definition of the term 'prostitute' through case law. It would thus appear that the Home Office requirement for a law that would 'clean up the streets' was still the essence of the remit and the central concern of the committee.

NOTES

1. The 'amateur prostitute' was frequently referred to in connection with the spread of venereal disease. She was usually a young woman who topped up her wages with intermittent prostitution, or one who was merely promiscuous, mostly with soldiers.
2. PRO. HO. 345/13/24. The Howard League.
3. *The King* v. *de Munck* (1918) 1KB. 635.
4. 'The first four counts of the indictment charged the appellant under s. 2, sub-s. 2 of the Criminal Law Amendment Act 1885, with attempting to procure her daughter, to be a common prostitute. Counts 5 to 8 charged the appellant with aiding and abetting prostitution, contrary to the provisions of the Vagrancy Act 1898, as amended by s. 7 of the CLA Act 1912. The particulars alleged being, that for the purpose of gain the appellant exercised control, direction and influence over the movements of a prostitute, to wit, Kathleen de Munck, in such a manner as to show that the appellant was aiding and abetting her prostitution. Counts 9 to 12 charged the appellant under s. 17 of the Children Act 1908, with causing or encouraging the prostitution of a girl under sixteen years of age, of whom the appellant had the custody, charge or care.'

5. Ibid.
6. The raising of the age of consent to sexual intercourse to 16 and the protection of girls from sexual abuse, procurement and trafficking.
7. The arrest and prosecution of children for loitering and soliciting under the Street Offences Act 1959 has been the subject of two large campaigns in the 1990s by the Children's Society and Barnardo's. See M. Lee and R. O'Brien, 'The Game's Up: Redefining Child Prostitution', The Children's Society (1995).
8. *Winter* v. *Woolfe* (1930), 1KB 549.
9. Ibid. 'There was no evidence that the women resorting to the premises were *convicted prostitutes* (my emphasis, as prostitution is not a criminal offence), or received any payments for the acts of indecency that had taken place, and there was no evidence that the respondent made any profit out of the conduct of the premises other than that arising out of the sale of teas and similar refreshments' (p. 550).
10. Ibid., pp. 549–50.
11. CLA Act 1885, s. 13, sub-s. 2. The appeal was allowed (that it was not necessary to show that the women were prostitutes or that money had exchanged hands) and the case remitted to the justices to hear and determine according to the law. The decision in *Winter* v. *Woolfe* has been criticized by Scion as being inconsistent with the definition of prostitution in *de Munck*, in that it contradicts the assumption that non-commercial sex is not the business of the law (A. A. Scion (1977), *Prostitution and the Law*, Faber and Faber, London). Nevertheless, *Winter* v. *Woolfe* was approved in *Kelly* v. *Purvis* (1983) 1 All E.R. 525. In this case the respondent was charged with assisting with the management of a brothel. Sexual services (masturbation) had been offered to customers patronising a massage parlour, but the additional fee was usually paid directly to the masseuse. Ackner L.J. reviewed *Winter* v. *Woolfe* and affirmed that for it to constitute a brothel it was not essential to show that it was used for the purpose of prostitution, involving payment for services rendered, or that normal sexual intercourse had taken place. 'It is sufficient to prove that more than one woman offers herself as a participant in physical acts of indecency for the sexual gratification of men' (p. 529). See also P. Rook and R. Ward (1993), *Sexual Offences*, Sweet & Maxwell, London, pp. 278–89.
12. 'I don't think that the matter of nuisance is of any importance, for it is too well known that these places are often kept in such a way as to be no nuisance at all, but kept perfectly private' Avory J., p. 555.
13. There has always been a class dimension to the discourse on prostitution, as it was seen by philanthropists and social commentators as a working-class problem. Men and women of higher social status did not need to resort to the streets, although middle and upper-class men were drawn to the excitement of uninhibited loose living. For a particularly compelling account of the Victorian low-life and prostitution see K. Chesney (1991), *The Victorian Underworld*, Penguin, London.
14. The decision in *Winter* v. *Woolfe* greatly widened the definition of a brothel, leading Lord Parker C.J., in *Gorman* v. *Stanton* (1949) 1. Q.B. 294, to define a 'brothel' as a 'house resorted to or used by more than one woman for the purpose of fornication' (p. 303.). The definition of a brothel was extended further in *Stevens* v. *Christy* (1987) 85 Cr. App. R. 249, to embrace a house or room, or set of rooms in any house kept for the purpose of prostitution. In *Donovan* v. *Gavin* (1965) 2 Q.B., it was established by Sachs J. that individual rooms within a single house may constitute a brothel if they were sufficiently close to each other to constitute what might be called a 'nest of prostitutes', 'be that nest large or small' (p. 659). At a personal level I find these rulings offensive. Lord Parker's ruling translates into law the cultural notion that promiscuous women are whores. Sachs J.'s comment is equally unacceptable, as women are not birds in nests any more than they are horses in stables. The whole area of definition is a confused muddle, which could, theoretically, allow for any hotel or student hostel to be deemed a brothel and any promiscuous woman to be labelled a prostitute.
15. PRO. HO. 345/10/Misc./9.
16. British Social Biology Council (1955), *Women of the Streets*, ed. C. M. Rolph, Secker & Warburg, London.
17. This comment echoed the message of Josephine Butler, which was expanded upon in her many speeches and pamphlets during the 1870s.
18. PRO. HO. 345/13/27.
19. PRO. HO. 345/6. 'Minutes of 8th meeting, 31 March 1955'.
20. Lord J. Wolfenden (1976), *Turning Points: The Memoirs of Lord Wolfenden*, The Bodley Head, London, p. 138.

21. PRO. HO. 345/12/10. Comment made by the Metropolitan magistrate Paul Bennett.
22. Wolfenden, *Turning Points*, p. 138.
23. Quoted in Frances Heidensohn (1985), *Women & Crime*, Macmillan, London, p. 30.
24. Anon. (1959), *Street Walker*, The Bodley Head, London.
25. *Tribune*, 27 November 1959.
26. *Shield*, September 1960, p. 31. Copy of article published in *Tribune*, 27 November 1959.
27. The impression given would vary according to who was being interviewed. Wolfenden assured the NCW, 'I am a moralist. I agree with high and moral standards . . . but we cannot spend too much time on moral and social issues' (HO. 345/13/ Trans./27). He told the AMSH, 'we are of course charged primarily with the task of considering the law and practice in these matters' (ibid., Trans./26). In a letter to Roberts, Wolfenden expressed a different sentiment, 'with an effort we could be rid of the moralists by 4 o'clock' (PRO. HO. 345/2).
28. PRO. HO. 345/6. 'Summary Record of General Exchange of Views at the 14th Meeting'.
29. PRO. HO. 345/6. 'Minutes of 26th Meeting, 25 & 26 July 1956'.
30. Ibid.
31. PRO. HO. 345/6. Discussion document undated (1956).
32. PRO. HO. 345/12/16. Alderman Charles P. Russell, Westminster City Council.
33. Ibid.
34. There was, presumably, nothing to prevent prostitutes from submitting written evidence to the Home Office, but it seems unlikely that there were many who would have known how to go about it, or what to write. The Society of Labour Lawyers tried to present a number of prostitute women to the committee, but the attempt failed.
35. PRO. HO. 345/6. Discussion document updated (1956).
36. PRO. HO. 345/6, 'Summary of Record of General Exchange of Views at the 14th Meeting'.
37. PRO. HO. 345/10/Misc./9. General discussion.
38. HO. 346/6. Discussion document undated (1956).
39. The double standard of morality is elaborated in many feminist texts, but the most respected rendition is by Keith Thomas, 'The Double Standard', *Journal of History of Ideas*, 20, (1959).
40. A. Neilans (1939), 'The Unity of the Moral Law', *Scottish Women's Temperance News*.
41. See, for example, Margaret Jackson (1994), *The Real Facts of Life: Feminism and the Politics of Sexuality, c 850–1940*, Taylor & Francis, London.
42. PRO. HO. 345/16/59.
43. PRO. HO. 345/12/11.
44. PRO. HO. 345/12/5, March 1955.
45. T. E. Jones (1951), *Prostitution and the Law*, Heinemann, London.
46. PRO. HO. 345/6. 'Summary Record of General Exchange of Views at the 14th Meeting' 1955.
47. PRO. HO. 345/13/26.
48. PRO. HO. 345/3.
49. PRO. HO. 345/16/16.
50. PRO. HO. 345/9/19.
51. PRO. HO. 345/4. Individual answers to Wolfenden's list of questions, March 1955.
52. PRO. HO. 345/10. Reservation by Mrs Cohen, Mrs Lovibond and Lady Stopford.

CHAPTER SEVEN

The Report

When the inevitable pressure came from the Home Office for the report to be published, Wolfenden grumbled that, 'the committee had a rather depressing tendency to change its collective mind about points that seemed to be settled'.[1] As for the testimony of 'experts' in whose knowledge he had expressed so much confidence, he declared himself to be disillusioned. 'One of our difficulties is to get at facts. A lot of people have views and are prepared to make generalised statements which are not substantiated when you begin to examine them.'[2] There is some irony in this remark, as there is little evidence to show that he tried to verify anything, and he was given to making unsubstantiated statements of his own. Mrs Cohen was equally disenchanted, complaining that 'they had not found out anything about anything', while collectively the group discussed the nature of the 'humbug' that the solicitation laws represented. Wolfenden commented: 'Where exactly is the "humbug"? I am still groping here. If it is said that the "annoyance" caused by prostitutes is quantitatively different from that caused by anybody else, the humbug then exists, does it not, in pretending in law that the annoyance is the same?'[3] The quantity and quality of the annoyance involved were a continual point of issue, as the justification for harsher penalties rested upon the argument that this particular form of annoyance was much greater than other forms, but without the committee getting trapped into admitting that it was related to communal moral values.

As the completing of the report dragged on, members of the committee became impatient. Mrs Lovibond thought that the draft was 'repetitive and woolly', Curran called it 'supercilious and superior'. Mr Mischcon felt that 'the anxiety to produce a report that might commend itself from the literary point of view to the man in the street could be overdone. Everybody on the committee wanted a readable report but it was necessary for them to produce something for the legislature to bite on.'[4] In the end Curran, Adair, Whitby and the three women all made reservations so the report was far from unanimous. Wolfenden describes the committee in his book rather differently, as 'a happy band of followers', 'their devotion was complete, their patience unwearying, and their industry unflagging . . . a remarkable corporate spirit'.[5]

The drafting committee consisted of Wolfenden, Wells and the Oxford theologian Canon Demant.[6] There were no women. As always Roberts was behind the scenes, constantly drafting and re-drafting, changing the text and fussing. On 28 August 1956 he wrote to Wolfenden stating, 'I have managed to get more of the re-draft through the machine, but I am hamstrung at present for paragraphs B1–B4 and B131–B160 which might be put in temporarily and replaced later if you agree . . . I have also made one or two minor amendments which seemed to me desirable as I went along.'[7] This was more than a year before the final report was published in September 1957, which hardly indicates a meeting of minds or an easy consensus of opinion. In the end far more time was spent quibbling over semantics and trying to convey ambiguously worded impressions than over the consideration of evidence or the analysis of data.

SEVENTH STAGE: THE REPORT

The publication of the report brought fame and notoriety and became known as the 'Wolfenden Report' instead of the 'Report of the Committee on Homosexual Offences and Prostitution'. Patrick Higgins writes of the two dons, Demant and Wolfenden, indulging their passion for 'linguistic fastidiousness and ambiguity'.[8] By contrast Sebastian Faulks finds the report's recommendations on homosexuality as 'a victory for intellectual process over personal distaste; it was a vindication of the disinterested mental disciplines of Oxford PPE'.[9] In reality it merely suggested that homosexual acts, conducted in private, should be given the same legal status as prostitution in the sense that private conduct was not criminalised. However, the process had involved a number of highly respected academics spending an unconscionably long time creating a bundle of transparently obvious contradictions.

The report runs to 155 pages in total, most of which is devoted to the discussion and recommendations relating to homosexuality. 'Part Three', Chapter VIII, covers 'Prostitution', beginning on page 79[10] with 'General Considerations' and ending on page 114.[11] This is a balance that reflects the concern shown and the time given to the two subjects. The committee knew from the beginning what the expectations of the Home Office were in connection with prostitution, but with homosexuality there were no preconceived designs, leaving the group free to explore the wider issues.

General Considerations: Paragraphs 222–8

Paragraph 222 of the report sets out the terms of reference, which were to consider: 'The law and practice relating to offences against the criminal law in connection with prostitution and solicitation for immoral purposes.'
Paragraph 223 refers to the limitations of this remit and places women at the centre of the discourse. 'It would take us beyond our terms of reference to investigate in detail the prevalence of prostitution or the reasons which lead

women to adopt this manner of life.' The report then proceeds to make unsubstantiated claims without the necessary backing of empirical data. 'We believe that whatever may have been the case in the past, in these days, in this country at any rate, economic factors cannot account for it to any large or decisive extent.' In the next sentence the report hesitates by suggesting that economic factors, bad upbringing, seduction at an early age or broken marriage might be precipitating rather than determining factors, although they should not be accepted as an 'excuse' since 'many women surmounted such disasters without turning to a life of prostitution. There must be some additional psychological element in the personality of the individual woman who becomes a prostitute.'

The committee had no evidence to support this theory, only the opinions of groups such as the BMA. It was conjecture based upon prejudice, which was freely acknowledged. 'Our impression is that the great majority of prostitutes are women whose psychological make-up is such that they choose this life because they find it a style of living which is to them easier, freer and more profitable than would be provided by any other occupation.'[12] These were Wolfenden's words, his own personal impression which he repeated freely. But to support this opinion they selectively quoted Mrs Wilkinson's comment that: 'Prostitution is a way of life consciously chosen because it suits a woman's personality in particular circumstances.' This remark was selected in the knowledge that Mrs Wilkinson had recorded many separate case histories of women and girls that demonstrated a wide spectrum of disadvantage and social exclusion influencing women who took up prostitution.

These statements, contradictory in themselves, do not sit comfortably next to the famous 'liberal' declaration (Part 1, para. 61) upon which the basic philosophical principle of the whole report was founded. 'Unless a deliberate attempt is to be made by society, acting through the agency of the law, to equate the sphere of crime to that of sin, there must remain a realm of private morality and immorality, which is, in brief and crude terms, not the law's business.' With regard to homosexuality this was a fairly clear statement. All that was required was for consensual acts between two adults to be made legal so long as they were conducted in private. But the issue of prostitution was more confused because the nature of the affront to the ordinary decent citizen was based upon his sense of morality, as many of the witnesses had testified. Therefore placing the reference to morality within the remit was confusing for the reader, since it applied only to men.[13] The report was not honest on this point, as the committee had spent a considerable amount of time discussing whether to attack prostitution through morality or annoyance. Nor did it seek to clarify the point by addressing male importuning.

Paragraph 224 underlines the fact that prostitution was not in itself illegal and the committee could not see any case for making it a crime. This, of course, would have involved making men liable to prosecution, with all the attendant problems of police costs and surveillance, not to mention the possibility of embarrassment, blackmail and loss of status. The committee therefore needed to choose between channelling the trade into off-street prostitution or leaving the street scene to continue as it was.

Paragraph 225 moved into the Augustinian rationalisation of this argument: prostitution was deplorable but had persisted through many centuries and could not be eradicated through the agency of the criminal law; no amount of legislation directed towards its abolition would eradicate it. Men, it was admitted, kept the trade alive but there would always be women who would choose this form of livelihood, even when there was no economic necessity. But although prostitution could not be eradicated and was not in itself illegal, society could not be indifferent. 'Prostitution was an evil of which any society claiming to be civilised should seek to rid itself.' Yet this was a solution which the committee never 'seriously' considered; it simply aimed at diverting it to off-street premises.

The text of the report was then used to ameliorate the sensitivities of the women's movement with words similar to those used by the AMSH. 'This end could be achieved only through measures directed to a better understanding of the nature and obligation of sexual relationships and to a raising of the social and moral outlook of society as a whole.' The responsibility for these ambitious objectives was deflected on to the churches and other organisations concerned with moral welfare, marriage guidance and the family. Nevertheless it was argued that the law had its place, as demonstrated by a quotation from an ambiguously worded paragraph from the Street Offences Committee Report of 1928.

> As a general proposition it will be universally accepted that the law is not concerned with private morals or with ethical sanctions. On the other hand, the law is plainly concerned with the outward conduct of citizens in so far as that conduct injuriously affects the rights of other citizens. Certain forms of conduct it has always been thought right to bring within the scope of the criminal law on account of the injury which they occasion to the public in general. It is within this category of offence, if anywhere, that public solicitation for immoral purposes finds an appropriate place.[14]

This passage was quoted despite the AMSH having repeatedly pointed out, to both committees, that the term 'immoral purpose' had never been used in legislation concerning the solicitation of men by women. If it had been, the courts would at some time have been obliged to define the meaning of an 'immoral purpose', which was an extremely nebulous concept. The excerpt was said to represent the Wolfenden Committee's approach to the problem, which was concerned 'not with prostitution itself, but with the manner with which the activities of prostitutes and those associated with them offend against public order and decency, expose other ordinary citizens to what is offensive and injurious, or involve the exploitation of others'.[15] This phraseology was a substitute for the term 'cleaning up the streets' which appeared in the report only once.

Paragraph 228 sets out the framework of the report as including:

(a) street offences;
(b) living on the earnings of prostitution;
(c) premises used for the purpose of prostitution;
(d) procuration; and
(e) miscellaneous.

The bulk of the time and attention was given to street offences, which were
seen as the major issue.

CHAPTER IX, *STREET OFFENCES*

Paragraphs 229–32, The Extent of the Problem

The report moved on to a discussion of the unreliability of official statistics,
appealing simultaneously to both orderly logical thought and moral outrage.
It was 'the presence, and the visible and obvious presence, of prostitutes in considerable numbers in the public streets' that caused the problem, not the isolated behaviour of individual women. Yet it was not possible to establish
through statistical data that the situation had actually deteriorated. The irra-
tional fear of crowds of women swarming through the streets of London was
then played upon, to the point of dishonesty, by means of an irrelevant quotation from the Report of the Select Committee of the House of Lords on the
Law Relating to the Protection of Young Girls, 1881. This paragraph related to
the evidence of a senior officer of the Metropolitan Police who stated that, 'at
half-past twelve at night a calculation was made a short time ago that there were
500 prostitutes between Piccadilly Circus and the bottom of Waterloo Place'.

There was no attempt in the report to examine this statement, or to place it
in the social and economic context of late Victorian society and of the relative
poverty of Victorian women. It was merely used to alarm the reader about what
might happen if the appropriate steps were not taken. Moreover, the committee had been given no real evidence on which to base its assumption that the
causes of prostitution in the 1950s were no longer economic, apart from comments about dress, the prejudiced remarks of people such as Frank Powell and
their own personal observations when wandering around the West End. These
were all aspects of the question that the NCW and the AMSH had tried to
explore with the committee, only to be dismissed as the 'Old Women's Society'.

Paragraphs 233–48, The Present Law, *and Paragraphs 249–56*, Defects of the
Existing Law

After setting out the law as it stood the report turned to the consideration of
reform. The committee had found a general consensus of opinion that the law
was in need of amendment, but the direction that it should take had been a

matter of controversy. The main justification for reform was the ineffectiveness of the law, as the refusal of the 'annoyed' citizen to appear in court had reduced it to 'a dead letter'. The committee concluded that, in the light of a general agreement over the necessity for reform, 'the needs of the "normal decent citizen" should take precedence over those of the prostitute and her client'. This approach had underscored all the proceedings of the committee, as the authority figures or 'experts' whose opinions had been courted viewed the prostitute and her client as an abstraction. The objectification of prostitute women reduced them to a problem of public order that needed to be solved rather than citizens with problems that might be addressed. The detached professionals, who were usually male, were assumed to have integrity and depth of understanding whereas prostitutes, with their varied life experiences, remained outside the framework of discussion and were automatically relegated to an inferior position. They became a category of persons with fewer rights, deserving a lesser standard of justice than the equally abstract and illusory 'normal decent citizen'.

The report moved on to a justification of the recommendations that were going to be made. The failure of the existing formula was used as a ground for rejecting the AMSH's Public Places (Order) Bill, which had proposed a single enactment directed towards 'Every person, who in a street or a public place, wilfully causing annoyance', etc. The frailty of the use of annoyance as the basis of a charge had been demonstrated in 1923 following the Almeric Fitzroy case at a time when the number of prosecutions had dropped to 595 as compared with 2,231 in 1922.[16] Similar reasons were given for rejecting the recommendations of the 1928 Street Offences Committee, which had advocated the dropping of the term 'common prostitute'. That committee had sought to distinguish between real annoyance in the form of molestation and a more harmless offence of 'frequenting' a public place for the purpose of prostitution, a proposal that was subsequently supported by the Royal Commission on Police Powers and Procedures 1929, which stated in its report, with reference to the earlier committee:

> We are in general agreement with the proposals submitted by them for a reformulation of the existing law as to solicitation. If their proposals obtain legislative approval, solicitation will become a matter, not of annoyance but of 'molestation by offensive words and behaviour' . . . We welcome the proposals of the Committee in this connection and think they should go far to lessen the difficulties of the police in dealing with these offences.[17]

One of the 'difficulties' referred to was in connection with allegations of police bribery by prostitutes. The Street Offences Committee went so far as to admit that 'instances of this must inevitably occur'.[18] The Royal Commission had been appointed the following year in response to a general lack of public confidence in the police due, it observed, to 'certain happenings and allegations of irregular procedures'.[19]

However, the Home Office had not endorsed the Street Offences

Committee's recommendations at the time and in 1957 the Wolfenden Committee considered them to be inconsistent, stating that both loitering and importuning were 'so self-evidently public nuisances that the law ought to deal with them'.[20] The report therefore advocated an increase in police powers by recommending that evidence of annoyance should be dispensed with, despite the Magistrates Association's insistence that 'annoyance must continue as an essential part of the offence of soliciting'.[21] The Wolfenden Committee did not share the earlier doubts about the possibility of police corruption but went out of its way to express confidence in the service. 'Suggestions have been made that the police are occasionally bribed by prostitutes with money or other favours . . . we do not, however, consider the risk is sufficiently serious to outweigh the advantages of the amendments we have proposed. Our opinion is that the general standard of the police in this respect is high.'[22]

This was the most extraordinarily complacent statement given that a major scandal had erupted in 1955 when it was revealed in the *Daily Mail*[23] that Detective Superintendent Bert Hannam had lodged a report with Sir John Nott-Bower, alleging bribery and corruption amongst police officers in the West End. The 'racket' was said to have involved club proprietors, gaming-house owners, prostitutes, brothel-keepers and men living on the earnings of prostitution.[24] Sir John predictably condemned the report as an 'unwarranted attack on a fine body of men and women'.[25]

Paragraphs 257–65, The Prostitute as the Subject of Express Legislation

As the dropping of 'annoyance' was going to leave an evidential gap, the report moved on to a discussion of the second major problem, which was the necessary retention of the defining term 'common prostitute' coupled with the legal immunity of the client. Mrs Cohen's assertion that the law was not concerned with morals was used as a reason for not implicating the client in the committal of an offence:

> If it were the law's intention to punish prostitution *per se,* on the grounds of immoral conduct, then it would be right that it should provide for the punishment of the man as well as the woman. But that is not the function of the law.'[26]

The justification for retaining 'common prostitute' as a category of persons was the protection of the innocent woman. This was not an entirely logical argument, as the close scrutiny required to ascertain whether or not a woman was loitering for the purpose of prostitution negated the 'self-evidence' of the annoyance given to the passer-by. A woman who was waiting in a busy thoroughfare would be unlikely to attract much attention, let alone annoy anyone, unless she persistently accosted people, which took the argument back to the 'potential' annoyance of women gathered in numbers. But as we have seen, the anxiety over the protection of innocent women was closely connected to the credibility of the police.

The Public Places (Order) Bill with its provision for an offence applying to 'every person' was rejected by the committee and the recommendation for retention of the term 'common prostitute' was deemed necessary for the effective operation of the law. The alternative use of an offence applying to 'any person habitually or persistently loitering', etc., had, it was claimed, been considered but was deemed to be far too expensive in terms of police resources and manpower. 'We have accordingly come to the conclusion, with regret, that no alternative formulation is preferable to that which is already familiar to those concerned.' This expression of regret was accompanied by the refusal to recommend that the official recording of a woman as a 'common prostitute' should be removed from police records after a lapse of time without any conviction. The reasoning used to support this was that, 'unless she is charged again, it never again comes to light'. This was a false assumption as the recommendation for prison sentences, if implemented, was bound to make rehabilitation and future employment more difficult.[27]

Paragraphs 268–73, Police Procedures

A comparison was made of the London system of cautioning and apprehension with those used in the Scottish cities of Glasgow and Edinburgh. The differences were marginal. The London system involved a street caution with particulars recorded in the official notebook. On the second occasion when the woman was seen soliciting she would be arrested and charged. If there was some doubt as to the intentions of the woman she might be arrested for 'using threatening, abusive or insulting behaviour . . . whereby a breach of the peace' was occasioned.[28] The Scottish system differed from that of the rest of the UK in a number of details. On the first occasion when a woman was seen 'loitering about, importuning or accosting people for the purpose of prostitution',[29] particulars of the offence would be recorded in the police notebook. On the second or third observation the woman would be taken to the police station and formally charged. In Glasgow the details of the first offence were reported to a moral welfare worker who would try to contact the woman involved. The penalties in Scotland were greater than those in England and Wales, with a £10 fine or up to sixty days imprisonment. It was suggested that these more elaborate steps might be needed in order to satisfy the court that a woman was in fact a common prostitute and to overcome any tendency that might develop, in the light of harsher penalties, for the London prostitute to plead not guilty.

The idea of formal charging at the police station and reference to a welfare worker had appealed to the committee. It was suggested that the intervention of court missionaries, welfare workers and probationary officers at an early stage of a girl's involvement (i.e. on the first occasion on which a woman or girl was observed soliciting) might bring a young woman 'up sharp' and have the desirable effect of preventing her from embarking on a life of prostitution.

There are a number of strands that need to be unravelled at this point which have relevance to what went on in the committee. Men such as Curran,

Whitby and, to varying extents, the rest of the committee were quite anxious to place girls and young women either on remand or under some form of detention, ostensibly for their own good, so that medical and psychiatric tests could be carried out. Yet they viewed with equanimity the exploitative potential of off-street outlets such as massage parlours, saunas and clubs, which posed dangers that were said by Curran to be 'very theoretical and would not deter the Committee from recommending that the streets be cleared'.[30] Similarly the so-called 'amateur prostitutes' were described by Adair as girls who 'infested camps'. At the same time the men on the committee tended to be dismissive of men's responsibility for what took place, often painting them as innocently tempted victims who were accosted when they were not looking for prostitutes. 'The man', claimed Canon Demant, 'is merely a consumer or customer, he is not quite in the same bracket . . . he is guilty of a private vice not a public offence . . . inveighed into prostitution when he is not looking for it.'[31] In contrast, the women on the streets were represented as free agents who enjoyed what they were doing and therefore did not need to be procured. And when challenged by authority, they were liable to resort to aggressive tactics.[32]

Paragraphs 274–84, Penalties

Once the dropping of the need for corroborative evidence and the retention of the label 'common prostitute' had been defended, the report was free to move on to its key recommendation, which was the imposition of harsher penalties. It was through these three measures that the committee sought to smooth out the processes of arrest and conviction and reduce the numbers of women on the streets. Consequently it was argued that the only realistic remedy to the 'revolving-door' syndrome was for increased and progressively higher fines followed by imprisonment for persistent offenders. This sanction was said to be a 'last resort'; nevertheless, it was to be made available for the third and subsequent offences. The harshness of this recommendation was tempered by a return to the old theme of redemption 'for women':

> We do not deceive ourselves into thinking that a short term of imprisonment is likely to effect reform where repeated fines have failed. But we believe that the presence of imprisonment as a possible punishment may make the courts anxious to try, and the individual prostitute more willing to accept, the use of probation in suitable cases. As the law at present stands, a probation order can be made in the case of an offender over fourteen years of age only if the offender expresses willingness to comply with its impositions and conditions.

Thus the redemptive possibilities of voluntary participation in a probationary period were made the central argument for imposing a prison sentence. 'The possibility that help of this kind might be accepted by some even of the most persistent offenders seems to us to be a strong argument for including imprisonment as an ultimate penalty.' There was an element of dishonesty in this proposal, as the committee's declared aim had always been 'cleaning up the streets' and there had never been any real concern shown for the well-being of prostitutes, who were viewed as unrepentant and shameless. This approach diverted the attention of the critical reader away from the reality of what was being recommended, as a prison sentence was to be imposed for attempting to accomplish something that was essentially legal.

It is difficult to see, from the evidence presented to the committee, quite where this confidence in the welfare and probationary services had come from. Looking at the files it seems more likely that Wolfenden was doing what he usually did, that is, minimising the possibility of criticism by placating the factions whose wishes he was disregarding (e.g. the women's movement), while at the same time rationalising the recommended solution.[33] This proved to be the case.

For the two doctors, Curren and Whitby, the detention of young women in a more clinical setting opened up interesting possibilities. In fact the willingness of the committee as a whole to pathologise women who were considered deviant was underlined in paragraph 297, under the heading of *Research*. It was suggested that as more 'case material' became available for clinical research, young women on remand for prostitution-related offences might be used for the purpose of 'deliberate scientific investigation' by teams of psychiatric social workers. 'We still do not know at all precisely what element it is in the total personality of a woman which results in her adopting a life of prostitution, and this, too, would seem to offer a fruitful field of research . . . we recommend that research into the aetiology of prostitution should be undertaken.'

As with homosexuality there was strong resistance to viewing prostitution as in any way a normal expression of human sexuality, and on the street in particular it was the openness of the invitation that the committee viewed with distaste because it jarred with ideological expectations of female behaviour. Consequently the possible advantages of probation and detention, compulsory or voluntary, especially for young prostitutes, were discussed at length. Many witnesses and members of the committee had expressed a wish for the age of 'care and protection' to be raised to 18 or 21. Other witnesses had advocated some special system of compulsory detention and punishment, which would have involved the creation of new official institutions catering specifically for prostitutes. However, with all of these suggestions there were certain difficulties. The courts had in the past been unwilling to use their powers to place convicted young women on remand for an offence that attracted only a small fine. But as the committee was about to recommend a prison sentence, it felt free to suggest that courts should be given explicit power to 'remand, in custody if need be, for not more than three weeks, any prostitute convicted for the first or second time of a street offence, in order to enable a social or medical report to be furnished'.[34]

Clearly this particular set of recommendations presented the committee with a difficult balancing act, since the report was constructed around the hypothesis that the law was not concerned with morality. Men's involvement, it was argued, although admittedly immoral, was not the cause of the problem. Therefore the detention of young women had to be justified upon the basis of social and medical reasons that were not applicable to men. However, the committee encountered some difficulty in justifying the severity of the sanctions that it wished to impose without reverting to the concept of protecting young women from 'moral danger'. But by pursuing this one-sided and contradictory line of argument the committee was precluded from making any critical assessment of the possible dangers facing young women who were subject to abuse and exploitation through the actions of unscrupulous men – for example, the girls who vanished into the nebulous world of long-distance lorry-drivers.

Paragraphs 285–90, Possible Consequences of Amending the Law

These sections returned the discussion to the need to maintain acceptable levels of decency on the streets of London and to the possible (moral) dangers of changing the law. It was accepted that street prostitution might be diverted into more exploitative off-street outlets, but:

> We think it possible, indeed probable, that there will be an extension of the 'call-girl' system and, perhaps, a growth in the activities of touts. These are dangers; but where they involve exploitation of the prostitute, we should expect the laws which already cover this kind of exploitation to be rigorously enforced.

The suggested disadvantages of emending the law were thought to be 'hypothetical' and when set against the benefits of clearing the streets, emendation was considered preferable. It was argued that this would relieve the ordinary decent citizen of the 'constant affront' to his sense of decency by the 'constant parading of the prostitute's wares'. It would also remove temptation from men and cease to be a bad example to young women who had not previously considered prostitution as a way of life. On this basis it was submitted that the overall amount of prostitution might diminish. On the other hand the laws that guarded against exploitation had not been discussed in any detail. Indeed, this had not been necessary, since the protective legislation had been consolidated in 1956 regardless of the committee's opinions.

The balance that was being struck went against the hopes and aspirations of local authorities, which had pressed for new powers to evict single women from flats. They had argued that women solicited on the streets and returned to the flat with their customers, creating noise and disturbance, upsetting neighbours and generally lowering the tone of residential areas. But the committee was convinced that these problems would be overcome if a more sophisticated trade developed in which telephone lines replaced the necessity for street appearances.

This was quite a difficult path to follow, as the local authorities had been some of the most forceful and vociferous advocates of harsher laws. But the committee had realised early on that it would be difficult to clear both the on- and off-street trade without making prostitution a crime in itself and upsetting the delicate balance within the liberal argument that left the customer free. Wolfenden himself had seen the need for a 'safety valve', which was the reason for placing so much emphasis upon the argument of the 'lesser evil' of pushing prostitutes off the streets and into private accommodation.

Paragraphs 291–96, Licensed Brothels

The obvious alternative in the minds of those who wanted to free both the street and the private residence was the setting up of licensed brothels. This was not advanced as a possible solution by the committee, as by the end of its life it had become more familiar with the global movement to abolish these establishments. Consequently it referred to the findings of the League of Nations 'Report of the Special Body of Experts', which had concluded that trafficking in women was sustained and generated by the tolerated brothel. There is no indication among the papers of the committee that individual members thought that brothels would be a good idea. It had never been an English solution and was not likely to be acceptable to the public. The report therefore set out the valid argument that the state ought not to be seen condoning vice. But once again this was not entirely truthful as the safety valve of call-girl flats had to be condoned, if only in a furtive way and as a lesser evil.

CHAPTERS X–XIII

Chapters X–XIII are concerned with the protective side of the law and consist mostly of a textual account of the newly consolidated legislation in the Sexual Offences Act 1956. This is accompanied by a definite attempt to deconstruct the (Victorian-Edwardian) 'feminist' version of gender relationships and replace it with a newly painted picture of the 1950s liberated prostitute. The passive victim of male lust, a woman driven by poverty, is replaced by a shameless, arrogant and aggressive woman whose activities are entirely voluntary. It was again argued that the economic need to resort to prostitution as a survival mechanism was no longer valid:

> The present law seems to be based on the desire to protect the prostitute from coercion and exploitation. When it was framed, the prostitute may have been in some danger of coercion; but today, through the effectiveness of the law or through changes which have removed some economic and social factors likely to result in a life of prostitution, she is in less danger of coercion or exploitation against her will.[35]

This was an inaccurate and misleading statement as the law had not been framed with the intention of protecting the prostitute but in order to protect the innocent woman from trafficking. Hence the need for Barbara Castle's CLA Bill in 1951, which the committee had failed to notice.

CHAPTER X, *LIVING ON THE EARNINGS OF PROSTITUTION*

Paragraphs 298–307

There were no reliable figures to indicate the prevalence of this offence prior to 1954, as statistical records had combined the offence of living on the earnings of prostitution with the offence of importuning by male persons. 'In 1954, in England and Wales, 114 men had been found guilty of the offence at the magistrates' courts and 11 at the higher courts. In 1955, the figures were 113 and 14 respectively. The number of women convicted of exercising control, direction or influence over a prostitute's movements were said to be negligible.' No figures at all were available for Scotland.

These figures, or lack of them, were not analysed in the way that soliciting statistics had been. The small number of convictions could have meant that the crime was not taken seriously or not investigated for administrative reasons. As the report explains, 'Detection of the offence is not without its difficulties, and calls for prolonged observation', but:

> There is little doubt that the number of prosecutions could be appreciably increased if sufficient manpower were available to undertake the prolonged observation necessary to obtain satisfactory evidence, but we are satisfied that with the resources available to them, the police do all they can to deal with this particular offence.[36]

'Prolonged observation' involved an intrusion into personal liberty as it entailed careful investigation of the couple's lifestyle: seeing if they lived together, noting whether the man was working or acting as a woman's ponce, noticing also whether the man watched the woman soliciting and was handed money. From a police point of view, this time-consuming performance was not only difficult and distasteful but far less effective than just picking up the women for soliciting, which fostered the impression that they were in control of the streets.

The report continues the pattern that had been established at the beginning of Part Three, that is, of making assumptions on the basis of evidence that had been admitted to be inadequate:

> Such evidence as we have been able to obtain on this matter suggests that the arrangement between the prostitute and the man she lives with is usually brought about at the insistence of the woman, and it seems to stem from the need on the part of the prostitute for some element of stability in her background life.[37]

The vision of the parasitic ponce or *souteneur*, so much despised by Lord Goddard, is transformed into a voluntary arrangement in which the woman takes on the active role. 'In the main the association between the "ponce" and the prostitute is voluntary and operates to mutual advantage.' The report goes on to dispel the notion, encouraged by the press, that vice rings and syndicates were involved in exploiting unwilling victims:

> The popular impression of vast organisations in which women are virtually enslaved is perhaps in part due to the indiscriminate use of words which suggest an entirely passive role for the woman concerned . . . It is in our view an over-simplification to think that those who live on the earnings of prostitution are exploiting prostitution as such. What they are exploiting is a whole complex of relationships between the prostitute and her customer.[38]

The committee did not doubt that there were commercial interests involved, including taxi-drivers, hotel porters, and so on, but the violent ponce was considered to be a thing of the past.

This section concludes with a return to a form of moralising, reminiscent of the nineteenth-century National Vigilance Association's pronouncements that abounded in its monthly journal, the *Vigilance Record*. Prostitution, it was argued, resulted not merely from the exploitative activities of ponces, but from a whole complex of evil practices that excited the demand. These including the consumption of alcohol, dubious advertisements, pornography, the sale of contraceptives and 'the stimulation of late hours and sensuous entertainment', a quotation that came from Abraham Flexner's *Prostitution in Europe* (1914).[39]

Flexner's book was a frequently cited text full of graphs and statistics used in an effort to establish the sort of 'facts' that Wolfenden felt were so sadly lacking. The book's Calvinistic tone chimed more with the nineteenth century than with the twentieth and was particularly concerned with the evils of regulation and with the waste caused by venereal infection. It attempted to strike a balance between the demand and supply sides of the business, expressing views that were contrary to the Wolfenden Committee's line of thinking. Flexner was not slow to castigate men and wrote of the 'universality of demand' condoned 'on the assumption that it represented an irresistible physiological impulse'.[40] He complained of the lack of respect for women, especially of the working class, and commented that, 'over and above all this, is an industry, deliberately cultivated by third parties for their own profit'. The Street Offences Committee 1928 had also quoted Flexner for its own purposes. In this instance it used it to underline the danger of the police becoming the guardians of public morals, a danger that did not bother Wolfenden.[41]

In many ways the Wolfenden Report is a collage, a synthesis of carefully selected texts which are intended to support the action being proposed. The section on brothels derives from the League of Nations documents, whereas Chapter X is a mixture of Phillip Allen's report on conditions in America and Mrs Wilkinson's views of prostitutes' relationships. Whenever a controversial statement is made, such as those that appear to minimise the involvement of men, the impact of the text is softened by reference to the views of the AMSH and the NCW; as Wolfenden put it, 'to be in good with the women's organisations'. The argument that the relationship between the prostitute and her ponce was a voluntary and mutually advantageous alliance was qualified by the assertion that, 'To say this is not to condone exploitation; the "ponce" or "bully" has rightly been the subject of universal and unreserved reprobation.'

Nevertheless Chapter X concluded with the recommendation that penalties for living on the earnings of prostitution (a maximum of two years) were quite sufficient. This was the point at which the three women rebelled, arguing that in prescribing penalties the law had to have regard for the worst case that could arise and that in their opinion a maximum of two years' imprisonment was quite inadequate. They, at least, had listened to Nott-Bower's warnings on the danger of a new class of middlemen developing and therefore recommended that the maximum penalty for 'living on the earnings of prostitution' should be increased to five years' imprisonment.

CHAPTER XI, *PREMISES USED FOR THE PURPOSE OF PROSTITUTION*

Paragraphs 308–36

For some reason not easily discernible discussion of the complexities of the legislation governing premises used for the purpose of prostitution was placed between living on the earnings of prostitution and procuration, whereas in the Sexual Offences Act 1956 the 'Suppression of Brothels' is left to the end. These sections are gender-neutral, so that it is just as likely for a woman to be prosecuted for managing a brothel as it is for a man, although a man is more likely to be the owner and may be difficult to trace. Roberts had expressed his feelings on the subject to Wolfenden in 1956. 'In balancing the interests of the prostitute and the "respectable" landlord, I think that the responsible landlord should come out on top, though this may be playing into the hands of the unscrupulous'.[42] At least the landlord was to be given the benefit of the doubt.

Two possible solutions had been put forward by the local authorities for the problems that they faced. First, the use of rented property by a 'convicted prostitute' for the purpose of her own habitual prostitution should be made an offence. Second, the legal distinction between premises used as a brothel and premises used for the purpose of habitual prostitution should be eliminated. The problem with the first, as the report explains, was that there was no such thing as a woman convicted for prostitution. The committee were well aware of the confusion among the public over this issue but the report explains, 'By "convicted prostitute" our witnesses presumably meant prostitutes convicted of some offence ancillary to their profession – for example, soliciting – since prostitution is not, of itself, an offence . . . but . . . as long as society tolerates the prostitute, it must permit her to carry on her business somewhere.'[43]

The second big issue to be skated over was the enormous range of circumstances dictated by case law (*Winter* v. *De Woolfe*, 1931), which could result in a premises being designated as a brothel. At one end was the full-scale brothel in which a large number of women might be genuinely exploited for profit by a third party, and at the other end a flat in which two women worked for themselves at an occupation that was, when it suited the argument, classified as a trade or profession. It seems that it was ethically acceptable to the committee to protect the client, on the grounds of expense and relative levels of annoyance, but at the same time legislate in a way that allowed women to work only in isolated and vulnerable circumstances. The balance of stigmatisation loaded upon the women was crucial to the presumptions of the report and depended upon public approval.

The statistics for the offences coming under the heading of 'premises used for the purpose of prostitution' were available only for the period between 1951 and 1955. Over the five-year period 387 men had been convicted for brothel-keeping as against 838 women.[44] The lack of statistics may have arisen partly from the difficulty of policing these offences and/or because they were not taken very seriously, or because most of the women working indoors had set themselves up independently.

A number of minor changes to the legislation were recommended. These included the prosecution of landlords who demanded extortionate rents, a series of offences connected with the assignment of leases, and prosecution of tenants who managed or knowingly permitted a premises to be used as a brothel. Finally, when a local authority wished to pursue a prosecution, the committee considered that it would be best to establish a uniformity of practice and therefore such prosecutions ought to be undertaken by the police.

CHAPTER XII, *PROCURATION*

Paragraphs 337–46

Procuration was dealt with in a very similar manner. There were no precise figures available and very few examples of procuration came to the notice of the police. This was attributed to the advances that had been made since the CLA Act 1885 had been enacted. It was stressed that the international activities of traffickers had been curbed through the machinery of the League of Nations and the United Nations in cooperation with voluntary bodies. And when a case did come before the courts it might be difficult to pursue a prosecution, as it was very likely that the woman concerned had embarked upon a life of prostitution voluntarily. The report continues:

> Very few cases of procuration come to the notice of the police in this country at the present time. It has been suggested that this is because the women or girls who become prostitutes do so because they want to and do not need to be 'procured'. In order to sustain a charge of procuration

it is necessary to establish that some persuasion or influence has been brought to bear on the woman or girl, and this may be negatived by the evidence that shows that she was not really 'procured' because she needed no procuring at all and acted of her own free will.[45]

This was not the impression that the League of Nations Special Body of Experts had wished to give. It had found that a considerable proportion of trafficked women had originally been induced to become prostitutes through some form of deceit or fraud even though they had been prostitutes in their own country.[46] The report of the Special Body of Experts pointed the finger of blame at the tolerated brothel and relentlessly denounced the *souteneur*, stating, 'If the third party could be eliminated, the battle would be largely won.'[47] These are, of course, issues that have returned to haunt us in the present day. All the same no evidence was put before the committee which persuaded it to recommend any changes in the laws against procuration.

CHAPTER XIII, *MISCELLANEOUS PROVISIONS*

Paragraphs 347–51, Refreshment Houses

A number of statutory provisions had made it an offence for a refreshment licence holder 'knowingly' to allow prostitutes to gather together, or assemble, for longer than it took to consume the refreshments they had purchased.[48] Where the licensee was the holder of a 'justice' licence to sell intoxicating liquor, he or she was not allowed to permit the premises to be 'the habitual resort of known prostitutes'. Repeated offences could result in the licence being withdrawn. These provisions have their roots in the historic notion of the 'disorderly' or 'bawdy-house', which was a tavern where a number of prostitutes might live, or alternatively might become the haunt of prostitutes and their customers.

It had been suggested by some witnesses that allowing prostitutes to gather in a known rendezvous might relieve the pressure on the streets. Being mindful of the Edinburgh coffee stalls, the committee suggested that too rigorous an application of these provisions might lead to more prostitutes on the streets and therefore recommended that they should be implemented only when the conduct of the prostitute gave offence to other users of the premises or to neighbouring residents. This was one of the rare occasions where, either by chance or by design, the committee recommended a course of action that showed some toleration of the prostitute and an extension of the liberal principle to women who were using public facilities without annoying other citizens.

Paragraphs 352–4, Aliens

A number of Aliens Acts[49] had been enacted at the beginning of the century, partly as a result of the alarm over 'white slavery' and partly in consequence

of anxiety over Jewish immigration. These Acts invested immigration authorities with quite sweeping powers, allowing them to refuse entry to people
deemed to be undesirable, and to board vessels so as to detain suspected passengers for medical examination. Foreign prostitutes and their souteneurs
were both 'undesirable' and possible carriers of disease, and immigration
officers and voluntary workers from vigilance societies were on the look-out
for suspicious characters who might come into this category. The links
between anti-Semitism, Jewish pogroms and trafficking have been well documented, most notably by Bristow.[50] These links are not a part of this study
except to indicate that their existence demonstrates the unsavoury 'hidden
agenda' that may underlie seemingly benign legislation and the licence that it
sometimes gives to prejudiced individuals.

Some of the witnesses who appeared before of the Wolfenden Committee
had suggested that marriages of convenience had been contracted between
foreign women and British men in order to allow 'undesirable' women into the
country. The committee had not found any evidence of this practice and consequently did not recommend any changes in the law.

Through this report most of Maxwell Fyfe's objectives were realised. But
while the recommendations on prostitution exactly mirrored his original
Cabinet memorandum, the recommendations on homosexuality demonstrate
that the committee had been an independent body and the subsequent media
interest given to the latter conveniently took precedence over the debate on
prostitution. Furthermore, Wolfenden and Roberts had neatly solved the
challenge of the women's organisations by reducing them to two groups represented by an even smaller number of spokeswomen. But although the representatives of the AMSH and the NCW were probably as unrepresentative of
the 'average woman' as the prostitute on the streets, their views and philoso-
phies were not invalid and should have been given more careful consideration.

NOTES

1. PRO. HO. 345/2, 'General Correspondence', Wolfenden to Newsam, Home Office, 6 May 1956.
2. PRO. HO. 345/16/61.
3. PRO. HO. 345/12/12.
4. PRO. HO. 345/10, Misc/10 & 11.
5. Lord J. Wolfenden, *Turning Points: The Memoirs of Lord Wolfenden*, The Bodley Head, London, p. 134.
6. PRO. HO. 345/10/8.
7. PRO. HO. 345/5. Roberts to Wolfenden, 28 August 1956.
8. See P. Higgins, (1996), *Heterosexual Dictatorship: Male Homosexuality in Post-War Britain*, Fourth Estate, London, Ch. 5 for a account of the drafting problems in relation to homosexuality.
9. S. Faulks (1997), *The Fatal Englishman: Three Short Lives*, Vintage, London, p. 243.
10. Cmnd. 247, para. 222.
11. Ibid., para. 345.
12. PRO. HO. 345/13, 13 July 1955. Wolfenden to Mrs Bligh of the NCW.

13. Sexual Offences Act 1956, section 32.
14. Cmnd. 247, para. 227.
15. Ibid., para. 227.
16. Ibid., para. 231.
17. Report of the Royal Commission on Police Powers and Procedures. 16 March 1929. Cmd. 3297, para. 200.
18. Report of the Street Offences Committee, 1928, Cmd. 3231, para. 59.
19. Cmd 3297, p. 127.
20. Cmnd. 247, para. 255.
21. PRO. HO. 345/7/64.
22. Cmnd. 247, para. 288.
23. *Daily Mail*, 17 November 1955 (cited by J. Morton (1998), *Bent Coppers: A Survey of Police Corruption*, Warner Books, London, p. 92).
24. Morton, *Bent Coppers*, p. 92.
25. *The Times*, 19 November 1955.
26. Cmnd. 247, para. 257.
27. The final difficulties to be overcome were (a) the objection to making the 'purpose' of an act that, if achieved, was not an offence, into an offence, and (b) the fact that a 'purpose' could not be substantiated by corroborative evidence. As no alternative solution had presented itself to the committee it appears to have given up: 'If, however, the law is to impose penalties in respect of a particular offence, it is necessary that the offence should be clearly defined, and while we recognise some force in the objection we are unable to suggest for this purpose any alternative to the present formulation.' Cmnd. 247, para. 265. This seems to be a nonsense as making the abstract 'purpose' of a legal act into a criminal offence cannot be described as a 'clear definition'. Paragraph 267, *Kerb Crawling*. The inclusion of a discussion about kerb-crawling was somewhat surprising as it was not a topic that had been raised at any length during the life of the committee. The rationalisation of this activity as a relatively insignificant aspect of some men's behaviour followed the usual pattern. Although it was said to pose a serious nuisance to many well-behaved women, the problems of obtaining proof were thought to be considerable and the possibility of a very damaging charge being levelled at an innocent motorist had to be borne in mind. Therefore no recommendation was made.
28. Metropolitan Police Act 1839, section 54 (13).
29. Edinburgh Corporation Order (1933), section 116 (A) (3). See Cmnd. 247, p. 84, fn. 2.
30. PRO. HO. 345/1/Misc.9.
31. PRO. HO. 345/13/26. Canon Demant to Miss Peto (interview with AMSH).
32. For example, Cmnd. 247, para. 272, 'Some aggressiveness on the part of a particular prostitute'.
33. Eileen McLeod argued that the combined efforts of police courts and social workers reflected the characteristic post-war approach to deviancy, but there was no guarantee that it would secure the intended results. See Eileen McLeod (1981), *Women Working: Prostitution Now*, Croom Helm, London, p. 95.
34. Cmnd. 247, para. 280.
35. Ibid., para. 304.
36. Ibid., para. 301.
37. Ibid., para. 302.
38. Ibid., para. 305.
39. Abraham Flexner (1914), *Prostitution in Europe*, Bureau of Social Hygiene, New York (reprinted 1917), p. 45.
40. Ibid., p. 44.
41. Cmd. 3231, para. 19.
42. PRO. HO. 345/3. Roberts to Wolfenden, 11 December 1956.
43. Cmnd. 247, para. 320.
44. Ibid., p. 145. There seems to be a confusing discrepancy between the statistics set out on p. 145 (387 men and 838 women) and those on p. 148. Both tables come under the heading of 'Brothel Keeping', but in the second table, showing the number of charges in respect of these offences which were proved over a five-year period (as opposed to the number of persons convected during the same five-year period) the figures add up to only 18 men and 29 women. If the first set of figures is correct then there were already a large number of women working indoors, indicating that sweeping the others off the streets might be counterproductive, and that the different venues serviced a different clientele.

45. Ibid., para. 344.
46. LN, Special Body of Experts, p. 18.
47. Ibid., p. 48.
48. Licensing Act 1953, s.139; Refreshment Houses Act 1860, s. 32; Metropolitan Police Act 1839, s. 44; City of London Police Act 1839, s. 28.
49. Aliens Act 1905 [5. Edw. 7. c. 21]; Aliens Restriction Acts, 1914 and 1919 [4 & 5 Geo. c.12. And 19 & 10 Geo. 5, c. 92] Aliens Orders, 1920; No. 448. 1920, No. 2262. 1923, No. 326, and 1925, No. 760.
50. E. Bristow (1982), *Prostitution and Prejudice: The Jewish Fight against White Slavery 1870–1939*, Clarendon Press, Oxford.

CHAPTER EIGHT

The Double Standard

The women's movement and supporters of the Public Places (Order) Bill had lost the battle to influence the committee's recommendations. They had been out-manoeuvred and outwitted. The AMSH and the NCW had been true to their feminist roots and clung firmly to their opposition to the 'double standard of morality' which they wished to see replaced by a 'high and equal' standard of sexual responsibility for men and women. 'From the 1880s onwards', writes Lucy Bland, '. . . the feminist demand for a single moral standard became central to the women's movement . . . Feminists sought transformed sexual relations between men and women in which women were equal and independent and men took responsibility for changing the oppressive aspects of their sexual behaviour.'[1] This exalted aspiration rested upon the hope that men would change the self-seeking and advantageous habits of centuries and aspire to the values of chastity before marriage and faithfulness in wedlock, hitherto expected of middle-class women.[2] Prostitution and rape had been the foundation upon which this monument to hypocrisy was erected.

Keith Thomas traces the history of the double standard back through many centuries finding, like Flexner, that it had become so universally accepted as an aspect of culture as to be perceived as 'natural'. But the dilemma that had always contributed a sense of urgency to the issue of prostitution was not that of sexual licence or moral integrity. It was syphilis and the disabilities inflicted by venereal infection. As some contemporary observers noted, the so-called feeble-minded were frequently the result of sexually transmitted disease. Numerous Victorian and Edwardian women had responded to this situation by demanding sexual autonomy, seeing chastity and spinsterhood or lesbian relationships as infinitely preferable to marriage. Indeed, it has been asserted that spinsters, rather than married women, 'provided the backbone of the feminist movement in the late nineteenth and early twentieth centuries'.[3]

In her polemic *The Great Scourge And How To End It*, Christabel Pankhurst (1913) wrote, 'A woman infected with syphilis not only suffers humiliation and illness which may eventually take the most revolting form, but is in danger of becoming the mother of deformed, diseased, or idiot children.'[4] She argued that marriage had become increasingly distasteful to women[5] and coined the slogan 'Votes For Women and Chastity For Men'. Margaret Jackson claims that the progress towards female sexual autonomy made by the early feminists, such as Pankhurst, was halted or reversed by the theories of sexologists. She argues that Havelock Ellis[6] and others overturned women's politicization of male sexual power and eroticised female submissiveness, leading to a decline in feminism following the First World War.[7] Sexologists had endowed the patriarchal model of sexuality with a new scientific legitimation. Thus the acts of lewdness so roundly condemned when performed by Katherine de Munck became wholesome and beneficial, indeed a positive duty, when performed by married women. Jackson contends that, 'What feminists had argued was *political*, sexologists redefined as *natural*' and therefore could not be changed.[8]

Bertrand Russell had viewed the changing moral scene quite differently.[9] Although he agreed with the premiss that prostitution had supported men's incontinence, he maintained that the moralists supported the institution of prostitution by reluctantly considering it better for a young man to have illicit intercourse with a prostitute than with a woman of his own class. In other words the moralist also supported the double standard on the basis of the Augustinian notion of the necessary evil. Russell argued that women's claim for equality between the sexes would lead them to demand the same level of sexual licence that men had traditionally enjoyed. He welcomed the development of contraception and saw the shift towards female sexual liberation as wholly admirable. He considered it to be far more healthy and creative than the earlier moralistic model. With this statement he foreshadowed the work of Alfred Kinsey, believing that instead of men aspiring to new ethical heights, the average respectable girl would be willing to delight in premarital intercourse. With our benefit of hindsight Russell appears to have been proved correct in his forecast of prevailing trends, although in his own life, with four marriages and numerous affairs, he seems to have manipulated social and political change for his own advantage.

The post-First World War generation of the 1920s and 1930s had developed its own brand of liberation, especially amongst the better-off. Some of the more adventurous younger women smoked and danced. They flattened their chests, cut their hair short, wore liberating clothes and experimented with free love. As time progressed even the older women began to copy many of the new fashions.[10] The post-Second World War period was different. The trends portrayed by Mort were counterbalanced in some quarters by a new prudery. One example of this is the way in which Donald McGill's naughty seaside postcards came under the censors' hammer in the 1950s while they had been ignored during the 1930s.[11]

Unfortunately for the AMSH, clinging to the moral imperative proved to be its downfall, as Mort comments, 'the Wolfenden Committee marked a long-term defeat for such traditional sexual politics. The hybrid version of liberalism championed by these campaigners, which mixed defence of the individual rights of women with an exacting regime of personal morality for both sexes, reinforced by coercive legislation, was marginalised by the Committee.'[12] Mort puts this defeat down to the institutional decline of the women's organisations after the war and to the increasing power of the professional expert.

Although I would agree that the committee was dismissive of all the moralists,[13] I would take issue with Mort over the women's alleged support for punitive sanctions. The AMSH had campaigned against the solicitation laws for many years and had worked for the enactment of Mrs Castle's Bill (1951) giving equal protection to prostitutes, but limited only to the offence of procuration. The evidence shows that Wolfenden was conscious of the criticisms of injustice directed towards him and was careful to rebut them. The AMSH analysis of the soliciting laws was thorough, but its mistake was in failing to give the same attention to the weaknesses in the protective legislation the women's movement had helped to secure in the past, and which it would like to have seen more rigorously enforced.

Wolfenden dealt with the moral issue, as we have seen, by insisting that the law was not concerned with morals, and then contradicted himself by demonstrating that it was. The associated issues were more difficult: the immunity of the client, the heavy penalties that were only to be applied to the prostitute, the dropping of the requirement to prove annoyance and the underpinning of the term 'common prostitute' with a cautioning system. Much of this had to be justified by falling back upon the moral argument. The subconscious survival of the double standard was demonstrated at every turn: the vociferous women who had to be mercifully silenced, the excusing of the client, Paul Bennett's 'cross-grained women' with 'nothing fallen about them', the proprietorial view of women in brothels, the playing upon public fears of women gathering in groups, through to Wolfenden's opinion that they 'did it because they liked it'. All these stereotyped assumptions flowed from the acceptance of the one principle. 'Not only was sobriety expected,' writes Thomas, 'but modesty, delicacy, bashfulness, silence and all other "feminine" virtues. For centuries the ideal woman was Griselda, passive and long suffering . . . and in courtship women existed to be pursued, not to do the pursuing.'[14]

The 'old women's society' had broken the rules just as much as the unashamedly brazen, flaunting women of the streets, and they were dismissed with as little consideration.

THE MAN AND HIS COMMITTEE

In his memoirs, *Turning Points*, Wolfenden recounts the details of his appointment as chairman of the committee. A surprise telephone call from the Home Secretary's private office was followed by a chance meeting with the Home Secretary on an overnight sleeper train from Liverpool to London during which Maxwell Fyfe explained the problems and the solutions that he considered appropriate. This was done in much the same terms as they appeared in his memorandum. It is also very likely that the possible personal advantages to Wolfenden of his accepting this potentially embarrassing and provocative assignment were hinted at. Within a week Wolfenden had a firm offer from the Home Office which, after some consideration, he accepted. The members of the committee were chosen with equal rapidity, and 'women' were seen as an interest that had to be represented. Wolfenden insisted that he did not know why he was thought to be suitable, but assumed that as an academic he was considered capable of an objective and dispassionate view of a controversial subject. He also speculated that his long experience of chairing committees would be an advantage.

This was a good example of a typically British process, which manages to sidestep the open democratic procedures that ought to have been respected.[15] Thus two well-established professional men had a quiet word together and agreed upon a course of action. There were no advertisements, no applications or shortlist, no interviews and no time for the public or the press to consider the suitability of prospective candidates. If democratic procedures had been honoured it would surely have been revealed that Wolfenden's own son, Jeremy, was an open homosexual at the time. The fact that this did not come to light demonstrates the level of deference shown to public figures during the 1950s. It seems inconceivable that none of the other members of the committee knew about Jeremy, who was studying at Oxford University and living a fairly dissolute life.[16] This was most likely the version of 'humbug' that eventually pushed Goronwy Rees (Principal of the University of Wales at Aberystwyth) to overstep the mark and place both his position on the committee and his career and reputation in jeopardy. Rees was by far the most lateral thinking and perceptive member of the committee, but in 1956 a series of articles were published in the *People* that revealed his connections with the homosexual traitor and spy Guy Burgess. It was discovered and exposed by the *Daily Telegraph* that Rees himself was the author. According to Higgins, the connection between Rees and the committee was not revealed, despite enquiries. The composition of the committee was not common knowledge and the Home Office was in no hurry to reveal anything. The carefully constructed 'public' front of the official committee was breached, revealing connections between the foreign service, the Home Office and the world of espionage and corruption. But this world of intrigue produced its casualties: Faulks gives a sad account of Jeremy's early death, his connections with the secret service, Russian espionage, blackmail, and the pressures put upon him by uncaring faceless civil servants.[17]

Wolfenden's account of the committee in his memoirs is very revealing, both of himself as a man and of the departmental committee process. Of the man we find not the committed public servant for whom one would hope in a public service position but a self-satisfied social climber. We move from his discussion with Maxwell Fyfe, to his interviewing of Lord Goddard and later to what he said to the Archbishop. Then we are told of the excitement of publication, the massive sales (15,000 in the first month) and the notoriety that

came with it. The book has pictures of himself with the queen and other dignitaries, but only the back view and a childhood photograph of his wife. Of
the committee only Adair was named in person with reference to his dissent
from the major recommendation on homosexual offences. There is no back-
wards glance at the result of the policies he sanctioned or at the women who
were in prison while he wrote his memoirs. The one thing that had 'nettled'
him was the accusation by a stranger that he had amassed a personal fortune.
He was careful to point out that the proceeds of the report went to Her
Majesty's Stationery Office and that he had personally found it necessary to
spend over £200 upon travel and entertaining. In retrospect that seems a small
outlay in return for a knighthood and a place in history.

Wolfenden's chapter on the committee is also revealing in the succinctness
with which it crystalizes both the problem and the solution. It was, as
Wolfenden frequently said, 'not a matter of morality'. It was, however, a matter
of power. Soliciting had become more open and persistent. 'Besides breaking
the law,' he writes, 'they were flaunting themselves and pestering passers-by,
causing intolerable embarrassment and giving to visitors a deplorable impression of London's immorality.' The police were suspected of operating a rota
system and arresting girls in turn. The women appeared in court, were fined a
nominal amount and then returned to the streets in order to recoup the money.
The law was being brought into disrepute and it had to be stopped.[18]

The solution was equally neat. Having established that it was not a matter
of morals, the client became a side issue. Women cluttered up the streets and
men did not; what people did in private was none of the law's business, but
what happened in public was. As an ex-headmaster, Wolfenden understood
the problem very well. Authority had, in the last resort, to be backed up by
coercion. The sanctions imposed needed to be sufficiently harsh to create a
plausible deterrent, and as it was acknowledged that prostitution could not be
abolished, it could at least be pushed out of sight. In his typically affected vein
Wolfenden wrote:

> We were accused by some highly respectable women's organisations of
> discriminating against the prostitute and doing nothing about her
> wicked client. Indeed one very distinguished ecclesiastic charged me with
> this conversation. 'Surely', he said, 'you would agree that a man who
> goes with a prostitute is just as guilty as she is.' 'My dear Archbishop, he
> may be just as guilty as she is of what you and I might call the sin of for-
> nication: he is not as guilty as she of cluttering up the streets of London'
> ... Nor were our withers rung by prophecies that to get the girls off the
> streets would inevitably lead to increases in call-girl networks, strip-clubs
> and other clandestine channels of assignation. We were not concerned
> with prostitution as such, or with immorality as such; we stuck to our
> last of public order and decency.[19]

Finding the right balance of members for a committee is obviously
difficult, although looking for clever and prominent people, over and above

actual experience, has some obvious disadvantages. Bertrand Russell was acknowledged to be a genius in his time. He certainly thought so, but he believed that you could generally tell if a man was clever or a fool by the shape of his head.[20] Russell was a man of his time and influenced by the thinking and prejudices of his time. The individual members of the committee each came with their own professional expertise and a willingness to endow prostitution with legal, moral, medical and psychiatric significance far beyond the reality of the situation. This 'professionalisation' of the enquiry was combined with a lack of any real knowledge of the problems faced by the women involved, whereas Miss Mackenzie had a far better grasp of what it was like to be a woman on the streets and what the dangers were for youngsters when they ventured into the public realm.

ASSESSMENT

Faced with a mountain of written submissions and contradictory evidence to sift through, it is perhaps understandable if a 'tunnel vision' solution seemed the only way through the labyrinth of detail. But the fact remains that the final recommendations were more or less exactly what Maxwell Fyfe had set out in his memorandum, which was based on Philip Allen's report and written before the committee was appointed. The general public would have assumed that the recommendations were arrived at as a result of examining the evidence, but Wolfenden's comment, quoted above, suggests otherwise. 'Nor were our withers rung . . . we stuck to our last of public order and decency.' Indeed, the consolidation in 1956 of all the previous protective legislation suggests that the government and the Home Office were interested in securing recommendations regarding prostitution that sanctioned its internal policy that they did not wish to encourage a public debate on this aspect of the legislation.

The position of Conwy Roberts was also a critical factor in the development of a desired result. Wolfenden and other members of the committee were involved with many varied activities and responsibilities but Roberts, employed as a government civil servant, busied himself continuously, advising, arranging, steering, manipulating and travelling to and from Reading. Wolfenden writes that 'every sentence in the final document has a history of discussion, re-wording, deletion, fresh approach, and eventual acceptance'. Yet he also writes that 'individual members submitted drafts of sections which might fall within their own particular specialisms; but the bulk of the composition naturally fell to the Chairman and Secretary'.[21] Certainly the creation of the report and the impression that it would convey to the public of academic excellence and carefully fashioned logical argument were at the forefront of Wolfenden's mind, and he saw himself as the 'expert' when it came to the written word. Writing the report took up the bulk of the time, yet there were six sets of reservations, which suggests a certain imbalance of power within the committee. How much disharmony there was is difficult to tell but the fact that they chose to conduct the proceedings in private made it possible for the authors to spin the final conclusions whichever way they pleased, as no one outside the committee was in a position to check up on the detail and criticise the results.

As with most official committees, much was made of the importance of sticking to the remit – understandably so, as it provides a great protection from unwanted criticism. 'We were not', Wolfenden repeats, 'concerned with prostitution as such, or with morality as such.' This was incorrect. The words 'in connection with prostitution and solicitation for immoral purposes' were within the remit. The fact that the remit was a confusing reflection of the legislation did not absolve the committee. The committee had a duty to examine the connections between 'the purpose of prostitution' and immorality. The severity of the penalties was justifiable only on the ground that the general public believed that soliciting for the purpose of prostitution was an immoral activity and that there was a relationship between morality and 'public order and decency', which required more coercive regulation. The remit was reduced, or subverted, to mean 'cleaning up the streets', and a deliberate choice was made to privatize prostitution in order to achieve that aim.

As the report unfolded much was made of the redemptive aspect of the law, that is, the hope that the prostitute would take advantage of the opportunity of cooperating with a court missionary or probation worker. 'We may have been misguided or over-optimistic,' wrote Wolfenden in defence of the penalties, 'but it is not the case that we were being viciously vindictive or draconian.' Care was also given to promoting measures for the detention and treatment of children and young women in order to prevent them from embarking upon a life of prostitution. But this did not reflect the debate within the committee, where it became obvious that the safety net was not working and that the institutions in which children were cared for needed closer inspection.[22] Nothing at all was said about the men who abused the children.

Wolfenden comments in his book that many people did not understand that the their recommendations on both homosexuality and prostitution were governed by the same logic. 'We have argued . . . that since one of the law's concerns was the preservation of public order and decency, steps should be taken to remove the affront to public order and decency which was presented by the obtrusive presence of large numbers of prostitutes on the streets. At the same time we argued that private morality or immorality was a private matter . . . There must remain a realm of private morality, that is, in crude terms, not the Law's business.' The 'logic' of the argument did not begin to explain why it was thought necessary to give the police powers to 'arrest without warrant' a woman (who had not annoyed anybody) because she loitered or solicited passers-by for a purpose that was legal. The reader is left with the law's prior ability to construct prostitutes as a special class in relation to the law.[23]

It is unlikely that those parties who were concerned with clearing prostitutes from the streets of London cared much about the logic of the argument so long as the recommendations fulfilled their expectations. From its own point of view the committee was fortunate as it stood on a bridge of time between the old morality and the new, before second-wave feminism had refined its challenge to the protection of the private sphere over individual freedoms.[24]

The extent of the problem that prostitution actually posed to the general public was also in question. It appeared, as Lord Lothian had remarked, to be very largely confined to the West End of London, yet the report played upon public fears and used exaggerated analogies to reinforce its argument. The committee was not even convinced that the problem had increased, only that it had become more visible by moving into residential areas. Despite the value that was placed upon listening to the 'expert', the advice of the two men who fell most readily into that category, Nott-Bower, Chief Commissioner of the Metropolitan Police, and Sir Lawrence Dunn, Chief Metropolitan Magistrate, was ignored. Both urged the committee not to pursue a policy of pushing women into off-street venues.

When the committee was being established, Roberts and Wolfenden were anxious to have a wide spectrum of opinions represented: political, medical, theological, and so on. Wolfenden added, almost as an afterthought, that it was very important that the committee should not be 'all-male'.[25] Women were included because it was politically correct for the committee to appear balanced. The difficulty that they had in establishing their identities and making their points of view respected is shown by the stand over the penalty for living on the earnings of prostitution and by the submission of a separate reservation. There was an undercurrent of misogyny, of mockery and complacency where women witnesses were concerned, as shown through the exchanges between Wolfenden and Roberts. There was also an acceptance of the stereotyped assumptions that emanated from the double standard of morality. 'I cannot see', said Wells (who was a lawyer), 'where equality comes into the question of prostitution and the law.' This is where the difficulty lies. There is so often an impenetrable stone wall of incomprehension.

In the end the solution that was arrived at rested upon the defining label of 'common prostitute', which was not only a demonstration of the double standard but a contravention of the cardinal principle of English law, 'that a person is innocent until found guilty'.

It broke the foremost rule created by men for their own governance.

NOTES

1. Bland, *Banishing the Beast: English Feminism and Sexual Morality, 1883–1995*, Penguin, London, p. xiii.
2. Keith Thomas argued that this strategy left a much larger proportion of poorer men for whom there existed no lower strata of socially inferior women 'at whose expense they may gratify their sexual appetites' outside of their own class. See K. Thomas (1956), 'The Double Standard', *Journal of the History of Ideas*, p. 208.
3. S. Jeffreys (1987), *The Idea of Prostitution*, Spinifex, Melbourne.
4. C. Pankhurst (1913), *The Great Scourge And How To End It*, Lincoln's Inn House, London.
5. Ibid., p. 96.

6. Havelock Ellis (1858–1939). Havelock Ellis was the best known of a number of Victorian and Edwardian writers who transformed the study of sex into what they believed was a scientific discipline and became known as 'sexologists'. He is best known for his seven-volume *Studies in the Psychology of Sex* (1897–1928) in which he promoted a more egalitarian relationship between the sexes and defended the erotic rights of women. These works were hugely successful and influential, stimulating a great deal of plagiarism and theoretical speculation about the 'natural' urges and responses of men and women. Havelock Ellis was a biologist who viewed sex and sexuality as reproductive rather than socially constructed. His views have been criticized by in S. Jeffreys (1985) *The Spinster and her Enemies*, Pandora, London and J. Weeks (1989), *Sex, Politics and Society*, Longman, London. A more positive view of his contribution towards the liberalisation of sexual expression can be found in R. Porter and L. Hall (1995), *The Facts of Life*, New Haven, CT, Yale University Press.

7. M. Jackson, *The Real Facts of Life*, Taylor & Francis, London.

8. Ibid., p. 3. Jackson argued that a number of early feminist writers and journalists, including Frances Power Cobb, brought to light some of the violence that occurred within marriage and the lack of judicial response to domestic crime. See Frances Power Cobb (1894), 'Wife Torture in England', *Contemporary Review*, 32, pp. 55–87. Jackson quotes a number of more extreme examples of writers who followed in the footsteps of Havelock Ellis and expanded upon the importance of female submissiveness, including Theodoor Van de Velde (1931), who suggested that the 'essential force of maleness expressed itself through a sort of violent and absolute possession' (*Sex Hostility in Marriage: Its Psychology and Technique*, Heinemann, London).

9. Bertrand Russell (1929), *Marriage and Morals*, George Allen & Unwin, London. A quotation from Russell's work was among the Wolfenden papers. 'Those who stimulate the appeal to harry prostitutes . . . those who denounce women for short skirts and lipsticks; and those who spy upon sea beaches in the hope of discovering inadequate bathing costumes, are none of them supposed to be the victims of sexual obsession. Yet in fact they probably suffer more in this way than do writers who advocate greater sexual expression. Fierce morality is generally a reaction against lustful emotions, and the man who gives expression to it is generally filled with indecent thoughts' (p. 225). Russell devoted a full chapter on Marriage and Morals to the subject of prostitution, which he saw as functional.

10. For a picture of life during the 1920s see, for example, Dora Russell's account of her life with Bertrand Russell. Dora Russell (1986), *The Tamarisk Tree: My Quest for Liberty and Love*, Virago, London; Virginia Woolf (1972), *A Room of One's Own*, Penguin Books, London.

11. John Windsor, 'Postcard from the edge', *Independent Magazine*, 28 November 1999.

12. F. Mort (1999), *Dangerous Sexualities*, Routledge and Kegan Paul, London.

13. This includes the Paddington Moral Reform Council and the Public Morality Council. Both groups gave evidence.

14. Thomas, *The Double Standard*.

15. For an amusing account of the process of selecting candidates who will arrive at an acceptable conclusion see Peter Hennessy (1986), *The Great and the Good*, Policy Studies Institute, London, pp. 11–29. This is a recurrent theme. For example, accusations of partiality were made against Jack Straw, Labour Home Secretary, in connection with his appointment of sympathisers of blood sports to an independent inquiry on rural pursuits. *Guardian*, 24 January 2000.

16. See S. Faulks, *The Fatal Englishman: Three Short Lives*, Vintage, London, p. 237. 'But however dissolute they were, they could be sure that Jeremy Wolfenden would be a little more so.'

17. Ibid., pp. 211–307.

18. J. Wolfenden, *Turning Points: The Memoirs of Lord Wolfenden*, The Bodley Head, London, p. 130.

19. Ibid., p. 142.

20. Russell, *Marriage and Morals*, p. 201.

21. Wolfenden, *Turning Points*, p. 138.

22. A Children and Young Persons committee was sitting at the time that the report was being written. The concerns of the Wolfenden Committee with regard to the young prostitute were conveyed to this committee (Cmnd. 247. s.281).

23. C. Smart (1995), *Law, Crime and Sexuality: Essays in Feminism*, Sage, London, p. 64.

24. From the late 1960s onwards feminist academics and women's groups have challenged the notion that the private was not political, pointing out that women's exclusion from the public

sphere (political and economic power) had been created by a political process that supported the nuclear family in which their labour was exploited and their poverty hidden. Government policies were based upon assumptions about a woman's role as carer and her dependence upon the family wage. Imbalance of power within the family was reflected in the public sphere, where her contribution to the economy was treated as less valuable than men's through inequalities in pay and segregation at work.

25. Wolfenden, *Turning Points*, p. 133.

PART III

The Law and Society

CHAPTER NINE

The Legislative Legacy

Media responses to the Wolfenden Report were varied, with most of the interest centring on homosexuality. Wolfenden himself obviously enjoyed being in the spotlight. His quiet holiday in Guernsey came to an end when the report was published on 4 September 1957 and the hotel he was staying in was invaded by BBC interviewers and journalists. He was obliged to return to London in order to talk to newspapers, parliamentarians and television commentators. 'It went on for weeks,' he recollected:

> It is difficult for me, and it must be nearly impossible for anybody else, to realise the to-do that followed. It entirely filled the front pages of Wednesday's evening papers, with VICE in inch-high capitals as the main headline. And Thursday's dailies, in their different styles, gave it more column inches than any of us had dreamt of.[1]

Many of the commentators, for example in the *Daily Mail*, represented the recommendations as a way of sweeping vice under the carpet. By contrast a *Daily Express* editorial enquired, 'Why did the Government sponsor this cumbersome nonsense? Anyone would think that prostitution and perversion were a widespread problem. In fact the majority of British homes never come into contact with either.' The *Daily Mirror* observed that the report had had an immediate effect upon the numbers of prostitutes in the West End, which had fallen to a quarter of the previous figure because the 'girls' had assumed that the recommendations were already law. It conducted a poll among its readers that revealed overwhelming support for the recommendations on prostitution in the belief that the evidence of its existence ought to be kept out of sight.[2]

The Times commented in a leading article[3] on the disparity between the suggested penalties for men and women. It noted that the committee had recommended a maximum penalty of ten years for indecent assault by a man on another man, as opposed to two years if the victim was female. On the other hand, it noted recommendations of two years' imprisonment for male (homosexual) soliciting but only three months for a woman. It also observed that the committee had proposed that the maximum penalty for seducing a youth over 16 but under 21 be raised to five years, whereas seducing a young woman of the same age remained non-criminal.[4] *The Times* applauded the committee for its 'necessary and proper determination to make it clear beyond doubt that the proposed exemption of adult inverts from legal penalty is in no sense a sign of tolerance of paederasts or corrupters of youth'.[5] This editorial comment underlined the assumption that what was thought of as the 'unnatural vice' (homosexuality) was a more serious transgression than a temporary lapse of moral fibre in the face of temptation that could be excused as natural (that is, heterosexual infractions such as prostitution or adultery). Moreover, the use of the word 'seduction' was misleading as it implied a measure of consent, although in many situations this had been a euphemism for rape, especially in Victorian times.

On 13 January 1957 R. A. Butler became Secretary of State for the Home Department. He was once described as 'both irreproachable and unapproachable' and likely to go down in history as one of the most progressive, thoughtful and dedicated of Tories.[6] He was born in India, where he spent his earliest years, the son of a conscientious colonial administrator and a devoted loving mother. Like many expatriate children he was sent home to England for schooling, first to a preparatory school in Hove when he was eight, then to Marlborough and to Cambridge University. Judging by his autobiography,[7] Butler followed in the footsteps of a long family tradition and was an academic at heart; he claimed that the one period in his life during which he found 'perfect and unalloyed happiness' was as Master of Trinity College, Cambridge. He served with distinction under six prime ministers, and, like Hugh Macmillan, appears to have been a hard-working cultured person who moved easily within the top social circles and enjoyed a very rewarding and privileged life. His autobiography contains a good balance of official and family photos, as well as cartoons. Despite his good intentions and reputation as a man of integrity it seems unlikely that he could have had any understanding of the pressures and causes leading to prostitution or the ability to empathise with street-women.

One of the lesser-known facts about R. A. Butler is that he was related to Josephine Butler through her husband, George. Josephine was his great-aunt. The AMSH, and its reincarnation as the Josephine Butler Society, always courted people with power and influence in political circles. This conferred certain advantages in that it provided very convenient links with influential politicians either in the House of Lords or the Commons. Annual general meetings were held in the House of Lords and MPs were encouraged to attend. Whenever the AMSH was in a flurry of campaigning it would use these links to influence members of parliament, and on occasions a lord or an individual MP could be induced to support or introduce a private members bill which the society had been involved in drafting. The status of the AMSH was further enhanced by the appointment of a president with an aristocratic pedigree such as Lord Balfour of Burleigh, and an array of vice-presidents who would be either titled people or politicians. In this way, and unlike the more moralising NVA, the AMSH continued to maintain a high political profile. But on the negative side of this arrangement was the danger that it catered for the 'social-climbing' instincts among the members and encouraged a degree of snobbery, which distanced the association from the women whom it wished to help.

Under these circumstances it cannot be surprising that the AMSH was pleased to have Butler as a vice-president. The links with Josephine made him an obvious choice. Considering his connections with the family and the association, he must have been well aware of what the AMSH stood for and the reasons for its long fight for the reform of the solicitation laws. He should also have been familiar with the arguments put before the Wolfenden Committee and, as a vice-president, had tacitly given his name to their support.

A further political strength could be found in the ability of the AMSH to forge a network of links with other organisations in a way that had become part of the ethos of the women's movement. Although not strictly an 'all-women' association, the AMSH was one of 19 national societies that were linked under the auspices of the Status of Women Committee, which Conwy Roberts had suspected of coordinating plans for putting pressure on the Home Office. Many women had multiple allegiances – for example, Lady Nunburnholme, who chaired the NVA as well as the NCW, and Chave Collinsson, who was a leading light in the International Alliance of Women (IAW).[8] The IAW and its associate members, including the AMSH, came under the umbrella of the Commission on the Status of Women, which had been established in 1949 as a functional commission of the Economic and Social Council of the United Nations.[9] There were, therefore, both national and international links of some significance of which Conwy Roberts had been aware when he decided not to burden the members of the committee with too much information. As Home Secretary and vice-president of the AMSH, Butler must also have known of these links and of their implication.

On 4 February 1957, seven months before the Wolfenden Report was printed, the AMSH wrote a long letter to *The Times* commemorating the half-century that had passed since the death of Josephine Butler[10] and restating its principles. The message remained the same as it had been in the nineteenth century: Josephine had issued a solemn warning that if the unity of the moral law were broken by the establishment of tolerated brothels that catered for the vice of men and if a class of women were created through unjust or unequal laws then moral chaos would inevitably follow. It was argued, as she had done, that men were just as responsible for upholding sexual moral standards as women and ought not to be regarded as 'predestined to licentiousness'.[11] The letter was signed by a long list of prominent figures including Lord Balfour of Burleigh, A. S. G. Butler (grandson of Josephine Butler), Lord Elton (Conservative peer), Clement Davis (leader of the Liberal Party), the suffragist campaigner F. W. Pethick-Lawrence (ex-Colonial Minister for India), R. V. F. Scott (who had resigned from the Wolfenden Committee when he became Moderator of the Church of Scotland), Dr Israel Brodie (the Chief Rabbi), the Archbishop of Canterbury, Professor Gilbert Murray (historian and philosopher, president of the League of Nations Union, 1923–28), Wilfred Kitchen (International Leader of the Salvation Army) and K. L. Parry (Moderator, Free Church Federal Council).[12] The fact that *The Times* was prepared to devote a quarter of a page to such a letter demonstrates that there was still a public constituency for the message it contained. It seems that Wolfenden's suggestion that the association was merely represented by a group of eccentric old women with too much to say for themselves showed a lack of judgement and was not a universally held opinion. But although his committee had no intention of recommending the legalisation of brothels, it conveniently sidestepped any suggestion that the male customer had a responsibility that should be addressable through legal means. Butler would have had to weigh up all of these factors and the strength of public opposition when deciding on his political approach to the passage of the Street Offences Bill.

Following the publication of the Wolfenden Report the AMSH suppressed its disappointment and got to work immediately. A deputation was organised for 29 January 1958, and representatives of 16 societies went to meet the Home Secretary to protest against the proposals. The familiar names headed the list. They were Mrs M. Bligh, the Dowager Lady Nunburnholme, Dame Rachel Crowdy Thornhill, Miss D. O. G. Peto and Miss Chave Collisson. With regard to the report the deputation complained that the scales had been weighted unevenly between men and women, and:

- That the proposed elimination of the need to prove annoyance would turn the prostitute into a criminal;
- that a single law applicable to all citizens should be substituted;
- that the heavy penalties proposed made the need for evidence much greater;
- that while the male kerb-crawler was not to be punished in case innocent motorists were penalised, the position of an innocent woman pestered by soliciting men was to be ignored;
- that the growth of the call-girl system envisaged by the report was highly dangerous;
- that the suggestion that the regulations relating to refreshment houses should not be too rigorously enforced might result in the equivalent of a *maison des rendezvous*;
- that the Scottish system of cautioning, if introduced into England, would require special legislation aimed at the prostitute;
- that the heavier penalties were excessive and imprisonment unjust;
- that the admirable work of the women police should be rooted in the principles and traditions governing the police service as a whole; and
- that the international reputation of the United Kingdom as leader in the field of social reform would be endangered.[13]

Once again the AMSH displayed a degree of ambivalence with regard to its own principles. For although the organisation wished to achieve what it considered to be justice and equality within the law, it did not want to encourage the practice of prostitution, which was seen as immoral and an abuse of male power over the bodies of women. So in some areas its aims were the same as those of the legislature. By attacking the recommendations on refreshment venues it was condemning the one recommendation through which the Wolfenden Committee had demonstrated some empathy with the needs of women, by suggesting that prostitutes should be allowed to use the facilities provided by all-night cafés unhampered by the police.

Butler met the deputation of women's organisations and assured them that their views would be carefully considered, but emphasised that as Home Secretary he had a duty to deal with the problem of soliciting on the streets of London. He commented that 'at a later date he might be able to rejoin the AMSH in its work'.[14]

The various women's organisations and their sympathisers (headed by the AMSH) continued campaigning. Meetings were held around the country, Chave Collisson appeared on television, memoranda were distributed to societies and numerous articles were written. Printed comments on the Wolfenden Report were sent to every MP and to many of the members of the House of Lords. None of this frenetic activity made the slightest difference. On 26 November the debate on the Wolfenden Report took place in the House and Butler announced that the government intended to implement the Wolfenden Committee's recommendations on prostitution. The AMSH sought the help of Miss Joan Vickers (NU), Mrs Lena Jeger (Labour) and Mark Bonham Carter (Liberal). A meeting was arranged in the House of Commons for 16 December with Lyon Blease (a barrister and professor of law at Liverpool University), at which Chave Collisson, Mrs Bligh and representatives of 19 societies were to be represented. As the delegates left the House it became apparent from the newspaper vendors' placards that Butler had already published the Street Offences Bill. By 18 December it had received its first reading. It began to be obvious that the government had every intention of pushing forward with the legislation regardless of any opposition.

The AMSH stepped up its attack. It sent protest letters to the Prime Minister and the Home Secretary, and every MP was sent a careful summary of its objections to the Bill. It was rewarded by being requested to gather together representatives of the various societies who had attended the deputation in January 1958 to meet Butler on 26 January 1959. The delegates were introduced by Miss D. G. O. Peto (an ex-policewoman) and Chave Collisson presented the arguments. Mrs Bligh spoke on behalf of the NCW, Mrs Coombs for the Mothers' Union, and Miss Charlotte Marsh (affiliation unknown) made a plea against imprisonment. Butler was 'courteous but uncompromising' and the delegation left feeling indignant and dissatisfied. The episode seems to have been nothing more than a democratic formality. Chave Collisson continued to put forward the views of the opposition through radio news and television appearances[15] but the House moved on to the second reading.

THE CHURCH OF ENGLAND MORAL WELFARE COUNCIL

One of the many supporters of the AMSH and other detractors of the Street Offences Bill was the Church of England Moral Welfare Council (CEMWC), which put together a very thoughtful and perceptive critique of the Bill's provisions.[16] It argued that sexually motivated behaviour in public could give rise to three forms of nuisance: (a) indecent behaviour, which was a nuisance in itself, (b) importuning, which was also a nuisance in itself, and (c) 'loitering or soliciting', which were nuisances only in certain circumstances. It claimed that loitering and soliciting were within the rights of every citizen and did not constitute a 'self-evident nuisance' punishable in all circumstances, as Wolfenden had argued. All three of the offences could be committed for both heterosexual and homosexual purposes. The CEMWC argued that all of these offences should come under a single, uniformly applicable national law and that they should be made gender-neutral. It was suggested that the statutory terminology should also be made neutral rather than emotional or moralising. The Calvinist term 'libidinous purposes', used in Scots law, was favoured as a replacement for 'the purpose of prostitution' as it would apply more broadly. The council also took issue over the concept of annoyance, stating that the requirement to prove annoyance had been misdirected towards the 'passer-by' who was rarely annoyed, whereas residents in an affected area were often extremely annoyed. It was suggested that the definition of annoyance should be widened so as to include recognition of the general public nuisance that soliciting for libidinous purposes constituted,[17] especially in public parks and commercial areas. This addressed the argument put forward by Roberts and Wolfenden that the possibility of prostitutes gathering together in numbers created a potential nuisance that had to be prevented. But as Miss Peto had remarked on behalf of the AMSH, it had been her experience as a policewoman that it was quite easy to respond to public complaints by 'moving people on' using the powers bestowed by the Police Acts.[18]

The CEMWC maintained that the aggrieved resident had a duty to cooperate with the police in the maintenance of law and order and did not hold with the 'dead letter' argument that had been put forward by both Macmillan and Wolfenden, declaring that 'residents, business occupiers, the clergy, and others who want their neighbourhood cleared of publicly visible prostitutes have their own responsibility as citizens to help the police to enforce the law. They should not too easily be allowed to transfer the whole responsibility to the police.'[19] This was a point picked up by *The Times* in its leading article on 19 December 1958, which expressed surprise that so few residents took advantage of the remedies available to them and argued that: 'Given penalties of unprecedented severity, residents aggrieved by the nightly haunting of streetwalkers will have exactly the incentive they now lack to help the police in contested cases, by testifying to their annoyance.'

The wider responsibility of the citizen to make an active contribution towards the creation of a safe and disciplined society had not been considered by the Wolfenden Committee. This was an aspect of the moral argument that related to the balance between rights and duties. Wolfenden had eschewed any such discussion, maintaining that the remit confined the committee to the law even though the individual members were continually making judgmental observations. Had there been an attempt to look at prostitution in its wider social context, this aspect of the debate might have been drawn out. But, as we have seen, the Wolfenden Committee sought to avoid the moral arguments, preferring to rationalise its recommendations on the basis of a need to protect the citizen. In contrast, the local authorities' responsibility for exploring other avenues of control, such as street lighting, the supervision of parks and public places, more police on the beat, and so on, was ignored. The CEMWC suggested that a start could be made by clearing bombed sites, dealing with abandoned property and restricting the activities of all-night cafés.

The CEMWC urged the government to implement the Wolfenden recommendations for stiffer penalties. It supported the creation of a prostitutes' cautioning system, suggesting that before bringing the first charge the police should be required to give at least two formal cautions on separate days, one of which should take place at the police station. It was sceptical of the argument concerning the danger of charging an innocent woman with committing a criminal offence, declaring that 'it implies a quite unjustifiable lack of confidence in the ability of the police to distinguish between loitering for libidinous purposes and the innocent loiter . . . No policeman required to caution a loitering woman on several occasions before arresting her is likely to make a mistake of this sort.'[20] The council favoured extension of the remand system for new offenders but opposed changing the existing definition of soliciting so as to make it an offence in its own right. It was also pointed out that the Bill went beyond the Wolfenden recommendations in that it proposed to make a third offence punishable by both a fine and imprisonment simultaneously. It agreed with the AMSH that although prostitution was a legal activity there was a grave danger of the prostitute herself being made into a criminal. An alternative formula was put forward, which was:

> it shall be an offence for any person to loiter or solicit in a street or public place for any libidinous purpose:
> (a) to the annoyance of the inhabitants, occupiers of non-residential premises, or passengers, or
> (b) so as to constitute a nuisance.

This formula was a feasible alternative that addressed a number of critical objections to the Bill and constituted an interesting mixture of both liberal and conservative measures. As with the Public Places (Order) Bill, it dispensed with the terms 'common prostitute' and retained annoyance. It also replaced 'for the purpose of prostitution' with 'libidinous purpose . . . to the annoyance of', which surmounted the problem of female stigmatisation and the making of an abstract notion into a criminal offence.[21]

THE PUBLIC MORALITY COUNCIL

The Public Morality Council had been among those who gave oral evidence to the committee, and members were referred to disparagingly by Wolfenden as the 'moralists'. In 1924 the London Public Morality Council had produced its own mixture of legislative recommendations.[22] These would have amounted to a law that would have made it an offence for '*any person* to solicit in a public place' regardless of the annoyance caused. Convictions would have been based upon the sole evidence of a police officer. This recommendation was not to be backed up by heavy penalties, as the council had concluded that fines were useless and imprisonment was counterproductive. The council advocated the setting up of separate courts on the American model to try sexual offences, along with an expansion of the probationary service. It was suggested that these measures be strengthened through substantial increase in the number of women probationary officers and policewomen. The state was advised to work in close cooperation with the voluntary and rescue agencies, which would be served by people with deep religious convictions. All of these measures were to be backed up by an increase in religious education in schools and a proliferation of church-based activities including Toc H, Scouts, Boys' Brigades, and so on. Real coercion was to be reserved for what it called the 'hardened offender', a category of women for whom the council advised that special institutions should be set up, with indeterminate sentences imposed upon those who did not respond to benevolent treatment.[23]

State cooperation with the voluntary sector has been a constant theme in relation to prostitution and needs to be approached with some caution. For the law also has a role in protecting the individual from the arbitrary control and rough justice meted out by overzealous sections of the community. Many of the homes and reformatories to which young women had been sent came into this category.[24]

The Public Morality Council and the CEMWC were motivated by religious moral doctrines, which they claimed were the basis of British legislation. The more liberal aspects of their recommendations concerning equality were accompanied by a desire for the Church to wield greater power and influence over the community. Proposals for reform were usually reinforced with an emphasis on the need for religious education and for solutions to prostitution that involved the use of church-based organisations staffed by committed personnel. As a result of this doctrinaire approach it was possible for the members of the Wolfenden Committee to dismiss such institutions as 'moralisers' and give scant attention to their ideas. The AMSH, however, was in a different category. Its strength lay in its ability to operate from within three different discourses – Judaeo-Christian morality, feminism and politics – without being solely committed to any of them. This versatility came from the enlightened nature of its founder, Josephine Butler, who had been a compulsive writer of letters, pamphlets and articles. Although she was deeply religious she was genuinely concerned for the welfare of poor women and did not allow piety to cloud her judgement.

Josephine Butler's arguments concerning women's equality within the law were not just feminist pique but, like those of John Stuart Mill,[25] founded upon a passionate belief in the constitutional right of all citizens to equal and just treatment under the law.[26] It was on the basis of this *political* argument that she condemned the creation of a legally defined category of women for whom a different discriminatory system of justice was reserved. She had a profound mistrust for the police, whom she viewed as an unelected and coercive arm of the state that had been given arbitrary powers over poor women.[27] These were subversive 'political' messages that were ignored by those who preferred to view her as the Church of England's only saint. It is inconceivable that, as a member of the family, R. A. Butler was unaware of the political nature of his great-aunt's career or that the AMSH was striving to continue her work. It appears that he was happy enough to be a vice-president of the AMSH when the position was only nominal but equally willing to put political expediency first when it suited the needs of the Conservative Party.

THE USE OF POLICEWOMEN

The final 'panacea' for controlling the 'problems' of street prostitution that I wish to highlight was the recommended use of policewomen. The Wolfenden Committee echoed the 1928 Street Offences Committee by praising the work of women police officers, judging them to be more effective than policemen in dealing with young prostitutes[28] and commenting in its report:

> We should not want to see the women police used exclusively, or even mainly, as *police des moeurs*; but we hope that every encouragement will be given to them to take every legitimate chance of dissuading young girls from adopting a life of prostitution, by advising and helping rather than involving them in the machinery of the law.[29]

The matter of policewomen was an issue over which the AMSH had reservations, doubts that had their roots in the society's history.[30] One of the main planks of the earlier campaign to repeal the CD Acts had been the hatred of the plainclothes special police force who, it was argued, had been given arbitrary powers over poor women. The campaign for women to be accepted as fully accredited police officers grew out of the associated movement for opposing the 'White Slave Traffic', and during the twentieth century this particular aspect of the crusade was headed by the NCW. To a very large extent the burden of the campaigners' argument had been that policewomen were necessary for the supervision of appropriate and just treatment in cases that involved sexual offences against women and children. They had insisted that a woman officer ought to be present on all occasions when women offenders were being questioned and that they should be employed on patrol duties in parks and other areas where vulnerable young women were to be found in order to give advice and prevent abduction for the purpose of trafficking. These arguments had eventually convinced the authorities that there was a role for women police officers[31] and the women's organisations lost no opportunity in promoting their advantage. There was, however, a fine line to be drawn between the policewoman's role as arbiter in dealing with matters concerning women and children and the temptation to slip into the middle-class busy-bodying role of a female version of the *police des moeurs* by attempting to supervise and control the sexual behaviour of other women. The AMSH encountered some difficulty in preventing itself from being hoist on its own petard and maintained that the police already had sufficient powers to clear the streets, stating:

> That the most admirable work of women police must be rooted in the principles and traditions governing the police service as a whole, and their work in the field of prostitution must not be accepted as affording a safeguard, still less a justification, for proposals which encroached on the rights and liberties of any section of the public.[32]

DEBATING WOLFENDEN

Homosexuality

Jeffrey Weeks has commented that 'the proposals relating to prostitution were rushed into law with indecent haste'.[33] However, there was a gap of a year during which nothing appeared to be happening and the AMSH suspected that the report had been shelved and legislation postponed. This was not the case. On 26 November 1958 the debate was opened in the Commons by R. A. Butler, who explained that the delay had been thought necessary in order to give the public time to consider the Wolfenden Report.

Butler began his opening speech[34] by praising the Wolfenden Committee and thanking it for 'a Report which set out the issues involved in the subject clearly, cogently and briefly'. He emphasised the importance of the remit, which had confined the committee to a discussion of the law and had therefore precluded it from embarking upon moral or theological discussions.[35] When summing up the report as a whole Butler elaborated upon the problems that attended the relaxation of strictures on homosexual offences, suggesting that many people still found the idea of homosexual relationships morally repugnant and would not sanction reform. He feared that the public would misinterpret liberalisation as a form of condonation by the legislature, if not the actual encouragement of homosexual conduct. He was concerned for those individuals who were outside the influence of religion but appeared to believe that the law might usefully stand as a replacement for abandoned moral values. In this way he reasoned that the weak-minded (latent homosexual) might be saved from yielding to temptation. 'Can we be sure', he asked the House, 'that if we removed the support of the law from these people they would find any other support?'[36]

The Home Secretary made it clear from the outset that the House was dealing with moral questions. He argued that although the committee had been concerned only with the law, parliament was bound to consider the social issues behind it, and he was painfully aware that the art of government could only be 'the art of the possible'. He believed that the law had a role to play in maintaining morally defined standards of behaviour and he put forward the Wolfenden Committee's criteria as a means for achieving these aims. In doing so he squared the contradictions inherent within Wolfenden's duplicitous argument. These were that with regard to sexual matters the function of the law was threefold: (1) to preserve public order and decency; (2) to protect the citizen from what was offensive and injurious; and (3) to provide sufficient safeguards against exploitation and corruption. It was, he suggested, the duty of the government to define the boundaries between the individual responsibilities of the private citizen on the basis of conscience and the necessary guidance provided by the legislature for the protection of society at large. Of course, in setting out these guidelines Butler merely highlighted the frailty of Wolfenden's argument, since a person's perception of what is 'offensive' and 'indecent' must be related to their moral values.

Butler went on to argue that much human suffering resulted from the operation of the law in relation to homosexuality leading to blackmail and prison sentences. With regard to imprisonment he observed:

> My own personal experience of visits to prisons which have in them those who have committed this type of what is called crime shows how very unsuitable in many cases a prison sentence is for the redemption of a person of this sort. I need not go into details, but in some circumstances, such treatment could hardly be regarded as more unsatisfactory.[37]

This was a curious statement; first because Butler had suggested initially that disagreement over the issue of homosexual offences meant that liberalising legislation was not appropriate, and second because he intended to approve of the imprisonment of women for loitering or soliciting. If he genuinely believed that imprisonment was an inappropriate penalty for homosexual men, why did he not support the Wolfenden recommendations for liberalisation? And why did he consider that a penalty that had proved to be so unsatisfactory for men should be appropriate for women? The answers appear to be grounded in political expediency. It would appear that he felt sufficiently confident that public opinion would support measures aimed at clearing the streets of prostitutes, but thought that there was less support among Conservative voters for homosexual reform. Apparently Sir David Maxwell Fyfe became so strongly opposed to homosexual law reform that he refused to sit at the Cabinet table when the subject was being discussed, and as Lord Kilmuir he issued dire warnings of the consequences of reform during the second reading of the Sexual Offences Bill in 1965.[38] This is a further indication that Maxwell Fyfe had been interested only in the prostitution measures when he set up the Wolfenden Committee and must have been annoyed by the recommendations on homosexuality when they were published.

Prostitution

With regard to prostitution Butler maintained that there was little disagreement about what was desirable, since everybody acknowledged that prostitution was a trade that they would like their country to eradicate. In comparison to homosexuality he saw prostitution in legislatively simplistic terms. 'For myself, I have no doubt of the need to clean up the streets.' His kinswoman Josephine Butler was remarked upon as he had been greatly influenced by reading the account of her life's work and influence. Butler assured the House that he had engaged in a great 'travail of thought' because he knew that the measures being recommended would not be approved of by his great-aunt, although he had been persuaded by the evidence of the committee that matters were now very different. To demonstrate this point he restated, out of context and without acknowledgment, Mrs Wilkinson's statement as quoted in the report:

> The Committee was in no doubt that nowadays *prostitution is a way of life deliberately chosen because it suits a particular woman's personality* and gives her both freedom from irksome routine and the means of earning much more than she would earn in regular employment. It is no longer a way of life which a woman adopts because no other is open to her, and the opportunities for rescuing women from it are consequently limited. All this is quite different to what happened in the time of Josephine Butler, when the girls she used to save were the poorest creatures in society.[39] (my italics)

Butler must have known that this was a very partial and misleading reference both to Josephine Butler and to the historical facts generally. His great-aunt's passionate concern was for the repeal of inequitable and oppressive legislation rather than rescuing women from a sinful life, although she would have recognised that extreme poverty was not always the motivation. Butler did not say to which account of Josephine's life he had been referring, but in 1953 another relative, A. S. G. Butler (Josephine's grandson), published a biography entitled *Portrait of Josephine Butler*[40] in which the author comments: 'Mrs Butler knew – and realised as well as anybody – that women lose their virtue in a weak moment with an attractive man. She knew, too, that some of them, having done so, sell themselves for money or other gain; and she realised that they always will.' In this context A. S. G. Butler made reference to the incident during the repeal campaign when 48 'professional harlots' from Colchester and 21 from Windsor had petitioned parliament in *support* of the CD Acts.[41] Some of these prostitutes liked to refer to themselves as the 'Queen's women', treating the medical certificate issued after inspection as a licence to trade.[42] The Home Secretary might also have been familiar with Dr William Acton's seminal work, *Prostitution*, first published in 1858, in which Acton created his own taxonomy of prostitution. He listed the many reasons why a woman embarked upon the life, the different types of personality and the rich variety of ways in which men and women met and bargained for the exchange of sexual services for sustenance or gain.[43] It is certainly true that there was as much outraged concern over the blatant display of female sexual availability during Victorian times as developed a century later, as well as a body of women who were unwilling to lose all vestige of self-respect by identifying with the stigmatisation society wished to impose upon them. They preferred instead to ascribe some dignity of purpose to their chosen occupation.

During his opening speech[44] the Home Secretary spoke continually in terms of sin and redemption. He turned the Wolfenden rationalisation on its head, arguing that moral guidance *was* the purpose of the law. It followed therefore that as both homosexuality and prostitution were sinful and abhorrent to the average citizen, it was right that the law should deal with them. This line of argument made it possible for the legislature to concentrate upon the redemptive aspects of the recommendations. 'As a preface,' he explained to the House, 'I would say that we propose to practise every art of redemption which we can practise in dealing with this problem.' The essential thing in legislation was, he believed, to find some means of reconciling the ethical, or moral, and the practical approach. 'I am convinced that we have a duty, particularly with the young, to bring every means of redemption to bear, before prostitution becomes a settled habit, and the law should, as far as possible, assist towards this end, although it cannot itself achieve it.' The Home Secretary anticipated immense obstacles in the path of government, the most important of which was the 'great moral problem'. His main criticism of the report was that 'it was so severely practical a document that it hardly introduced morals at all'. But:

> When a Committee like this reports, its report is set out in severely practical language. Nothing could be clearer, nothing could be straighter, nothing could be more straightforward than this Report. However, it leaves the great moral question, of whether if we take action to clear our streets we are doing anything in the end to do away with the evils, difficulties, sorrows and tragedies of prostitution.[45]

Balancing the ethical, moral and practical became the essence of Butler's approach, although he found himself persuaded by the arguments in the report, upon which he felt he could not improve. He couched his own arguments in compassionate terms: 'Each girl who becomes a prostitute, with all that entails, of eventual degradation and misery, is a reproach to our society.' Yet at the same time he was quite happy to make regular use of the phrase 'cleaning up the streets', and did not see that there was any contradiction. He argued that the law had to be adequately defined in order to simplify the task of the police and avoid the 'very great danger' of accusing an innocent woman who might behave 'indiscreetly'. 'In any definition in the Bill,' he insisted, 'the woman must be so described that the police and the court can perform their duty.' This would require retention of the legal definition of 'common prostitute', and those who would not accept redemption would have to face the consequences.

Two constitutional points were picked up at this early stage by Sidney Silverman (Nelson and Colne): (1) that in a disputed case the record of the defendant's past would be used as evidence for the prosecution, which was wrong in principle; and (2), that it was morally wrong to treat the sale of a thing as a crime when its purchase was not.[46] The Home Secretary evaded the first question as it related to the cautioning system and the Bill had not yet been published. On the subject of equality he endorsed the double standard, enquiring, 'How, then, can the demand for equality between men and women be satisfied? Of what offence, in fact, is the man to be guilty? . . . He appears once on the scene and is gone?' Anthony Greenwood (Rossendale) challenged this acceptance of the double standard of morality.[47] 'I would not have thought it impossible to devise a form of words which would ensure that if a woman solicits a man and the man accepts her solicitation, he should be made an accessory to the act for which she has been found guilty.'

With regard to the protection of women the Home Secretary maintained that in the rare case that a man was arrested for persistently importuning a woman, he could be prosecuted under section 32 of the Sexual Offences Act 1956, which states that, 'It is an offence for a man persistently to solicit or importune in a public place for immoral purposes'. This was a very contentious point. The 1956 Sexual Offences (Consolidation) Act was only two years old. Section 32 had its origin in the Vagrancy Act of 1898, which had been enacted as a measure to deal with the prostitute's tout. In the event it had been applied almost exclusively against homosexuals. The CEMWC had drawn attention to this in its pamphlet, commenting that, 'save in two recent cases, this law has never been used to protect women and girls'.[48]

The Home Secretary had also been vague about what he referred to as the offence of 'living on immoral earnings'. As with the terms 'common prostitute' and 'cleaning up the streets' the constant use of this phrase created a negative impression of women that was not reflected in the words of the legislation, as section 30 of the Sexual Offences Act 1956 defined the offence as that of a *man* 'living on the earnings of prostitution'. The immorality of the woman's behaviour was an assumption based upon moral judgements about women. The amendment put forward by the three women members of the Wolfenden Committee for an increase in penalties for section 30 was supported by Butler, who believed the offence to be particularly reprehensible and easier to deal with than trying to apprehend and criminalize the customer. He suggested that this measure might balance out the members' anxieties over inequality and the constitutional issue that Mr Silverman highlighted, hoping 'that in some respects that would be a consolation and balance for some other things we may have to do'.

Some MPs, including Walter Edwards (Stepney), expressed their attitude towards the pimp in a predictable manner. 'I would make it ten years, because they are the dirtiest filthiest lot in creation.'[49]

Butler's political philosophy was summed up in his favoured phrase 'the art of the possible', which he used as the title for his memoirs. He claimed that he was required to draw lines between what was morally acceptable, politically expedient and administratively practicable. When he wrote his autobiography he explained the motivations behind his actions:

> I was moved to take such action by the condition of the streets around Mayfair and Piccadilly which were literally crowded out with girls touting for clients. This gave a very unhealthy look to the centre of our great capital city. But my position in clearing up this state of affairs was made peculiarly difficult by the fact that I was related to Josephine Butler, the great social reformer who in 1870 had founded the Association of Moral and Social Hygiene. Of which I was Vice-President. It had been her cardinal principle that in matters of prostitution the woman is not alone responsible and must not be the target of punitive action; the responsibility of the man must be established. I pointed out to the Association that there were provisions in my Bill against pimps, but could not convince them, as the Commissioner of Police had convinced me, that whereas the police knew and could trace the women who had regular abodes, they simply could not identify the men, who were unknown transitory, and very often from out of town.[50]

This excerpt is notable for a number of inaccuracies, one of which is the fact that the AMSH had not come into existence until 1915, when the Ladies National Association combined forces with the British branch of the International Abolitionist Federation, both of which had been founded by Josephine Butler. What is most curious is that Butler believed that members of the AMSH might be placated by increased penalties for pimps, as if this concession to the minority report of the three women could be traded against the negation of 40 years of campaigning to reform the solicitation laws.

Butler's attitudes and behaviour were in keeping with his conservative political philosophy, but he should not have allowed himself to be vice-president of the AMSH, which would have been no more convinced by the rhetoric of redemption than would Josephine Butler herself. After concluding his speech on behalf of the government the Home Secretary disappeared from the debate and seems to have left the chamber for a large part of the time. But he had set the scene for what was to follow in 1959.

NOTES

1. J. Wolfenden, *Turning Points: The Memoirs of Lord Wolfenden*, The Bodley Head, London, pp. 140–1.
2. P. Higgins, *Heterosexual Dictatorship: Male Homosexuality in Post-War Britain*, Fourth Estate, London, Ch. 5, 'Meet the Press', pp. 116–22.

3. *The Times*, 5 September 1957.
4. See Cmnd. 247, paras. 90–1.
5. *The Times*, 5 September 1957.
6. *Chambers Biographical Dictionary: Centenary Edition* (1999), ed. Melanie Parry, Chambers Harrap, Edinburgh and London.
7. R. A. Butler (1971), *The Art of the Possible: The Memoirs of Lord Butler, K.G. C.H.*, Hamish Hamilton, London. R. A. Butler (1902–82); Minister of Education 1941–45; Chancellor of the Exchequer 1951–55; Lord Privy Seal 1955–59; Leader of the House of Commons 1955–61; Home Secretary 1957–62, First Secretary and Deputy Prime Minister 1962–63; Foreign Secretary 1963–64. In 1965 he was appointed Master of Trinity College, Cambridge. Butler is probably best remembered for his time as Minister for Education (1941–45), and the Education Act 1944, which reorganised secondary education and introduced the 11-plus examination for the selection of grammar school pupils. There is an interesting chapter about him in Roy Jenkins (1993), *Portraits and Miniatures*, Macmillan, London, pp. 1–15.
8. The International Alliance of Women was founded in 1904 and had been involved with the League of Nations work for the prevention of trafficking in women and children. For reference to the International Alliance of Women see A. Whittick (1979), *Women into Citizens*, Athenaeum, London, L. J. Rupp (1997), *Worlds of Women: The Making of an International Women's Movement*, Princeton University Press, Princeton, NJ.
9. See 'Basic Facts About The United Nations' (1992), p. 128.
10. For references to the life of Josephine Butler see G. W. and L. A. Johnson (1909), *Josephine E. Butler: An Autobiographical Memoir*, J. W. Arrowsmith, London; L. Hay-Cooper (1921), *Josephine Butler and her Work for Social Purity*, London Society for Promoting Christian Knowledge; Millicent Fawcett and E. M. Turner (1927), *Josephine Butler: Her Works and Principles, and their Meaning for the Twentieth Century*, AMSH, London; E. Moberly Bell (1962), *Flame of Fire*, Constable, London; Rover (1970), *Love, Morals and the Feminist*, Routledge and Kegan Paul, London. Glen Petrie (1971), *A Singular Iniquity: The Campaigns of Josephine Butler*, New York; Annemieke van Drenth and Franciskia de Hann (1999), *The Rise of Caring Power*, Amsterdam University Press.
11. *The Times*, 4 February 1957.
12. Ibid.
13. AMSH (1959), 'The Street Offences Act 1959', reprinted in the Congress issue of *Shield*, September 1960.
14. Ibid.
15. Ibid.
16. Church of England Moral Welfare Council (1959), 'The Street Offences Bill. A Case for its Amendment', published for the Church of England Moral Welfare Council by the Church Information Board, Church House, Westminster.
17. Ibid.
18. PRO. HO. 345/13/Ch. 26/p. 16.
19. C. of E. Moral Welfare Council, 'The Street Offences Bill'.
20. Ibid.
21. Both the AMSH Public Places (Order) Bill and the C. of E. Moral Welfare Councils' recommendations were discussed during the parliamentary debates on the proposed legislation.
22. London Public Morality Council, '"Women's Courts": Committee of Enquiry 1924', Report, Vacher & Sons Ltd, London (1924).
23. Ibid.
24. For an expansion of this topic see P. Bartley (2000), *Prostitution Prevention and Reform in England, 1860–1914*, Routledge, London, E. J. Bristow (1977), *Vice and Vigilance*, Gill and Macmillan, Rowman and Littlefield, Dublin; L. Mahood (1990), *The Magdalenes: Prostitution in the Nineteenth Century*, Routledge, London.
25. John Stuart Mill (1806–73); MP for Westminster 1865–68; author, philosopher and journalist; appeared before the Royal Commission upon the Administration and Operation of the Contagious Diseases Acts 1871. From the point of view of the Women's Movement, his most important work was his essay *The Subjection of Women* (1869). He argued that the moral regeneration of mankind would take place only when the most fundamental of social relationships (marriage) was placed under the rule of equal justice. To be found in *Mary Wollstonecraft: A Vindication of the Rights of Women* (1985), Everyman Classic, Dent, London, p. 311.
26. See, for example, Josephine Butler, 'The Constitution Violated: An Essay', Edinburgh,

Edmondson and Douglas (1871); ibid., '"The Constitutional Iniquity": Speech of Mrs Josephine Butler at BRADFORD, January 27th 1871', Douglas, Edinburgh.

27. See for example Josephine Butler (1879), '"Government By Police", An Essay "Respectfully Dedicated to The Town Councillors of the United Kingdom"', printer unknown (Beverley Grey Collection).

28. Cmd. 3231, para. 28, 'Women Police'. The committee recognised that there was a special sphere of usefulness for women police and emphasised their value in preventative work.

29. Cmnd. 247, para. 273, 'Women Police'.

30. This subject is a study in itself. There are a great many references to be found in the *Vigilance Record*. See also Alison Woodeson, 'The First Women Police: a Force for Equality or Infringement?' *Women's History Review* Vol. 2, No. 2, 1993, pp. 217–32.

31. Two government committees of enquiry were set up in order to look into the matter of the employment of women on police duties. Report of the Committee on the Employment of Women on Police Duties 1920, Cmd. 877. Report of the Departmental Committee on the Employment of Policewomen 1924, Cmd. 2224.

32. AMSH (1959), 'The Street Offences Act 1959'.

33. J. Weeks (1989), *Sex, Politics and Society: The Regulation of Sexuality since 1800* (Second Edition), Longman, London, p. 244; E. Wilson (1977), *Women and the Welfare State*, Tavistock Publications, London, p. 67.

34. P.D. 5th Ser. Vol. 596, col. 366, 26 November 1958.

35. As I have already argued, this was not entirely accurate because the committee's attention had been drawn to the offence of 'solicitation for immoral purposes' (which was within the remit although it applied only to men importuning).

36. PD. 5th Ser. Vol. 596, col. 370, 26 November 1958.

37. PD. 5th Ser. Vol. 596, col. 370, 26 November 1958.

38. Stephen Jeffery-Poulter (1991), *Peers, Queers & Commons: The Struggle for Gay Law Reform from 1950 to the Present Day*, Routledge, London, pp. 54, 70.

39. P.D. 5th Ser. Vol. 596, col. 372, 26 November 1958.

40. A. S. G. Butler (1953), *Portrait of Josephine Butler*, Faber and Faber, London.

41. Ibid., pp. 88, 137.

42. Rover, *Love, Morals and the Feminist*, p. 80.

43. W. Acton (1887), *Prostitution* (Peter Fryer edition, reprinted, 1968), MacGibbon and Kee, London; L. Bland '"Cleansing the Portals of Life": The Venereal Disease Campaign in the Early Twentieth Century', in M. Langan and B. Schwarz (eds), *Crisis in the British State, 1880–1930*, London (1985); J. R. Walkowitz (1992), *City of Dreadful Delight: Narratives of Sexual Danger in Late Victorian London*, Virago, London.

44. PD. 5th Ser. Vol. 596, cols. 365–82, 26 November 1958.

45. Ibid., cols. 373–82.

46. Ibid., col. 382. When Sir Hugh Linstead was pressed to answer this point at a later stage in the debate, he commented that he almost entirely agreed with Mr Silverman, but that the committee had come to its conclusion reluctantly on account of the women's unruly behaviour and the sheer numbers involved.

47. PD. 5th Ser. Vol. 596, col. 386, 26 November 1958. Anthony Greenwood opened for the opposition, but gave an independent view because the subjects involved matters of public morality and a free vote was to be allowed.

48. C. of E. Moral Welfare Committee, 'The Street Offencs Bill'.

49. PD. 5th Ser. Vol. 596, col. 403, 26 November 1958.

50. R. A. Butler, *The Art of the Possible*, p. 204.

CHAPTER TEN

Moral Matters

It is impossible to draw a hard-and-fast line between crime and sin. So far as the right standards of behaviour are concerned, I say most emphatically these standards and these morals are the concern of the law whether done in private or in public. Without religion there can be no morality and without morality there can be no law. (Lord Justice Denning[1])

In 1871, that is, a couple of years after she had founded the Ladies' National Association (LNA) as an organ through which to oppose the CD Acts, Josephine Butler wrote one of her many extended essays, 'The Constitution Violated'. On the opening page she wrote: 'The moral side of the question is undoubtedly the most important, and has been dwelt upon by the religious portion of the community, almost to the exclusion of all others, although it may be truly said that it of necessity includes all others.'[2] Josephine Butler would certainly have agreed with Lord Denning that law and morals were inextricably linked together. But she would also have argued that in its interpretation of religious doctrine the law had privileged one sex over the other, and in the case of the CDAs the law itself was guilty of promoting immorality and condoning sin.

There were a great many moral questions embedded within the Home Secretary's presentation in November 1958, when the House first debated the Wolfenden Report, most of which he failed to confront or enlarge upon. Yet R. A. Butler made it quite clear that in his opinion the government was faced with a moral problem for which women were largely responsible, and that the public display of immorality had to be prevented through legislation. In brief, he supported the Wolfenden argument that it was the women's presence on the streets that caused offence and that the matter of equality between the sexes was irrelevant. He went on to argue that the Bill was only a limited measure, which he hoped would contribute towards the solution of a much larger social problem that had to be addressed by society adopting higher moral standards, although he realised that the extent to which legislation could influence matters would be constrained by the limits of what was practicable.

When introducing the Street Offences Bill on 29 January 1959, Butler adopted the opposite approach to Wolfenden and presented the problem of prostitution as a gender-specific moral dilemma which demanded Parliament's compassion. Yet in following this line he still needed to persuade MPs of the legitimacy of the legislation that he had in mind, which was harsh and pro-scriptive. In order to balance these contradictions he employed five arguments:

- that harsher penalties would act as a deterrent and persuade women to accept help from probationary officers as an alternative to ending up in prison;
- that the introduction of the Scottish cautioning system would provide a redemptive route by which young women would be helped towards a more wholesome and honest way of life;
- that the innocent or indiscreet woman would be protected from false accusation;
- that section 30 of the Sexual Offences Act 1956 (living on the earnings of prostitution, etc.) would protect women from sexual exploitation; and
- that section 32 of the same Act (a man persistently soliciting for an immoral purpose) would protect women from the unwelcome immoral solicitations of men in public places.

The justification for what he described as a 'harsh definition' was that there was no longer any economic necessity for women to resort to 'immoral earnings' in order to keep themselves alive, and therefore there was no 'excuse' for their behaviour that he felt obliged to take into consideration. So although prostitution in itself was not illegal he believed that the government had a duty to provide, as far as possible, for the redemption of the women involved in the practice.

When the economic basis of the Home Secretary's argument was challenged the largely 'male' House was reduced to laughter. F. J. Bellenger (Bassetlaw)[3] remarked that although he had 'never been inconvenienced by these ladies'[4] he believed that the alleged increase in the number of women on the streets was due to an increase in demand, as the greater dispersal of money meant that many more of the customers could afford the price and consequently the rewards of prostitution were greater. In other words, an improving economy was reflected in an increase rather than a decrease in prostitution and the demand fuelled the supply.[5] The economic argument was taken up again when, after four and a half hours of debate, Mrs Evelyn Emmet (East Grinstead) made the first substantial contribution by a woman MP. In her opinion many of the young women involved in prostitution were poorly educated and had left school early, with the result that they found it difficult to obtain remunerative work. Moreover, they experienced problems finding affordable accommodation in the city, the availability of which had decreased since the war had ended.[6] She argued that if anything more than repression was intended, it was necessary to take a longer view. But, as is often the case, long-term solutions were not part of the government strategy, the only politically acceptable solution had to be cheap, effective and foolproof.

JUSTIFICATIONS (IMPRISONMENT)

If Lord Denning's words are to be accepted at their face value and religious precepts translated into immutable law, then the transparency of the justice that they embody needs to be irrefutable. The basis from which the logic springs must have its own integrity and the law its legitimacy. Nowhere was the precariousness of official reasoning clearer than in relation to the recommendation for imprisonment. Yet there was no real clarity as to the exact nature of the offence that the Home Office wished to penalise so heavily. Roberts had reduced it to the presence of the women on the streets, Wolfenden had clothed it in intellectual ambiguity, Butler vacillated from one extreme to another, while Sir Hugh Linstead insisted that it was solely a matter of civil disobedience. All took refuge behind the contentious term of 'cleaning up the streets', a phrase that had no moral integrity in its definition and was based upon the age-old perception of women as polluting.

It became obvious during the second reading of the Bill that the Home Secretary himself was not clear in his own mind of the true nature of the offence but was puzzling over it as Roberts and Wolfenden had done before him. When debating the merits of the proposed cautioning system, he commented: 'I am perfectly well satisfied that the police are able to distinguish by the activities of a woman and by the evidence of not only one policeman, but of two policeman, of what a woman is up to when they condemn her as a common prostitute and bring her before the court.'[7] In Butler's mind prostitution was the offence, and the woman was to be 'condemned' as a 'common prostitute', rather than being 'charged' with loitering or soliciting for a legal purpose. Hers was therefore essentially a moral offence, hence the importance of safeguarding the 'indiscreet' but 'innocent' woman.

Butler followed in the footsteps of Wolfenden by using the questionable argument that the threat of imprisonment might encourage more prostitutes to accept probation, and thereby have access to a court missionary, social worker, probationary officer or a member of a voluntary society. Yet, as Mrs Lena Jeger (Holborn and St Pancras South) observed, this list included many of the individuals and bodies who were most opposed to the Bill.[8] The court missionary was a case in point. Many of the women who took up this type of work would have been trained at the Josephine Butler Memorial House in Liverpool,[9] founded in 1920 in order to train young women for moral welfare work. As late as 1970 the college produced 94 students who became moral welfare workers and 15 who entered the probationary service. Throughout its existence the college had strong links with both the AMSH and the International Abolitionist Federation, both of which organisations adhered to the 'principles' that Roberts and Wolfenden had found incomprehensible. Mrs Jeger was wise when she counselled caution because the perennial complaint about discrimination between the sexes became more pertinent as the seriousness of the penalty increased. More revealingly, the opposition to imprisonment came predominantly not from women's organisations but from respected male-dominated bodies such as the Howard League for Penal Reform, the National Council for Civil Liberties, the Magistrates' Association and the National Association of Probation Officers.[10]

Having established at the beginning of the Second Reading that the House was discussing a problem that was largely confined to a specific area of London, Kenneth Younger (Grimsby) argued that the government was resorting to panic measures. For whereas the problem of prostitution on the streets was limited, localised and possibly temporary, the solution being proposed was national and permanent.[11] While ignoring these arguments the Home Secretary continually rationalised his position by resorting to the moral standpoint, but qualified it with the suggestion that harsh punishments would achieve a moral and compassionate end:

> I hope that we shall not only deal with conditions in the street which constitute a public nuisance, but also make a positive and valuable contribution to the discouragement of vice and the redemption of those who are in danger of adopting it as a way of life. The main purpose, as I said, is to clear the streets of prostitutes plying their trade and give the police effective powers to that end.[12]

With this argument Butler returns to the justification provided by the double standard. It was the 'woman' who adopted prostitution as a way of life, whereas the regular customer inhabited a different moral space. The Labour opposition was not impressed. Anthony Greenwood (Rossendale) became impatient with Butler's moralising and accused him of using his kinswoman, Josephine Butler, as a 'gimmick' when it suited his purpose.

The efficacy of imprisonment was frequently challenged. To begin with, probationary services, welfare workers and voluntary agencies were already available and could have been used to better effect. Furthermore, imprisonment was available as a penalty outside the London area and the value of this penalty had not been researched. Greenwood made his own investigations and suggested that it had proved to be an ineffectual deterrent, and in any case it did not seem appropriate to many MPs to overload the prisons with young prostitutes.[13] In addition there was no evidence to show that prison would have a beneficial effect on the women, whereas their presence in prisons might be detrimental to the other inmates. Most of all it seemed unfitting, even immoral, to imprison one sex for offering the other a legal service when it was frequently welcomed and readily accepted.

THE MORAL IMPLICATIONS OF SECTION 30 OF THE SEXUAL OFFENCES ACT 1956

Critics of the Bill who, like the AMSH, saw little government concern for the safety of women were answered with reference to sections 30 and 32 of the newly consolidated Sexual Offences Act 1956, which imposed heavy sentences upon men. As the 1956, Act had not been subjected to parliamentary scrutiny, it is worth looking more closely at the nature of these offences and the justifications that underpinned them.

Section 30(1) of the Sexual Offences Act 1956 states:

> It is an offence for a man knowingly to live wholly or in part on the earnings of prostitution.

Section 30(2) states:

> For the purpose of this section a man who lives with or is habitually in the company of a prostitute, or exercises control, direction or influence over a prostitute's movements in a way which shows he is aiding, or abetting or compelling her prostitution with others, shall be presumed to be knowingly living on her earnings, unless he proves to the contrary.

The subject of this offence is a man and only he can commit the crime, but he cannot be charged unless it is shown that the woman involved is a prostitute. The offence is officially and unofficially referred to as 'living on immoral earnings', although it is the woman's immorality that is in question rather than the man's. Through this offence the law is saying that it is dishonourable for a man to live on the earnings of a woman whom society has condemned as an immoral person. However, before a man profits from a woman's prostitution other more serious crimes (abduction, rape, violent abuse, coercion and theft) may have preceded the main offence, but they need not be proved in order to obtain a conviction under section 30(1), in which the profit motive is paramount.

The complexities of sections 30(1) and 30(2) were considered in 1982 by the Criminal Law Revision Committee (CLRC),[14] which commented on the dilemma that poncing presented for the legislature, arguing that: 'The statutory definition itself suggests that the rationale of the offence is that this is a disgraceful way for a man to get his living, or part of it.' Yet 'the offender is liable to be severely punished for conduct which need not be proved as an element of the offence at all'. That is:

> He may in practice be punished chiefly for compelling the woman to work as a prostitute, and for using threats and force against her or for taking her earnings by compulsion. Yet these are offences involving assault, robbery or blackmail with which he is not charged. The point is brought out by the second part of the presumption set out in section 30(2): aiding, abetting and compelling prostitution is, one would have thought, much more objectionable than living on the earnings of prostitution, yet the former does not constitute the offence but is to be treated as evidence of it.[15]

Section 30(2) extends the provisions of section 30(1) and again applies only to a man. The obligation to prove innocence is imposed upon him rather than on the prosecution, inverting one of the cardinal principles of British law. But the man who lives with, or is habitually in the company of, a prostitute may be her father, brother, son, husband or partner. He may be a violent exploiter or the only stable influence in the woman's life. Whereas 'aiding and abetting' suggest willing cooperation in a joint enterprise, 'controlling' and 'compelling' imply the possibility of force. Once again we are faced with a contradiction, as the wording of these sections allows the law to pull simultaneously in two different directions. Whereas section 30(1) and section 30(2) may be used to prosecute the man who exploits a woman, they also isolate the prostitute, denying her the right to a lawful private family life by preventing her from living in a stable relationship with a male partner of her choice. When these provisions are set beside those in *Winter* v. *Woolfe* (1930) and the case law that extends them,[16] the prostitute is 'legally' condemned to live and work in a state of isolation and vulnerability.

The perception of financial gain as the essence of the exploitation involved in this offence seems to reflect gender-specific values and social expectations. For a woman to live on a man's earnings is considered normal and correct.[17] What appears to give offence in the eyes of the law is that the man has profited from the woman's (immoral) prostitution instead of by his own efforts. The woman's inferior status adds to the repugnancy with which many men view this offence. However, for most women the financial gain that the pimp obtains is a secondary consideration when placed beside the betrayal of trust and the mental and physical abuse that are frequently a part of this type of relationship. These circumstances add another layer of paradox and contradiction to a woman's life when quite frequently she has entered prostitution in order to gain independence and escape from poverty only to find herself swept up into a world of violence and exploitation.[18] She may then enter into a state of denial and be unwilling, or afraid, to give evidence against the men who abuse and exploit her. This was the message of the book *Street Walker*, published anonymously in 1959, which Wolfenden regretted not having had the opportunity to read.[19] But also from an administrative point of view, the offence of 'living on the earnings of prostitution' requires a great deal of time and effort on the part of the police and it is more difficult to prove than a soliciting offence. On the whole these are hidden crimes, as the Wolfenden Committee hoped and suspected, and prosecutions are comparatively infrequent.[20]

Section 30 (1) and section 30(2) do not deal satisfactorily with coercion and exploitation and conversely come down too heavily upon men who have only a limited involvement in a woman's occupation. Problems with these offences came to light when they were tested in court. For example, *Donald Theodore Wilson* (1983)[21] was charged under section 30 (2) of the Sexual Offences Act 1956. Wilson was a caretaker of a block of flats where he lived with a woman. The prosecution gave evidence to the effect that she was a prostitute who had admitted giving sums of money to Wilson towards maintenance payments for his children. He was convicted and appealed on the ground that 'living on' meant living on 'parasitically'[22] and that the trial judge had failed to point this out to the jury. The appeal was dismissed but the prison sentence reduced from three months to seven weeks on the ground that the appellant was to some extent the victim of the woman's predilection for drink and the selling of her body in order to pay for the habit. Kilner Brown J. commented that matters logically began with the necessity of establishing ('as the Act makes quite plain has to be established') that the woman is a prostitute.[23] Section 30 can be difficult to prove when the man involved is a marginal character and pleads that he did not know that the woman was a prostitute.

As the law report reveals no evidence of exploitation or coercion on the part of Wilson the case seems to have been brought in order to prevent prostitution, which is not the purpose of the law. But so long as prostitution is not illegal there must be ways in which it can be legally practised. The personal consequences of the case might have been considerable. It is quite possible that Wilson lost his job and his accommodation as well as the support of the woman with whom he was living.

In the course of time a number of appeals were made against the length of sentencing on the ground that coercion had not taken place. In the case of *Farrugia* (1979)[24] Lawton L. J. was uncertain as to why the penalty for such offences had been increased: 'the court can only speculate as to why'. He advised that for offences under section 30 of the Sexual Offences Act 1956 that: 'In the absence of any evidence of coercion, whether physical, mental, or of corruption, a maximum sentence of two years was probably enough'. Lawton L.J. deplored the fact that the case had lasted 73 days. It is hardly surprising that such confusing legislation should cause problems.

The equivalent 'female' offence found in section 31 is also linked to the profit motive. It makes it an offence 'for a woman for the purpose of gain to exercise control, direction or influence over a prostitute's movements in a way which shows she is aiding, abetting or compelling her prostitution', but it leaves out the reference to 'living with or being habitually in the company of a prostitute'. This prompts further criticism on the ground of gender discrimination favouring women.[25] The problem that then arises is that women who run escort agencies or manage small brothels may be caught under this provision, although they are not usually responsible for the violent abuse that is the scourge of prostitution. Moreover, the women who want to work in the sex industry often feel safer in this type of situation than working on their own, even though it might be financially exploitative. A number of high-profile and well-publicized cases have resulted from prosecutions under this section.[26]

SHAW v. DPP (1961) OR *THE LADIES DIRECTORY*

The defining case with regard to 'living on the earnings of prostitution' was *Shaw* v. *DPP* (1961).[27] The case, which is better known as the *Ladies Directory*, involved the publication of a booklet containing the names, addresses and telephone numbers of prostitutes along with coded abbreviations indicating the various sexual practices in which they were willing to participate. The appellant was convicted at the Central Criminal Court on 21 September 1960 of (a) conspiracy to corrupt public morals, (b) living on the earnings of prostitution, and (c) publishing an obscene publication contrary to section 2 of the Obscene Publications Act 1959.[28] The case was referred to the House of Lords, where it was considered by Viscount Simonds, Lord Reid, Lord Tucker, Lord Morris of Borth-y-Gest and Lord Hodson. William R. Rees-Davis (barrister) represented the appellant.

In his role as Conservative MP for the Isle of Thanet Rees-Davis made an extensive contribution to the second reading of the Street Offences Bill.[29] He had informed the House that from the beginning of his professional career in Treasury Chambers he had covered over 300 cases for the Church Commissioners, dealing with all the legal aspects of prostitution including pimping and brothel-keeping. Although he supported the Bill and appeared to have little sympathy for the prostitute (whom he described as 'a hard girl who knows exactly what her value is'), he was concerned to protect the taxi-driver, hotel porter and the anonymous middle-men who passed on information to potential customers, arguing that they should not be prosecuted for living on the earnings of prostitution. He pointed out that it would be counterproductive deliberately to push the women off the streets and then make 'off-street' operations equally hazardous. Like Wolfenden, he realised that the state could not have it both ways and appreciated that deliberately to privatise prostitution and then persecute the operator was hypocrisy . Rees-Davis argued that there was a subtle difference between 'living on the earnings of a prostitute' and 'living on the earnings of prostitution'. The first of these two suggested a greater degree of coercion so the formulation of the offence need not be interpreted too harshly.

When he appeared before the Law Lords[30] Rees-Davis explained that section 30 of the SOA 1956 derived from the Vagrancy Act 1898 as amended by section 7 of the CLA Act 1912. He argued that 'the Act was not an Act dealing with public morals. It was designed to give the police power to enter a house where a man who was an idle and disorderly person within the meaning of the Vagrants Act 1824, and who was living on the earnings of women of the streets, cohabited with a prostitute or where he was known to frequent.'[31] Furthermore, he claimed that there had been no case that had defined the meaning of the words 'living wholly or in part on the earnings of prostitution'. It had never been suggested that a landlord or person who rendered services to a prostitute should come within this sub-section. Rees-Davis submitted that these men were living upon their own earnings. He argued that there was a distinction between men who supplied services for reward to a prostitute and those who in the course of their own business merely received the prostitute's earnings.[32]

A large part of the Law Lords' discussion turned on this point. 'The heart of the issue', observed Lord Reid, 'is whether a person can provide a normal service to a prostitute.' The Lord Chancellor, Viscount Simonds, elaborated:

> The grocer who supplies groceries, the doctor or lawyer who renders professional services to a prostitute do not commit an offence under the Act. It is not to be supposed that it is its policy to deny to her the necessities or even the luxuries of life if she can afford them. I would say, however, that, though (*sic*) a person who is paid for goods and services out of the earnings of prostitution does not necessarily escape from its provisions by receiving payment for the goods and services that he supplies to the prostitute. The argument that such a person lives on his own earnings, not hers, is inconclusive. To give effect to it would be to exclude from the operation of the Act the very person, the tout, the bully or protector, who it was designed to catch . . . Somewhere the line must be drawn and I do not find it easy to draw it.[33]

I would suggest that for a discussion of this nature to take place indicates that there is a fundamental flaw in the legislation. The judgment focused upon the entitlement of prostitutes to essential goods and services, although the law was initially enacted in order to protect women from exploitation. Viscount Simonds' choice of a prostitute's access to doctors and lawyers as an illustration of his point indicates a lack of understanding because it presupposes that she enjoys a normal recourse to these services. However, the isolation and stigmatisation that prostitutes encounter and the chaotic and often illegal nature of their working lives[34] mean that many of them are inhibited from obtaining either legal or medical advice.[35]

The judgment in the case of *Shaw*, that there was a common law offence of 'conspiracy to corrupt public morals', did not lead to a flood of prosecutions for supplying goods and services that were required for the purpose of prostitution.[36] It is also arguable whether 'living on the earnings of prostitution' is correctly described a *sexual* offence, because it is not in itself a violation of the person even though sexual violence may be an aggravating ingredient of the crime.

XENOPHOBIA

The case of the *Ladies Directory* was one of the first indications that a closer organisation of the trade, which included a new breed of middle-men, was emerging. It resembled the circumstances surrounding the enactment of the Vagrancy Act 1898.[37] The crack-down on small lodging-house brothels after the passage of the CLA Act 1885 had resulted in an increase in the number of homeless women who became prey to bullies and touts. As these men were generally believed to be foreigners it fuelled a wave of xenophobia.[38] The tendency to equate the offence of living on the earnings of prostitution with unwelcome immigrants was also apparent during the 1958–59 parliamentary debates.

A number of MPs emphasised their belief that the problem arose from colonial immigrants who ought to be sent back to their country of origin.

Norman Parnell (Liverpool) offered statistics to the House claiming that in 1956 106 convictions had taken place in the London Metropolitan area, 70 per cent of which involved immigrants from the Republic of Ireland, colonial or Commonwealth countries. In 1957 there were 130 cases, 82 of which involved men from the Republic of Ireland, the colonies and the dominions. Even if these figures were correct they did not necessarily reflect the true situation.

During the second reading of the Bill the commentary was moderated but by the third reading it had descended into undisguised racism. Rees-Davis, for example, was anxious to defend the British male. 'The great majority of ponces and pimps in this country are not Englishmen. They are principally Maltese, Ghanaians and Jamaicans . . . they are a pest to this country, and the crime of poncing is a singularly un-English crime.'[39] Walter Edwards went a step further referring to 'these stinking people who come to this country and earn money from the bodies of women'.[40]

The answer to Lawton L. J.'s question as to why the penalty for living on immoral earnings had been increased lay in the similarity between a stigmatised group of 'prostitute' women and a stigmatised group of 'black' male immigrants. Once they have been removed from the generality of 'ordinary decent people', as portrayed in the Wolfenden Report and the Commons debate, they can be treated differently and prosecuted more readily.

LORD DEVLIN AND THE ENFORCEMENT OF MORALS

Wolfenden's proposition that 'there must remain a realm of private morality and immorality which is not the law's business'[41] prompted a considerable amount of academic discussion concerning the enforcement of morality through law. The most famous of these became known as the Hart–Devlin controversy. In 1958 Lord Devlin was asked to deliver the second Maccabaean Lecture in Jurisprudence for the British Academy, the first having been given by Lord Evershed, then Master of the Rolls. Lord Devlin accepted with some misgiving, but was fortified by the knowledge that he had a topical subject at his disposal with which he could deal competently. He had given evidence before the Wolfenden Committee and supported reform of the law so long as youths could be protected from corruption. When the report was published he found himself in complete agreement with 'its formulation of the criminal law in matters of morality'.[42]

In the preface to the publication of his lectures, *The Enforcement of Morals*, he refers to the homosexual man and expresses a considerable amount of sympathy for his situation. 'I do not think that there is any good the law can do that outweighs the misery that exposure and imprisonment cause to addicts who cannot find satisfaction in other ways of life. Punishment cannot cure and because it is haphazard in its incidence I doubt if it deters.' In saying this Lord Devlin showed empathy with the remarks made by Butler in connection with the imprisonment of homosexuals, but equally there was no admission of the illogicality of the opposite formula being found appropriate for prostitutes.

On reflection Lord Devlin decided to use the Wolfenden proposition as the basis of his lecture and determined to apply its hypothesis (that the law was not concerned with public morals) to other areas of private behaviour and show how it influenced the criminal law; and to suggest reforms. But he was discomfited to find that his examination destroyed rather than confirmed the simple faith with which he began. Consequently his Second Maccabaean Lecture became a confirmation of the place of law in the imposition of morality. But although Devlin's initial interest was stimulated by the application of the Wolfenden proposition to homosexuality, he sought to rationalise his argument by reference to prostitution. He claimed that even if Wolfenden's proposition was stretched to breaking point it still would not cover the recommendations that the report made in connection with prostitution. Therefore he asked his audience: 'if prostitution is private immorality and not the law's business, what concern has the law with the ponce or the brothel keeper or the householder who permits habitual prostitution?' Lord Devlin concluded: 'there may be cases of exploitation in this trade, as there are or used to be in many others, but in general a ponce exploits a prostitute no more than an impresario exploits an actress'.[43]

This is a curious statement that can be interpreted as either naive or dishonest as it belies the reality of violent abuse that is endemic to prostitution, and so graphically portrayed in *Street Walker*. Nor does Lord Devlin say on what evidence he based such a confident statement. There was only the report, which he did not think to question. Instead he used it to support his comment by quoting the reformulation of Rosalind Wilkinson's observation, which Wolfenden had embellished with his own opinions,[44] saying: 'The Report finds that "the great majority of prostitutes are women whose psychological make up is such that they choose this life because they find it a style of living which is to them easier, freer and more profitable than would be provided by any other occupation" . . . in the main the association between prostitute and ponce is one of mutual advantage'.[45] I quote this again because it *was* quoted *again and again* by each succeeding commentator. Lord Devlin appears to have accepted it without question although, as we have seen, there were no references in the report to any empirical evidence supporting these assertions and no prostitute interviewed. Yet he writes:

> All sexual immorality involves human weaknesses. The prostitute exploits the lust of her customers and the customer the moral weakness of the prostitute. If the exploitation of human weakness is considered to create a special circumstance, there is certainly no field of morality which can be defined in such a way as to exclude the law.[46]

Speeches by people of the standing of Lord Devlin can be influential, yet he seems to have been ambivalent over the weaknesses of men, as in 1965 he was one of eight signatories (five bishops and three peers) to a letter to *The Times* supporting reform of the law on homosexual offences.[47] As Lord Simonds discovered, drawing a moral line is often very difficult.

MRS ROSALIND WILKINSON

The story of Rosalind Wilkinson seems appropriate at this stage. She was engaged by the British Social Biology Council in 1949 to research prostitution in London. Part of her work was done in conjunction with the London School of Economics. Her report was eventually edited by C. H. Rolph, the pseudonym of an ex-Chief Inspector (Hewitt) of the City of London Police. In his autobiography *Living Twice* Rolph records that Mrs Wilkinson had lived among the prostitutes of the West End and some of the inner suburbs and 'had come up with a manuscript that was so vivid and human and at the same time so factual and carefully documented that I should like to see it published unchanged. But it ran to about 200,000 words and the Council felt unable to publish a book of more than 90,000 words.' Rolph was soon regretting having accepted the assignment, which he described as 'butchery'. 'I think that if anybody decimated a book of mine in that fashion I should raise the roof.' Mrs Wilkinson did exactly that, and a long legal tussle over copyright ensued. The Council went ahead with the publication, referring to Mrs Wilkinson as 'the Research Worker' and placing C.H. Rolph's name on the cover as 'Editor'. Consequently many people believed that he was the author of the report.

The members of the Wolfenden Committee were aware of this but avoided being embroiled in the controversy (or embarrassing the members of the BSBC mentioned above). Instead they referred to Mrs Wilkinson as 'one of our witnesses'. Nevertheless her unguarded comment was quoted and discussed by the Wolfenden Committee, then printed in its report, quoted again by Butler in his opening speech, discussed during the parliamentary debate and quoted once more by Devlin. In each instance the comment was taken out of context and without reference to the rest of her work, much of which contradicted this particular statement. The BSBC's behaviour was probably legal in that it had employed her to work on its behalf, but I would have thought it was morally indefensible either to abridge Mrs Wilkinson's work without her consent or to continually quote her out of context in order to support a point that could not be substantiated. Although her fate cannot be described as corruption, in Devlin's terms it certainly involved exploitation and an abuse of power. The law can, on occasions, be used to enforce injustice as well as society's current version of morality.

THE HART–DEVLIN DEBATE

In his lecture Lord Devlin posed a number of questions. First, if society had the right to pass judgements based upon collectively held moral values, did it also possess the right to impose those values upon individuals through the mechanisms of the law? Second, if the answer was yes, how could society distinguish between those moral values that were to be enforced by law and those that were not? Professor Hart responded to Devlin's analysis and submitted a slightly different formulation of the question: 'Is the fact that certain conduct is by common standard immoral sufficient to justify making that conduct punishable by law?'[48] Devlin answered 'yes' and Professor Hart 'no'.[49] But there is a further unasked question that applies to prostitution and grows naturally out of the Church of England Moral Welfare Council's criticism of the Bill. If society decides that it has a collective right to impose moral behaviour through the law, then does it also have a duty to make a contribution towards the solution of the problems rather than invest arbitrary powers in the police and stand aside? The trouble with the answer to this question is that society's attempts to grapple with prostitution were frequently highly coercive, unregulated and aimed almost entirely at reforming women.[50] The practice of placing prostitutes in homes of redemption had not only institutionalised them[51] but confirmed the distinction between the good and the bad woman, a distinction that the Street Offences Act 1959 was to enshrine in law.

Hart's response to Devlin is intriguing for other reasons. He found the resurgence of what he termed 'legal moralism' curious and wondered what had provoked it.[52] Yet it is also curious that Devlin made the case of *Shaw* v. *DPP* the central theme of his first lecture. It appears that it was easier to discuss morality in terms of female prostitution than in connection with the homosexual activities of men. Hart suggested that the adoption of three separate charges in order to ensure the conviction and imprisonment of Shaw was excessive in that he was concerned by the 'vastly comprehensive' nature of the offence of 'corrupting public morals', which he considered to be an 'exceedingly vague and obscure idea'. He observed that legal writers in England had not yet worked out the relationship between this common law offence (whose existence was doubted by many) and those that defined certain specific offences concerning sexual morality, and suggested that it was arguable that the prosecuting authorities might avail themselves of this common law offence in order to avoid the restrictions imposed by statutory law.[53] I would submit that, on the contrary, vagueness and lack of precision were the hallmarks of British statutory law on prostitution-related offences, leading to ever-widening definitions for terms such as 'common prostitute' and 'brothel', which create anomalies and increase the possibility of judicial error and injustice.[54]

Professor Hart made another very pertinent comment that has some relevance to this study. With reference to the legislative complexities of American law on immorality (which might vary from state to state as well as under local ordinance),[55] he noted that although much of the legislation represented a dead letter the facts of law enforcement were hard to establish. He argued that the existence of unenforced criminal sanctions combined with inadequate statistics placed formidable and discretionary powers in the hands of the police and prosecuting authorities.[56] This is an observation of importance to women,

because the nature of the arbitrary powers bestowed by a largely male legislature on a predominantly male administration had always been at the heart
of the feminist complaint over legal moralism that privileges men.

ANNOYANCE

In his opening speech on the second reading of the Street Offences Bill, Butler
was anxious to reject objections to the removal of the need to prove annoyance, stating: 'In my view this is essential if the provisions of the Bill are to be
effective for the purpose of clearing the streets', and that he did not want to
be responsible for the enactment of a dead letter. The Home Secretary
informed the House that the term 'dead letter' had been coined by Hugh
Macmillan, but did not comment on the Street Offences Committee's proposal for the enactment of two offences, the lesser of which, 'for solicitation',
should retain the need to prove annoyance.[57]

The *Times* printed a leading article that severely criticised the proposed Bill,
and in particular the proposal to drop the requirement to prove annoyance:

> Until the effect in London of these stern penalties has been tested, it
> would seem dangerous to accept the Bill's fourth purpose of, in addition,
> changing the law simply to read: 'It shall be an offence for a common
> prostitute to loiter or solicit in a street or a public place for the purpose
> of prostitution.' As the Macmillan Committee concluded in 1928,
> instances of bribery of the police by prostitutes either with money or
> with favours . . . must inevitably occur. To choose the occasion when
> really severe penalties may enlarge that danger also to enlarge police
> powers to arrest loiters and, in contested cases, to secure convictions
> without convincing evidence is to invite both trouble and injustice. The
> Bill seems, moreover, to single out one class of citizen – those who have
> acquired the label of 'common' prostitute (often by somewhat dubious
> procedures) – to be denied everyone else's right to loiter, provided no
> obstruction or annoyance is caused. It seems to ignore the fact that men,
> as well as women who are not (or not yet) 'common' prostitutes, may also
> loiter for libidinous purposes and thereby cause annoyance. There is an
> unconvincing air about Mr Butler's argument that if the ingredient of
> annoyance remains, the law will be unenforceable, while if the offence is
> not restricted to common prostitutes there will be 'a very great danger'
> of the police arresting virtuous women.[58]

The *Times* leader concluded that: 'Parliament should throw out the attempt
to abolish the annoyance ingredient, as it had done repeatedly ever since 1885.'
In this the paper was correct, for to retain the label of common prostitute but
withdraw the requirement to prove annoyance both increased the arbitrary
powers invested in the police and at the same time removed the prostitute's
only defence against false accusation. The already small likelihood of 'not

guilty' pleas was even further reduced and the registered prostitute who was in the street but not loitering for a purpose could be arrested with impunity. The significance of the *Times* leader was not just that the Home Secretary ignored the advice it contained, but that the criticisms made were precisely the same as those that had been so passionately put forward by the AMSH and circumvented by the Wolfenden Committee. On this occasion the criticisms could not be so easily set aside by the use of sexist witticisms, since *The Times* of the 1950s was not administered by a group of old women, and was very much the premier establishment paper directed by and for educated men.

The Home Secretary had justified the omission of 'proof of annoyance' by employing the Roberts–Wolfenden argument that it was not so much the individual prostitute who caused annoyance, but the general nuisance caused to the community at large by numbers of prostitutes.[59] In doing so he admitted that in many cases the claim of nuisance might be disputed, in which case the police required a measure that enabled them to arrest a woman who was not, at the time in question, creating a problem. In these circumstances the essence of the offence would become 'being a prostitute' rather than 'loitering for the purpose of prostitution'. The labelling procedure and registration provided by the caution was to make this possible.

MORALITY AND THE POLICE

The dangers of arbitrary powers being placed in the hands of the police, and accusations of corruption with regard to prostitutes and sexual offences, represent a constant theme that can be traced back over the years. For example, the *Morning Post* in 1855[60] complained of over-zealous police action in clearing the streets of prostitutes,[61] stating that 'such proceedings harshly carried out by the ordinary police will be an unmanly and unwarrantable wrong done to the wretched women, unless some place be at once provided for their reception'. Similarly, when Josephine Butler wrote her essay on 'Government by Police' (1879), she advocated the need to curb the powers of the police, whom she saw as a 'threatening tyranny'.[62] During the parliamentary debate on the 1885 Criminal Law Amendment Bill, C. H. Hopwood warned of the danger of dropping 'proof of annoyance'.[63] He believed this omission would automatically increase the powers of the police. In 1910 a tract issued following the publication of the Royal Commission on the Metropolitan Police (1908–09) complained of wrongful arrest and misconduct towards prostitutes,[64] and in 1928 the Macmillan Committee had admitted that such things must happen.[65]

Wolfenden and Butler had gone to the other extreme, taking care to demonstrate their confidence in the integrity of the police force. 'In passing,' remarked the Home Secretary, 'I would like to pay a sincere tribute to the policemen in their handling of this matter. They have shown great tact and efficiency in dealing with it, especially in the West End.'[66] This reassurance must have given rise to some cynicism, as during the course of the Wolfenden

Committee's hearings, rumours and accusations of bribery and corruption had abounded in the press.[67] Indeed, letters had passed between Roberts and Wolfenden,[68] referring to 'general accusations made in certain quarters against the police', which in turn referred to 450 men being transferred from C Division. Notwithstanding, the Parliamentary Under-Secretary of State announced in the House that these rumours were unsubstantiated, while Nott-Bower, Chief Commissioner of the Metropolitan Police, was reported by *The Times*[69] as denying all suggestion that 'the Metropolitan Police as a body were corrupt'. He maintained that this was an unwarranted attack on 'a fine body of conscientious men and women'. The Chief Commissioner stated that he had been in close personal touch with the Home Secretary, 'who had authorised him to say that he had complete confidence in the Metropolitan Police'.[70]

In his biography, *Living Twice*, C. H. Rolph made the most uncompromising statement, alleging that any policeman in disciplinary trouble would always lie if he was guilty, and often even if he was innocent. He compounded this statement by declaring:

> The police system, no doubt like many other systems of which I know less, is therefore rotten in important parts of its foundations. But what is unusual about this is that the rot has spread downwards from the summit which is obscured from the policeman by clouds. Not even, that is to say, from venial chief officers but from departments of State and their readiness to lie for the common weal. And this is the atmosphere in which corruption comes to seem excusable, if not inevitable.[71]

One of the main arguments for changing the legislation so as to simplify arrest procedures was that the police were thought to be operating a rota system that rested upon a tacit agreement between the police and the women.[72] This added to the general perception that the criminal justice system was being brought into disrepute. It is significant that although much of the anxiety over police procedures arose from the conduct of police officers towards homosexuals, rather than towards prostitutes, incriminating papers concerning these practices have been removed from Home Office files.[73] However, this deficit has been filled in by other writers who give more detailed descriptions of entrapment methods.[74] For example the historian and MP H. Montgomery Hyde gave some further indication of the unsavoury practices used by the police in order to secure convictions.[75] These included extensive use of *agents provocateurs* in plain clothes to trap men in public lavatories, raiding properties without a search warrant in the hope of finding incriminating evidence, persuading accomplices to turn 'Queen's evidence' in return for immunity from criminal proceedings and, 'most objectionable of all', the revival of the conspiracy charge. 'Counts under this head', he explains, were 'added to the indictment, thus making the words and acts of each of the defendants accused jointly admissible in evidence against all others.' It seems reasonable to speculate that the use of these practices by the police, some of which appear to be of doubtful legality, must have influenced the committee when it made its recommendation to liberalise the law on homosexual offences, even though it did not extend this empathy to the women.

I am not arguing here that the police were or were not corrupt, only that as it was felt necessary to remove temptation from the sight of men, it might have been equally sensible to protect the police from future accusations of corruption by requiring them to obtain the evidence of an aggrieved citizen before prosecuting women for loitering or soliciting.[76] The possibility of police corruption is an appropriate concern considering the extent to which the integrity of the police has always been defended by politicians. For example, in 1953 the Home Secretary, David Maxwell Fyfe, signed the death warrant for Derek Bentley, who was subsequently hanged. Bentley was a mentally retarded young man who was accused of being the accomplice to the murder of a policeman. Christopher Craig, who shot the policeman, was 16 at the time and Derek Bentley was 19. Bentley was alleged to have shouted 'Let him have it'. Both were found guilty of murder and their appeals were dismissed by the Court of Criminal Appeal. Maxwell Fyfe wrote in his memoirs: 'In the Bentley case I had the additional question of the possible effects of my decision upon the police forces, by whom the murder of a police officer is justly regarded as the most heinous of crimes. The Home Secretary cannot – or should not – reach his terrible decision as if it were merely a matter of studying legal, medical, and personal files in his office'.[77]

It is clear from this remark that it was the desire to maintain police morale and public respect for their integrity that swayed his judgement. Because of the danger they faced, the police expected a level of support and protection from the establishment that was not always extended to other sections of the community. Therefore, the police, in so far as they were defined as a social category of citizens, were given protection, just as the social category of 'common prostitute' was made vulnerable.

PROTECTING WOMEN: THE SEXUAL OFFENCES ACT 1956, SECTION 32

The women parliamentarians came up against the same problem of gender imbalance as those of the Wolfenden Committee. For instance, Mrs Eirene White (Flint East) wondered 'whether if the House of Commons consisted of 602 women and 28 men, this Bill would have come before the House today'?[78] It seems unlikely, but a gender imbalance in the opposite direction would have created a different arena for the women to work in. All social arrangements would be expected to have been different, and what was or was not annoying or immoral would have emerged from an alternative social reality and a different order of moral values. This does not mean that the case against the Bill was not well and fairly argued by the men who opposed it, but does mean that on occasions, and when the debate touched upon personal experience, the women had great difficulty in establishing the validity of their case.

The Home Secretary had three main lines of defence against adverse criticism, all of which played upon the general dislike of prostitutes, their stigmatisation as a class, and the prejudice they confronted within society. The first
two arguments related to the protection of the 'innocent woman' who would
be shielded from harassment and wrongful arrest, and the third to the redemptive component of the cautioning system, which would provide a means for
rescuing prostitutes from degradation and depravity. In the face of a mainly
male parliament, the complaint by Mrs Lena Jeger that 'no cognisance was
taken of the responsibility of men for the social evil' made little headway.[79] It
was in this context that Butler had argued that men did not constitute a serious
nuisance and wondered 'of what offence is he to be guilty?' In a similar vein
Walter Edwards commented on the 'very sweet way' in which Mrs Jeger spoke
of prostitutes – it 'even leaves a lot of people with the impression that a prostitute is a very decent person' – but stated that what he liked about the Bill was
'the provision for imprisonment' because it would 'grip the girls at the right
time'. Lieutenant-Colonel Cordeaux followed this by arguing that 'the punishment for the man was incomparably greater than for the prostitute'[80] since
he placed his marriage, his employment and his social status in jeopardy.

As always, the use of the term 'common prostitute' came up against fierce
opposition, but the Home Secretary could see little cause for complaint. He
maintained that to substitute the words 'any person' or 'any woman' for
'common prostitute' was open to grave objection that would be aggravated by
the adoption of 'libidinous purpose', because in those circumstances *any
woman* waiting for a man for a libidinous purpose (without expecting financial
reward) might be committing an offence. He argued that in order to avoid
unfortunate mistakes the definition should be made quite clear. 'Furthermore,
so far as it is right and proper for the criminal law to deal with men who pester
women for immoral purposes, the necessary provision exists in section 32 of
the Sexual Offences Act 1956, as consolidated, which states: "It is an offence
for a man persistently to solicit or importune in a public place for immoral
purposes."' He assured the House that: 'It has been a matter that has concerned me from the start that we should not appear simply to be legislating
against women, but that we should keep the legislation against men in existence.'[81] This offence also carried severe penalties: with six months' imprisonment on summary conviction and two years' imprisonment on indictment.

The Home Secretary must have been well aware that this section was rarely
used and had not been properly tested in the courts in relation to the protection of women. He compounded this weakness by being unable to give any
figures for the number of convictions. Therefore, in reply to Elwyn Jones (West
Ham), he announced, 'I have not got any figures, and it is very hard to get
them. There have been much fewer prosecutions under this section dealing
with men than under the section dealing with women.' There were other
important differences between this offence and the proposed offence in the new
Bill. To 'importune' was a more serious transgression, which had been disregarded with reference to women. It required persistence, which would have to

be proved, and therefore the court would demand more reliable evidence. The possibility of any difficulty occurring as a result of the woman's defence claiming that the man had solicited her had been overcome by the inclusion of the passive act of loitering in the Street Offences Bill. Moreover, if a man was prosecuted, he was not already branded before he came to trial. As Anthony Greenwood commented, 'The Right Hon. Gentleman knows perfectly well that this procedure under section 32 of the Sexual Offences Act 1956 is normally only used in cases of men importuning men . . . I think I am right in telling the House that until recently, there were no examples of that having happened.'[82] Indeed the Home Secretary had no figures, and was again absent from the House when Mrs Jeger referred to his assurance that section 32 created equality as 'hypocritical' and 'absolutely farcical'.[83] The lack of statistics for this offence illustrates Professor Hart's observations on the creation of arbitrary police powers, as the Home Secretary had admitted that they were not available because they had not been separated out from other sexual offences and were therefore not known[84]. The glossing over of women's concerns was picked up by Mrs Eirene White (Flint East) who, like Chave Collisson before her, spoke of her personal experience of harassment by men in public places: 'All I can say is that any woman who lives in Central London knows perfectly well that one does not need, I trust, to look like a prostitute to be solicited by men . . . or for a man to come up and make some remark from which his intentions were quite as clear as the intentions of a prostitute.'[85] Eirene White was evidently making a point that was submerged in the family-orientated world of the 1950s and drawing the attention of the House to the fact that a large number of Wolfenden's ordinary (male) citizens presumed that any woman, respectable or otherwise, was sexually available to them.[86]

When Josephine Butler addressed a conference in 1870 on the 'Moral Reclaimability of Prostitutes' she made much the same point: 'It would have been easier for me, and more in my line, to read a paper before two or three hundred prostitutes on "the reclaimability of profligate men".' Prostitutes, she argued, were not hypocrites, they did not act a *double part*, 'going about doing vile things under cover of the darkness of night' then taking their place smilingly in the daytime and going to church on Sunday! The women themselves had spoken to her of their disgust: 'For young men there is more temptation; but, oh, it is shocking, disgusting, to see the crowds of married men, of middle-aged, or grey-haired fathers of families, who come to us.'[87] No wonder R. A. Butler neglected to quote his great-aunt!

RESOLUTION: *CROOK* V. *EDMONDSON* (1966)

In 1966, after the Bill had become law, section 32 of the Sexual Offences Act 1956 was tested in court, creating a notorious precedent. In the case of *Crook* v. *Edmondson* (1966),[88] a kerb-crawler called Fred Edmondson was arrested in Percy Street, London, for persistently soliciting known prostitutes for an immoral purpose. The case came before the court and was dismissed on the ground that there was no case to answer. The magistrate had considered it shocking that a man of unblemished character could run the risk of being brought before the courts and charged with soliciting on the basis of inconclusive evidence, which in this case was being seen speaking to a prostitute.

The Crown's appeal was heard in the Divisional Court before Lord Parker C.J., Winn L.J. and Sachs J. In his summing up, Winn L.J. clarified the issue:

> In the widest sense of the phrase we think that the conduct of the defendant was immoral, but having regard to the objects of the section in our view the immoral purpose must be one that is prohibited by law; e.g. unnatural acts which outrage decency, exploitation of women and girls for the purpose of prostitution, and procuration etc. It would seem that the legislature does not choose to enforce morals in every instance, but when some form of conduct goes beyond the bounds of toleration of a reasonable man, it is made illegal.[89]

This presumably meant that adultery did not go beyond the bounds of what a reasonable man found tolerable, which was reflected in the fact that it was not a crime. But in relation to the original purpose of the offence, which was for apprehending the bully or the prostitute's tout, there was little difference between section 32 and section 30 as both were initially intended to prevent exploitation. Winn L.J.'s reasoning was based partly upon the fact that section 32 attracted a greater penalty than 'soliciting for the purpose of prostitution' and that the woman involved in the case was a prostitute who was later charged under the Street Offences Act, so Edmondson's solicitations were presumed to be acceptable to her. This reasoning begged the question that whereas the 1959 Street Offences Act was used liberally, section 32 of the Sexual Offences Act 1956 was not, despite the complicity of the man who solicited the prostitute. Section 32, it was argued, ought to be used more cautiously because something more was needed in order to justify the penalty, and therefore the purpose had to be defined as 'immoral' *in law*.

Winn L.J.'s tangential reference to section 30 appears to have been unguarded, as although it ought to have been about the protection of women and girls against exploitation it was, as I have argued, more accurately about profiting from a woman's immorality, whereas procuration was rarely punished. The appeal against the verdict was dismissed, with Sachs J. concurring on the ground that the decision as to what constituted an 'immoral purpose' ought to be left to the jury. In the meantime women were left without any protection from public harassment by men, even when it was for the purpose of prostitution. 'The punter,' remarked Susan Edwards, 'happily for him, is beyond the law.'[90]

The vagueness of the application of section 32 to a variety of offences, including homosexual soliciting, men touting for customers on behalf of prostitutes, or the supposed protection of women from harassment in public places, became apparent during the judicial discussion of the *Crook* v.

Edmondson appeal. It underlines two points. First, the Victorian–Edwardian collection of sexual offences (CLA Acts, 1885, Vagrancy Act 1898, Incest Act 1908, CLA Acts 1912 and 1922) ought not to have been consolidated within one Act without being subjected to full parliamentary scrutiny, especially since the Act brought together many complex and contentious provisions that covered a wide range of offences, including incest, rape, homosexual offences as well as those relating to prostitution. And second, Butler must have known that section 32 was not enacted for the purpose of protecting women, but was merely the reinstatement into an overarching consolidated Act of a measure originally intended to deal with pimps.

When it came to kerb-crawling, which was the source of many complaints regarding public solicitation for immoral purposes, the government had been given no encouragement to pursue the issue through legislation, as the Wolfenden Committee had displayed its usual reticence when it came to male offences. The committee insisted that, although they appreciated the reality of the problem, 'the difficulties of proof would be considerable, and the possibility of a very damaging charge being levelled at an innocent motorist must also be borne in mind'.[91]

The application of the law to prevent procuration, brothel-keeping and 'living on the earnings of prostitution' presented a similarly confusing profile. Nott-Bower had testified to the Wolfenden Committee that the charge of procuration was rarely used, as only six men and five women had been found guilty in 1954 and four men and three women in 1955. For the same years there were 102 and 118 imprisonments for 'living on the earnings of prostitution' (which included four women in 1955). For brothel-keeping, 26 men and 43 women were imprisoned in 1954, and 37 men and 43 women in 1955.[92]

DEFINITIONS

Notwithstanding the old adage that statistics can be used to prove anything, this particular pattern of legislative application, presented by the preventative and offensive sides of the legislation, fits neatly into Steven Box's[93] analytical framework of 'radical reflectiveness' or 'artful' criminal definitions. He reasons that 'criminal law categories are artful, creative constructs designed to criminalize some victimising behaviours, usually those more frequently committed by the relatively powerless, and to exclude others, usually those frequently committed by the powerful against subordinates'. Box argues, however, that not all legislation fits this equation as individual laws may reflect the temporary victories of interest groups. 'Some laws are passed purely as symbolic victories which the dominant class grants to inferior interest groups, basically to keep them quiet; once passed, they need never be efficiently or systematically enforced.'[94] Many years earlier George Orwell[95] made much the same point when writing of the English respect for constitutionalism and legality and his belief in 'the law' as something incorruptible and unchanging.

'It is not', he observed, 'that anyone imagines the law to be just. Everyone knows that there is one law for the rich and another for the poor. But no one accepts the implications of this, everyone takes it for granted that the law, such as it is, will be respected, and feels a sense of outrage when it is not.' [96] The long years of campaigning for equality of treatment and protective legislation are made a mockery through the selective application of the law, as the above figures show.

THE MORAL RATIONALISATION OF THE
CAUTIONING PROCEDURE

R. A. Butler's remaining line of defence against accusations of injustice involved the adoption of a prostitutes' cautioning system, which was intended to protect the innocent woman from arrest and create an avenue for newly recruited prostitutes to exit from the trade. The novelty of this procedure, which was to be non-statutory, created a great deal of questioning and confusion. The Home Secretary made it quite clear that he did not want there to be any question of arrest for the purpose of cautioning or for it to be made a constituent part of the charge. He assured the House that the practice of informal cautioning would be adopted generally within the Metropolitan Police district, and it would be commended in other areas to chief constables over whom he did not have authority. The Home Secretary understood the implications of making it statutory, as a formal caution would have required the police to arrest a woman and take her to the police station even though they did not intend to bring a criminal charge. It would also prejudice the case if a woman was subsequently brought before the court and denied the charge.[97]

On the 22 April 1959, the Attorney-General, Sir Reginald Manningham-Buller, introduced the cautioning system enthusiastically to the House, as a redemptive measure: 'I should like to remind the House that the main object of the cautioning system as we see it is that it should operate as a system to rescue those about to embark on a a career of prostitution.'[98] It was to be 'a work of salvation', a 'kind of fender' that would help to prevent women from coming into the clutches of the criminal law. The Attorney-General explained that when a police officer saw a woman loitering or soliciting for the purpose of prostitution, who was not known to him as a common prostitute who had convictions, he would obtain the assistance of another police officer. They would then watch the woman together and if they were satisfied that she was loitering or soliciting for the purpose of prostitution she would be cautioned. The woman would then be asked if she was willing to have her name and address given to a moral welfare organisation or to return to the police station and speak to a policewoman who would put her in touch with a welfare officer. The Attorney-General insisted that it was essential for the caution to be administrative in character and not embodied in any statutory code or regulation.[99]

Of course, to have done so would have made it necessary to have a more formal set of procedures, which would have left the police open to valid criticism if they did not follow them conscientiously.

This was another area in which the government was following the recommendations of the Wolfenden Committee, but although the committee had discussed the possibilities of redemption it was, on balance, more impressed by the indications that the Scottish system had been successful in keeping the problem of soliciting under control, although there was far more emphasis on redemption in the official report than there had been in committee meetings. In practice, the reality was to be that women would be withdrawn from the streets through the creation of an identifiable group who would be registered as common prostitutes. After two cautions and a third sighting they would be prosecuted for the first time and after the third conviction committed to prison. The possibility of wrongful arrest was to be covered by giving a woman the right to appeal against a caution within 14 days; the police would then be obliged to provide evidence that she had been 'loitering or soliciting for the purpose of prostitution'. This procedure was to provide an official legal channel through which a woman could appeal *in camera* against an informal caution, which suggests that there was more to the caution than its 'informal' non-statutory redemptive purposes would imply.

Reginald Paget (Northampton) did not believe that a lonely and frightened girl, who was probably a foreign immigrant, would be willing to return to the police station with an officer in order to have a talk with a policewoman and be put in touch with a moral welfare worker or a middle-class member of a voluntary agency. He reasoned that once the women realised that they were not being arrested they would refuse to give their names and addresses and tell the police officer to 'buzz off', or worse still they might give the name and address of somebody else. He was scathing about the evidential safeguards provided by making the caution non-statutory: 'What hypocrisy! Does anyone really imagine that magistrates are so dumb that they do not know the procedure? Does anyone think there is a single magistrate who will not know that any girl brought before him has been through the cautioning procedure?'[100]

The irony of this process was drawn out by Winn L.J in his summing up in *Crook* v. *Edmondson* when he argued that the caution had been introduced in order to protect the 'innocent woman', whereas an 'innocent man' accused of soliciting did not have that protection. It seems unlikely that parliament would have proposed and passed a measure creating a stigmatised group of men whose names were to be recorded on a police register and whose behaviour was to be monitored across the country through the close surveillance of specially appointed plain-clothes police squads. On the other hand, if the two preliminary prostitutes' cautions were to be withdrawn without the reintroduction of 'persistence' or the need to prove 'annoyance', the prostitute's situation would not improve. Only the injustice of the labelling process that transformed them into 'common prostitutes' would be more apparent.

The non-statutory nature of the caution was to increase the arbitrary powers of the police still further by creating greater flexibility and a general uncertainty as to what the rules really were. The vagueness of the process resulted in new tactics being adopted by both sides, including not using the caution at all but arresting a woman in order to frighten her, arresting a woman two or three times in one night[101] and, once she had been registered, arresting her when she was not working. Prostitutes were to respond in a variety of ways, such as by giving the police false names and addresses, disguising their appearances and evolving into an increasingly mobile and peripatetic body of women.[102] In addition, the use of plain-clothed police officers created further possibilities for irregularity. But, perhaps more significantly, once a prostitute had been proceeded against for an offence of 'loitering or soliciting' the cautioning system became redundant.[103] The importance of this was that the women whom the Home Office wanted to clear from the streets were not the young and uninitiated, but those whom Butler had described as having taken up prostitution as a settled way of life.[104]

ENACTMENT

The Street Offences Bill became an Act on the 16 July 1959 and the wishes of David Maxwell Fyfe became a reality. In his autobiography he makes no reference to the Wolfenden Committee, the Bill or the Act.[105] They need never have happened; the twilight world of sex and sensuality were too abhorrent to be mentioned.[106] The bulldozing through of the 1959 Street Offences Act bears his stamp and reflects his reputation for inflexibility, but as the Bentley case shows he was more interested in preserving the existing system of authority than investigating the causes of social unrest. 'Why moulder in the valley', he concluded, 'when you can climb the hills?'[107]

Butler has a better reputation for innovative social reform, but as far as the Street Offences Act was concerned his contribution was inglorious and bumbling. He seems to have been anxious to be seen as principled, compassionate and caring, while he ushered in a very repressive measure of questionable justice. Consequently he extolled the redemptive virtues of the cautioning system and rationalised the repressive and discriminatory nature of the Street Offences Act as a partial and practical measure aimed at cleaning up the streets. In his closing speech he admitted that it had been 'an extremely hard tussle' and that in facing up to the conclusion reached he also had to face up to his own family tradition.[108] He assured the House that he had taken the very best advice and had been convinced that they were dealing no longer with the poor pushed out by the circumstances of a capitalist society to earn a living by prostitution, but with women of a very different type who were making considerable fortunes. The AMSH remained unconvinced of his integrity and he was obliged to resign from his position as vice-president of the society, but he consoled himself with the knowledge that in a very short period the Act had achieved exactly what it had set out to do and the streets had been cleared of prostitutes.[109] The AMSH concluded that the government victory was attributable solely to the use of the Whip.

In the mean time there had been very real doubts expressed about the Bill; the *New Statesman* suggested that 'society was planning to make its vice more discreet, probably more profitable and certainly more corrupt'.[110] Anthony Greenwood quoted a letter of Edmund Burke to Charles James Fox: 'People crushed by law have no hope but power. If laws are their enemies, they will be enemies of the law.'[111] Leslie Hale (Oldham West) protested, 'Never before in the history of this country has a grave criminal charge . . . carrying a loss of reputation and three months' imprisonment been put in terms so vague and so impossible to describe.'[112]

One of the main frustrations for the opposition was that the Bill had not been open to a free vote on the government side. This was referred to by the *News Chronicle* as 'the prostitution of Parliament',[113] suggesting that, with an general election impending, the appeal of 'family values' was being used to sway the electorate. This mode of proceeding created inbuilt inconsistency as the opposition declined to use the Whip, regarding the affair as a moral matter affecting the individual consciences of MPs. Voting after the second reading came to 235 ayes and 88 noes and after the third reading it was reduced to 131 ayes against 25 noes. On both occasions the vote was taken late at night, and according to the AMSH, many of the opposition members had left the House. The Bill had an equally stormy passage through the House of Lords with strong opposition, on identical grounds, from several notable peers, including Lord Balfour of Burleigh, Lord Denning, Baroness Wootton, Lord Pethick Lawrence and the Archbishop of Canterbury. A large number of amendments were put forward, all of which were rejected by the Lord Chancellor, Viscount Kilmuir (*né* Maxwell Fyfe).

Lord Brabazon of Tara complained:

> We have seen and admired the skill and persistence of the noble and learned Lord Chancellor in resisting every amendment that has been raised . . . I must say that it is very remarkable that there has emerged from another place a piece of legislation which is such a jewel that it cannot be altered in any way . . . I should rather like to hear whether the idea was that, if we amended it at all, it would have to go back to another place, and consequently there might be a risk of losing the Bill altogether . . . I do not think the noble and learned Viscount has ever appreciated how shocked many of us are by the provisions in the Bill. In many cases it seems to offend the basic principles of justice.[114]

Chave Collisson had continued to campaign throughout the process, having prepared more than sixty special briefs for MPs, attended and provided advice at standing committee meetings, interviewed peers and MPs and had a special meeting with Anthony Greenwood. All to no avail. The government had been totally inflexible over the issue and there was nothing more to be done.

Two points worth considering here emerged from the parliamentary debate. First, given the strength of the opposition to the Bill, it seems to have been a tactical mistake for the official opposition to have allowed a free vote, even though the legislation touched upon profound matters of individual freedom and justice. Second, Lord Brabazon of Tara was probably correct in his observation over the timing, as the passage of the Bill came perilously close to a general election. Significantly, Maxwell Fyfe says nothing in his autobiography about the Street Offences Bill, but he does give an accurate picture of the difficult time that the Tories had experienced during the 1950s when the Suez crisis had 'shaken the party to its foundations'.[115] However, the people of Britain were grateful to the politicians for a buoyant economy and were beguiled by the Macmillan slogan 'You've never had it so good.'[116] The election came on 8 October 1959 and 'cleaning up the streets', like most 'law and order' issues, had great popular appeal. The Conservative government was returned with a majority of a hundred.

The Act itself differed in a number of ways from the Wolfenden recommendations, making the overall impact still harsher. The courts were enabled to fine *and* imprison repeat offenders. Section 3 increased the penalties incurred by keepers of unlicensed refreshment houses (all-night cafés) for harbouring prostitutes. Section 4 increased the penalty for 'living on the earnings of prostitution' from two to seven years.

The Act made both the passive and the active acts of loitering or soliciting into criminal offences that only the registered 'female' prostitute could commit, making it impossible for her to step outside her own home without risking the possibility of arrest. That an arrest was not for 'being a prostitute' but that 'being a prostitute she had been observed loitering for a purpose' was a point carefully underlined in the Wolfenden Report. But even Butler made this error when he spoke of the police knowing what a woman was up to when they 'condemned her as a common prostitute' and brought her before the court. In the end the question as to whether the act of prostitution was immoral became almost immaterial because the determination to get rid of its outward manifestation was uncompromising. Nevertheless the issue of morality remained a central element of the discourse.

JUSTIFICATIONS

As I have noted previously, Wolfenden had argued that there should remain an area of private morality and immorality which was not the law's business. This argument was used to justify the liberalisation of the law on homosexuality and, conversely, to tighten up the law on prostitution so as to protect the public from the 'offensive spectacle' of prostitutes loitering and soliciting on the streets. At the same time it was argued that prostitution was an *evil* of which any society that claimed to be civilised would seek to rid itself. Thus the 'harm' done to the population at large through the visibility of soliciting women was weighed up against the 'possible' but 'less visible' harm that might be done to an increasing numbers of prostitutes through their exploitation by third parties and a closer organisation of the trade. This balancing argument could be sustained only by minimising the responsibility of men, which narrowed the debate (and therefore the pressure for legal intervention) to a simplified set of problems centred around the dichotomy between 'good' and 'bad' women; in other words, the limited objective of 'cleaning up the streets'.

Butler's reasoning was less subtle. He saw the issue as essentially a moral problem and used his allegiance to Josephine Butler and to the society founded to continue her work to support the credibility of the position that he was taking. In doing so he was forced to confront the dilemma of equality and the moral responsibility of the client, but he evaded this entanglement by falling back on the assurance of Nott-Bower, who convinced him that whereas the police knew and could trace the women they simply could not identify the men.[117] In these circumstances he chose expediency or what he called 'the art of the possible' and evaded the logical point, that if the law *was* about morals then men were equally at fault and prostitution itself ought to be made illegal, or at the least, men and women should be treated equally. In the course of the parliamentary debates he admitted that the purpose of the Bill was the limited purpose of cleaning up the streets, using this metaphor almost as frequently as Wolfenden, although the latter had the sense not to use it liberally in the official report. Thus at the heart of the legislation there was to be a dishonest formula that linked street soliciting with public order while the limited protection of women from exploitation through prostitution was linked with their immorality, as seen through the ubiquitous use of the term 'living on immoral earnings'.[118]

'How can sex (of all things) be obscene?' queried Joel Feinberg.[119] 'The question is not whether explicit depictions of sexual behaviour as such are in fact obscene, but rather, how could sex, a department of life so highly valued by almost all of us, *possibly* be obscene?'[120] Feinberg places a similar question mark over the suggestion that an erotic interest represented a 'human' or 'moral' weakness. In his commentary on the Wolfenden Report, he quotes the passage that seeks to diminish the offence of 'living on the earnings of prostitution', in which it is argued that it is not the prostitute as such who is exploited, but the whole complex of relationships between customer and client; that is, they were exploiting human weakness. 'I assume', wrote Feinberg, 'that both Lord Devlin and the authors of the Wolfenden Report considered sexual congress with prostitutes to express a 'human weakness' because they thought of it as something typically opposed to the customer's interest, his prudential judgement, and his conscience; the customer typically only succumbed because of the enticement and allure of the commercial exploiter'.[121] To illustrate his argument Feinberg cites the case of the *United States* v. *Ginzburg*, in which a five-year prison sentence was imposed for publishing obscene material. It was not, he suggested, the sin of obscenity that was being punished but 'pandering', or the sordid business of profiting from the erotic interests of customers.[122]

It seems to me that the same arguments apply to section 30 and section 32 of the Sexual Offences Act 1956. Many women would agree with the magistrate in the case of *Crook* v. *Edmondson*[123] that for a man to solicit a woman for sexual intercourse is not an immoral purpose, or at the least, that it is not the 'immorality' that bothers them. While a man who is solicited by a woman may be annoyed, a woman in the same situation often suffers aggravating circumstances, including anxiety and fear. These were aspects of a problem that the law-makers were reluctant to acknowledge during the debates that took place in the 1950s and (as we shall see) continued into the mid-1980s. It is significant that although the terms 'immoral earnings' and 'immoral purpose' are used liberally by judges and writers of official documents, they are used very sparingly in the legislation, since immorality is virtually indefinable and when it does come up it is left to the jury to decide.

The Wolfenden Committee endorsed Mill's principle of 'harm to others': 'The only purpose for which power can be rightfully exercised over any member of a civilised community against his will is to prevent harm to others.'[124] Some feminists[125] have adapted Mill's notion of harm and applied it to pornography and prostitution, claiming that both represent the abuse of men's economic power through the purchase and objectification of women's bodies. Andrea Dworkin, for example, addresses the male strategies for denial that were evident in both the Wolfenden Committee's discussions and the parliamentary debate, both of which avoided any serious appraisal of the role of men in the prostitution of women.[126] She demands that her reader confronts the reality of prostitution, which she considers to be 'intrinsically abusive' and to result from male dominance rather than from female nature. 'It is a political reality', she insists, 'that exists because one group of people has maintained power over another group of people.' She writes, rather crudely perhaps, but to the point, 'I want to say to you that you can't think about prostitution unless you think about the man who wants to fuck the prostitute. Who is he? What is he doing? What does he want? What does he need?'[127] These are difficult and infrequently addressed questions, although the new fashion for 'john schools' has given greater access to the customer and the accumulation of empirical evidence.[128] But in the context of rights, and on either side of the feminist controversy over whether there is or is not a 'human right' to be prostituted, it is worth noting that feminists are unanimous in pressing for legislative reform.[129] Which is where I stand.

Simon Lee considers the notion of 'harm' to be a necessary, but insufficient, condition for the construction of law. Quite reasonably he asks what is 'harm' and what do we mean by 'others'?[130] Once again, definition is the problem. 'Our language', writes Thomas Szasz, 'informs and even defines our perceptions.'[131] The notion of 'harm', 'significant harm' and 'identifiable harm' have been developed by feminists in order to redefine the impact of pornography, prostitution and the sexual objectification of women and children.

These perceptions focus upon the long-term repercussions of abusive treatment upon the individual woman or child, recognising the impact of inequity and power within society.[132]

Lee's writing is helpful in leading us towards a better understanding of the Hart–Devlin debate, especially as he seems to find it inconclusive. He argues that Hart's focus is on the individual whereas Devlin's focus was society. He likens the debate to Monet's 20 studies of Rouen Cathedral, which he painted in different lights and at different times of the day. All of them revealed something different about the timeless structure without conflicting with each other. I find this a helpful metaphor that could be applied to much analysis.

When Lord Denning retired he announced that nothing upset him more than a wrong decision but he had his trust in God to sustain him. 'If you have this trust, you don't have to worry, as you don't have the same responsibility.'[133] It would appear from this remark that God and Lord Denning were on the same footing, although it is comforting to realise that whereas both may be right, both may be wrong. That which we incorporate in law, whatever its provenance, is still worthy of periodic scrutiny in order to determine whether or not it reflects human prejudice and error.

NOTES

1. P.D. 5th Ser. Vol. 596, col. 463, 26 November 1958, quoted by Cyril Black (Wimbledon). Denning (of Whitchurch), Alfred Thompson Denning, Baron, 1899–1999; Magdalen College, Oxford; called to the Bar in 1923; King's Counsel (1938); judge of the High Court of Justice (1944); Lord Justice of Appeal (1948); Lord of Appeal in Ordinary (1957); Master of the Rolls (1962–82). In 1963 he conducted the enquiry into John Profumo's resignation as Secretary of State for War.
2. Josephine Butler (1871), 'The Constitution Violated: An Essay', Edmondson and Douglas, Edinburgh, p. 1.
3. F. J. Bellenger (Bassetlaw), Labour Secretary of State for War, October 1946–47.
4. P.D. 5th Ser. Vol. 596, col. 422, 26 November 1958.
5. Ibid., col. 423.
6. Ibid., cols. 451–2.
7. PD 5th Ser. Vol. 598, col. 1281, 29 January 1959.
8. Ibid., 1326.
9. See Kathleen Heasman (undated) 'Josephine Butler House: A History', typed and bound copy in WL.
10. PD 5th Ser. Vol. 598, cols. 1293, 1298, 1313, 29 January 1959.
11. PD. 5th Ser. Vol. 596, cols. 489–491, 26 November 1958.
12. PD 5th Ser. Vol. 598, col. 1267, 29 January 1959.
13. Ibid., col. 1297. Anthony Greenwood had looked at the Prison Commissioners' Report and found that during 1955, 235 women had been imprisoned for non-indictable offences related to prostitution, 128 had been in prison for previous convictions, 27 had been in prison twice for previous convictions, 16 had been in prison between 6 and 10 times, and 14 had been in prison between 11 and 20 times. In 1956 165 had been to prison for previous convictions, 89 had been in prison for previous convictions, 20 had been in prison twice for previous convictions, 15 had been in prison three times for previous convictions, 7 had been in prison four times for previous convictions, 13 had been to prison between 6 and 10 times for previous convictions, and 8 had been to prison between 11 and 20 times for previous convictions. In 1957 211 women had been to prison for previous convictions, 89 of these had served previous prison sentences, 18 had two previous prison sentences and 13 had three prison sentences.

14. The Criminal Law Revision Committee was set up on 2 February 1959 by the Home Secretary, R. A. Butler, 'to be a standing committee to examine such aspects of the criminal law of England and Wales as the Home Secretary may from time to time refer to the committee . . . to consider whether the law requires revision and to make recommendations'. On 8 July 1975, the then Home Secretary, the Rt Hon. Roy Jenkins, asked the committee to review, in consultation with the Policy Advisory Committee on Sexual Offences, the law relating to, and penalties for, sexual offences, including prostitution.

15. CLRC, 'Working Paper on Offences relating to Prostitution and allied Offences', December 1982, para. 2.19.

16. *Winter* v. *Woolfe* (1930), confirmed and extended by *Kelly* v. *Purvis* (1983), 1 All ER 525; 'it is not necessary to prove provision of normal sexual intercourse'. *Durose* v. *Wilson* (1907), 96 LT 645; *Donovan* v. *Gavin* (1965), 2 Q.B. 648, a block of flats in a building, each used by one woman only for purpose of prostitution may constitute the whole building a brothel (known offensively as a 'nest of prostitutes').

17. Gender disparity appears again when the possibility of a woman committing a similar crime is covered. Section 31 makes it an offence: 'for a woman for the purpose of gain to exercise control, direction or influence over a prostitute's movements in a way which shows she is aiding, abetting or compelling her prostitution'.

18. Joanna Phoenix (1999), *Making Sense of Prostitution*, Macmillan, London, p. 2.

19. This is also the message conveyed by organisations such as 'Women Hurt in Systems of Prostitution Engaged in Revolt' (WISPER), which states: 'We believe that the function of prostitution is to allow males unconditional sexual access to women and children limited solely by their ability to pay for this privilege.' Quoted by S. S. M. Edwards (1996), *Sex and Gender in the Legal Process*, Blackstone Press, Oxford, p. 165. For a study of the myths surrounding violence against prostitutes see Jody Miller and Martin D. Schwartz (1995), 'Rape Myths and Violence Against Street Prostitutes', *Deviant Behaviour: An Interdisciplinary Journal*, 16 (1): 1–23, Taylor and Francis. For a study of the grooming process through which a child or young woman is converted into a prostitute, see the work of Sara Swann in Barnardo's (1998) 'Whose Daughter Next: Children Abused Through Prostitution, Barnardo's, pp. 21–31.

20. In 1954 there were 122 men convicted for living on the earnings of prostitution and two women convicted under section 31 for 'exercising control, direction or influence over a prostitutes movements' for the purpose of gain (see below). Similarly, in 1955 there were 127 men and four women. This compares dramatically with the 11,518 and 11,878 convictions for street offences Cmnd. 247, 'Official Statistics', pp. 143–4.

21. *Donald Theodore Wilson* (1983), Cr. App. R. 247.

22. Lord Reid in *Shaw* v. *DPP* (1961), Cr. App. R., stated that 'living on' normally meant 'living on parasitically'. Later approved in the Court of Appeal in *Stewart* (1986), 83 Cr. App. R. 327 at p. 322.

23. *Donald Theodore Wilson* (1983).

24. *Farrugia* (1979) 69 Cr. App. R. 108, confirmed in *Stewart* (1986), 83 Cr. App. R. 327. For appeal against length of sentence see, *Dennis Dixon and Frank Dixon* (1994), 16 Cr. App. R (S). 779; *Christopher Sinclair Smith* (1995), 16 Cr. App. (S).

25. See CLRC (1982), paras. 2.2–9 and CLRC (1986) Cmnd. 9688, para. 2.6.

26. See Helena Kennedy (1992), *Eve Was Framed: Women and British Justice*, Vintage, London for commentary on the cases of Cynthia Payne and Jani Jones.

27. *Shaw*, pp. 113–14.

28. Obscene Publications Act, 1959 [7 & 8 Eliz. 2, c. 66.], s.1.

29. PD 5th Ser. Vol. 598, cols. 1346–56, 29 January 1959.

30. *Shaw*, at p. 129.

31. Ibid., p. 129.

32. Ibid., p. 129.

33. Ibid. Viscount Simonds, at pp. 143–4.

34. See Phoenix, *Making Sense of Prostitution*, passim; Tiggy May, Mark Edmunds and Michael Hough (1999), Street Business: 'The Links Between Sex and the Drug Market', *Police Research Series Paper* 118, Home Office Reducing Crime Unit, Clive House, Petty France, London, p. 12. This research team commented that 'both professionals and workers stated that the latter's chaotic lifestyle effectively excluded them from services offered in normal office hours', p. 12.

35. Anxiety over the spread of AIDS, coupled with the problem of accessing working

prostitutes, has stimulated the growth of outreach working, health clinics and drop-in centres for sex workers. See, for example, Helen Ward and Sophie Day, 'Health Care and Regulation: New Perspectives', in G. and A. Scambler (1997), *Rethinking Prostitution: Purchasing Sex in the 1990s*, Routledge, London, pp. 139–63. This is the story of the Praed Street Project, begun in 1986 at St Mary's Hospital, Paddington, London. Ward and Day write: 'Many women requested help and professional counselling with work and other problems . . . But there is a widespread lack of trust by women in prostitution of other professions. Social workers are feared most, but others, including doctors, health advisers and psychologists are also threatening. Women expect, and their fears are all too often confirmed, a prejudiced and unhelpful response.' See also Neil McKeganey and Marina Barnard (1996), *Sex Work on the Streets: Prostitutes and their Clients*, Open University Press, Buckingham, who comment: 'Prostitutes are known not to make much use of conventional services; furthermore, such services are usually health-based and cannot cater for the plethora of prostitutes' concerns' p. 100. In April 1982 the English Collective of Prostitutes initiated Legal Action for Women (LAW), in order to provide advice and support for prostitutes with legal problems and launched a national campaign encouraging women to plead 'not guilty' when they had been arrested while not working. See English Collective of Prostitutes (1997), 'Campaigning for Legal Change', in Scambler and Scambler, *Rethinking Prostitution*, pp. 86–7.

36. Paul Ferris, for example, comments that if this section were to be enforced, it ought logically to apply to the chemist who supplied condoms to the prostitute. Paul Ferris (1993), *Sex and the British: A Twentieth Century History*, Michael Joseph, London.

37. See S. Petrow (1994), *Policing Morals: The Metropolitan Police and the Home Office, 1870–1914*, Clarendon Press, Oxford, for an analysis of the Vagrancy Act 1898, pp. 161–3.

38. See E. J. Bristow (1977), *Vice and Vigilance*, Gill and Macmillan, Dublin, pp. 168–71.

39. P.D. 5th Ser. Vol. 604. col. 542, 22 April 1959.

40. Ibid., col. 541.

41. Cmnd. 247, para. 61. Full text: 'Unless a deliberate attempt is to be made by society, acting through the agency of the law, to equate the sphere of crime with that of sin, there must remain a realm of private morality and immorality which is, in brief and crude terms, not the law's business.'

42. Patric Devlin (1965), *The Enforcement of Morals*, Oxford University Press, Oxford.

43. Ibid., p. 12.

44. Ibid. See, for example, the exchanges between the Wolfenden Committee and the NCW. PRO. HO. 345/13/27, pp. 21 and 23. Quoted in previous chapter.

45. Devlin, *The Enforcement of Morals*.

46. Ibid., p. 12.

47. *The Times*, 11 May 65.

48. H. L. A. Hart (1968), *Law, Liberty and Morality*, Oxford University Press, Oxford, p. 4.

49. Simon Lee (1986), *Law and Morals: Warnock, Gillick and Beyond*, Oxford University Press, Oxford, p. 27.

50. One exception to this rule can be found in the work of Ellice Hopkins, the Victorian social purity worker who founded the White Cross League in order to promote higher moral standards for men. See Bristow, *Vice and Vigilance*, p. 138.

51. The efficacy of such homes was challenged as early as 1917, in the *Shield*, 'Is Rescue Work a Failure? Some Opinions', pp. 176–5, June 1917. Some modern historians have been very critical of rescue work – see, for example, P. Bartley (2000), *Prostitution Prevention and Reform in England, 1860–1914*, Routledge, London, and L. Mahood (1990), *The Magdalenes: Prostitution in the Nineteenth Century*, Routledge, London. On the other hand, members of the Salvation Army and others who devoted their lives to the care of prostitutes and homeless girls would probably have viewed these efforts in a more positive light, if only because there was no alternative except the workhouse when rescue homes were at their most prolific.

52. Hart, *Law, Liberty and Morality*, p. 6.

53. Ibid., p. 10. The House of Lords confirmed the existence of an the offence of conspiring to corrupt public morals, which J. A. G. Griffith (1985), has described as an 'invention' in *The Politics of the Judiciary*, Fontana Press, Cornwall, p. 152. The charge of 'conspiracy to corrupt public morals' was used in the case of *Knuller* v. *D.P.P.* (1973) AC. 435. In this instance the House of Lords upheld the conviction of a man who had agreed to insert advertisements in a magazine for the purpose of facilitating homosexual acts between consenting

adults. Lord Reid maintained that there was a difference between exempting certain conduct from criminal penalties and making it lawful in the full sense. See P. Rook and D. Ward, *Sexual Offences*, Criminal Law Library 13, Sweet & Maxwell, London. This case demonstrates the way in which the law relating to prostitution has been widened so as to encompass behaviour that has been considered immoral. Although Lord Reid dissented in the case of *Shaw* he upheld the conviction in the case of *Kunller*, stating, 'on reconsideration I still think that the decision was wrong . . . But I think that however wrong or anomalous the decision may be it must stand and apply to cases reasonably analogous unless or until it is altered by Parliament'. Lord Diplock found himself in a similar position. See Griffith, *The Politics of the Judiciary*, p. 189.

54. See the cases that I have already cited including *Shaw*, *de Munck*, *Winter* v. *Woolfe*. For *Crook* v. *Edmondson* see below. The CLRC commented that, 'in some instances judicial decisions have given a wider meaning to the statutory language and in others a narrower one than the words bear in ordinary English usage'. CLRC (1982), para. 1.5.

55. Hart in *Law, Liberty and Morality*, noted that in California the penal code did not make prostitution a crime, yet persons had been convicted in Los Angeles for many years under a local ordinance for 'resorting' solely on proof that they had used a room for fornication. Also, in many states the statistics for sex crimes were only broken down into 'Rape' and 'Other Sexual Offences' (p. 27).

56. Ibid., p. 27.

57. Cmd. 3231, para. 66.

58. *The Times*, 19 December 1958.

59. P.D. 5th Ser. Vol. 598, col. 1277, 29 January 1959.

60. *Morning Post*, 1 February 1858, 'Sin in the City'.

61. Emsley comments that 'the power of the police in the streets, and their use of this power, probably contributed to the belief amongst many members of the working class that there was one law for the rich and another for the poor'. C. Emsley (1991), *The English Police: A Political and Social History*, Harvester Wheatsheaf, New York.

62. J. Butler (1879), '"Government By Police". An Essay: Respectfully Dedicated to The Town Councillors of the United Kingdom', printer unknown, p. 5.

63. Quoted by Anthony Greenwood MP. PD. 5th Ser. Vol. 598, col. 1294.

64. David A. Mathieson and Antony J. Walker, Social Enquiry Reports No. 7, *The Royal Commission on the Metropolitan Police: The Truth About the Enquiry*, Police and Public Vigilance Society, possibly 1910.

65. See also the work of Petrow, passim.

66. See P.D. 5th Ser. Vol. 596, col. 375, 26 November 1958.

67. *News of the World*, 20 November 1955.

68. PRO. HO. 345/2, 22 November 1955.

69. *The Times*, 18 November 1955.

70. Ibid.

71. C. H. Rolph (1974), *Living Twice: An Autobiography*, Victor Gollancz, London, p. 269.

72. Cmnd. 247, para. 271. J. Wolfenden (1976), *Turning Points. The Memoirs of Lord Wolfenden*, The Bodley Head, London, p. 130.

73. P. Higgins (1996), *Heterosexual Dictatorship: Male Homosexuality in Post-War Britain*, Fourth Estate, London, p. 10.

74. See S. Jeffery-Poulter, *Peers, Queers and Commons: The Struggle for Gay Law Reform from 1950 to the Present Day*, Routledge, London, pp. 59–61; Higgins, *Heterosexual Dictatorship*, pp. 45–9 on policing public lavatories, pp. 113–14 on corrupt police practices F. Mort (1987), *Dangerous Sexualities: Medico-moral Politics in England since 1830*, Routledge and Kegan Paul, London, pp. 100–4.

75. H. Montgomery Hyde (1970), *The Other Love: An Historical and Contemporary Survey of Homosexuality in Britain*, Heinemann, London, p. 215. Hyde supported the Wolfenden recommendations on homosexual law reform.

76. The ECP have been assiduous in their constant accusations of corrupt and uncaring police practices. See, for example, *Some Mother's Daughter: The Hidden Movement of Prostitute Women Against Violence* (1999), Crossroads Books, London, pp. 45–7.

77. David Maxwell Fyfe (1964), *Political Adventure: The Memoirs of the Earl of Kilmuir*, Weidenfeld and Nicolson, London, pp. 106–210. Derek Bentley's conviction was thrown out by the Court of Appeal on 31 July 1998.

78. P.D. 5th Ser. Vol.598. col. 1337, 29 January 1959.

79. Ibid. Lena Jeger, col. 1319.
80. Comment by R. A. Butler, P.D. 5th Ser. Vol. 598, col. 1284. Comment by Edwards, P.D. 5th Ser. Vol. 604, col. 503, L. C. Cordeaux, col. 534.
81. Ibid., col. 1283.
82. Ibid., cols. 1295–96.
83. Ibid., col.1325.
84. Ibid.
85. Ibid., col. 1334.
86. A considerable amount of second-wave feminist literature, especially on the subject of rape, covers this point. One of the best-known books is Susan Brownmiller (1997), *Against Our Will*, Martin Secker and Warburg, London. More recent work includes Sue Lees (1997), *Ruling Passions*, Open University Press, Buckingham. On prostitution with reference to male sex tourism, see Julia O'Connell Davidson (1998), *Prostitution, Power and Freedom*, Polity Press, Cambridge.
87. Josephine Butler (1870), A Paper on 'The Moral Reclaimability of Prostitutes', read by Mrs Butler at 'A Conference of Delegates from Associations and Committees formed in Various Towns for Promoting the Repeal of the Contagious Diseases Acts', held at the Freemason's Tavern, 5 May 1870 (Beverley Grey collection). The ECP made a similar point, when lambasting feminists for claiming that prostitution encouraged men to believe that all women were sexually available, while 'conveniently forgetting that men already thought that'. See G. and A. Scambler, *Rethinking Prostitution*, p. 83.
88. *Crook* v. *Edmondson* (1966), 2 Q.B. 81.
89. Ibid.
90. S. S. M. Edwards (1984), *Women on Trial*, Manchester University Press, Manchester. Edwards discusses *Crook* v. *Edmondson* in the context of pre-kerb-crawling legislation as well as a number of other examples of anomalous case law.
91. Cmnd. 247, para. 276.
92. Ibid., p. 143–7.
93. Steven Box (1989), *Power, Crime and Mystification*, Routledge, London.
94. Ibid., pp. 7–8.
95. George Orwell (1953), *England, Your England*, Martin Secker & Warburg, London.
96. Ibid., p. 201.
97. P.D. 5th Ser. Vol. 598, cols.1273–75, 29 January 1959.
98. P.D. 5th Ser. Vol. 604, col, 420, 22 April 1959, 604.
99. For the final wording see, Home Office Circular No. 108/59.
100. P.D. 5th Ser. Vol. 604, col. 416, 22 April 1959.
101. Catherine Benson and Roger Matthews, 'Police and Prostitution' in Ronald Weitzer (ed.), *Sex For Sale*, Routledge, New York, London (2000), p. 249.
102. Interview with Ron Holmes, Area 1, Clubs and Vice, Charing Cross Police Station, Agar Street, London, 1995.
103. Edwards, 'The Legal Regulation of Prostitution: a Human Rights Issue', in A. and G. Scambler (eds), *Rethinking Prostitution*.
104. P.D. 5th Ser. Vol. 598, col. 1275, 29 January 1959.
105. On the other hand his involvement in the Nuremberg Trials was extensively covered.
106. After Maxwell Fyfe moved to the House of Lords he continued to fight against any relaxation of the law on homosexuality. See Richard Davenport-Hines (1990), *Sex, Death and Punishment: Attitudes to Sex and Sexuality in Britain Since the Renaissance*, Collins, London, p. 304; Jeffery-Poulter, *Peers, Queers and Commons*, pp. 54, 70; A. Grey, *Quest for Justice: Towards Homosexual Emancipation*, Sinclair-Stevenson, London, pp. 94–5, 105.
107. Maxwell Fyfe, *Political Adventure*, p. 328.
108. P.D. 5th Ser. Vol. 604, cols. 550–54, 22 April 1959.
109. R. A. Butler, *The Art of the Possible*, Hamish Hamilton, London, p. 204.
110. The *New Statesman:* quoted in the House by Anthony Greenwood, P.D. 5th Ser. Vol. 604, col. 534, 22 April 1959.
111. P.D. 5th Ser. Vol. 604, col. 533, 22 April 1959.
112. P.D. 5th Ser. Vol. 604, col. 488, 22 April 1959.
113. PD. 5th Ser. Vol. 598, col. 1289, 29 January 1959. Quoted by Antony Greenwood.
114. Quoted by the AMSH in its account of the proceedings, 'The Street Offences Act 1959'.
115. Maxwell Fyfe, *Political Adventure*, p. 288.
116. Ibid., p. 311.

117. R. A. Butler, *The Art of the Possible: The Memories of Lord Butler, K.G, C.H.*, Hamish Hamilton, London, p. 204.
118. Section 30 of the SOA 1956.
119. Joel Feinberg (1985), *Offences to Others: The Moral Limits of the Criminal Law, Vol. Two*, Oxford University Press, Oxford, p. 138.
120. Ibid.
121. Joel Feinberg (1988), *Harmless Wrongdoing: The Moral Limits of the Criminal Law, Vol. Four*, Oxford University Press, Oxford, pp. 187–9.
122. Ibid., pp. 187–8.
123. *Crook* v. *Edmondson* (1966)
124. John Stuart Mill (1975) [1859], *On Liberty and Other Essays*, Oxford University Press, Oxford.
125. Andrea Dworkin (1997), *Life and Death: Unapologetic Writings on the Continuing War Against Women*, Virago, London; Eveline Giobbe (1990) in Leidholdt, Dorchen, and Janice G. Raymond (eds), *The Sexual Liberals and The Attack on Feminism*, Pergamon Press, New York; Catherine Itzin (ed.) (1992), *Pornography, Women, Violence and Civil Liberties*, Oxford University Press, Oxford; K. Barry (1995), *The Prostitution of Sexuality*, New York University Press, New York; S. Jeffreys (1997), *The Idea of Prostitution*, Spinifex, Melbourne.
126. Dworkin, *Life and Death*.
127. Ibid., p. 147.
128. The 'john school' began in San Francisco. It provided a programme of education for first-time offenders, which could be chosen as an alternative to other penalties. See Martin Monto (2000), 'Why Men Seek out Prostitutes' in Ronald Weitzer (ed.), *Sex for Sale, Prostitution, Pornography and the Sex Industry*, Routledge, London, Ch. 5. The idea has been copied by members of the Leeds Metropolitan University, Research Centre on Violence, 'Kerb-crawlers Rehabilitation Scheme' in cooperation with West Yorkshire Police. The schemes in both San Francisco and Leeds are defunct, due to a lack of funding and support. These schemes have fuelled feminist controversy.
129. Laurie Shrage (1994), *Moral Dilemmas of Feminism: Prostitution, Adultery and Abortion*, Routledge, New York, p. 82.
130. Lee, *Law and Morals*, p. 22.
131. T. Szasz (1983) in Richard E. Vatz and Lee S. Weinberg (eds), *Thomas Szasz, Primary Values and Major Contentions*, Prometheus Books, Amherst, NY, p. 131.
132. See, for example, Liz Kelly (1985), 'Feminist', *Trouble and Strife*, 7, Summer; Maureen O' Hara (1991), 'Making Feminist Law?' *Trouble and Strife*, 21, Summer; Itzin, *Pornography*, pp. 557–76; Barry, *The Prostitution of Sexuality*, pp. 70–1; S. S. M. Edwards, (1996), 'Significant Harm' in *Sex and Gender in the Legal Process*, Blackstone Press, London, pp. 297–303.
133. Denning (1982), retirement speech, quoted in *Chambers Dictionary of Quotations*, Chambers, Edinburgh.

PART IV

Change and Continuity: The Consequences of Legal Reform

CHAPTER ELEVEN

Legal Reform

The law is not to be compared to a venerable antique, to be taken down, dusted, admired, and put back on the shelf; rather it is like an old but still vigorous tree – firmly rooted in history, but still putting out new shoots, taking new grafts, and from time to time dropping dead wood. That process has been going on, is going on now, and will continue. (The Earl of Kilmuir, David Maxwell Fyfe,1957)[1]

Not surprisingly, the legitimacy of the new Act was rejected by the women involved in prostitution, who preferred to see it as a challenge to their ingenuity. Thus after a satisfactory start from the government's point of view, the problem of a closer organisation of the trade by middlemen began to be realised.[2] The result was an increase in less visible problems that were more difficult for the police and social workers to deal with, including single-girl flats and brothels masquerading as clubs. These developments, it was presumed, led to an overall increase in prostitution and a general lowering of sexual morality, as prostitution became increasingly attractive to a middle-class and 'respectable' clientele who had previously felt inhibited about picking up women on the streets. There was also an expression of concern for the safety and welfare of young women who had developed a variety of strategies for avoiding arrest and consequently could no longer be approached by the voluntary care agencies. In addition there was a perception that the non-statutory 'cautioning system' was being abused by the police and was failing miserably as a redemptive mechanism. These anxieties were shared by some officials who moved in government circles, as in the course of time, two further departmental enquiries took place and five parliamentary bills were introduced in an effort to amend the legislation.

But to begin with I return briefly to mid-twentieth-century social policy and to the social setting within which the legislation evolved. The contrast in attitudes towards women in society accepted by politicians such as Beveridge and those of the latter part of the century places the developments of the 1960s–1980s into more conspicuous relief. I also look at a number of research projects that, although available, failed to influence the Wolfenden Committee findings.

SEX AND SENSIBILITY

The Beveridge Report

During the 1950s voices within the establishment became concerned by the loss of certainties[3] that governed the outlook of men such as Sir William Beveridge, whose ground-breaking report, *Social Insurance and Allied Services*, was published in 1942.[4] He argued that marriage gave women a new economic status that reduced their claim to insurance benefits. He declared that 'during marriage most women will not be gainfully occupied' and that 'the attitude of the housewife to gainful employment outside the home is not and should not be the same as that of the single women. She has other duties.' Women were expected to marry and raise a family, and their economic dependence upon their husbands was seen as 'natural' and 'normal'. Consequently, the Anomalies Act of 1931[5] was introduced in order to deal with what Beveridge described as the 'undoubted scandal' of married women claiming unemployment benefit when they were in no real sense in search of employment.[6]

This economic arrangement was probably acceptable for couples who rejoiced in stable loving marriages, but as the decades progressed the upheavals of the two world wars were to accentuate the drawbacks of the nuclear family,[7] within which the weaker members were economically dependent upon the earning power of the male breadwinner and the coercive powers of the husband were protected through a policy of 'non-interference'. Official support for the nuclear family was an ideological stance that was strengthened by the findings of the Royal Commission on Population, which reported in 1949. Among its conclusions was that the opening up of careers for women had brought money-earning into conflict with motherhood and weakened the traditional dominance of the husband. Recommendations focused upon making motherhood more attractive by providing larger family allowances, nursery schools and children's playgrounds.[8] This official endorsement of the notion that women ought to be contented with a life of economic dependency, regardless of the success or failure of their marriage, reflected an acceptance of gender-biased attitudes upheld by the Church and many politicians. These were manifested through social policy objectives concerning education, employment, marriage and divorce, property rights and the expectations of women's role in caring for the wider family.[9] In the decades to come, as sexual mores and attitudes towards women evolved, these viewpoints would come under severe pressure for change.

Mass-Observation, Little Kinsey and post-war adjustment

During the Second World War the research organisation known as Mass-Observation conducted surveys into sexual behaviour. At the time there was concern over the spread of venereal disease and over the fall in the national birth rate. Liz Stanley[10] explains that, 'By the end of the war, many people who worked in or headed voluntary or statutory organisations concerned with marriage, child birth, and birth control within and outside marriage, were increasingly aware that the war had brought with it major changes to sexual attitudes and behaviour, with attendant effects on the national birth rate.'[11] This statement ought not to be accepted without some reservations as the birth rate had been declining steadily since the 1870s, beginning with the middle classes,[12] which suggested that long-term factors such as a desire for economic improvement had influenced people's choices.

One of the indicators of change was the popularity of Marie Stopes' best-selling book *Married Love*,[13] first published in 1918, which had encouraged women to expect and demand sexual enjoyment within marriage. Stopes was at the centre of the controversy over the movement that fought to make birth control available to married women. The easy availability of contraception, alongside 'entertainments of a suggestive character, dubious advertisements, pornographic literature, drugs, alcohol and "aphrodisiacs"' were cited by Wolfenden as 'evils' that encouraged prostitution.[14] Hardly the sort of comment that one would expect from a man who eschewed moralising.

In 1949 Mass-Observation carried out a survey of sexual habits and attitudes that became known as 'Little Kinsey'. It introduced random sampling and computerised methods of quantitative data analysis. The survey seems to have been very much ahead of its time and of a completely different genre from the personalised comments of Rowntree and Lavers. The opinions of ordinary people revealed a fairly conservative picture, which conforms with the comment made by the *Daily Express* that the majority of British citizens never came into contact with either homosexuality or prostitution. The views of interviewees on the practice were very traditional and often judgmental in character.[15] 'Vice, Vice!' sang the music-hall comedian. 'They don't know what vice is here. That's what's the matter with Churchtown.'[16]

Worktown, Seatown and Churchtown were the pseudonyms for a number of northern towns, including Bolton and Blackpool, where the research was carried out. The overall impression given by the interviewees was that of fairly close-knit communities that had settled down to a similar way of life and set of moral values to those that had applied before the war, except that society was more open and honest about sexual matters. People behaved more freely when on annual holiday, but the young women were still careful to emphasise that they were not flighty like the London girls. Although the upheavals caused by war had been the cause of a substantial rise in illegitimacy and divorce, Mass-Observation's National Panel concluded that the post-war developments should also be seen as part of a historical trend rather than a drop in moral standards. Women had been socialised into monogamous fidelity, and most of them preferred to wait for the return of the man they loved rather than risk the stigma attached to infidelity.[17] Sex had not been the defining issue; it was the experience of work and of some degree of financial independence that had the greatest impact upon women's lives and their changing attitudes to domestic confinement.[18]

John Costello[19] painted a more racy picture of female sexual liberation, but argued that many women chose in the end to return to domestic drudgery after the war had finished because they were simply exhausted and did not relish the double burden of work and home. Not surprisingly, the jobs into which they had been conscripted were often frustrating and unpleasant, some-times dangerous and invariably lower in pay and status than the men's.[20] These were the women who mothered the post-war 'baby boom', children who were raised in the increasing affluence of the 1950s and enjoyed a level of economic power that had been denied to previous generations. 'It was teenage spending which fuelled the phenomenon of "Rock 'n' Roll", whose ostentatious eroti-cism ensured its wide appeal amongst a sexually mature and rebellious younger generation and provided the emotional context for their dating, courtship and generally permissive lifestyle.'[21] Although for many women eco-nomic gains were given up in the retreat to post-war domesticity, the seeds of sexual revolution had already been sown and were to germinate and flower two decades later in the movement for women's liberation. It seems that although attitudes towards sexuality and family life were changing and that the war had taken its toll, the majority of people outside the big city were still fairly conservative.

These were the sorts of issues that troubled Maxwell Fyfe during the post-war period and were subsequently recorded in his memoirs. But although he had nothing to say about his role in the appointment of the Wolfenden Committee, he did mention his concern over marriage and divorce. 'We were sorely troubled by the serious increase in the number of broken marriages after the war, with their inevitable damage to domestic life, and repercussions in juvenile delinquency.'[22] The Royal Commission on Marriage and Divorce published its findings in 1955 and recommended that the courts should ensure the welfare of the children whose lives were devastated by their parents' failed marriages. Maxwell Fyfe recalled that he was subsequently concerned with ten Acts of Parliament dealing directly or indirectly with these problems and with revision of the law of illegitimacy. His concern for the preservation of the family swept him up in social policy changes driven by circumstances that he could not restrain. His career came to an abrupt end in 1962 during 'the night of the long knives' when the ailing Prime Minister, Harold Macmillan, dis-missed many of his Cabinet. As Macmillan was to say in response to a jour-nalist's question on what prompted his actions, 'events, dear boy, events'. Maxwell Fyfe was very conservative in his outlook, with set ideas and class interests to defend; he was in power for a long time and, as with Beveridge, the ideologies that he espoused influenced social policy.

THE FLIPSIDE

When Alfred Kinsey visited Britain during the 1950s he recorded a very different set of impressions after visiting Piccadilly Circus on a Saturday night. He commented: 'I have never seen so much nor such aggressive behaviour anywhere else.' He estimated that he had seen at least a thousand prostitutes (with both males and females accosting) between 8 p.m. and 3 a.m. He observed 'trim and neat' girls in Piccadilly and 'worn out old hags' in Soho. By two and three in the morning the invitations had become sexually blatant. Consequently he concluded that prostitution was alive and well in Britain and that America had inherited many of its sexual attitudes from its English forebears.[23] In Kinsey's terms Britain was a sexually repressed and prurient society. In particular he had been distressed to see the pitiful state and harsh treatment of imprisoned homosexuals, finding that fully 30 per cent of the inmates of the institutions he visited were imprisoned for sexual offences. His two world-famous books on sexual behaviour, which were based upon his research work in America, were influential in breaking down inhibitions and challenging prejudice.[24]

It would appear from the evidence available that although sexual attitudes had been moving gradually in a more liberal direction from the First World War onwards, prostitution was not, at the time of enactment of the 1959 Act, a generalised national problem. London seems to have been a special case. The Street Offences Act 1959 was therefore used to suppress a localised problem that had been amplified out of all proportion by the media. It was a sledgehammer to crack a nut. But, unfortunately, it was also instrumental in creating a much larger national dilemma.

ACADEMIC RESEARCH INTENDED TO INFLUENCE POLICY

The Cambridge Report on Sexual Offences, 1957

In 1950 the Cambridge Department of Criminal Science initiated an inquiry into sexual offences under the direction of Leon Radzinowicz. Its final report was published in 1957, the same year as Wolfenden's.[25] This research paralleled the work of the departmental committee and was in progress when the government consolidated sexual offences in 1956. The Sexual Offences Act was reviewed in the Cambridge Department's final report. Accordingly, acknowledgement and thanks were extended to the Home Office and the Metropolitan Police (including Philip Allen and Sir John Nott-Bower) for their cooperation, with the qualification that the opinions expressed in the report did not necessarily represent those of the Home Office or any other authority.

The Cambridge study was carried out in 14 districts, which included rural agricultural locations, as well as industrial and urban areas. The main section of the report centred upon 2,000 cases of conviction. Details of age, occupation, marital conditions and previous convictions were investigated in order to provide information that had formerly been lacking. In his preface Radzinowicz commented on the public awakening of interest in sexual delinquency, an area of law he considered to have been neglected, but regretted the current concentration on homosexual offences. He explained that: 'The aim of the Cambridge enquiry has been to provide facts which have hitherto been difficult to come by, and to correlate them so as to throw light on the many facets of sexual misconduct which seem to have escaped notice or which could not be fully appreciated through lack of adequate data.'[26] It seems that the Cambridge Department of Criminal Science was attempting to produce a broadly based scientific investigation of a specific area of law that the government appeared to consider unnecessary or, at least, failed to take into consideration.

Radzinowicz discovered that statistical analysis revealed a disturbing picture of 'a very substantial increase in every form of sexual misconduct reported to the police', but he stressed the difficulty of using police statistics as a basis for extrapolating the facts. 'The very methods adopted by the police authorities in recording and classifying crimes that come to their knowledge may have the effect of increasing or decreasing the final figures as they appear in the annual criminal return.' He concluded that changes in public attitudes towards sexual crime had a direct influence upon the number of crimes reported to the authorities; also that there was an enormous 'dark figure' of criminal offences that never came to light and could not be substantiated. In making these comments Radzinowicz highlighted some of the deficiencies of the departmental committee. The Wolfenden Report had emphasised the fact that official statistics were an unreliable reflection of the number of actual offences committed, but failed to recognise the general increase in the prosecution of sexual offences, either as a reflection of police practice or as an evolving social trend. Instead the government chose to react to political pressures emanating from public and private opinion fuelled by the media.

This deficiency becomes more apparent when the conclusions of Radzinowicz's study are examined. Under the heading 'Proposals for Amendment of the Existing Law', the report warns against 'over-astuteness in interpreting the law so as to impose criminal sanctions for sexual acts, the immorality or even impropriety of which may be the subject of widely divergent opinions'.[27] No opinion was expressed in the report regarding street offences, partly because the departmental committee was already reviewing the area and possibly because it was not viewed as a 'sexual' offence. Section 32 of the Sexual Offences Act 1956, respecting 'a man importuning for immoral purposes', was only covered in a very limited form. The shortcomings of the law that the Cambridge Department chose to highlight were: indecency with girls and boys under 16 years of age; the age of consent; the defence of reasonable cause to believe that a girl was over 16 in relation to sexual intercourse or indecent assault; indecent exposure; homosexual offences and maximum punishments. The Cambridge Report suggested that society had a problem not only with public demonstrations of sexual availability but also with offences committed by men against young women and children, in that these were hidden offences that were more difficult to detect and were not being adequately dealt with. The disappearance and abuse of children were points that had been emphasised by a number of the witnesses who appeared before the Wolfenden Committee (for example the headmistresses, Miss Brown and Mrs Jackson, testified that girls absconded from school and disappeared, often travelling on lorries for up to twelve months). However, this testimony, which came mostly from women, was treated with some complacency.

The Association of Moral and Social Hygiene / Josephine Butler Society: history and response to the Cambridge Report

The Draft Sexual Offences (Amendment) Bill 1958, and the Children and Young Persons Committee

The AMSH studied the Cambridge Report and prepared a draft Sexual Offences Amendment Bill addressing offences against children. The Bill was intended to repeal the law that provided a 'reasonable cause for belief' for men under the age of 24 (with no previous convictions), that a girl was over the age of 16 when he had illegal intercourse with her.[28] The Bill also covered the situation where the child was persuaded to become the dominant partner. The AMSH sought the cooperation of the Law Society and considered the possibility of asking an MP to introducing a Private Members Bill.[29] Nothing seems to have come from this exercise, probably because the society was overtaken by the more troubling event of the enactment of the Street Offences Act 1959. [30]

The relevance of the Cambridge Report to the legislation under consideration is that it highlighted graver and more complex social issues around the area of sexual offences, which were disregarded by the government in favour of consolidating previous legislation. Despite cooperating the Home Office did not await publication before acting and the report was too late to influence policy. The Wolfenden Committee was given evidence of deeper problems, but it did not see the wider picture as part of its remit. As a result of reacting to the more visible provocation of street soliciting, the government lost the opportunity for initiating a comprehensive review of the whole area of law and for creating legislative balance.

Through the latter part of the 1950s and into the 1960s, the AMSH experienced financial problems and internal disagreements and the *Shield* remained unpublished for a couple of years.[31] The members established an uneasy peace and the society's image was updated by renaming it the Josephine Butler Society (JBS) in 1962.[32] The Josephine Butler Educational Trust (JBET) was established in 1966 in order to raise funds to support or conduct research projects into prostitution.[33]

In 1960 the AMSH considered the Report of the Committee on Children and Young Persons (Ingleby Committee).[34] This Committee was referred to in the Wolfenden Report[35] with reference to the concern expressed by some witnesses who had recommended that the age at which a young person might be brought under compulsory supervision should be raised to 21. The Wolfenden Committee placed its views on the matter before the Ingleby Committee and recommended that the age limit should be raised to 18 or, if practicable, even higher.[36] However, the Ingleby Committee observed that the majority of those who recommended this reform were concerned with wayward girls of 17 who were thought to be in 'moral danger'. The maximum age of admission to an approved school was 17 and no boy or girl could be detained after the age of 19. The Ingleby Committee therefore accepted the view of the Home Office that an extension of the age limit would create great difficulties and that approved school training would not be a suitable form of training for young prostitutes. The committee felt that foster care or local authority homes, hostels or borstals would be equally unsuitable and therefore declined to recommend any change to the existing system. The only procedure that it considered to be of any use for the young prostitute was for the court to make an order for supervision by a probation officer.[37]

The Ingleby Committee was a very different body from the Wolfenden Committee. Instead of making coercive recommendations it launched itself into colourful hyperbole on the uncertain state of the world in the aftermath of two world wars. It commented on the uncertainty of modern life, the fundamental insecurity of the individual, the material revolution and the changes in the basic assumptions that governed behaviour.[38] This type of rhetoric would certainly have appealed to the AMSH, but it appeared that the Ingleby Committee was working its way towards a more liberal recognition of the changes that had been taking place within society during the 1950s, many of which had escaped Wolfenden.

One interesting link between the various perspectives on young people and sexual behaviour was the work of Professor T. C. N. Gibbens of the London School of Economics, who had also given evidence to the Wolfenden Committee. In 1956 he published a paper in the *British Journal of Delinquency* entitled 'Juvenile Prostitution', in which he provided an optimistic assessment of the prospects for young prostitutes. He deconstructed many of the accepted stereotyped notions associated with the prostitute, including the Wolfenden conviction that they 'do it because they like it'.[39] He argued that the main problem facing policy-makers was 'whether something could be done for the prostitutes between 17 and 21'. Gibbens claimed that extending the age at which care and protection proceedings could be taken would mean taking action against 95 per cent of wayward girls for the sake of 5 per cent who were in danger of prostitution.[40]

It seems that the Macmillan government of 1959 was not, after all, sufficiently concerned about the 'redemption' of young women to await the findings of the Ingleby Committee before enacting the Wolfenden recommendations, even though there was a lack of consensus between different departments within the Home Office. This gives added weight to the assertion that the Street Offences Act 1959 was an electioneering tactic congruent with the Conservative 'law and order' ideology that was popular with the public during the 1950s.[41]

However, the negative aspect of neglecting the issue of how best to deal with teenage girls[42] gave rise to a long-standing problem with the prosecution of children, and of young women of 17 and under, for loitering or soliciting, especially as a prison sentence was available to the courts after a third conviction.[43] It also meant that while a child or young woman might acquire a criminal record, the problem of older men taking illegal advantage of under-age youngsters was neglected.[44]

NOTES

1. The Earl of Kilmuir, David Maxwell Fyfe, quoted in the *Journal of Business Law*, April 1957, from an address given to the Mansfield Law Club. See D. Maxwell Fyfe (1964), *Political Adventure: The Memoirs of the Earl of Kilmuir*, Weidenfeld and Nicholson, London, p. 298.
2. See Cmnd. 247, para. 286, 'It has been suggested to us that to "drive the prostitutes from the streets" is to encourage the closer organisation of the trade, with greater opportunities for exploiting prostitutes and greater dangers that a new classes of "middlemen" (e.g., taxi-drivers and hotel porters) will arise. We think it possible, indeed probable, that there will be an extension of the "call-girl" system and, perhaps, a growth in the activities of touts . . . Another possible consequence is an increase in small advertisements in shops or local newspapers, offering the services of "masseuses", "models" or "companions"; but we think that this would be less injurious than the presence of prostitutes on the streets.'
3. See, for example, Maxwell Fyfe, *Political Adventure*, p. 300, in which he expresses his concern for the stability of the family, the rising divorce rates and the care of children whose parents have separated.
4. William Beveridge (Report), *Social Insurance and Allied Services* (1942), Cmd. 6404, pp. 50–1. Beveridge was made a baron in 1946. For an excellent but straightforward account of Beveridge's political career see José Harris (1977), *Beveridge: A Biography*, Oxford University Press, Oxford (Chs 16 and 17 cover the report). For a feminist approach see E. Wilson (1977), *Women and the Welfare State*, Tavistock Publications, London, p. 148. Beveridge's opinions were in keeping with the ideas and concerns of his time and with the government's anxieties over family poverty and the falling birth rate.
5. Unemployment Insurance (No. 3) Act 1931 [21 & 22 Geo. 5. Ch. 36] known as the Anomalies Act 1931.
6. Beveridge, pp. 50–1.
7. Further drawbacks include the isolation of the wife and the insularity of the family.
8. Report of the Royal Commission on Population, 1949, Cmd. 7695, para. 102. Also Jane Lewis (1992), *Women in Britain Since 1945*, Blackwell, Oxford, pp. 16–17. This report ought not to be dismissed too lightly as a backwards-looking. The committee had the benefit of three sub-committees set up to study and give advice on the statistical, economic, biological and medical aspects of demographic change. It is full of carefully thought-out commentary and well worth reading.
9. It is important to recognise the extent to which law and social policy are grounded in ideological belief and a 'taken for granted' expectation of what is assumed to be 'normal' and 'natural'. See, for example, K. O'Donovan (1979), 'The Male Appendage – Legal Definitions of Women', in Sandra Burman (ed.), *Fit Work for Women*, Croom Helm, Great Britain; Jan Pahl (1989), *Money and Marriage*, Macmillan, London, Ch. 9; Gillian Pascall (1986), *Social Policy: A Feminist Analysis*, Routledge, London. Pahl examines the *economic* inequalities within marriage. On the basis of her research she writes (p. 169): 'Patriarchal ideologies have the effect of legitimating the power of husbands, even when couples express the desire for greater equality, and of constraining the power of wives, even if they earn more than their partners.' Pahl found that many married women whose economic situation appeared to be comfortable had nevertheless lived in a state of personal private penury. The demoralising effect, for many women, of relative poverty, both at work and within marriage, in a society where money is the measure of success, was not understood or considered by men such as Beveridge, Wolfenden or Butler. Historically one of the results of these ideological assumptions has been the constant reproach that women prostituted themselves in order to obtain luxuries. Wolfenden adopted this approach (see his exchanges with the NCW in an earlier

chapter), which he would also have seen developed by Gladys Hall. See Cmnd. 247, para. 302: Gladys Hall (1933), *Prostitution: a Survey and a Challenge*, Williams and Norgate. Hall referred to 'dress, drink, dainties and gay times' (p. 86). Hall was quoting the educational psychologist, Dr Cyril Burt, 'Causes of Sex Delinquency in Girls' pamphlet from *Health and Empire* (1926), p. 19. Hall's book was based on a thesis submitted to the University of Liverpool in which she argued (p. 13) that promiscuity was a substitute or intermediate stage leading to prostitution, which made it difficult to distinguish between the two. Many of her more controversial statements were footnoted as 'private evidence'. R. A. Butler in 1959 rationalised the controversial legislation on the ground that women no longer suffered from economic need.

10. Liz Stanley (1995), *Sex Surveyed, 1949–1994: From Mass Observation's 'Little Kinsey' to the National Survey and the Hite Reports*, Taylor & Francis, London. Mass-Observation was founded in 1937 by Tom Harrisson, Charles Madge and Humphrey Jennings as a mass popular sociology that would carry out sufficiently detailed empirical research to form an 'anthropology at home'. It was run from Blackheath in London and appointed a 'National Panel' of volunteer observers who studied many aspects of social life in Britain. During the war it worked for the government through the Home Intelligence Department of the Ministry of Information. Stanley argues that it used innovative research techniques that were important for women, pre-dating by 45 years the epistemological frameworks developed by feminists in their search for women-friendly ways for establishing data. See pp. 4 and 19–26. I came across no mention of the British Mass-Observation surveys or of 'Little Kinsey' among the Wolfenden papers.

11. Ibid., p. 5.

12. Pat Thane (1982), *The Foundations of the Welfare State: Social Policy in Modern Britain*, Longman, London.

13. Marie Stopes (1995), *Married Love*, Victor Gollancz, London. First published in 1918, the book sold 2,000 copies in the first two weeks after publication and went through seven editions in its first year. More than a million copies were sold during the next two decades and it was translated into 14 languages and into Braille. It was once placed sixteenth among the twenty-five most influential books ever to be written (John Peel, in the Introduction to 1995 edition). Stopes' writing and her promotion of contraception were instrumental in challenging the Victorian double standard of morality and promoting the idea that sexual intercourse could be a life-enhancing experience for both women and men, which enriched and cemented the marital relationship.

14. Cmnd. 247, para. 306.

15. Stanley, *Sex Surveyed*, Ch. 8.

16. Ibid., p. 178.

17. A. Sinfield (1997), *Literature, Politics and Culture in Post-War Britain*, The Athlone Press, London, p. 8.

18. Penny Summerfield (1998), *Reconstructing Women's Wartime Lives*, Manchester University Press, Manchester, passim.

19. John Costello (1985), *Love Sex and War: Changing Values, 1939–45*, Collins, London, pp. 355–72.

20. Sinfield, *Literature, Politics and Culture*, p. 8.

21. Costello, *Love, Sex and War*, p. 370.

22. Maxwell Fyfe, *Political Adventure*, p. 300.

23. James H. Jones (1997), *Alfred C. Kinsey: A Public Private Life*, W. W. Norton, New York, p. 754. Alfred Kinsey is probably the most famous of the early twentieth-century researchers into sexual behaviour. His Institute of Sex Research was based at Indiana University, USA. Kinsey began his project in 1938 and gained financial support from the National Research Council and the Rockefeller Foundation. Sixteen people were employed at the Institute and hundreds of medical and other specialists were consulted and gave advice and information. Case histories from 5,300 white males and 5,940 white females were analysed. Many more supplied data. Although Kinsey was interviewed by members of the Wolfenden Committee and his views preserved among the transactions (PRO. HO 345/9/19), the committee viewed him with caution and his name is not among the contributors to the report. His evidence suggests that he did not believe that legislation was required, as changes in social mores meant that prostitution would no longer be necessary. The work of early sexologists has been criticized by feminists such Stanley for having being based upon a patriarchal concept of sexual normality, eventually challenged in the *Hite Report*, which analysed 4,000 women's relation-

ships. Shere Hite (1987), *The Hite Report: Women and Love, a Cultural Revolution in Progress*, Penguin, London.

24. Alfred Kinsey (1948), *Sexual Behaviour in the Human Male* (1953), *Sexual Behaviour in the Human Female*, W.B. Sanders, New York.

25. Report of the Cambridge Department of Sexual Offences (1957), ed. L. Radzinowicz, 'Studies in Criminal Science', Macmillan, London.

26. Ibid., p. xiii.

27. Ibid., p. 405.

28. Section 6 (3) of the Sexual Offences Act 1956.

29. AMSH, August 1958. (1) Copy of Memorandum on (draft) Sexual Offences Amendment Bill, 24 July, 1958; (2) copy of (draft) Bill; and (3) copy of letter to Law Society, August 1958, JBS collection.

30. Section 6 (3) of the Sexual Offences Act 1956 remains unaltered.

31. Correspondence concerning this issue was destroyed by a relation of Mrs Bligh, although the occasional hint of strained relationships with other members of the society remain. For example, Mrs Bligh eventually wrote to her friend, Mrs White of the Liverpool Diocesan Moral Welfare Board (18 April 70), that 'the situation was most unsatisfactory'. She had apparently fought it for as long as she could and would have resigned but for the fact that 'it would have made matters even worse!'

32. The AMSH/JBS office was moved from 129 Kennington Road, London, to 83 Denison House, 296 Vauxhall Bridge Road, London in 1967 and to the private residence of the Secretary, Miss Margaret Schwarz, in South Mimms, Hertfordshire, in 1971.

33. The 'Josephine Butler Educational Trust' had the advantage of creating a tax-free way of holding funds and depositing legacies, but had the obvious disadvantage of redirecting the society's monies. In 1971 the Inland Revenue queried the charitable status of the Trust on the ground that it was not doing anything except employing a secretary (JBS, minutes of meeting, 2 September 1971).

34. Report of the Committee on Children and Young Persons (Ingleby Committee, 1960), Cmnd. 1191. See also AMSH Report, 'Ingleby Committee, 1960'. 3JBS2, Box 123, WL. The committee was appointed in 1956 by the Home Secretary, Gwilym Lloyd-George, 'to be a Committee to inquire into, and make recommendations on; (a) the working of the law, in England and Wales, relating to (i) proceedings, and the power of the courts, in respect of juveniles brought before the courts as delinquent or as being in need of care and protection or beyond control; (ii) the constitution, jurisdiction and procedure of juvenile courts; (iii) the remand home, approved school and approved probation home systems; (iv) the prevention of cruelty to, and exposure to moral and physical danger of juveniles; and (b), whether local authorities responsible for child care under the Children Act 1948 in England and Wales should, taking into account action by voluntary organisations and the responsibilities of existing statutory services, be given new powers and duties to prevent or forestall the suffering of children through neglect in their own homes.'

35. Cmnd. 247, para. 281.

36. The problem here, as far as Wolfenden was concerned, was that a non-statutory caution that did not provide powers of arrest, and an offence that on the first two occasions only attracted a fine, did not provide a suitable mechanism for compulsory detention. Additionally, it was not the loitering that the authorities wished to detain the young prostitute for, but the 'immoral' act of prostituting herself. Cmnd. 247, paras. 278–82.

37. Ingleby Report, paras. 98–103.

38. Ibid., para. 11.

39. Gibbens (1956), 'Juvenile Prostitution', *British Journal of Delinquency*, VIII: 3–12.

40. Ibid., pp. 11–12.

41. C. Smart (1981), 'Law and the Control of Women's Sexuality: The Case of the 1950s', in B. Hutter and G. Williams (eds), *Controlling Women: The Normal and the Deviant*, Croom Helm, London, pp. 52–3.

42. The problems posed by adolescent sexuality and prostitution as well as the causes and possible solutions are discussed by Susan Moore and Doreen Rosenthal (1993), *Sexuality in Adolescence*, Routledge, London, pp. 169–200.

43. This was an area of continuing concern for Lord Stonham, who became president of the AMSH in 1960. In May 1961 he moved an amendment to the Criminal Justice Bill to delete a proposal for a detention centre for girls. He pointed out that only girls given short sentences would be eligible. Therefore half of the inmates would be detained as a result of prostitution

offences. He claimed that they were mostly 'mentally ill or seriously disturbed girls, for whom a "short sharp shock – knees-bend" treatment was unsuitable', thus demonstrating that he too was prepared to pathologise the young women involved. See *Shield*, 1961, p. 1. Gibbens cited the cases of a number of girls who had been convicted by the court before it was realised that they were under age. See Gibbens 'Juvenile Prostitution', p. 6.

44. This problem was eventually highlighted as a result of campaigns run by the Children's Society and Barnardo's. See Mark Lee and Rachel O'Brien (1995), 'The Game's Up: Redefining Child Prostitution', The Children's Society; Barnardo's, 'Whose Daughter Next? Children Abused Through Prostitution', Barnardo's (1998); David Barrett (ed.), 'Child Prostitution in Britain: Dilemmas and Practical Responses', The Children's Society (1997).

CHAPTER TWELVE

Assessing the Effects of the Street Offences Act 1959

PRESS REACTION

Following the passage of the 1959 Act convictions for street offences plummeted from an all-time high of 19,663 in 1958 to 2,828 in 1960. The day after it became law the *Guardian*[1] revealed that police forces in the principal cities of the country had reported that the Act had produced the desired effect, although it was clearly too early to make a full assessment. As the clock chimed in the new Act, crowds of sightseers lined the streets of Piccadilly to watch three policemen make an uninterrupted tour of the area that twenty-four hours earlier had been paraded by at least forty-five prostitutes. All had vanished. The paper's legal correspondent was more sceptical, arguing that with a penalty of imprisonment at stake the police would have to satisfy the courts that a woman *was* a common prostitute. Failure to do this might lead to fewer convictions. The prostitutes themselves would be looking for protection from imprisonment and more assistance with contacting clients. 'We will think of some way round it,' commented one of the women. Within a fortnight the *Guardian*[2] was reporting that 'prostitution is learning to advertise'. Crowds of men had been seen clustered around a tobacconist's window behind which fifty or so cards were displayed. There were telephone numbers and messages such as 'exciting new model gives French lessons'. A reader from the Paddington area complained that a genuine advertisement placed in a shop window by her French visitor had resulted in the phone ringing continuously for three days. The Lord Chief Justice, Lord Parker, commented that the type of laws passed against prostitutes in England tended to drive 'evil' underground.[3]

By 1960 a more distinct picture was beginning to emerge. The peeress Lady Ravensdale (personal friend of the Prime Minister, Harold Macmillan) made a tour of the East End and communicated her distress to the House of Lords.[4] She demanded swift action from the government to stamp out clubs and cafés used for the purpose of prostitution and for other forms of vice. Clubs were 'popping up everywhere', she insisted. 'The street woman of 1959 is the club woman of the 1960s.' She had discovered that the 'wretched girls' were being rushed from one striptease venue to another and the audience was made up of men in the standard city dress of black coats and pinstriped trousers.

Prostitution had not ceased to cause anxiety for the Church. The *Daily Telegraph*[5] reported that almost all of the April issue of the *London Churchman* had been devoted to the problem of prostitution in the East End. The Reverend Joseph Williamson, Vicar of St Paul's, Dock Street, Stepney, had launched a personal crusade against the conditions in his parish, which was plagued by slums, derelict housing and prostitution.[6] He described the environment as 'a hotbed of vice on the gutter level . . . humans are like rats living in filth', and he urged the Housing Ministry to 'send the bulldozers in'.[7]

The Reverend Williamson came to the attention of the media as a result of an address he delivered to the London Diocesan Conference,[8] but although his speech was largely about the evils of poor housing and prostitution, the motion, which was carried unanimously, was for the government to call a halt to the 'flood of immigration into Britain' on the ground that racial violence was likely to develop.[9,10] Father Williamson's willingness to connect immigration with prostitution echoed the concerns of the late nineteenth and early twentieth centuries, which had linked the growth of trafficking with Jewish immigration. As a result of the various revelations Anthony Greenwood was prompted to write to the *Evening Standard*[11] suggesting that the Street Offences Act had proved to be the failure that many people had prophesied.

A similar situation was developing in parts of Birmingham, and the notorious Varna Street was eventually pulled down. The police had been accused of a lack of vigilance and allowing streetwalking to go unhindered.[12] Complaints also came from the residents of Balsall Heath, while the Anderton Park Residents Association initiated a national debate when it recommended municipal brothels.[13] Mrs Bligh of the JBS wrote to Alderman Frank Griffin[14] expressing the shock that the proposal had caused the Society. The *News of the World*[15] reported that two bishops (the Anglican Dr Leonard Wilson and Roman Catholic Archbishop George Dwyer) had spoken out against the plan. The Lord Mayor of Birmingham's secretary wrote to Mrs Bligh[16] assuring her that the city had no intention of building flats for prostitutes.[17] The *Birmingham Post* wrote of the 'head in sand' attitude towards the city's vice, but the following year it was able to report that the police had set up a secret 'vice squad' to deal with the increasing menace.[18]

At the same time anxiety over sexually transmitted diseases began to re-emerge and was mingled with concerns over permissive teenage sex and pregnancies. Headlines appeared in the *Daily Mirror* revealing 'The Terrible Truth' and 'Shame of a Big City'.[19] 'What can be done', it asked, 'to turn back this grim tide now creeping up on the young of Britain?'

ASSESSING THE EFFECTS OF THE STREET OFFENCES
ACT 1959: MRS ROSALIND WILKINSON (1960)

Four months after the Act came into operation the *Sunday Times*[20] commissioned Mrs Rosalind Wilkinson to investigate the working of the Act. They published the results in two stages. Her conclusions were based on interviews and consultations with police officers, welfare workers and other professionals in London and Manchester.

She considered the Act to be a victory for short-term expediency. The people whom she consulted had found the immediate effect dramatic, with a 90 per cent drop in convictions in London, although her interviewees felt that it was too early to make an accurate assessment. Courts were imposing fines well below the maximum but expecting immediate payment. Under the new provisions few new prostitutes were coming before the courts. Therefore she assumed that the drop in convictions was partially due to the operation of the cautioning system.[21] Prostitutes were resentful at being arrested 'for having a purpose' when they were not annoying anybody, and she suspected that the Act made it difficult for them to plead 'not guilty'.

She found that very few of the cautioned women had responded to expressions of concern for their welfare, and that they had not been willing to be interviewed by women police officers or put in touch with social agencies. She reasoned that, having abandoned the dull life, the new prostitute was in no hurry to return to a routine existence. She found that probation officers were seeing hardly any prostitutes as few came before the magistrates, and that no action had been taken to implement the Wolfenden recommendation that the courts should be given explicit powers to remand first offenders in custody. In other words the success of the Act was militating against the welfare objectives that were used to justify the harsh terms of the legislation. She reiterated the probation officers' unease concerning the contradiction between the use of imprisonment as a means for persuading women to choose the alternative of probation, and the stated need for 'willing cooperation' on the part of the prostitute if rehabilitative measures were to be successful.

In the second of her two articles, Wilkinson looked at the ways in which women were adapting to the new constraints, and found that they were extremely inventive and resourceful. Girls had told her that the West End was 'finished' and they were moving out to the country. Trains, underground stations and bus stops were being used as alternative venues for finding customers and a greater use was being made of late-night soliciting from cars. Prostitutes were moving around the country, wrong addresses were being given and a variety of disguises were used in order to evade the caution. Women who had always worked indoors found that the Act had improved trade: business had 'never been so good' and 'the Act has played right into my hands'. Wilkinson found no evidence to support the fear that touts or bully-boys had increased, as they were deterred by the heavy penalties, but there had been a proliferation of small-time middle-men, including taxi-drivers, café-owners and barmen who were willing to give addresses.

Wilkinson concluded that the socially expedient had triumphed over the socially constructive: 'prostitutes are being obliged to avoid official rehabilitative machinery now they have to work in ways that will keep them out of court'. She also observed that, although the Act contained no statutory guidelines on how to administer a caution, it did provide the statutory right for a woman to appeal against it, thus creating another grey area of ambiguity.

ASSESSING THE EFFECTS OF THE STREET OFFENCES ACT 1959: THE AMSH/JBS WORKING PARTY REPORT 1962–63

In February 1962, the AMSH/JBS set up a working party to investigate the effects of the 1959 Street Offences Act. Although the members were to remain anonymous, the 'interim' report[22] states that there were six members, including a psychiatrist with specialised experience of prostitution,[23] a barrister, two social workers and two officers of the society. The witnesses included statutory and voluntary workers involved in the problem of prostitution. A questionnaire covered the areas under investigation. These included:

1. (a) clearing the streets, (b) alternative methods of solicitation, (c) the cautioning system, (d) other preventative measures, (e) increased organisation of prostitution;
2. (a) Effects of increased penalties, (b) imprisonment; and
3. soliciting by men.

The working party acknowledged that the Act had been successful in dealing with the nuisance of soliciting on the streets, but argued that this had been achieved at a considerable price. It claimed that it was difficult to estimate the extent of the problem because much of the trade had gone underground. 'It has been impossible to ascertain whether there is more or less prostitution than before the passing of the Act, or whether more or fewer prostitutes are engaged in the trade.' Two prostitutes interviewed on ITV television's 'This Week'[24] were quoted as saying that there were more women involved than formerly. New and less obtrusive methods of solicitation were said to be developing, mainly through the congregation of people in clubs, cafés and bars, while others were being induced to work as hostesses who encouraged male customers to drink. Welfare workers testified that they had experienced greater difficulty than previously in intercepting young girls who had run away from homes, as ponces were on the look-out at railway stations for stray girls and persuading them to work in clubs, or to become call-girls. And once installed in clubs and bars the women were discouraged from contacting the police or social workers for fear of what might happen to them. This last anxiety was confirmed by the Central After-Care Association in its annual report, August 1960, sent to the Home Secretary. It stated:

The introduction of new laws concerning soliciting has resulted in the homeless and friendless girl being in an ever-more dangerous position than hitherto, since once she has been picked up and introduced to the call-girl system she is not likely to be seen on the streets by the police-women, who have in the past rescued many such women from a life of prostitution.[25]

The JBS Working Party Report claimed that a system of organised prostitution was developing along a variety of undesirable lines, which increased the number of persons involved. For example, women who lived in flats were now employing maids who would organise arrivals and departures. They had adopted the practice of displaying their names under a lighted bell, which would help the taxi-driver to find the address supplied by other intermediaries such as barmen or hotel porters. In some places, and in particular Notting Hill, the area was said to have deteriorated. Girls who used to solicit on the streets and return with men two or three times a night now employed a male runner, or protector, who would bring men back to the flat until the early hours of the morning. There was also evidence of growing mobility. For example, girls living in Stepney were being taken to the West End in an organised manner, while residents in Knightsbridge had been shocked by phone-calls from middle-men requesting a supply of 15-year-old girls at £25 each. The overall picture indicated the development of a more closely organised trade. In addition the women themselves were resorting to new methods for attracting customers, including advertising their telephone numbers with their 'vital statistics' on cards displayed in shop windows. Others overcame the restrictions by establishing a clientele of regular customers who made contact by telephone.

It was argued by the JBS that although the Licensing Act of 1961[26] had enabled the police to raid and close down clubs, the continued proliferation of these establishments,[27] alongside cafés and bars that offered a variety of attractions, provided a greater temptation than an uninspiring row of women lined up in Hyde Park. Men who emerged from the premises, stimulated by drink and pornography, would be confronted by a queue of clients waiting their turn to visit a prostitute. All that had really happened was a reversal of roles, with a line of women replaced by a queue of men.

Among the witnesses quoted were Dr Mary Beveridge, of the Royal Hospital Sheffield, and Professor Gibbens. Dr Beveridge wrote of 'the burgeoning array of problems' in the *British Journal of Venereal Disease*, September 1962. She explained that the Sheffield version of a 'call-girl' was one who called at the door of the customer offering some other service, but in reality was engaging in prostitution. Some women appeared to be 'on tour' servicing Pakistani Muslims and commuting between Hull and Nottingham. One girl had escaped after being beaten up by a teddy-boy gang. Dr Beveridge assumed that Muslim men were denied access to prostitutes as a result of the prohibition placed upon the consumption of alcohol and believed that this had accelerated the growth of the 'call-girl' system. This theory was supported by

Nicholas Swingle in *New Society*,[28] who found that the concentration of unattached Pakistanis in Bradford was being exploited by English prostitutes, one of whom had moved there after a year at the London School of Economics.

Professor Gibbens, who had conducted research with prostitutes' clients, argued that street solicitation did not play any considerable part in tempting men to visit prostitutes.[29] He found that the men made the decision to use the services of a prostitute first and then allowed themselves to be solicited afterwards. In other words, street prostitution merely speeded up the process. The professor also reported that men tended to visit prostitutes as a form of group activity and would spur each other on, so that an element of bravado was involved. On this basis he suggested that a proliferation of clubs could provide an additional, if unforeseen, temptation. The most worrying aspect was probably the increased availability of drugs, from barbiturates to heroin. The main consequence of all these developments was that the prostitute had acquired a ponce who made it more difficult for her to extricate herself from the game. During a discussion about possible research projects at the National Institute of Social Workers Professor Gibbens outlined some of the aspects of the problem that interested him. He was impressed by the different patterns of behaviour adopted by different prostitutes and thought that it would be interesting to construct a pathology, or several different pathologies, on the subject. Another doctor thought that the medical model for investigation of disease might be fruitful.[30] This shows that even a sympathetic medical practitioner and academic such as Gibbens was still prepared to identify and categorise the prostitute in terms of medical symptoms that could be scientifically observed, diagnosed and treated.

The working party was critical of the cautioning system, which had been introduced on the basis that it would give women the opportunity of withdrawing from a degrading lifestyle before they became entangled with the law. It drew attention to the fact that a system of cautioning and referral had been practised before the new procedure was introduced; all that had changed was that the women were to be cautioned twice.[31] On investigation the team found that it had been agreed in the first instance that all cases in London should be referred to one central social worker, but that only four women had been officially referred and all of them had supplied false addresses. A few older women had asked to see a probation officer whom they already knew and had abandoned prostitution rather than face imprisonment. The working party concluded that the cautioning system had failed in its welfare objectives, as the Act had succeeded in pushing women off the streets. It also became apparent that although the Home Secretary had insisted that he did not wish the caution to become part of any charge preferred against a woman if she pleaded 'not guilty', it had enabled the police to present her to the court as a 'common prostitute' and, consequently, the court knew that she had already been cautioned twice and was left without any defence.

Imprisonment was judged by the working party to be equally futile as a reformative measure. In 1960 the Prison Commission had reported that prostitute women created a special problem.[32] They did not settle down in prison or respond to prison discipline, and they were reluctant to work or to cooperate with attempts to rehabilitate them because they intended to return to prostitution after release. The prison management did not want to start classifying women according to the nature of their offences, but found the prostitutes a disruptive force inside the system. After discharge, the prostitute ex-prisoner remained uncooperative, was usually unwilling to accept offers of accommodation and experienced difficulty in finding or keeping a suitable job that required some level of discipline. It was felt that the Act had played into the hands of third parties and, although the team was aware of the incompleteness of the investigation, it was impressed by the unanimity of the views that it had encountered.

As president of the AMSH, Lord Stonham had actively supported the Working Party. In March 1961 he wrote to the secretary suggesting that the JBS should adopt a number of strategies, including setting up a 'Street Offences Repeal Fund'; appointing a panel of speakers;[33] compiling evidence through the monitoring of newspapers and collecting reports of prosecutions; lobbying prospective candidates at by-elections; and appealing for support to the electorate. In opposition to his own government's policy Lord Stonham set up an All-Parliamentary Group of members of both Houses, to consider modifying the Street Offences Act.[34] He anticipated that it would have approximately thirty members and that most of the women MPs would join, including the future Prime Minister, Margaret Thatcher.[35] He was quoted by the *Daily Telegraph*[36] as saying: 'I believe the Act presents scandalous injustices to women, which should not be tolerated.' This was also reported in the *News of the World*[37] and in the *Daily Herald*.[38]

By April of 1963 he appears to have become somewhat disillusioned with the in-fighting of the AMSH/JBS, as the Working Party had not, at that stage, published a report. He declined to put his name forward for re-election as president, and complained that he had expected that most of the society's energies would have been devoted to a vigorous campaign for the repeal of the Street Offences Act, but that 'almost no evidence had been produced on which the Parliamentary Group could get to work. On some occasions my own efforts seem to have been misunderstood and even resented by members of the Committee.'[39]

CORRUPTION

In commenting on the increase in the call-girl phenomenon, Mrs Bligh made reference to the sensational trial of Dr Stephen Ward in 1963. Ward was an osteopath with many prominent clients (including Winston Churchill), who, it was alleged, took particular pleasure in grooming attractive young women from humble backgrounds and introducing them to high society. According to Lewis Baston he also dabbled in security matters for the sake of the excitement.[40] Ward eventually became involved in the 'Profumo Affair', one of the biggest scandals ever to hit British politics. The cast of this extended drama included two high-class prostitutes, Christine Keeler and Mandy Rice-Davis, War Minister John Profumo and a Russian spy, Yevgeny Ivanov. Ward, who was eventually tried for living on the earnings of prostitution, committed suicide while the jury considered its verdict. Baston observes that Profumo was singularly unfortunate in being 'found out' indulging in behaviour that was unremarkable in high society. He also implied that Lord Denning's reportof the saga was a 'cover-up' that suppressed evidence of the sexual excesses of prominent politicians with prostitutes, or of the fact that they were homosexuals.[41] On the other hand, Ludovic Kennedy's account, which was written just after the trial, is highly critical of all concerned, including the police, the judge, Mr Justice Marshall and Lord Denning whose report he considered to be full of unnecessary gossip and damaging inaccuracies.[42] The case of Stephen Ward and the prurient fascination it attracted is a further example of the misuse of the charge of 'living on immoral earnings'.

    Stephen Ward and Christine Keeler were deeply involved in the colourful Notting Hill scene, which appears to have been far more raffish than Mrs Bligh's passing comment would suggest. During the early 1960s Notting Hill was the centre of a vibrant black night life involving music, drinking and drugs. The area contained a cosmopolitan society and, according to Keeler, many of the white residents were convicts, pimps or prostitutes.[43] In retrospect one can see that the early 1960s was a time during which there was a breaking up of social barriers and a mixing of people who would not have socialized together a few years earlier.[44] The JBS working party had picked up on some of these developments and was anxious to blame them on the deficiencies of the 1959 Act, but they should also be seen as part of a long-term evolution in sexual mores.

ASSESSING THE EFFECTS OF THE STREET OFFENCES ACT 1959: THE *PEOPLE* INVESTIGATION, 1965–69

During April 1965, following the interim conclusions of the JBS working party, representatives of the JBS met the Minister of State for the Home Department, Miss Alice Bacon, in order to impress upon her the need for reforming the Street Offences Act 1959. Miss Bacon explained that there was no hope of early legislation and that the case for amendment could only be sustained by the production of evidence. The minister, who was reported to be particularly concerned with the protection of young girls and preventing them from becoming prostitutes,[45] asked the JBS if it could produce evidence to support its claim that the Street Offences Act was not working as intended.[46] The society was anxious to conduct further research but had been unsuccessful in its attempts to raise funds.[47] In 1966 the trustees to the Educational Trust decided to approach the *People* newspaper, suggesting that they might undertake the project. An agreement was reached that involved the setting up of a group of reporters under the direction of Ken Gardner, who addressed the following questions posed by the society:

1. Has the Street Offences Act 1959 increased the number of known prostitutes in the 10 years of its operation?
2. Has it been made more difficult to find young missing girls who have been drawn into prostitution, but who have been pushed off the streets?
3. Has the amount of third-party profiteering and the number of people living on immoral earnings increased?
4. To what extent has the sweeping of the girls off the streets into club premises of one kind or another increased the number of drug takers and the number of people suffering from VD?
5. How big is the menace of the "kerb-crawler" to ordinary women walking home at night or queuing at bus stops?
6. What assessment, if any, can be made of the effect on the country's social scene of 100 years of work started by Josephine Butler and carried on by her supporters today?

Although it would seem unlikely that the *People* reporters would be in any position to address the final question, they came up with some interesting findings, which were published in a series of articles between 5 October and 2 November 1969. The first instalment reported that the merging of various police forces, the rearrangement of divisional boundaries and a general shortage of police had made statistical 'facts' hard to come by. Chief constables established their own priorities and there was an argument that other areas of crime, such as violence, ought to take precedence over vice.

The *People* investigators found that one of the strange side-effect of banishing girls from the streets of Mayfair was that prostitution had become more respectable. Men who had previously been too embarrassed to be seen speaking to a 'blatant tart' were willing to ring a discreetly positioned doorbell; thus a new market had opened up for businessmen. 'Today, however,' it commented, 'a man can sin in private, in the full knowledge that there is unlikely to be an unwelcome visit from the law.' The result of this development was the proliferation of the type of flat that they had been investigating in Maddox Street, which seven men had entered within half an hour. Reporters also found that high rents were being charged for flats by some landlords and protection money paid. It would seem that Wolfenden's suggestion that the law would be expected to deal with any adverse consequences had not materialised.[48]

The second article concentrated upon the developing problem of kerb-crawling and on the cost of hiring a girl in a flat or hotel. Hotel prices were more lucrative: up to £25 in London, £20 in Glasgow and £15 in Manchester.[49] Clients' cars were increasingly being used. One woman had been observed picking up lorry-drivers while out walking with her toddler and using the child as a cover for her activities. Anthony Greenwood MP, who was by this time the Housing Minister, commented that it was 'humbug' to attempt clearing women from the streets while the men remained untouched.

A further article dealt with the growth of venereal disease.[50] Gonorrhoea was said to have increased from 31,344 cases in England and Wales in 1959 to 41,829 in 1967, while an unnamed venereologist suggested that oral contraception had resulted in an increase in unprotected sex.

This comment did not, of course, prove anything about prostitution but rather it reflected the changing sexual habits of the population. Nevertheless the point was supported and illustrated by repeated press coverage of adolescent sex resulting in the spread of venereal disease and teenage pregnancies. For example, the *Daily Mirror* revealed 'The Terrible Truth' and featured what it described as 'a grave and growing menace'.[51] It reported that schoolgirls of 14 and 15 were presenting themselves to the doctors with venereal diseases and that there had been steep rises in infections among young people in many major towns. It concluded that society had become more tolerant of promiscuity.[52] When the venereologist Dr R. D. Catterall delivered the tenth Alison Neilans Memorial Lecture for the JBS on 2 November 1967, his approach to the subject demonstrated that wartime attitudes were still influential by conflating prostitution with promiscuity and by referring to women as a 'reservoir of infection'.[53] He even made the extraordinary suggestion that prostitutes might be refused treatment because their continued reinfection contributed to the growth of penicillin-resistant strains.[54] In this way Catterall contributed towards the general willingness to pathologise the prostitute and to classify her as a member of a distinct group of women. Although the *Shield* published the lecture in 1968 it remained uncritical of Catterall's provocative comments.

With reference to the increase of prostitution the *People* reporters investigated the conviction rates of four cities: London, Cardiff, Manchester and Bradford. Manchester alone had shown a steady increase in the number of convictions for street offences while the other three had declined until 1963, and then rallied. The average yearly total for these cities during 1960 was 1,798 convictions and for 1968 it was 1,106. This contrasted with the convictions for men living on the earnings of prostitution, which showed that only Bradford had decreased from 11 convictions in 1960 to one in 1968. The other three cities exhibited a steady increase with an overall average total of 190 convictions in 1960 and 266 in 1968.

Even this rather small sample suggested that the trade was adapting to the new parameters. The JBS concluded that there were probably more nightclubs in London than in Manchester, and although the pattern of prostitution had changed, the total amount of prostitution had increased since most of it took place under cover.[55] These findings may not have been of any great concern to the Home Office as the problem of women on the streets had greatly diminished.

Surprise was expressed by the *People* at the casualness with which this way of life was being adopted by young girls, as if no shame were attached to it any more.[56] It assumed that 'the Pill and the general atmosphere of our increasingly permissive society both play a part'. Mrs Bligh was reported as saying that even street solicitation was 'no longer mainly a London problem as it was once supposed to be. It has spread to almost every city in the country.'[57]

In conclusion the *People* claimed that the 1959 Act had had a 'boomerang' effect, encouraging vice rather than suppressing it. The increase in the number of clubs meant that girls were being corrupted without the welfare agencies being able to help them, or even being aware of their existence. Third-party profiteering, especially by landlords, had increased, as had kerb-crawling. The spread of sexually transmitted disease was also a cause for concern.[58]

It seems fair to assume that a newspaper, especially one like the *People*, which aimed at a broad popular audience,[59] had its own commercial agenda, but that does not necessarily mean that its findings were invalid, especially when they confirmed the evidence acquired from other sources. For example, they concurred with the conclusion of Mrs Wilkinson and Miss Judith Priceman (below). Of course, there were the usual titillating stories and plenty of value-laden commentary, with the paper adopting a high moral tone, but that is to be expected.[60] The JBS would have been very upset if it had done otherwise and it is most likely that this was understood by the *People* when it agreed to embark on the project. As we shall see, the publication of the articles was timed to coincide with Lord Chorley's second Street Offences Amendment Bill, and it was hoped that they would have maximum impact upon public opinion.

CONSOLIDATING THE STREET OFFENCES ACT 1959 AND EXTENDING ITS REMIT THROUGH CASE LAW

What must surely be seen as the inevitable extension of the definition of 'soliciting in a street or a public place' came when the legislation was challenged in the courts. In *Smith and Another* v. *Hughes and Others*[61] it was established that soliciting from a doorway, window or balcony was to be regarded as the same as 'soliciting in a street or a public place' and in *Behrendt* v. *Burridge*[62] this precedent was extended to the woman who sat motionless in a window in order to advertise her availability. In the case of *Smith* v. *Hughes*, Lord Parker C. J. stated that:

> Everybody knows that the Street Offences Act 1959 was intended to clean up the streets, to enable people to walk along the streets without being molested or solicited by common prostitutes. Viewed in this way, it can matter little whether the prostitute is soliciting while in the street or is standing in a doorway or on a balcony, or at a window, or whether the window is shut or open or half open; in each case her solicitation is projected to and addressed to somebody in the street.

Although the logic of this statement is obvious, if a little strained, the inaccurate reference to molestation in the first sentence and use of the colloquial idiom of 'cleaning up the streets', so beloved by Wolfenden, seems inappropriate when it comes from a High Court judge. The term 'molestation' had been deliberately omitted from the Street Offences Act because it required active and obtrusive forms of annoyance to passers-by involving actions such as touching and pulling. Consequently 'molestation' was regarded as a more serious offence, which merited a heavier penalty. It was for this reason that the Street Offences Committee in 1928 had suggested that molestation should be classified as a separate offence, distinguishable from just standing about or strolling around, nodding and winking. The omission of 'molestation' from the 1959 Street Offences Bill was one of the criticisms directed at the government by the CEMWC. It seems to me that an element of personal judgement crept into Lord Parker's ruling.

The *New Statesman* complained of the absurdity of these decisions, commenting that the 1959 Act had fulfilled its aim in clearing the streets of prostitutes.[63] It reported that a Marylebone magistrate, Mr Geoffrey Raphael, had held that displaying a prostitute's card in a confectioner's window constituted 'soliciting in the street' and fined the woman £25 (*Wies* v. *Monahan*).[64] It wondered if a threepenny stamp stuck on a ground-floor window could be interpreted as soliciting if the message were generally understood. It argued that this sort of development had been forecast by some MPs, who ought to take the matter further. The placing of cards in shop windows had become a growing practice and a number of summonses had been brought under the Street Offences Act, answerable at Bow Street Court, which had resulted from raids made by Scotland Yard's Obscene Publications Department.[65] Lord Parker overturned Raphael's ruling, stating that advertisements in shop windows did not constitute soliciting as the physical presence of the prostitute was necessary.[66]

The intricacy of the emerging entrepreneurial scene was highlighted by the case of *Geoffrey Anthony Quinn and Samuel Bloom*,[67] who were prosecuted for keeping a 'disorderly house' contrary to common law. The premises in question was Raymond's Revuebar, Soho, which gave 'striptease' performances. The Court of Criminal Appeal upheld the convictions at the County of London Sessions, on 14 April 1961, and laid down that a disorderly house did not have to amount to a common nuisance, as it was sufficient to prove that the performances or exhibitions that took place there (a) amounted to an outrage of public decency; (b) tended to deprave or corrupt; or (c) otherwise were calculated to injure the public interest so as to call for condemnation or punishment. *Shaw* v. *D.P.P.* was cited. It was argued by the defence that the prosecution of *Quinn and Bloom* represented an extension of the law and that there was no need for the prosecution to dig up an offence from its grave.[68] An analogy was made with the judgment in the trial of Penguin Books in 1960 for publishing D. H. Lawrence's *Lady Chatterley's Lover*, in that the performance as a whole had to be assessed before coming to a decision. The *Daily Herald*[69] supported the London Sessions condemnation of the striptease performances as 'filthy and disgusting', stating that the very name 'striptease' was indecent with its suggestion of 'leering and prurience', and insisting that 'what the police must be concerned with is public morality'.

The legitimacy of the judgment in *Shaw*, based upon the belief that the judiciary had a role in upholding standards of public morality, was used to support the conviction in *Quinn and Bloom* but was increasingly subjected to criticism. Bernard Levin, writing in *The Times*, launched into a series of furious articles attacking the Attorney-General for his support of a common law misdemeanour, which, Levin argued had been invented by the Law Lords in order to ensure the prosecution of Shaw for a prostitution-related offence.[70] In 1972 the publishers of a magazine called *IT* (*International Times*) were prosecuted for 'conspiring to corrupt public morals' after publishing advertisements by homosexuals looking for partners. Levin argued that the Law Lords were creating law independently of parliament in order to convict persons whom *they* deemed to be guilty of immorality. He claimed that at least thirty prosecutions had taken place on this dubious basis since 1962 and that it was being used to catch people who could not be successfully prosecuted under the Obscene Publications Act 1959 where there was a need to prove that the 'article'[71] in question tended to 'deprave and corrupt'. The point that annoyed him most was that Lord Reid, who had dissented in the case of *Shaw*, voted with the majority in *IT*, not because he had changed his mind but because the offence had been established and must therefore stand until parliament legislated. Levin's accusations were rejected by the Law Officers Department on behalf of the Attorney-General (Sir Peter Rawlinson) on 23 and 28 June. It was argued that the advertisements, which were not obscene in themselves, constituted a threat to adolescent boys.

These cases highlight the overlap between the law on prostitution and the tendency of some activists (for example the NVA) to use it as a launchpad for the suppression of sensuality. Many aspects of popular culture, from the nineteenth-century music hall to Donald McGill's saucy seaside postcards, have come under the prurient gaze of the moralists, their thesis resting upon the theory that lewd and libidinous thoughts would stimulate illicit sexual activity and encourage prostitution.

The complexity of the emerging situation was highlighted by A. E. Jones (a magistrates' clerk), writing for the *Criminal Law Review* (1960). He had found that inventiveness was keeping pace with the law's attempts to control the trade. One so-called 'shop' had the whole of its window devoted to prostitutes' advertisements, with the women given false names and described as models. The police were dealing with the situation by prosecuting men for obstructing the footway. He found that brothels were being advertised as clinics offering 'manipulative services' by a 'therapist'[72] but providing unorthodox treatment. 'Sham' prostitutes were acting as 'hostesses' and inveigling men into 'near-beer' establishments with promises of sexual intercourse later but did not honour the agreement. In the case of *Bryan v. Robinson*[73] it was decided that there was not likely to be a breach of the peace if a young woman smiled at and beckoned to men in the streets. Lord Parker C.J. said that 'the appellant is merely touting for this refreshment house. There was no suggestion that it was a disreputable establishment or a brothel, or that solicitation was for the purpose of prostitution.' A number of refreshment houses had become a focus of anxiety as they had developed into alternative centres of immoral activity. This matter was addressed through the Refreshment Houses Acts 1964 and 1967, which awarded licensing authorities the power to impose conditions on grant or renewal of a licence.[74] Jones concluded that:

> legislation had failed to keep pace with the ingenuity of the business of vice. As soon as a restrictive practice is passed, certain people always set to work to try to find a way round it; and too often when they are successful, Parliament does not find time to deal again with that particular subject until a number of evil-doers have enjoyed many years of anti-social activities. . . . The present danger is that the Street Offences Act will lead to more living on the earnings of prostitution and more thrusting of prostitution on the attention of the public than ever before.[75]

It seems that both the police and the courts were dealing with an enormous diversification of outlets for sexual activity and finding it increasingly difficult to deal with them. As on previous occasions there was a tendency for case law to extend the impact of the legislation by allowing moral considerations to influence judgments. The inadvisability of rapid enactment of harsh legislation to regulate complex expressions of social behaviour was becoming painfully obvious, and the outcome was being dealt with by fairly inventive use of legislation. The result of pushing prostitution off the streets and then endeavouring to prevent it flourishing had its own inevitable outcome in a rash of demands for the legalisation of brothels.[76] One of the less palatable ways in which the police attempted to deal with the situation was to return to the questionable practice of acting as 'agent provocateur'. In *Sneddon* v. *Stevenson*[77] Lord Parker upheld the conviction at Nottingham Magistrates Court of Mary Sneddon. She had been picked up by a policeman who was impersonating a kerb-crawler, who drove her to a colleague and then arrested her for soliciting. The Nottingham magistrates found nothing improper in this action. The rationale for this decision was that the officer was acting on the instructions of his superior.

As prostitution adapted and diversified the police and the judiciary tried to cover loopholes and stem the tide of creativity. Wolfenden had insisted that his committee was concerned only with law and not with public morals, but many of the magistrates and judges clearly believed that they were dealing with offences of immorality and made this quite clear when summing up. The result, as in *Shaw*, was that a concern to convict offenders of prostitution-related offences was spilling over into other areas of public life and had implications for civil liberties. One writer to *The Times*[78] asked 'whether the puritanical zeal with which we are currently persecuting 'vice' in this country is worth the price of freedom', while another suggested that the offence of 'conspiring to corrupt the public morals' could be used against those conspiring to promote racial hatred (a proposition that might have appealed to the supporters of civil liberties). The impact of the law was being broadened through case law and, as demonstrated by *Sneddon*, discredited police practices were creeping back in.[79] While the 1959 Act was passed in order to push women off the streets, parliament attempted to block new outlets through legislating against licensed premises and refreshment houses. At the same time the judiciary tried systematically to make the alternative outlets for prostitution untenable by preventing the women from advertising. Lord Butler, however, was well satisfied, stating 'my Bill was completely successful: because the streets were completely cleared.'[80]

NOTES

1. *Guardian*, 17 August 1959.
2. *Guardian*, 2 September 1959.
3. *Guardian*, 3 and 5 September 1959, report of Lord Parker's attendance at the annual meeting of the Canadian Bar Association.
4. *Daily Mirror* and *Daily Sketch*, 2 June 1960.
5. *Daily Telegraph*, 25 June 61.
6. *Church of England Newspaper and the Record*, 17 February 1961.
7. *Daily Herald*, 14 February 1961.
8. London Diocesan Conference, 13 February 1961.
9. *News of the World*, 29 October 1961.
10. One delegate to the conference pointed out that the situation was the result of government policy, on three points. 'In 1954, 300,000 houses had been built. Since then there had been a steady and continuing decrease. Housing subsidies had been cut, interest rates raised, and the task of the local authorities had been made almost impossible.' See *Church of England Newspaper and Record*, 17 February 1961.
11. *Evening Standard*, 3 March 1961.
12. *New Society*, 16 January 1969.
13. *News of the World*, 2 July 1967; *Guardian*, 7 and 19 July 1967.
14. Mrs Bligh to Alderman Frank Griffin, 19 July 1967.
15. *News of the World*, 2 July 1967.
16. Lord Mayor of Birmingham's secretary to Mrs Bligh, 19–20 July 1967.
17. Assorted correspondence between Mrs Bligh and Birmingham City Council, 3/JBS2, WL.
18. *Birmingham Post*, 21 July 1967, 20 April 1968.
19. *Daily Mirror*, 18 August, 5 December 1961.
20. *Sunday Times*, 13 and 20 December 1959.
21. S. S. M. Edwards (1984), *Women on Trial: A Study of the Female Suspect, Defendant and Offender in the Criminal Justice System*, Manchester University Press, p. 31. Edwards argued that when prosecutions and cautions were taken together for 1960 the difference between the pre- and post-1959 number was not so dramatic, indicating that many women who would previously have been arrested were merely cautioned for the first time. The Act forced women to pursue other ways of contacting clients.
22. Report of the Working Party set up by the JBS in 1962 to Study the Effects of the Street Offences Act 1959. Document undated, but signed by Mrs Margaret Bligh, pre. *Crook* v. *Edmondson*, 3/JBS2, WL.
23. This is most likely to have been Gibbens.
24. ITV programme 'This Week', 18 April 1963.
25. Quoted by Anthony Greenwood, see *Shield* 1961, p. 11.
26. Licensing Act 1961 [9 & 10 Eliz. 2. c. 61]. The object of the Act was to extend the granting of justices' licences in respect of restaurant and residential premises, in order to vary and extend the permitted hours during which intoxicating liquor could be sold. Part 3 of the Act was of interest to the JBS, because it dealt with the sale of intoxicating liquor on club premises. It established that a club must apply annually for renewal of registration. Objections to registration or renewal could be lodged by the police, the local authority or neighbouring residents, on the ground of disorderly conduct, indecent displays or the use of the club as a resort for prostitutes. See *Shield* (1961), p. 14.

27. Although some premises were raided by the police, the Licensing Act 1961 did not appear to make much difference, as the increase of 'undesirable' premises remained a problem. Alan Fitch asked the Home Secretary what he intended to do about the considerable increase following the 1959 Act. See PD. Vol. 675, col. 606, 4 April 1963. On 28 May 1963, Lord Morrison of Lambeth moved an amendment to the Local Government Bill, intended to increase the powers of the London County Council to deal with clubs. The amendment was withdrawn when the Lord Chancellor promised to study the question further. Lord Morrison considered that Soho had become the most disreputable place to be found in Europe; see *Shield* 1963, p. 12.

28. *New Society*, 16 January 1969.

29. Professor Gibbens created a taxonomy of prostitute types, which included: those who associated with coloured men, indolent and passive girls, mercenary girls and middle-class girls fascinated by prostitution. He reported his finding that an unusually high proportion of juvenile prostitutes had menstrual difficulties. See T. N. C. Gibbens (1956), 'Juvenile Prostitution', *British Journal of Delinquency*, VII and (1959). 'Supervision and Probation of Adolescent Girls', *British Journal of Delinquency*, X (2): 84–103. Gibbens' work influenced the Home Office research study, 'Girl Offenders Aged 17 to 20 Years' (1972), A Home Office Research Unit Report, London: HMSO. The conclusion of this report suggested that a 'successful' outcome, i.e., 'one that did not lead to re-conviction', was to be found in the maintenance of a steady relationship with a man. Failure, on the other hand, was associated with sexual problems, including lesbianism. Success was therefore measured in terms of the young women's endorsement of the generally accepted social norms and ideological framework.

30. Professor Gibbens and Dr Arie (1976), comments made at a seminar held at the National Institute of Social Work Training, 28 February 1967. Gibbens was impressed by the different patterns of behaviour adopted by different prostitutes and thought that one might construct a pathology, or several different pathologies, of the subject. He found that older prostitutes had come to terms with the 1959 Act and were not greatly affected by it, but was curious to know why girls had disappeared from borstals. Arie thought that the medical model for studying a disease would be useful: 'The procedure should be to trace the natural history of the disease by studying its evolution at various stages. There would have to be some way of getting hold of the subjects and getting them to talk.' See J. E. Hall Williams (1976), 'Report on Discussion About Research Into Prostitution and the Law', 3/JBS2, WL.

31. This was not entirely true, as the previous system of cautioning was very informal, whereas the new system was non-statutory but more formalised. It was open to abuse both by prostitutes who evaded it and by police officers who failed to observe it, or who recorded a woman on successive occasions in one day. See JBS 'Working Party Report', p. 4.

32. Ibid., p. 6.

33. Among the public figures to be approached was Chave Collisson, who declined on the ground that 'she did not normally go to small groups in far distant suburbs' and now charged a high fee in order to fund her work with the International Alliance of Women. See C. Collisson to M. Schwarz, 17 February 1961, 3/JBS/2, Box 135, WL. Chave was not a member of the EC at this point, but reappears on the list in 1966.

34. Lord Stonham to Margaret Schwarz, 3 March 1961, 3/JBS/2, Box 135, WL.

35. A circular letter was sent by Lord Stonham, on behalf of the AMSH, to all women MPs during July 1961, inviting them to attend a meeting of an All-Parliamentary Group of both Houses, which would campaign for an amendment of the Street Offences Act. Reply from Margaret Thatcher, 3 August 1961, 3/JBS/2, Box 135, WL.

36. *Daily Telegraph*, 31 October 1961.

37. *News of the World*, 4 February 1962.

38. *Daily Herald*, 31 October 1961.

39. Lord Stonham to Miss Schwarz, 26 April 1963. The 'Interim Report' was produced in an effort to persuade Lord Stonham to continue and his resignation was held in suspense until 20 October 1964, when he wrote to the Society stating that he had accepted a ministerial appointment as Parliamentary Secretary to the Home Office, 3/JBS/2, Box 135, WL.

40. Lewis Baston (2000), *Sleaze: The State of Britain*, Macmillan, London, Ch. 4.

41. Lord Denning (1999), *John Profumo and Christine Keeler 1963*, The Stationery Office, London. First published in 1963 as Cmnd. 2152.

42. Ludovic Kennedy (1964), *The Trial of Stephen Ward*, Victor Gollancz, London, pp. 133–251.

43. See also Christine Keeler with Douglas Thompson (2001), *The Truth at Last: My Story*, Sidgwick & Jackson, London.

44. Baston, *Sleaze*, p. 62.
45. J. E. Hall Williams, 'Memorandum on Research into Prostitution and the Law' (undated, 1965?), 3/JBS2, WL.
46. Henry Toch (1970), 'Summary of Report of Investigation into Prostitution by the People', 5 October–2 November 1969, *Shield*, July, pp. 5–6.
47. The JBS was in a poor state financially and by 1970 it faced the possibility of closure. Several members called for its dissolution during the AGM. An appeal for funds was launched through the *New Statesman* (2 October 1970), signed by members of the executive committee and Lord Soper, Dame Joan Vickers, Lord Sorensen and Lord Stonham. Lord Stonham declared that the 'common prostitute' clause in the 1959 Act remained a source of 'complete and vicious injustice'. *The Times* published an article (7 October 1970), and noted that 'equal moral standards' was no longer a popular cause. The *Sun* (8 October 1970), featured an appeal for £10,000.
48. Cmnd. 247, para. 286. 'There are dangers; but where they involve exploitation of the prostitute, we should expect the laws which already cover this kind of exploitation to be rigorously applied.'
49. *People*, 12 October 1969.
50. *People*, 19 October 1969.
51. *Daily Mirror*, 18 August 1961.
52. Press revelations that prostitutes were 'getting younger' represented a recurring theme. For example, see the *Daily Mail*, 10 November 1977, 'Teenage girls pushed into sex'. Organisations sponsored by the government, such as the Family Planning Association, were accused of enabling 14-year-old girls to have affairs, by providing contraceptives to children; *Daily Mail*, 4 August 1979, 'Selling Sex . . . Now younger and younger and doing it by choice'; *Daily Mirror*, 3 December 1981, 'Scandal of the Vice Girls, 14 . . . No-hope kids cash in on sex'. By this time girls were said to be earning up to £1,000 a week.
53. Two attempts were made to introduce legislation on VD during the 1960s. The first was through Richard Marsh's Private Members Bill, 3 July 1962. For adjournment debate see PD. 5th Ser. Vol. 679, cols. 1920–36, 28 June 1968. See also *Shield* (1963), p. 13. Marsh's Bill contained regulations similar to the 1940–44 wartime regulation 33B (which encouraged VD specialists to pass on information concerning the sexual partners of patients to the local medical officer of health). The Marsh Bill proposed compulsory treatment for people suspected of suffering from VD. Another attempt was made in 1969 by Sir Myer Galpern in his 'Control of Venereal Disease' Bill. See PD. 780, cols. 944–976, 21 March 1969. The Minister of State for Health and Social Security read a letter from the JBS to the House (cols. 974–5); see also the *Shield* (1970), p. 30. The issues of VD, promiscuity and prostitution were concerns which were kept in the public eye through the 1960s and 1970s. For example, see the *Daily Mirror*, 5 December 1961, 'The Shame of the Big City', which amplified the problem of teenage sex life and pregnancies and suggested a connection between venereal diseases and immigration; *Guardian*, 26 April 1971, 'Poster warns bed-sitter girls'; *Guardian*, 26 April 1971, 'Routine VD tests sought'.
54. Dr R. D. Catterall, 'Prostitution and the Venereal Diseases', Summary of Tenth Alison Neilans Memorial Lecture given at the House of Commons, 2 November 1967, *Shield*, 1968, pp. 5–9. Dr Catterall published an article in the *Lancet* in 1963, referring to the 'great reservoir of infection in women', *Shield* (1963), p. 13.
55. Toch, 'Summary', p. 5.
56. *People*, 26 October 1969.
57. Mrs Bligh, reported in the *People*, 19 October 1969.
58. Toch, 'Summary', pp. 5–6.
59. The format was copied by the *News of the World*, 4, 11 and 18 June 1972, which featured a series of articles based upon three months of investigation. The paper concluded that Britain was in the grip of a new 'vice boom', which was making an 'ass' of the law. Girls were earning a fortune (more than the Prime Minister), and advertising freely in magazines as members of a club. Shopkeepers were displaying cards in shop windows without repercussions and girls were diversifying into other areas, such as sado-masochism and bondage (correction). Manchester was reported to be one of the new centres for vice. An unnamed divisional London police chief was quoted as saying, 'All we have done is stick our heads in the sand' and 'What we don't see doesn't matter'. The Chief Constable of Bristol, Mr George Twist, criticised the law for a 'lack of success'. Sir Hugh Linstead, QC (Wolfenden Committee) thought that the government should review the law. Mr Peter Archer MP (a future president

of the JBS) commented, 'Girls are entirely at the mercy of exploiters nowadays. But no-one in authority seems to care.' The Salvation Army complained that they could no longer contact the girls now that they had been driven underground. The Bishop of Southwark, the Right Reverend Mervyn Stockwood, felt that the 1959 Act should be reviewed. Sir John Wolfenden commented that people did not understand that the committee was concerned only with the law and not with public morals. R. A. Butler maintained that the government had set out not to end prostitution but to clear the streets of the capital, and had succeeded. The following year the *News of the World* (29 April 1973), was back to the familiar pre-1959 story of 'Vice Kings Exposed'. Landlords were charging £150 a week for call-girl flats: 'Sin-for-Sale Girls'. The landlord in question was Maltese. Next to this article was a picture of two scantily dressed twin girls: 'Tasty Dishes' who were featuring in TV commercials.

60. As with the *News of the World*, the ambivalence of the *People's* attitude towards women and towards sexuality could be seen in an almost indistinguishable but apparently serious and unrelated article, 10 October 1969. This featured a series of pretty girls (one in bunny costume) who were being employed as waitresses by restaurants in order to encourage trade.

61. *Smith* v. *Hughes* [1960] 2 All. E.R. 859.

62. *Behrendt* v. *Burridge* [1976] 3 All E.R. 285.

63. *New Statesman*, 17 February 1961.

64. *Wies* v. *Monahan* [1962] 1 All E.R. 664.

65. *News of the World*, 8 January & 5 February 1961.

66. *Observer*, 4 February 1962.

67. *Quinn and Bloom* (1962) 2 QB 245.

68. Presumably meaning that in the opinion of the defence council there was no such offence as 'conspiracy to corrupt the public morals'.

69. *Daily Herald*, 15 April 1961.

70. *The Times*, 20–23–27 June 1972.

71. The definition of a 'article' included any 'matter to be read or looked at or both, any sound record, and any film or other record of a picture or pictures'.

72. Prostitution as 'sex therapy' was a recurrent theme. For example, the *Sunday Times* (25 April 1971), featured the story of Dr Martin Cole, described as 'Britain's most liberated apostle of liberated sex'. Cole had produced a 'sex education' film, 'Growing Up', intended for school children. He advocated the use of 'seductive female therapists' to help men with impotence problems, see the *Daily Mail*, 17 and 20 January 1972; *Daily Express*, 20 January 1972. Sex therapy was promoted by Dr Ken Russell, senior lecturer at the Leicester Polytechnic School of Law, in an article in the *Sunday Times*, 13 February 1977. Russell argued that research evidence from the United States supported this claim and that British society was hypocritical in its attitudes towards prostitution. He claimed that the Street Offences Act was no longer working, as the girls were back on the streets, and supported licensed brothels, believing that unlicensed prostitution encouraged exploitation. The therapeutic advantages of prostitution are also claimed, on occasions, by prostitutes themselves. The *Daily Star*, 19 November 1980, featured 'Charity', who described herself as a 'sex teacher'. Her clients were men with sexual hang-ups that she tried to solve. See also Claud Jaget (ed.) (1980), *Prostitutes Our Life*, Falling Wall Press, Bristol, pp. 195–13.

73. *Bryan* v. *Robinson* (1960) 2 All E.R. 173.

74. Refreshment Houses Act 1860 [23 & 24 Vict. c. 27], section 32, provided that: 'Every person licensed to keep a refreshment house under this Act . . . who shall knowingly suffer prostitutes, thieves, or drunken and disorderly persons to assemble at or continue in or upon his premises shall . . . be subject to a forfeiture of his licence.' However, a number of cases including *Belascose* v. *Hannant, Barton* v. *Hannant* (1862) 3 B & S 13, 26 JP 823; *Whitfield* v. *Bainbridge* (1866) 30 JP 644 established that prostitutes had the same rights to refreshment as other people (see 6–780: *Stone's Justices' Manual*, p. 1828).

For an offence to be committed it must be established: (1) that the premises is the *habitual* resort of prostitutes; (2) that they are allowed to remain longer than is reasonably necessary to consume refreshments. Also, the defendant must know the women are prostitutes. It is for the prosecution to prove that the reputed prostitutes remained beyond the time reasonably necessary for them to take refreshments. See *Greig* v. *Bendeno* (1858) E.B. & E. 133, p. 137. The Town Police Clauses Act 1847, section 35, provides that an offence is committed by: 'Every person keeping any house, shop, room, or place of public resort . . . for the sale or consumption of refreshments of any kind, who knowingly suffers common prostitutes . . . to assemble at and continue in his premises.' This section now applies throughout England and Wales.

The Refreshment Houses Act 1964 [12 Eliz. 2. c. 88].

The Refreshment Houses Act 1967 [15 Eliz. 2. c.38], empowered licensing authorities to impose conditions on the grant or renewal of a licence for a refreshment house.

See also the Licensing Act 1964 [12 Eliz. 2. c. 26]. Section175 (1) provides that: 'The holder of a justices' licence shall not knowingly allow the licensed premises to be the habitual resort or place of meeting of reputed prostitutes, whether the object of their so resorting or meeting is or is not prostitution; but this section does not prohibit his allowing any such person to remain on the premises for the purpose of obtaining reasonable refreshment for such time as is necessary for that purpose.' Section176 on 'Permitting Licensed Premises to be a Brothel' provided that: (1) If the holder of a justice licence permits the licensed premises to be a brothel (a), he shall be liable to a fine not exceeding level 2 on the standard scale; (2) If the holder of a justices' licence is convicted of allowing his premises to be used as a brothel he shall forfeit (b) the licence. (See *Stone's Justices Manual*, pp. 1827–8.)

The Late Night Refreshment House Act 1969 [17. Eliz. 2. c. 53], section 9(1) provides that 'If the licensee of a late night refreshment house . . . knowingly permits prostitutes . . . to assemble at, or continue in or upon, his premises, he shall be guilty of an offence.'

75. A. E. Jones (1960), 'The Law Versus Prostitution', *Criminal Law Review*, October: 794–9.
76. Proposals for the legalisation of brothels recur periodically when the intractable nature of the problem makes it appear insurmountable, or when a government committee is reviewing the subject. For example, Arthur Storer, a magistrate from Wolverhampton, was reported in the *Daily Telegraph*, 10 September 1979, as supporting the adoption of licensed brothels which should be properly controlled by the Home Office. He believed this would solve the problem of teenage prostitution. The matter was covered again by *The Times*, 26 and 27 November 1981, in relation to the licensing of sex shops and to the forthcoming report of the CLRC, which was to cover the possibility of legalising brothels. Matthew Parris MP (West Derbyshire) suggested that if prostitutes were allowed to set up business in a legitimate way, it would be easier to control them. James Hill MP (Southampton) agreed, and argued that brothels would alleviate the problem of kerb-crawling. But the *Daily Telegraph*, 19 October 1979, reported that the prostitutes were not enthusiastic. Similarly, in its evidence to the CLRC, the Haldane Society of Socialist Lawyers recommended legalisation, believing that it would 'clean up' areas which were notorious for soliciting (*The Times*, 14 September 1983).
77. *The Times*, 7 July 1967.
78. *The Times*, 10 and 11 May 1962.
79. A prime example of this is to be found in the case of *Webb* [1964] 1. Q.B. 375. Although the appellant was a man who ran a massage parlour, the case revolved around whether or not the women employed were prostitutes rather than whether they were exploited. Lord Parker C.J. said: 'It cannot matter whether she whips the man or he whips her: it cannot matter whether he masturbates himself or she masturbates him . . . it includes, at any rate, such a case as this where a woman offers herself as a participant in physical acts of indecency for the sexual gratification of men' (p. 376).
80. *Evening Standard*, 12 October 1971.

CHAPTER THIRTEEN

'Any Person': Attempting to Reform the Street Offences Act 1959

Undaunted as ever, the AMSH/JBS saw the various legal and social developments as a challenge and an opening that would enable it to campaign for the repeal or the amendment of the 1959 Act. Thus it revived its old crusade for a gender-neutral offence aimed at any (or every) person who loitered or solicited in public places to the annoyance of other people. In the course time the shortcomings of the Act became more generally apparent to politicians and the media. Consequently, it was suggested by the AMSH/JBS and their supporters that a widely defined public order measure, aimed at limiting the annoyance caused by soliciting for the purpose of prostitution, could be made gender-neutral and applied to 'any person' rather than to a legally constructed group of women labelled as 'common prostitutes'.

THE STREET OFFENCES AMENDMENT BILLS, *LORD CHORLEY*

The window of opportunity which provided a way forward for the JBS was the case of *Crook* v. *Edmondson* [1966] in which Winn L.J. had established that for a man to solicit a woman for the purpose of prostitution was not an 'immoral purpose' within the meaning of the Act, even though the conduct of the defendant was considered to be immoral. The 'immoral purpose', it was ruled, had to be a purpose that was expressly forbidden by law, such as unnatural acts (homosexual acts before 1967)[1] or procuration. As noted earlier, *Crook* v. *Edmondson* was an important case because it contradicted the repeated government assurances that women would be protected by section 32 of the Sexual Offences Act 1956.[2]

The infrequency of prosecution for this purpose became apparent during the parliamentary debate in 1959. Indeed, Butler was unable to obtain any figures for convictions. By contrast, as *Crook* v. *Edmondson* shows,[3] the sexual harassment of women might be defined by legislators and the courts as normal masculine behaviour and therefore unrelated to commercial sex.[4] Even as late as 1974 the Working Party on Vagrancy and Street Offences was reluctant to criminalize men for soliciting women, commenting that, 'Care would . . . have to be exercised to make sure that an offence did not extend to approaches by men to women which are accepted by society . . . for example chatting up a young woman after a dance.'[5]

Following the decision in *Crook* v. *Edmondson* the JBS launched a renewed attempt to introduce a Bill that would apply to 'any person' and would drop the use of the term 'common prostitute'. The society wrote to the chairman of the Law Commission explaining its position and inquiring, somewhat provocatively, whether a reform that legalised homosexual acts between consenting adults in private would also mean that soliciting for homosexual purposes would cease to be 'for an immoral purpose'.[6] The inference here was that the stigmatization associated with the term 'common prostitute' underpinned the legislation that was used to convict her, and that the term should therefore be removed.

The JBS held that section 32 was unjust towards men in that the maximum sentence of two years was disproportionate to the penalty of three months for women soliciting men. It therefore proposed a reform of section 1 (1) of the Street Offences Act by substituting the words: 'Every person commits an offence who, in any street or public place or in view thereof, persistently importunes for an immoral purpose.' The word 'importune' was to mean molestation by offensive words or actions and 'immoral purpose' included the purpose of both heterosexual and homosexual prostitution.[7] In this way it was hoped to achieve equality before the law for women and men.

During the early 1960s the criminologist J. E. Hall Williams became a member of the executive committee of the JBS. Meetings were held at the London School of Economics and for a time the LSE was the focus of activity for research and investigation into the problems of prostitution legislation.[8] The society cultivated its connections with members of the House of Lords in order to press for the reforming measure, and it was agreed that Hall Williams and Lord Sorensen would cooperate in drafting an amending Bill.[9] Promoting the Bill posed some difficulty, as in October 1964 Lord Sorensen[10] became a member of the government and was consequently debarred from taking part. Lord Stonham,[11] who had opposed the 1959 Bill, was already a minister at the Home Office and was also excluded. Consequently Lord Chorley,[12] who was one of the few peers left to have opposed Clause 1 of the Act in 1959, was asked to introduce the Bill to the House of Lords, where it would have a better legislative run than in the Commons. He accepted the invitation to take Lord Sorensen's place with some reluctance, feeling that his political experience was inadequate and that the subject matter was outside his range of interests.[13] However, the case of *Crook* v. *Edmondson* influenced his judgement. He had been persuaded that the 1959 Act was directly responsible for a rapid and substantial increase in kerb-crawling, a practice that by the mid-1960s was being described by the Home Office as a 'menace'. He reasoned that this was directly related to the decrease of women on the streets which had encouraged 'sexhungry' men to go looking for prostitutes and solicit in their own turn. He also remarked that the Act had been an incentive for pimps and was responsible for the country-wide spread of highly organised prostitution outlets, which were flourishing in the increasingly amoral atmosphere of the 1960s.[14]

The position of the campaigners was to be strengthened by the press coverage of events in Birmingham and by a return of the familiar stories of street soliciting in respectable residential areas. The *Guardian*[15] reported that a Mrs X had organised a public meeting in support of the Anderton Park Residents' Association, which had called for the legalisation of brothels. Birmingham's 13 MPs were invited to attend. The arguments were familiar: prosecutions for soliciting had steadily increased[16] and a Pakistani boy in grammar school uniform was alleged to have been pimping, but although it was maintained that men required an outlet for their pent-up feelings, councillors felt uncomfortable with the idea of municipal brothels. It transpired that Mrs X rented out 65 lock-up garages situated on a large site behind her desirable property and that this lonely darkened area was being used for the purposes of prostitution. Five MPs, including Mrs Jill Knight (Edgbaston), attended the meeting, but none of them supported the proposal.[17]

In a similar vein the *News of the World*[18] had reported that following the display of prostitutes' cards in a shop window, girls who had been advertising baby-sitting services had received improper phone-calls. The shopkeeper was convicted for living on immoral earnings. In another incident a café owner was convicted for running a disorderly house when it was discovered that youngsters smoking Indian hemp had been using the rear of his property for acts of gross indecency.[19] A Mexican Catholic priest from San Miguel who worked for the rehabilitation of prostitutes fuelled the old anxieties by reporting in the *Catholic Herald* that a vast nationwide white-slave organisation was victimising girls from 10 to 19 years of age. He alleged that he had received death threats for reporting these activities.[20]

On the other side of the divide were those who argued that prostitution was a form of therapy. For example, the Swedish psychiatrist Dr Lars Ullerstam, from Gothenburg, recommended the re-establishment of state-controlled brothels, arguing that they fulfilled an important social function similar to that of hospitals and clinics by treating men with sexual problems such as impotency.[21] A correspondent from the Wirral considered that the JBS was overly optimistic in its aspirations for an equal moral standard.[22] Men, she declared, 'will never be advanced enough to achieve the civilised outlook of a normal woman because they will always have the brute strength (with accompanying lack of sensibility), and this power corrupts them'.

Having accepted the challenge Lord Chorley's first concern was with the drafting, which he described as an 'esoteric exercise'. He amended Hall Williams' Bill and submitted it to the Home Office for scrutiny where, he observed, it was 'torn to pieces'.[23] In reality criticisms of the Bill were sent to him privately by Lord Stonham but did not reach him until after he had introduced the bill to the House on 30 November 1967. The Second Reading came on 8 February 1968. The Bill was portrayed in the press as a measure intended to bring men into the net of soliciting law[24] and as an anti-kerb crawling measure.[25] Lord Arran informed the *Sun* that he would probably try to wreck it as it gave too much power to the police.

The essence of Chorley's Bill was slightly different from the JBS's original suggestion and replaced section 1 (1) of the Street Offences Act with: 'It shall be an offence for any person in a street or public place either to loiter for an immoral purpose or to solicit.'[26]

The offence of 'soliciting' was to apply to the behaviour of either sex and to include any form of persistent importuning for immoral purposes and molestation by offensive words or behaviour. An 'immoral purpose' was to include male or female prostitution, whether heterosexual or homosexual, and 'loiter' was to include loitering in a vehicle. The new clause was already a watering down of the JBS proposal, as it lacked the safeguard of 'persistently', retained 'loitering' and left the undefined offence of 'to solicit' hanging in the air.

Lord Chorley opened the debate by emphasising the problems posed by the verdict in *Crook* v. *Edmondson*.[27] He quoted the Wolfenden Report, in which it was argued that although kerb-crawling represented a serious nuisance to many well-behaved women, it did not appear to fit into any existing category of offences.[28] This suggests that the Wolfenden Committee and their legal advisers did not believe that section 32 was an appropriate measure for dealing with the matter of kerb-crawling. Lord Chorley's contention was that if the problem of women soliciting could be effectively solved by one Act, the problem of men soliciting could be solved by another. But there were difficulties concerning Lord Chorley's argument in that he and his supporters already considered the 1959 Act to be an injustice to women. The proposal to criminalize similar behaviour in men risked either extending those injustices to men or creating a partial or ineffectual measure. Lord Chorley hoped that once the principle of the Bill had been accepted he would be given the benefit of a parliamentary draftsman, which he felt he needed.

Although the government stance was said by Lord Stonham to be neutral, the Home Office appears to have been unwilling to accept the policy of the Bill and did not come forward with any offers of draftsmanship. This is hardly surprising as the Home Office was not in any way dissatisfied with the operation of the 1959 Act, which was judged to have been successful in its primary objective.[29] Under these circumstances Lord Stonham was put in the peculiarly difficult position of having to reply for the government as Minister of State for the Home Office even though he had opposed the Street Offences Act and privately sympathised with the aims of the new Bill. He admitted in his opening speech that an offence of 'soliciting', which could be committed only by a person who, when charged, was described as a common prostitute, made it impossible not to import prejudice into the decision as to whether the woman was guilty or not.[30] He disposed of the contradictions inherent in his position by criticising the drafting of the Bill and arguing that it would be difficult to enforce although he sympathised in principle with the aims of the Bill. He maintained that although there was a good case for putting right the deficiency shown up by *Crook* v. *Edmondson*, amending the 1959 Act so as to accuse 'any person' made the offence too vague. He stated that the matter would be referred to the Criminal Law Revision Committee.

The main objection to the Bill (as set out by Lord Arran) was that it gave insufficient protection to ordinary users of the streets against arrest by the police, who might misconstrue the intentions of citizens who were lingering in a public place or engaged in normal social intercourse. This point had also been underlined by the National Council for Civil Liberties.[31] The second objection was the difficulty of proving an 'immoral purpose'. The Bill would have enabled the police to arrest without warrant 'any person' who loitered in a 'street or a public place' for an 'immoral purpose' and as this phrase was defined in section 2 as 'including' the purpose of prostitution, it left vague and undefined what else was included within the meaning of immorality, thus still leaving the measure open to be used for the purpose the Bill had been designed to amend (that is, targeting the female prostitute). Defeat came when Lord Arran moved an amendment proposing that the bill should be read again in six months time and this was carried by 50 votes to 29.

Despite the disappointment Lord Chorley did not feel disheartened. Meetings were held with the chairman and secretary of the JBS and it was decided to redraft the Bill. Baroness Birk and Lord Foot gave advice and it was decided to reintroduce the Bill early in the following session.[32] In preparation Lord Chorley addressed the annual general meeting of the JBS, the drafting panel began reworking the Bill and a press conference was held on 13 November 1968. Lord Chorley consulted the Home Office and a second letter was received from Lord Stonham. In the meantime the society circularised peers who were thought likely to take an interest in the measure. Articles placing the emphasis on kerb-crawling appeared the following day in *The Times*, the *Guardian*, the *Sun* and the *Daily Express*. Feature articles discussing kerb-crawling appeared in the *Daily Express* and in the *Yorkshire Evening Post*.[33]

The amended Bill was introduced on 23 January1969 and the second reading took place on 4 March, when the attendance at the debate was much larger than on the previous occasion. But although Lord Chorley's second Bill appeared more cumbersome that the first, it had the similar aim of replacing section 1 (1) of the 1959 Act with a non-discriminatory offence and widening its application to cover kerb-crawling:

> (1a) It shall be an offence for any person in a street or public place per-sistently to accost any person or persons with a view to offering sexual services for payment or reward. (1b) It shall be an offence for any person in a street or public place to importune any other person so as to cause annoyance to that person or a nuisance to any other person who resides in or uses the street or public place. Provided that no one shall be con-victed of this offence without evidence having been heard from a person thus importuned or a person to whom such a nuisance has been caused.

Sexual services were deemed to include heterosexual or homosexual services and 'to importune' was to mean 'persistently for sexual purposes to molest by words, by behaviour, by any obstruction or by pestering or following, whether in a vehicle or on foot'.[34] In retrospect Lord Chorley observed that the debate followed very much the same pattern as on the previous occasion, with the emphasis of his argument resting upon the growing menace of kerb-crawling. On this occasion he was supported by Lord Arran, Lord Foot, Lord Soper, Baroness Summerskill and the Bishop of Leicester, who approved of the principle of the Bill. Lord Stonham agreed that it was an improvement but still open to objections. The majority of speakers supported the Bill and the division resulted in 61 votes to 48 in favour of the measure.

This was to be Lord Chorley's only victory. Subsequent time-tabling proved unsatisfactory and he was unable to get a date for the committee stage until 17 April 1969. At the last minute Lord Stow Hill supported by Viscount Dilhorne (i.e. Sir Frank Soskice, the former law officer, and Sir Reginald Manningham-Buller) had submitted a series of amendments designed to wreck the Bill. Lord Chorley decided to fight the opposition by means of one of Lord Stow Hill's amendments, which retained section 1 of the 1959 Act, albeit extending it to male prostitutes. However, Lord Chorley considered this to be a reversal of the approval given to the principle of the Bill during the second reading and the term 'any person' would have naturally included the male prostitute. When it came to the final vote many of the peers who had supported the Bill on second reading were absent and the day was lost, giving the opposition a majority of nine. Following this defeat Lord Chorley decided that the best course of action was to drop the measure for the session.

This series of events provides a salutary lesson in the ability of a small number of determined opponents to undermine a Bill which they do not like, through the device of well tried wrecking tactics. Lord Stow Hill resorted to a familiar blend of ridicule, suggestive humour and time-wasting. 'There are, no doubt,' he informed the House, 'unbalanced women who are firmly convinced that their often very modest charms are far more enticing to the male sex than anybody else would conceivably think that they would be. I think they are sometimes known as "ingrowing virgins"'.[35] He believed that a measure to criminalize kerb-crawling was unnecessary. 'There are some ladies who will always think they are being molested . . . and . . . if they rode past the Sphinx on a camel, would be sure that it was ogling them.'[36] Of the transgressions of the kerb-crawler, he observed, 'He says something to one lady, who says nothing and passes on and forgets it, and he goes to a second or a third, who do the same, who take no notice and pass on. People ought not to be dragged into court and the time of the police and everybody else wasted if that is all they have done.'[37] Experience had told him that 99 women out of 100 acted in that way, although he did not explain how he knew this, apart from consulting his wife.[38] These were arguments that Lord Stow Hill must have realised applied equally well to prostitutes and to the passers-by whom they 'accosted', especially as he had fiercely opposed the Street Offences Bill when it had been debated in the House of Commons, commenting at the time that the magistrate would find it difficult not to accept a policeman's evidence that a woman was a common prostitute.[39] Furthermore he had sought to eliminate the term 'common prostitute' and to substitute it with the word 'person'.[40]

The *New Statesman*[41] printed letters complaining at the wrecking of the Bill, suggesting that the 'House of Lords sank lower than one would think possible' and had ignored the fact that a prostitute could be arrested for loitering when she was doing nothing more than looking in a shop window, whereas a man could solicit any number of women and the police could take no action.

Following this second defeat the JBS analysed the situation and chose to risk one more attempt. Lord Chorley had calculated that, overall, 70 members had voted for the Bill and it was possible that more might be persuaded to follow as a result of the interest that the debate had aroused. A few small modifications were made, which included elements of Lord Stow Hill's amendment.[42] Clause 1 required that there should be evidence of a second witness in addition to that of the complainant and Clause 3 conferred the right to trial by jury.[43] The second reading took place on 3 February 1970. By this time Lord Stonham had ceased to be Minister of State at the Home Office and was free to speak on behalf of the Bill, but Lord Stow Hill and Viscount Dilhorne strenuously opposed it and the measure was finally lost by a vote of 23 to 68.

I have covered this episode in some detail because it demonstrates the difficulty that can be experienced when trying to amend legislation once it has been put into place, as well as the hazards that can face a private members bill. Lord Chorley's bills were not the private whim of a single individual but the concerted effort of a group of people who did their best to raise public awareness of what they believed to be unjust and counter-productive legislation. Similarly, Lord Stow Hill and Lord Dilhorne highlighted some of the inherent weaknesses within a widely defined offence directed at 'any person', which they believed might be unjustly applied. But it seems strange that the JBS should have so far forgotten its roots that it sanctioned a Bill that contained an offence built around the concept of an 'immoral purpose', especially as the power to 'arrest without warrant' would have necessitated some form of moral policing. This left Baroness Gaitskell free to quote Josephine Butler's repudiation of that principle. 'Our laws do not permit, and it is hoped they never will, the arrest of persons, either men or women, because they are known to the police as immoral characters.'[44]

Lord Chorley regretted the lack of a professional draftsman, which he clearly believed he should have been granted after the policy of the Bill was approved in March 1969. In his summing up of the episode in the *Shield* he commented that:

> The drafting of legislation in the United Kingdom is a highly esoteric craft. The efforts of armature draftsmen are heavily criticised by the professionals, especially if the department particularly concerned with the Bill is hostile. The first hurdle which the protagonists of a private member's Bill have to confront therefore is the drafting.

> If the Government themselves want a Bill to be passed, or even if it
> becomes clear that it has a good chance of being accepted by Parliament,
> which in practice means if it looks like passing in the Commons, it will
> lend the services of one of its own Parliamentary draftsmen: at the time
> when I succeeded in my Second Reading in 1969 I had some hope that I
> might be offered such assistance, but it was not to be.[45]

However, the confidential letters that passed between himself and Lord
Stonham reveal that there were aspects of the affair that he was not prepared
to make public through the channels of the *Shield*. These letters give some
indication of the difficulties posed by legislation, which was open to wide
interpretation. They also confirmed the ideology that sustained the policies
embodied in the law, about which he appears to have been ambivalent. With
these problems in mind Lord Stonham wrote to Lord Chorley in August 1968
outlining some of the difficulties that his Bills would present:

> It seems to me that a major defect of the draft Bill is its lack of
> definitions of the terms 'solicit' and 'prostitution' . . . because of this we
> cannot reach any firm view of how the new offences you propose to
> create would be interpreted; and there must be some doubt as to whether
> your proposals would be as effective as the present law in dealing with
> the nuisance caused by prostitutes on the streets, and whether your pro-
> posals would enable effective action to be taken against 'kerb-crawlers'
> . . . much depends upon on how the terms 'solicit' and 'prostitution' are
> interpreted. It is true that these terms are not defined in the present law;
> but since the offence under section 1 (1) of the Street Offences Act 1959
> applies only to a common prostitute loitering or soliciting in a street
> or public place for the purpose of prostitution, the difficulty does not
> arise – the law is clearly intended to apply only to a prostitute who plies
> her trade.[46]

On 3 December Lord Stonham wrote again:

> I assume that the offence is aimed at catching activities of prostitutes and
> their customers in the street and public places generally. I doubt,
> however, whether it would do so. One limb of the offence is that an 'offer'
> of 'sexual services' for hire must be made. The interpretation of these
> terms is not free from doubt, but we feel it possible that the courts would
> hold that to constitute an 'offer' there would have to be an explicit indi-
> cation of the services being made available and that payment was
> expected, so that a mere gesture and *a fortiori* the mere presence of the
> prostitute awaiting custom would be insufficient.[47]

This mere gesture [or] presence of the prostitute was of course exactly what
the Street Offences Act had been intended to criminalise, as confirmed in the
judgments in *Smith* v. *Hughes* and *Behrendt* v. *Burridge*. 'Hanging around' and
'being', smiling and waving, or sitting motionless in a window could be made

into criminal offences, so long as they applied only to women labelled as common prostitutes and where a policeman's testimony provided sufficient evidence for a conviction.

During the final debate in February 1970 Lord Stonham was relieved from the strictures of office. He then reversed the arguments that he had been obliged to use when presenting the government case in February 1968. He condemned the injustices of the 1959 Act and used newly released figures to demonstrate the futility of imprisonment:

> Quite apart from the injustice built into the 1959 Act which my noble friend's Bill would remove, what earthly benefit is it to society constantly to send these women to prison? . . . One in five of all women and girls in prison are there for prostitution offences . . . the Act has not swept them off the streets, it has merely victimised them because they have no one to fight their case.[48]

The Earl of Cork and Orrery supported him and rejected both the 1959 Act and the new bill, stating:

> What I find particularly repugnant . . . is that it requires a police officer to preface his evidence with a statement of the previous record of the defendant; in other words, to begin a piece of evidence which in a criminal case of any other kind is inadmissible before conviction is secured. I think that is wrong and I think it ought to be put right. Habitual prostitution can no longer be adduced in court as material evidence.[49]

The problem that had sharpened the debate was the application of discriminatory law to 'any person' rather than to an artificially created category of stigmatised women, described as 'common prostitutes'. As Lord Stow Hill commented, 'It can touch every one of us.'

ANY PERSON

In a search for a feminist jurisprudence, Smart[50] examined the equality/difference problem of women within a legal system that has privileged men, seeing men as the norm against which women-as-different or women-as-equal have been measured. The stigmatisation of woman as 'whore' takes that distinction a step further in that it divides women into those who are 'normal' and those who are sexually promiscuous and dangerous. In a similar vein Gail Pheterson[51] provides an illuminating analysis of the constraining force of what she calls the 'whore stigma' as it applies to the 'category prostitute'. She describes the 'stigma' as the 'social and legal branding of women who are suspected of being or acting as prostitutes' and maintains that sex workers accuse a broad range of authorities, including police, judges, law-makers and researchers, of reinforcing this stigma and subsequently legitimising the persecution of prostitutes as opposed to clients and 'normal' women. She argues that prostitutes are alluded to in journals, articles and research papers as if the label described a fixed and homogeneous sample of the population, of whom a reliable profile could be provided. Presumptions are then made upon the basis of this profile and allowed to influence social policy and law. They also legitimate discriminatory behaviour, which may include questionable police procedures, violent abuse by pimps and clients, and on occasions, murder, since the isolation into which the prostitute is forced makes her an easy target for a man with violent inclinations.[52]

In his analysis of prostitution Lars O. Ericsson asks whether the risks that a hustler runs (violence, abuse, exploitation and criminalisation) are a good enough reason for maintaining that prostitution is undesirable.[53] He finds, like Pheterson,[54] that it has proved impossible to prevent prostitution without violating fundamental rights and liberties,[55] arguing that general contempt for whores and contempt for women are closely related.

The reference to prostitutes as deviant has been apparent in much of the value-laden terminology quoted throughout this narrative and in the constant use of terms such as 'innocent' and 'guilty', 'flagrant' and 'flaunting', 'respectable' or 'brazen', 'vulgar' or 'victim'. Ideological assumptions about deviance were revealed in Manningham-Buller's creation of opportunities for 'redemption' and Butler's 'innocent but indiscreet', Roberts' 'hanging around and being' and the *People*'s reference to 'blatant tarts'. The well-meaning reformists were little better: Lord Chorley referred to 'well-behaved women' and Lord Stonham displayed a paternalistic concern for the prostitutes in Holloway prison.[56]

Despite his tolerant attitude the same type of thinking was evident in Professor Gibbens' professional interest in prostitution as a pathological or medical condition 'in itself' rather than in prostitution as a peculiarly stressful and dangerous way of life that might 'of itself' produce stress-related symptoms. Variations of the same theme and the need for detention were promoted by Wolfenden and considered by Ingleby. It is to the credit of the Ingleby Committee that they were rejected.

As Smart observed:

> the law entitles state agencies to intervene, not only to punish but also to control physically by curtailing the woman's or girl's liberty. Persistent promiscuity or public prostitution, even though the female subject is defined as victim, invariably leads to some form of restriction for young women.[57]

The prostitute's constant engagement with the law and her strategies for avoidance are accompanied by the criminalisation of a way of life that sets her apart and confirms difference in the eyes of others. Thus the law itself both confirms and perpetuates the perception of the prostitute as a labelled and stigmatised 'other' of inferior value who cannot be included within the collective term 'any person'. There is no doubt that despite the posturing and rhetoric Lord Stow Hill and Lord Dilhorne were perfectly well aware of the dangers of applying this legislation to 'any person' as opposed to an artificially constructed category of stigmatised women.

In his confidential letter to Lord Chorley Lord Stonham explained that the Home Office did not have time to make a detailed study of the draft Bill or to undertake any consultations with people outside the department who might have views on it – for example, the Director of Public Prosecutions or the police. He made the reasons for this fairly clear in his second letter when he apologised for his lack of encouragement and a degree of inconsistency in his comments:[58]

> On the one hand I have pointed to the lack of definitions as a major defect. On the other hand I have criticized the definitions you have included as being too wide. This highlights what may be an insuperable obstacle in drafting a Bill with the objects you have in mind. I appreciate that it is extremely difficult to devise satisfactory definitions of the terms used. Yet without definitions the Bill would create an undesirable uncertainty in the law.[59]

As Lord Stonham had pointed out during the debate in February 1968, it was the lack of any need to prove persistence or molestation that had provided the 1959 Act with its deterrent effect.[60] He could have also included dispensing with the proof of annoyance, the escalating fines and the prison sentences, which he was to condemn in 1970. It seems likely that the Home Office was well aware of the criticisms of the 1959 Act and did not wish to expose them to scrutiny, especially as it recognised that the Act had providing the police with effective powers for clearing the streets of prostitutes.

The attitudes of the two main challengers to the measures, Lord Stow Hill and Lord Dilhorne, are instructive. As we have seen, Lord Stow Hill had opposed the Street Offences Bill in 1959 whereas Lord Dilhorne, in his role as Attorney-General, had defended the cautioning system as a means of redemption for prostitutes. Yet in 1969 Lord Dilhorne claimed that, 'the Act was not an Act which purported to deal with moral questions. We tried to keep all moral questions out of it.' The trouble was that the streets of London were 'infested' with prostitutes.[61] Yet at the end of the 1960s both men detected flaws in a Bill that could incriminate 'any person' and they agreed (as did Lord Stonham) that the measure would introduce areas of uncertainty and injustice into the law. The Earl of Cork and Orrery also struggled with his conscience. 'If they repeal the only law that ever succeeded in keeping them off the streets . . . then the first thing that will happen is that the women who were swept off the streets in 1959 will return – not "may" . . . but "will".' It seems that a number of their lordships were unhappy with the provisions of the1959 Act, but while they were willing to tolerate the categorisation of the 'common prostitute' they were not prepared, in the interest of justice or of non-discriminatory terminology, to extend the injustices within that Act to the vaguely defined category of 'any person'.

NOTES

1. In the case of *Ford* (1978) 1 All E.R. 1129, it was confirmed that a homosexual act was still 'immoral' within the meaning of section 32 of the Sexual offences Act 1956, despite the fact that it was no longer a criminal offence.
2. Two years' imprisonment on conviction for a man 'to persistently solicit or importune in a public place for immoral purposes'.
3. *Crook* v. *Edmondson* was cited in the case of *Dodd* (1978) 66 Cr. App. R. 87, when it was confirmed that a man who solicited a woman over the age of 16 for the purpose of prostitution was not committing a criminal offence under section 32 of the Sexual Offences Act 1956. In this instance three 14-year-old girls were solicited by Dodd and his conduct was deemed to be both immoral and criminal. In the case of *Goddard* (1991) 92 Cr. App. R. 185, it was deemed that the decision as to whether an act constituted an 'immoral purpose' should be left to the jury, which would reach its decision in the light of 'contemporary standards of morality'. See also S. S. M. Edwards (1996), *Sex and Gender in the Legal Process*, Blackstone Press, Oxford, p. 160. A similar nexus of problems concerning consent to intercourse has always bedevilled rape cases.
4. Women's campaign to have this problem recognised legislatively was to take until the 1990s, when the Criminal Justice and Public Order Act 1994 made intentional harassment in the street or at work a criminal offence, and the Protection from Harassment Act 1997 made it a civil tort enabling the victim to obtain an injunction and damages against the harasser. See Jeanne Gregory and Sue Lees (1999), *Policing Sexual Assault*, Routledge, London, p. 21. See also Edwards, *Sex and Gender*, p. 328.
5. Working Party on Vagrancy and Street Offences Working Paper (1974), para. 268.
6. Sexual Offences Act 1967 [14. Eliz. 2. c.60]. The Act decriminalised certain homosexual acts between consenting adult males in private. It did not apply to the armed forces.
7. JBS to the Lord Chancellor (Chairman of the Law Commission), undated, possibly1967, JBS collection. The writer listed six occasions on which assurances had been given that section 32 would provide protection for women. Attention was drawn to the case of *Doherty* (18 August 1959) which preceded *Crook* v. *Edmondson*. The defendant appeared before the West London Magistrates Court charged with soliciting five women. The magistrate had no doubt that Doherty did solicit, but was not satisfied that this constituted an offence under section 32 of the Sexual Offences Act 1956 (which, as I have demonstrated, was not a clearly defined offence). The defendant was granted an absolute discharge.
8. J. E. Hall Williams, 'The Reform of the Law of Sexual Offences: Offences Connected with Prostitution' (undated paper, probably 1971–72, giving details of background of personal involvement with the AMSH and account of the progress of the drafting legislation, with comments on the legislation), 3/JBS2, WL. In June 1961 Hall Williams received a phone call from Mr Norman Marsh, the director of the British Institute for International and Comparative Law (BIICL), asking him if he would be prepared to help in the drafting of a model law on the traffic in women and girls which would be suitable for introduction in the common law countries. The AMSH had approached the BIICL with the aim of providing draft legislation that could be adopted by countries adhering to the 1949 United Nations Convention for the Suppression of Traffic in Persons. Professor George Levasseur of the Sorbonne in Paris was working on a parallel draft that would be applicable to civil law countries. Professor Levasseur had spoken at a conference held in Cambridge in autumn 1960, during which he stressed the urgency of adapting existing legislation dealing with the traffic in persons so as to conform with the legislation currently in operation in the UK. (This project was eventually abandoned, as it was thought that too many friendly states dealt with prostitution under vagrancy laws, as the UK had originally done, see letter from C.H. Leigh (LSE) to the JBS, 28 February 1966, 3/JBS2, Box 131.) It was through this series of events that Hall Williams became involved with the AMSH and cooperated with Lord Chorley in the drafting of the Street Offences Amendment Bills.
9. Lord Balfour of Burleigh died in 1963. Lord Stonham became president in 1960 and Lord Sorensen in 1965. Various well-known political figures were vice-presidents, including Viscountess Astor, Dame Joan Vickers and Eirene White, MP. During 1961 both Anthony Greenwood and Dame Rachel Crowdy Thornhill (see previous chapter on Wolfenden) were on the executive committee and in 1963, Alan Fitch MP was also on the committee.
10. Reginald William Sorensen, b.1891; MP for Leyton West 1929–31 and 1935–50 and for Leyton 1950–64; created life peer as Baron Sorensen of Leyton 1964.

11. The Baron Stonham (Victor John Collins) Earl Stonham Suffolk, 1903–71. Educated London School of Economics; MP for Taunton Division Somerset 1945–50, and for Shoreditch and Finsbury 1954–58; Parliamentary Under-Secretary of State for the Home Office 1964–67; Minister of State for the Home Office 1967–69, Chairman of South West Regional Board Mental Health Committee 1950–54; President of Psychiatric Rehabilitation Association; Chairman Advisory Council on the Probation and After Care Service. Worked for prison reform over many years. For obituary see *The Times*, 23 December 1971.

12. Robert Samuel Theodore Chorley (1895–1978).1st Baron *cr* 1945, of Kendal; Barrister-at-Law, Inner Temple 1920; QC 1961; Junior Clerk Foreign Office 1916–17; employed in Home Office 1940–41; Assistant Secretary Ministry Home Security 1941–42. Tutor at the Law Society's School of Law 1920–24, Lecturer in Commercial Law 1924–30; Sir Ernest Cassel; Professor of Commercial and Industrial Law in the University of London 1930–46; Dean of the Faculty of Laws, London University of London 1939–42; Vice-President of Howard League for Penal reform, from 1948; President of Society of Public Teachers of Law 1954–5; President of Institute for the Study and Treatment of Delinquency from 1956; General Editor of *Modern Law Review* 1937–71.

13. Lord Chorley, 'The Reform of the Street Offences Act 1959: An Account of an Attempt that Failed', *Shield* (1970), pp. 7–13.

14. Ibid., p. 4.

15. *Guardian*, 19 November 1968.

16. Prosecutions for soliciting offences in Birmingham rose from 168 in 1965, to 209 in 1966 and 351 in 1967.

17. The MPs present included included Harold Green (Selly Oak), Reginald Erye (Hall Green), Sir Edward Boyle (Handsworth), and Dennis Howell (Small Heath). See *Guardian*, 19 November 1968.

18. *News of the World*, 26 November 1967.

19. *Evening News*, 15 June 1967.

20. *Catholic Herald*, 8 September 1967.

21. *Observer*, 6 September 1964.

22. *Observer*, 26 February 1966.

23. Ibid.

24. *Evening News*, 1 December 1967.

25. *The Times & Guardian*, 7 February 1968; *Sun*, 8 February 1968.

26. Street Offences [H.L.] 'An Act to Amend the Street Offences Act 1959', *The Lord Chorley*, 30 November 1967.

27. HL Deb. Vol. 288, No. 38, col. 1280, 8 February 1968.

28. Cmnd. 247, para. 276.

29. Home Office complacency was challenged in the House on a number of occasions. For example, Alan Fitch asked the Secretary of State if he was aware that the call-girl racket had increased, and was informed that the purpose of the Act had been to drive the women off the streets, and Members would agree that it had been remarkably successful. See PD. 5th Ser. Vol. 612, col. 1194, 5 November 1959. Mr Fitch asked the Secretary of State if he would introduce legislation to restore the need to prove annoyance, and Mr R. A. Butler replied. 'No Sir'. See PD. 5th Ser. Vol. 626, col.1582, 14 July 1960. On a query concerning imprisonment Alan Fitch was informed that between August 1959 and September 1962, 1,185 women had been sentenced to terms of imprisonment. No case had been made out for further legislation. See PD. Vol. 675, cols. 606–7, 4 April 1963. See also the *Shield* 1963, p. 12. Dame Joan Vickers, asked the Secretary of State, 4 February 1965, whether the Street Offences Act would be amended and was told that the Home Secretary had no plans for amending legislation on the subject. See PD. Vol. 705, col. 310, 4 February 1965. See also *Shield* 1965, p. 13.

30. HL Deb. Vol. 288, No. 38, col. 1289, 8 February 1968.

31. Chorley, *The Reform of the Street Offences Act 1959*.

32. A drafting committee was set up headed by Lord Chorley. It was comprised of Lord Foot, Lady Birk, Mrs Bligh, C. R. Hewitt, Hall Williams and Antony Grey (secretary of the Homosexual Law Reform Society, known as the Albany Trust, and member of the National Council of Civil Liberties, *Shield* 1970, p. 31.

33. *Daily Express*, 27 November 1968; *Yorkshire Evening Post*, 26 November 1968.

34. Street Offences [H.L.] 'An Act to amend the Street Offences Act 1959', *The Lord Chorley*, 23 January 1969.

35. HL Deb. Vol. 301, No. 55, col. 218, 17 April 1969.
36. HL Deb. Vol. 307. No. 33, col. 581–2, 3 February, 1970.
37. HL Deb. Vol. 301. No. 55, col. 263, 17 April 1969.
38. Ibid., col. 223.
39. PD 5th Ser. Vol. 604, col. 511, 22 April 1959.
40. Ibid., col. 513.
41. *New Statesman*, 25 April 1969.
42. HL Deb. Vol. 301. No.55, cols. 214, 253, 255, 267 and 276, 17 April 1969. Lord Stow Hill put down a long series of complicated amendments with the intention of wrecking the Bill.
43. Street Offences [H.L.] 'An Act to amend the Street Offences Act 1959', *The Lord Chorley*, 18 December 1969.
44. HL Deb. Vol. 288, No. 38, col. 1320, 8 February 1968.
45. Lord Chorley, *Shield* (1970), p. 9.
46. 3/JBS2, WL. Lord Stonham to Lord Chorley, 19 August 1968. This letter makes reference to phrases such as 'offering or obtaining prostitution', which do not occur in the printed Bill. Therefore the drafting committee must have adapted the 1969 bill in the light of Lord Stonham's suggestions.
47. 3/JBS/2 Lord Stonham to Lord Chorley, 3 December 1968, Home Office.
48. HL Deb. Vol. 307. No. 33, col. 591, 3 February 1970.
49. Ibid., col. 594–5.
50. C. Smart (1989), *Feminism and the Power of the Law*, Routledge, London, pp. 82, 93–4.
51. Gail Pheterson (1990), 'The Category "Prostitute" in Scientific Inquiry', *Journal of Sex Research*, Vol. 27, No. 3, August, 1990, pp. 397–407.
52. Most present-day commentators regard violence against prostitutes as endemic. See, for example, Maggie O'Neill, 'Prostitute Women Now' in G. and A. Scambler (1997), *Rethinking Prostitution: Purchasing Sex in the 1990s*, Routledge, London, p. 28.
53. Lars O. Ericsson (1980), 'Charges Against Prostitution: An Attempt at a Philosophical Assessment', *Ethics*, 90, April 1980: 335–66.
54. See Gail Pheterson (1993), The Whore Stigma: Female Dishonour and Male Unworthiness, *Social Text*, 37, pp. 43–5. Pheterson lists the civil rights that she maintains may be lost by whores as a result of their stigmatisation, which include freedom to travel or emigrate, loss of custody of children, loss of sexual self-determination and sexual privacy, denial of health insurance, forced medical checks, denial of the right to expand her business, lack of police protection from violence, excessive tax demands, etc.
55. Ericsson, 'Charges against Prostitution', p. 361.
56. By the term 'paternalistic' I am inferring that Lord Stonham viewed women as children, but I would not wish to devalue his undoubted commitment to the cause of prison reform.
57. C. Smart (1981), 'Law and the Control of Women's Sexuality', in B. Hutter and G. Williams (eds), *Controlling Women: The Normal and the Deviant*, Croom Helm, London, p. 56.
58. Stonham to Chorley, 19 August 1968.
59. Stonham to Chorley, 3 December 1968.
60. HL. Deb. Vol. 288, No. 38, col. 1294, 8 February 1959.
61. HL Deb. Vol. 301, No. 55, col. 229, 17 April 1969.

CHAPTER FOURTEEN

Resolving New Problems
with More Legislation

As time progressed the complexity of the social scene increased and the effectiveness of the Street Offences Act was seen to diminish, while at the same time a colourful saga of events flowed from its implementation. The JBET commissioned a small research project into the working of the Act and official concern over the issue of prostitution prompted the setting-up of two more government committees. The penalty of imprisonment was abolished in 1982, and two more Private Members Bills were introduced in an attempt to change the legislation. In contrast to official expectations it seems that the Street Offences Act had exacerbated the difficulties of regulating prostitution, leading to a new set of problems and additional legislation in 1985. The efforts to reform the 1959 Act had highlighted the increasing nuisance of kerb-crawling which, to some extent, had resulted from the scarcity of street prostitutes and their dispersal to lonelier places. But as with previous legislation, the Sexual Offences Act 1985 made the lives of prostitutes even more perilous.

ASSESSING THE EFFECTS OF THE STREET OFFENCES ACT 1959

Judith Priceman: Research Project into the Working of the 1959 Act (1972)[1]

The defeat of Lord Chorley's third Bill was a demoralising blow for the JBS, which was under financial strain as a result of its activities. Calls were made during the following AGM for the society to close down, but it responded by launching a new appeal for funds and continued to operate.[2] Miss Priceman from the London School of Economics was appointed in January 1972 to be a temporary research worker 'for the purpose of examining the working of the Act, and related matters'.[3] The initial appointment was for one month, which was to be extended for a second month if necessary.[4] The purpose of the research was to present the Home Office with some new evidence of the effects of the Act on the practice of prostitution, with a view to influencing a movement towards reforming the legislation on lines similar to those that had already failed. The JBS was under the impression that girls who had been reported missing were drawn into prostitution without the knowledge of the police, and hoped that if this could be demonstrated it might generate sufficient concern to influence public opinion and official attitudes.[5]

Miss Priceman found that the field of enquiry did not lend itself to what she believed was the more usual method of social research, and the marginal nature of the subject proved to be a barrier to establishing direct contact with practising prostitutes. She interviewed or corresponded with a variety of professionals including probation officers, welfare workers and police officials, but found that many of them approached the subject in the light of their own moral convictions and prejudices.[6] In her final report she divided the respondents up into those who looked favourably on the 1959 Act and those who considered it to have had negative consequences.[7]

Among those who approved was Chief Administrative Police Officer, Mrs Becke, of New Scotland Yard, who thought that the legislation had worked satisfactorily as it had succeeded in reducing the number of women on the streets.[8] She endorsed the Wolfenden objectives, which she viewed as a compromise, but condemned the cautioning system because it could easily be evaded. The evidence given by Miss Bleaby, a senior probation officer, who wrote on behalf of the Birmingham Aftercare Service, supported this reservation.[9] Miss Bleaby felt that the concepts of nuisance and morality had become confused, leading to public bewilderment about the purpose of the legislation, and therefore she recommended that proof of nuisance should be restored. In her opinion the police were still operating a corrupt rota system, most girls were uninterested in reform, and sending them to prison was a complete waste of public money.[10]

Like Mrs Becke the members of the Aftercare Association felt that the cautioning system was being abused by the police, who sometimes entered cautions in the register without a woman's knowledge and when she was not working. The cautioning system was also criticised by welfare workers who made similar complaints. The overall judgement was that prostitutes were very much at the mercy of the police since the new Act had enabled them to arrest women solely on the basis of police evidence.[11] Inspector Williams from Leman Street Police Station, London E1, was equally frustrated but for rather different reasons. He found that girls just laughed when they were asked if they wanted help and did not regard themselves as lawbreakers. He thought that attempts to reform them were hopeless and that the labelling had an adverse effect.[12]

One retired probation officer, Mrs M. A. Weaver, considered the Act to be 'the worst piece of legislation ever to pass through Parliament'. She argued that before it came into being, the women were known by name to the police, the probation officers and the Salvation Army, as well as to other organisations interested in the women's physical and mental well-being, and that an estimate could be made of the numbers working in a particular district. Women were now being forced into areas where living was cheap, and where landlords hoping to benefit from their trade were willing to afford them accommodation. These areas, Mrs Weaver regretted, were predominantly immigrant locations and she had found through examining conviction records that the majority of the men living on the earnings of prostitutes were in the main West Indian, Maltese and Indian. Mrs Weaver believed that far from decreasing the amount of prostitution the Act had probably led to an increase that was screened not only by bricks and mortar, but by those who wished to use their trade for personal gain.[13]

Professor Gibbens was interviewed on his work with women in Holloway Prison in 1967–68. He found that many of the prison inmates had worked either full-time or sporadically as prostitutes and stressed the casualness of their recruitment. He found little evidence of the existence of professionalism and argued that the pimp was frequently the boyfriend and not the demon he was made out to be.[14] This view of the pimp was supported by Dennis Powell, Principal Probation Officer, Brixton, who was also concerned by police corruption.[15] Powell concluded that the legislation was unsatisfactory and that the term 'common prostitute' had a negative effect on the women, whereas Professor Gibbens believed that the Act served no useful purpose and ought to be repealed.

Captain Hutchins of the Salvation Army reported that girls were still absconding from approved schools.[16] His colleague, Brigadier Scott, confirmed that the women were now more difficult to find.[17] One respondent from the 'London Haven', King's Cross, stated that there were virtually no cases of girls being referred to them by the police.[18] She judged prostitution to be sporadic, thought that exploitation had probably increased and claimed (as always) that the average age of the girls was decreasing. Some of them, she observed, came by train or lorry from Glasgow or the North of England. Father Joseph Williamson argued that driving the women off the streets had made the trade more lucrative for the men. He backed his assumption with the prosecution statistics for men living on the earnings of prostitution in London, which were 202 during 1970, that is, over 100 more than ten years earlier. He concluded that there was probably more prostitution in total than before the Act and believed that 'the government had done nothing to help prostitutes get out of that life'.[19] It was left to A. E. Cox, a solicitor from the Magistrates Court in Great Marlborough Street, to make the familiar comments about hardened girls from rough areas who knew their price. He was in favour of the Act and thought that the women need not be exploited if they did not want to be. He was also true to form in believing that trying to convict the men was impractical.[20]

Miss Priceman concluded that the information gained through official sources derived from the unsuccessful prostitutes who came into conflict with the law. She estimated that these represented only a fraction of the women who were actually involved. She was aware of the limitations of her project and regretted the lack of empirical data, commenting, 'there is much reason to be cautious about the degree of subjectivity implicit in the information and opinions transmitted'. Even so, she felt sufficiently confident to conclude with some certainty that, 'To isolate the simple process of solicitation and the ensuing market transaction from a vast and complicated network of social and psychological variables with which it is associated is unlikely to be a fruitful exercise.'[21]

But this is what she had been obliged to do and, more significantly, it reflected what the Wolfenden Committee had recommended and what the government had implemented so that street soliciting appeared to be the only variable that influenced policy.

SOCIAL CHANGE

During the early 1970s the usual cocktail of concern and titillation kept the subject of prostitution and society's changing moral standards in the public eye. The *Daily Telegraph*[22] asked, 'Isn't It Time We Made Our Streets Safe For Women? . . . Kerb-crawling is one of the persistent menaces of our big cities . . . a change in the laws is vital'. On the medical front, Dr John Slome, a Harley Street physician, read a paper to the Third International Congress of Psychosomatic Medicine and Gynaecology entitled 'Abortion – The Unmarried Mother'. He informed his colleagues that the kiss of the 1940s and 1950s had become the sexual intercourse of the 1960s and 1970s. Many unmarried women became pregnant as a result of casual friendships and resorted to abortion as a solution to their problems.[23] The dating or escort agency was added to the hierarchical list of prostitution outlets, 'Girl Offered for Night'.[24] At the same time drugs, and especially heroin, became a cause for anxiety, as in the 'Secret of Vice Girl Sally' whose life was ruined by addiction.[25] 'The sexually liberated atmosphere of the 1970s', wrote Baston, and 'the confusing laws concerning prostitution did not seem worth enforcing, which with social trends led to a boom in all forms of commercial sex. Call-girl operations flourished just as they had done in the early 60s but in a much less clandestine way.'[26]

By 1975 the writer and journalist Alan Mankoff felt free to publish a report on the pleasures of 51 European cities entitled 'Lusty Europe: The Only All-Purpose Guide to Sex, Love and Romance'.[27] The Director of Public Prosecutions answered a letter of complaint from the JBS secretary, Margaret Schwarz, which inquired if there were grounds for prosecution. The DPP replied: 'In my view no criminal offences are disclosed.'[28]

The driving force behind much of this shift in social mores was the production of the contraceptive pill in the 1960s, which placed in women's hands the power to control their own fertility. The impact upon attitudes towards marriage, family life and the importance of virginity, especially among the young, was enormous. One of the best indicators of this development was the case of Victoria Gillick, who in 1981 took her local area health authority to court in an attempt to prevent doctors from giving contraceptive advice to girls under the age of consent. Gillick won her case in the Court of Appeal in 1984[29] but lost it in 1985 when the Department of Health and Social Security (DHSS) appealed successfully to the House of Lords.[30]

In 1974 the DHSS had issued a 'Memo of Guidance' to doctors advising them to prescribe the contraceptive pill for young people under 16 and to respect confidentiality but to consult parents if possible. The DHSS memo in 1974 and their Lordships' judgment in 1985 were an acknowledgement of a glaring reality. Many young people below the age of consent were having sexual relations on a fairly casual basis without the slightest intention of getting married. It was the very state of affairs that Alfred Kinsey had forecast. Doctors therefore made what they presumably concluded was the sensible and pragmatic decision that it was better for girls to have confidential medical advice and treatment than to give birth to unwanted children.

REVIEWING THE WORKING OF THE STREET OFFENCES ACT 1959

The Vagrancy and Street Offences Committee (VSOC)

The deficiencies of the Street Offences Act had become apparent very rapidly. Hall Williams recorded that during the first seven weeks only one person was placed on probation out of 264 convictions and only ten pleaded not guilty, while the majority of women received fines of £25.[31] In the first two months of the Act's operation, 33 women were sent to prison for persistent soliciting and 53 for default of fines. He claimed that the Metropolitan Police reports had shown a continual decline in the use of the cautioning system and an almost complete failure of any attempt to place prostitutes in touch with the probationary service.[32]

Although the Criminal Law Revision Committee (CLRC) was to review the issue of prostitution, Lord Chorley's Bills and the problems that had arisen over the decade must have influenced government thinking sufficiently for the Home Office to consider that the subject needed looking at more urgently. Consequently the Working Party on Vagrancy and Street Offences[33] was appointed in 1971 by Home Secretary Reginald Maudling.[34] The 'Foreword' to the committees' Working Paper[35] states that it was decided to include street offences in its review since there was some overlap between the provisions of the Vagrants Act 1824 and the Street Offences Act 1959. On this occasion the problem of prostitution was coupled with a review of vagrancy, confirming that soliciting for the purpose of prostitution was viewed as a matter of public order rather than as a sexual offence. 'It was thought that this question and other problems concerning soliciting by men and women were best considered in the context of the whole body of law relating to street offences'.[36]

The committee reviewed the 1959 Act, which was said to have been 'a considerable success in its aim of clearing prostitutes from the streets'.[37] Prostitution was declared to be 'a trade like any other trade', which must, therefore, be regulated. It confirmed the notion implicit in the Wolfenden Report that: 'The conduct with which the law seeks to deal is conduct which people find offensive precisely because it is committed by prostitutes in pursuing their calling.'[38] The VSOC decided that the public had a legitimate right to protect itself from nuisance, but whereas begging had to be 'persistent' for it to be seen as a nuisance, the law on prostitution incorporated an element of persistence through the operation of the cautioning procedure. It supported the system although it was admitted that it had failed as a rehabilitative mechanism and had actively encouraged prostitutes to become peripatetic. Moreover, it was considered useful in that it provided the evidence that a woman was a 'common prostitute'.[39] The logic behind this reasoning was the principle of 'potential nuisance', originally put forward by Roberts, which legitimated the arrest of a prostitute for merely 'hanging around and being'.

In order to overcome the ineffectiveness of the cautioning system as a means of rehabilitating prostitutes, it recommend an extension of police powers so as to enable officers to arrest a women when cautioning her and require her to see a probation officer (a procedure which Butler had sought to avoid). However the committee was ambivalent over the possible efficacy of this idea not because it was unethical but because it was assumed that a woman was already 'case-hardened' by the time she first appeared in court.[40]

With regard to kerb-crawling there was some contradiction. It was argued that 'a man moving around in a car or on foot and talking to a woman is not *prima facie* creating a nuisance, as is a woman dressed as a streetwalker, and the terms of the offence would require much observation'.[41] Yet two pages later the report repeats Lord Stonham's comment that 'while the woman prostitute in the street can be an offensive nuisance, the soliciting male can be a menace'[42].

The final recommendations included: (19) 'A new offence should be created to control kerb-crawling and related behaviour on the lines that it should be an offence for a man persistently to accost a woman or women for sexual purposes in a street or public place in such circumstances as are likely to cause annoyance to the public, such as residents and users of the streets', and, (21), that section 32 of the Sexual Offences Act 1956 should be retained.

The committee continued to uphold the official Home Office view that any relaxation of the law on soliciting would result in a return of large numbers of prostitutes on the streets and that the public preferred to maintain the status quo.

CRITICISMS

Following the publication of the report the inevitable criticisms found their way into the press and were primarily aimed at the proposed penalties[43] and the deficiencies of the cautioning system. The National Association for the Care and Resettlement of Offenders (NACRO) wrote to *The Times*[44] complaining at the absurdity of inflicting prison sentences on vagrants and beggars as it did not provide a meaningful deterrent to severely deprived and impoverished people. At the same time the imprisonment of prostitutes had no rehabilitative value and only resulted in women exchanging information about the best areas for soliciting and recruiting inmates.

The Howard League for Penal Reform[45] produced a more comprehensive appraisal of the Working Paper, which it described as 'complacent'. The Working Party, it complained, had seen no reason for recommending any reform of the provisions of the Street Offences Act 1959, the only innovation suggested being an increase in fines. The League took a very different view of the legislation, which it considered to be unethical. In many respects it supported the position of the JBS and, in particular, Lord Chorley's second Bill, which had proposed making it an 'offence for any person in a street or a public place persistently to accost any person or persons with a view to obtaining sexual services for payment or reward' and similarly, 'to importune any other person so as to cause annoyance or nuisance to any person who resided in or used the street or public place'. With regard to the recommendation in the Working Paper, the Howard League considered it wrong to make the 'conduct' (loitering or soliciting) that was designed to lead to a legal transaction, that is, prostitution, into a criminal offence. It proposed instead that the phrase 'unreasonable nuisance and affront' (suggested by the Working Party in relation to begging) should be used to define the offence of soliciting. This phrase, it was argued, could cover persistent importuning and should be supported by the evidence of an aggrieved person. 'It seems to us absolutely wrong that a woman can be in danger of a custodial sentence without a shred of evidence being produced in court that anyone has been affronted by her actions.'[46]

The lack of sound and reliable evidence against loitering prostitutes was the central theme of the Howard League's analysis, which contended that if a woman pleaded 'not guilty' the evidence that she had already been cautioned twice would be produced to convict her. Moreover, the same policeman might be involved at every stage of the process. In the League's opinion a caution could be more damaging to a woman than a conviction, as it was not convinced that an innocent woman was automatically informed of the procedure available for expunging it from police records. Prison sentences, it complained, were being imposed for a crime which only amounted to 'loitering with intent'. The League considered that far from helping a women to resist the temptation of entering prostitution the process of labelling encouraged her to identify with a sub-culture, and that police harassment, connivance and bullying were part of this process. Finally it agreed with probation officers that it was wrong in principle to use the criminal law as a means for bringing more women within the reach of the social services.

The JBS submitted evidence in the usual way covering the history of the society's fight for justice and equal moral standards. However it made one new point of interest which was an objection to the use of the heading 'Offences by Prostitutes' within the official statistics, stating that 'all other categories are classified under the offence and not under that of the person who committed it'.[47] This practice, as with many other procedures for dealing with prostitution, served to reinforce the labelling process that defined prostitutes as a legal category of women who were different from normal women.

The VSOC of the 1970s was an extremely conservative body and did not respond in any way to criticisms of the 1959 Act or to the changing moral atmosphere within society. Both the Working Party Paper and the final Report [48] endorsed the position set out in the Wolfenden Report in 1957. It had been charged with assessing developments since 1959, but as with the Wolfenden Committee it claimed that it did not fall within its remit to make a study of the causes of prostitution. The emphasis therefore remained on maintaining 'law and order' in the street and on protecting the public purse from excessive expenditure and time-consuming procedures such as gathering evidence of 'persistence'. The committee remained 'stoically complacent'[49] and so another opportunity was lost for recommending reform or for equalisation of the legislation. This was left to the Criminal Law Revision Committee.

A RENEWAL OF CONFIDENCE

The continuing pressure for change was both relentless and confusing. It can only have been increased by the fact that prostitutes had begun to campaign for legal recognition of their occupation. This development was appreciated by Lady Joan Vickers MP, who organised a conference in London on 27 August 1978 to which magistrates, probation officers, social workers and members of the Home Office were invited.[50] The proceedings were reported in *The Times* on the following day.[51] The English Collective of Prostitutes (ECP)[52] had demanded an end to laws that made prostitutes dependent on pimps, the use of the term 'common prostitute', the criminalisation of two prostitutes living together, police harassment and the lack of police protection against rape, theft, battery and deformation of character. The organisation claimed that a massive number of women had at some time resorted to prostitution and that many families survived only because a mother, daughter or wife was on the game.[53] In response to this campaign Maureen Colquhoun, Labour MP for Northampton North, said that she would attempt to introduce a Ten-Minute Rule Bill in the Commons to back these demands.[54]

THE PROTECTION OF PROSTITUTES BILL 1979

During 1979 and 1981 there were two more attempts to change the law. The first bill,[55] the 'Protection of Prostitutes Bill', was launched in the House of Commons by Maureen Colquhoun[56] and had a double purpose. First it proposed to make it an offence for:

any person in a street or a public place (whether on foot or in a vehicle) persistently to accost, solicit or importune any other person or persons so as to cause annoyance to those persons or a nuisance to any other person who resides in or uses the said street or public place.

Evidence was to be presented by the person who had been annoyed. The second purpose addressed the problem that had been created by sections 33 to 36 (suppression of brothels) of the Sexual Offences Act 1956. These sections restricted prostitutes to isolated working conditions, which left them vulnerable to abuse from violent punters, since premises where two women worked together constituted a brothel. Clause 4 of the Bill provided that:

premises shall not be deemed a brothel for the purposes of the Sexual Offences Act 1956 by reason only of the fact that they are inhabited by more than one prostitute, unless it is proved that the inhabitants are practising prostitution under a system of common direction or control.

The parliamentary debate took place on the 6 March 1976. Ms Colquhoun argued that the Street Offences Act 1959 had been a mistake, which succeeded only in victimising inadequate and unsuccessful prostitute. Prostitution had grown rather than diminished as a result of the Act and it was time 'that the degradation, the harassment, imprisonment and fining of these women stopped.'[57] However, Ms Colquhoun encountered opposition of biblical proportions from the Reverend Ian Paisley, who must have endeared himself to second-wave feminists when he declared that: 'The person who had been caught up in prostitution through exploitation, victimisation, or by her own choice, has lost the greatest thing in life – the purpose for which she came into the world. She had lost her goal.' This goal, he believed, was attained through motherhood and the sanctity, joy and peace that flowed from family life. The Bill, he assured the House, was a scheme to undermine what lay at the very heart of the moral fabric of our society.[58]

Unfortunately the Protection of Prostitutes Bill reintroduced some of the problems that had been experienced with Lord Chorley's Bill, including the definition of 'any person' and the need to prove 'persistently'. It would not have been approved by the JBS which, despite its support for justice and equality, was not anxious to do anything that might make it easier for the women to practise. The Bill was unsuccessful.

CLIVE SOLEY MP AND THE IMPRISONMENT OF PROSTITUTES (ABOLITION) BILL 1981

A further attempt at reform was the Imprisonment of Prostitutes (Abolition) Bill presented by Clive Soley.[59] Although this Bill was unsuccessful at the time it was influential in achieving the abolition of imprisonment for soliciting,[60] a measure that was incorporated in section 71 of the Criminal Justice Act 1982.[61]

THE CRIMINAL JUSTICE BILL 1982

Following Soley's Bill the repeal of the penalty of imprisonment had become an achievable aim. The parliamentary debate (11 March 1982) was opened by Miss Jo Richardson (Barking) who returned to the pre-Butler argument that prostitutes were usually poor and uneducated women. She argued that the offence of soliciting was discriminatory because it impacted upon the least successful women who worked on the streets, many of whom were mothers.[62] Alex Lyon (York) emphasised the profound change in the moral climate since the early 1950s, when the only place a man was likely to find a woman of this sort was on the streets. He supported Kinsey's prophesy saying that, 'people now are much freer in their relationships and do not need the services of a prostitute in the same way', but argued that as there was still a residue of women on the streets there would probably always be some irreducible minimum.

The abolition of imprisonment did not meet with universal approval. For example, *The Times*[63] reported the comments of Mr David Hopkins, Chief Metropolitan Stipendiary Magistrate, who called for effective penalties to be found. 'Fining prostitutes left magistrates with the feeling of being an accomplice, as one knows that the money to pay will be earned by the lady on her back.' Hopkins remarked that one solution was to make it an offence for a man to solicit a prostitute's services. Indeed, the Justices' Clerks' Society, which proposed this in its evidence to the CLRC, considered that prostitution was on the increase and that this measure would greatly decrease the incidence of street soliciting. [64] It therefore suggested that there should be a new offence of 'accepting unlawful solicitation'. At the same time fines would be retained and the cautioning system abandoned.

These proposals had a mixed reception. The *Daily Telegraph*[65] reflected the divergent views on the controversy. A spokesperson for the Police Federation thought that it might lead to blackmail, as a man could be ruined if he were prosecuted. On the other hand the Magistrates Association's Legal Committee recommended a reform that would make it an offence for 'any person' to solicit for the purpose of prostitution. The Law Society thought that it would be sufficient to tighten up on kerb-crawling, while the Sexual Law Reform Society believed that there was no need for any special laws to control sexual behaviour on the street since this was considered to be an unwarranted interference with the liberties of individual citizens.

THE EMERGING STREET SCENE, 1980–85

As the 1980s progressed the economic recession was blamed for an increase in the number of women entering prostitution and many of the English Collective of Prostitutes' complaints were reflected in the media. The *Daily Mail* and the *Daily Star*[66] ran similar features on the seedy world of the streets: 'Selling Sex' and 'Vice for Sale'. They argued that the slump had encouraged more women and girls to move into prostitution and that they were getting younger and younger. The *Daily Mirror*[67] exposed the 'Nightmare World of a Teenage Prostitute: Shocking Exposure of a Booming Trade', revealing the 'frightening growth in the number of school children and youngsters taking to the game'. The children's charity Barnardo's complained that organised gangs of pimps were recruiting vulnerable children from local authority homes.[68] Councillors in Birmingham responded to a worsening situation by debating the possibility of designating a red-light area. This plan was opposed by the Bishop of Birmingham, the Right Reverend Hugh Montefiore, the Chief Constable of the West Midlands, Sir Philip Knights and the prostitutes themselves.[69]

The campaign to do something about kerb-crawling began to match the intensity of the 1950s drive against streetwalking. The *Observer*[70] reported on the level of anxiety experienced by the residents of Tooting in London, who were 'unable to go anywhere for fear of being attacked by pimps'. Complaints and responses came from around the country, claiming that females of all ages were being accosted and that the constant activity was making respectable residents' lives a nightmare. *The Times* and the *Daily Telegraph*[71] reported that the police in Hyson Green, Nottingham, used the 600-year old Justice of the Peace Act against 13 kerb-crawlers who were bound over to keep the peace. Their names, addresses and photographs received widespread publicity. The *Times* article makes it clear that the problem had escalated and was affecting many of the larger cities around the country including Sheffield, Manchester and Leicester. On the following day *The Times* reported the concerns of the National Council for Civil Liberties, which disapproved of the Nottingham police force's use of policewomen as decoys. The situation was further confused when the London police decided to take action in the King's Cross area. A thousand people were prosecuted within ten weeks, mostly women charged with loitering. The prostitutes responded to police harassment by occupying Holy Cross Church in central London, ensuring that the problems of prostitution would become national news. Local residents blamed the pimps for the violence and disturbance and the police for being unresponsive to the needs of the area. Frank Dobson, Labour MP for Holborn and St Pancras, blamed the pimps for 'changing a cottage industry into big business'. He criticized the police and the Home Office for being 'stunningly complacent'.[72]

It was at this stage that the fear of sexually transmitted disease returned with the emergence of AIDS. There had been 14 cases in Britain and five victims had died.[73] The result was predictable and by 1988 Edwards was writing that, 'Today prostitutes are further vilified as one of the main carrier groups for the AIDS virus, though there is hard evidence to refute this belief.'[74]

THE CRIMINAL LAW REVISION COMMITTEE (1982, 1984, 1986)

In 1975 the Home Secretary, Roy Jenkins, asked the CLRC: 'to review, in consultation with the Policy Advisory Committee on Sexual Offences, the law relating to, and penalties for, sexual offences' including offences related to prostitution.[75] On this occasion the committee comprised 17 judges and lawyers (including two women)[76] whose combined interests and expertise covered a wide spectrum of law. The Policy Advisory Committee (PAC), half of whom were women, represented a cosmopolitan sweep of professional experience including the probation service, journalism, psychiatry, social work, education and sociology. The PAC offered a degree of balance to the review and provided a reference point for the CLRC to draw upon. The committee observed the same basic formula as the VSOC in that it printed questionnaires and invited interested parties to submit evidence, after which it published a working paper, followed at two-year intervals by conclusions and recommendations.[77] Prostitution was to be looked at in relation to sexual offences rather than as a matter of public order or as a corollary to homosexuality.

There was a refreshing willingness to acknowledge social change, if not to act upon it. 'During this century attitudes to and thinking about sexual morality and prostitution have changed. Moralising, condemnatory language about sexual behaviour is generally disliked and is certainly disliked by members of this Committee. But dislike of the ways ideas are expressed does not necessarily connote dislike of the ideas themselves.'[78] The committee found that, 'each time the task of persons reviewing the law has become more difficult',[79] although 'with the important exception of street offences the law on prostitution is, today, substantially the same as it was at the beginning of this century'.[80] This reference to the 'important exception of street offences' seems strangely inaccurate as the Street Offences Act 1959 was essentially a 'tightening-up' of legislation that had remained much the same since the Vagrants Act 1824. The CLRC was presumably acknowledging the need for reforming the Sexual Offences Act 1956 but felt that the 1959 Act was satisfactory.

The CLRC was inevitably caught up in the usual tangle of contradictions. Wolfenden was quoted on the need 'to preserve public order and decency', but it was not the function of the law to intervene in the private lives of citizens. It was claimed that 'we tried to follow the Wolfenden Committee's approach . . . but that has not exempted us from the necessity of making moral judgments . . . So why single out the prostitute? . . . The answer to this question may be that the criminal law intervenes to abate or minimise any mischief when public opinion insists that it should.'[81] Some of the group maintained that the words 'being a prostitute' were offensive and prejudicial, 'making it difficult, almost impossible, for a defendant to get a fair trial if the accusation of loitering or soliciting is contested, and also that these words offend against one of the fundamental rules of our criminal law'[82].

The use of the pejorative term 'common prostitute' had been considered by all previous committees. In 1928 the Macmillan Committee had recommended that the term 'any person' should be substituted in two separate offences, whereas the Wolfenden Committee regretted that it was indispensable. The VSOC, in its turn, acknowledged the criticisms of this term but claimed that it had been presented with no evidence to show that the label had led to any injustice. Indeed, it was convinced that the motivation of the prostitute went much deeper than a simple reaction to the criminal law and commented: 'We were impressed by a suggestion made to us that the way of life of a prostitute is so remarkable a rejection of the normal way of society as to bear comparison with that of a drug addict.'[83] This demonstrated the usual willingness to pathologise prostitutes and to see them as different from other women.

But although the CLRC displayed a generally more enlightened attitude to the subject, the answers, as far as street soliciting was concerned, remained much the same. The court, it was argued, needed to have proof that the woman was a prostitute as it was this that gave her a 'potential' for making a nuisance of herself and lent significance to actions such as smiling at men approaching her. 'Were the court to be denied this knowledge, its task of reaching just and fair decisions would be severely hampered.'[84] These observations encapsulated the essence of the issue of 'justice and equality' that the AMSH/JBS and its predecessors had battled over from the beginning of the campaign to repeal the Contagious Diseases Acts.

POLICE EVIDENCE

As on previous occasions, the Metropolitan Police submitted evidence that demonstrated their frustration at what they perceived as a steadily deteriorating situation:

> The Street Offences Act 1959 initially reduced the West End of prostitutes but they are now returning in ever greater numbers . . . many move from one district to another; the West End, Paddington, Kings Cross and elsewhere. The use of hotels for prostitution has become increasingly popular and there are now so many other types of premises used by prostitutes and their associates that it could reasonably be argued that it is the women who have exploited the changing situation over the past years . . . were it merely street prostitution with which the law had to contend it is feasible that the subject could be decriminalised. But that time has vanished: prostitution has broadened its spectrum and is now so closely associated with other crimes that it would be disastrous to divorce one form of prostitution from another.[85]

The police no longer felt in control of the situation, and their feelings of impotence and insecurity were exacerbated by regional and court variations in the imposition of penalties, which resulted in a system lacking in national continuity. This was increased by wide variations in police practice, which depended on the seriousness with which prostitution was viewed by commanders and applied particularly to off-street prostitution. As one chief inspector commented, 'invisibility itself tends to reduce police interest'.[86]

A further indication that the procedure had broken down was an admission that the cautioning system had failed as an avenue for reformation and rehabilitation, its main function becoming the dubious one of providing evidence of a woman's status. The Metropolitan Police confirmed this, stating that "cautions and charges" appeared to have little deterrent effect. 'When a woman appears in court it is accepted that she has already been cautioned twice, so there must be a presumption of guilt.'[87] It was observed that the women had no desire to receive a lecture from members of the social services who had 'less knowledge of the world' than themselves.

The various tactics that had been adopted in order to avoid the caution contributed towards a decline in the old accommodation between police and prostitute, while the adoption of various disguises and a peripatetic mode of life were combined with a greater willingness to accuse the police of abusing their authority. The police no longer had the benefit of being acquainted with the women who worked on their beat. The main advantage of this, as far as the force was concerned, was that in the prevailing atmosphere of suspicion and mistrust the 'present system acts as a safeguard to protect police officers from possible unfounded allegations'.[88]

CLRC SIXTEENTH REPORT, 'PROSTITUTION IN THE STREET' 1984: RECOMMENDATIONS

In response to pressure from the government the CLRC published its report on prostitution in two stages, beginning in 1984 with 'Prostitution in the Street'[89] and explaining that while its preliminary report on sexual offences was at the printers, 'the Home Office Minister asked our chairman whether, in view of continuing public concern, it would be possible for us to publish a short report dealing with the nuisance of kerb-crawling in advance of our full report on offences relating to prostitution'.[90] The government was again responding to public and media pressure since, despite the 1959 Act, the nuisance element of street prostitution had increased considerably and convictions for 'loitering or soliciting' were steadily rising, with 5,811 in 1982.[91] The use of cars by men as vehicles for kerb-crawling had developed initially in consequence of the scarcity of prostitutes on the streets, while some women had resorted to this method of picking up customers in order to avoid arrest. The inconvenience caused to residents was aggravated by late-night visits to flats, door-banging, screeching of brakes, congestion and an increase of offensive litter, while noise, arguments and squabbling added to the disturbance. Interestingly the report states for the first time that although the Street Offences Act 1959 'did for a short time rid the streets of the nuisance caused by prostitutes plying their trade, the nature of the trade made it likely that the nuisance would start again'.[92]

The evidence of Clive Soley MP (an ex-probation officer) expanded on this point. He argued that the current law, accompanied by the penalty of imprisonment and doubtful police practices, created more social problems than it solved. He believed that the 1959 Act had exposed prostitutes to new forms of exploitation and that it would be better to allow the social services to deal with the problems.[93]

The committee was divided among itself over the matter of imprisonment following the dropping of the penalty in 1982 while it was in sitting. This had been followed by a steep rise in convictions in 1993, amounting to10,000.[94] But despite the many cogent arguments against the penalty it was thought by some of the members that detention ought to be kept for persistent offenders.[95] Indeed, it was stated that, 'For the present time we are content to draw one safe conclusion. This is not the time to amend the law to make it less effective in dealing with street prostitution.'[96] This view was shared by a number of magistrates, and the Magistrates Association had been against abandoning imprisonment. Quentin Campbell, writing in the *Justice of the Peace*, considered the practice futile and wrong, although he still claimed that it was necessary to retain the penalty for persistent offenders.[97] The subject had obviously not lost its potential for contradiction and the irony of the situation was that the numbers of women imprisoned increased due to the non-payment of fines.[98]

With regard to cautioning the committee recommended that the formal recording of cautions should be discontinued when a woman had not admitted (when cautioned) that she had been soliciting, 'although the police should not be discouraged from cautioning a woman informally or from administering a formal caution after admission of guilt'.[99] The CLRC had been persuaded that the dropping of a custodial sentence had made the caution less appropriate as it had reduced the apparent gravity with which loitering for the purpose of prostitution was viewed. On the other hand it noted that the introduction of a woman to the court as 'being a prostitute' fulfilled an evidential function, since it demonstrated that she had already been cautioned twice. Quite clearly the committee was divided over this issue, but commented:

> Although it is not for us as a committee to say what evidence a court should or should not accept as tending to show that a woman is a prostitute, evidence of the administration of a caution, which is no more than evidence of what a police officer did and does not depend on admission of guilt by the woman, is not the most satisfactory evidence available.[100]

Thus the dilemma remained the same. But despite expressions of concern, some members of the committee accepted the need for evidence that facilitated a prostitute's conviction on her first appearance in court.

Further recommendations included: (1) the replacement of the term 'common prostitute' in section 1(1) of the 1959 Act with the phrase 'being a prostitute'; (2) the operation of the Act should not extend to cases where both prostitute and client were in a building (hotels, etc.); (3) the power of arrest without warrant should be retained; (4) all offences should be punishable with a fine at level 3 on the standard scale.

The report concluded with recommendations for a new law covering kerb-crawling, which included the suggestion that it should be an offence for a man to solicit a woman for sexual purposes in a manner likely to cause her fear (by which it meant being 'frightened' rather than merely annoyed).[101] This was intended to address the more generalised problem of men harassing women in a sexual manner regardless of whether payment was offered. It was a significant suggestion that reflected the influence of the Policy Advisory Committee on the thinking of the CLRC.[102]

CLRC SEVENTEENTH REPORT, 'PROSTITUTION OFF-STREET ACTIVITIES'

The Working Paper and the Seventeenth Report provided the first detailed official survey of the privatised world of indoor prostitution, which the Wolfenden Committee had admitted was likely to be encouraged if its recommendations were followed. Even so, no connection was made by the CLRC between the working of the 1959 Act and the development of alternative outlets. Yet in many ways the reports were sympathetic towards the complex nature of the problems of prostitutes and the difficulties created for them by the law. Significant recommendations were made involving the amendment of sections 30 and 31 and 33 to 36 of the Sexual Offences Act 1956 (living on the earnings of prostitution[103] and the suppression of brothels),[104] which suggested making them gender-neutral and dispensing with the definition of a 'brothel'.[105] However, no action was taken to implement these recommendations, which represented the culmination of ten years' work. It seems that the outcome of the review was to be, as on the previous occasion, the enactment of legislation that the Home Office had already determined upon.

THE SEXUAL OFFENCES ACT 1985[106]

The CLRC report 'Prostitution in the Street' was published in August 1984, and the Sexual Offences Act became law in July 1985 without including the suggested offence of soliciting a woman in a 'manner likely to cause her fear'.

The Act, which is generally referred to as the Kerb Crawling Act, made it an offence for a man to solicit a woman (or different women) for the purpose of prostitution:

(a) from a motor vehicle while he is in a street or public place;
(b) in a street or public place while in the immediate vicinity of a motor vehicle that he has just got out of, persistently or . . . in such manner or in such circumstances as to be likely to cause annoyance to the woman (or any of the women) solicited, or nuisance to other persons in the neighbourhood.

The parliamentary debate covered the predictable grey areas of what was or was not an acceptable social exchange between men and women and at what point an amorous advance became a matter of fear and anxiety for any particular woman. Speaking for the Home Office, David Mellor made the usual distinction between the prostitute and the 'normal' woman and commented on the need to protect the 'innocent' woman who was not a prostitute but an 'ordinary woman – one's sister or wife, or someone else's daughter . . . not dressed in a way that could be described as extravagant or sexually provocative'.[107] Matthew Parris (Derbyshire West), on the other hand, argued that there was no possibility of an 'innocent' woman who was not a prostitute giving evidence of being solicited. This left open the related problem of protecting men from false accusations, which Tony Marlow (Northampton North), among others, argued might have a catastrophic effect on a man's family life and reputation.[108] Consequently a House of Lords amendment was adopted that made proof of 'persistence' by men a necessary condition, although proof of 'persistence' by women had been ruled out by the CLRC, since it would have made a successful prosecution too difficult. The argument put forward by the CLRC to support the need for proof of persistence in the case of men was that they often made innocent overtures to women and did not have the safeguard of the cautioning system[109] leading, in the opinion of Clive Soley, to the danger of introducing the concept of a 'common kerb-crawler'.[110] Accordingly, and as a result of these reservations, new inequalities were built into the legislation.

Although campaigners had fought for over a century for equality in this area of law the 1985 Act seemed to please nobody outside the government. Susan Edwards had forecast in the *Justice of the Peace*[111] that feminists would welcome the proposed changes in the law, but in the event the failure to embrace the wider issue of the sexual harassment of women in public places meant that they were disappointed. However, some predictable problems emerged. The obvious difficulty of proving 'persistence'[112] in a situation where persistence was rarely necessary (since a prostitute offered her services willingly) meant that there would be a wider differential between the numbers of prosecutions for male and female soliciting.[113] By contrast, the lack of a power to arrest men who solicited women meant that it remained easier for the police to deal with the problems by continuing to apprehend prostitutes. But as a consequence of this new Act, the lives of prostitutes themselves were made more hazardous as they were compelled to make a rapid assessment of the nature of a client's intentions before entering his car.

The ECP identified the Act as a 'sus' law, which was merely designed to provide a public order measure that extended to heterosexual men (especially black) some of the injustices inflicted upon women.[114] However, the 'safeguards' inserted into the Act, that is, the need to establish the man's 'persistence' and the intentional failure to provide a power to arrest, hampered the police in their attempts to use the legislation. It meant that they were obliged to issue a summons if they wished to prosecute a kerb-crawler. Consequently they generally settled for administering a caution. And when they did venture to 'crack down' on troublesome areas the result was frequently the displacement of the problem into the neighbouring district. Finally, Lord Stow Hill's worst nightmare of 'a tragedy beyond measure'[115] came to pass when a high-status member of the establishment was prosecuted for soliciting, leading to a personal outcome that far exceeded any punishment deserved by the nature of the offence.[116]

AN OVERVIEW

When the second reading of the Sexual Offences Bill took place on 6 July 1956 it lasted approximately three minutes. The Attorney-General, Sir Reginald Manningham-Buller, explained that the bill had been brought forward under the Consolidation of Enactments (Procedure) Act 1949 and involved only minor corrections and improvements. Consequently it would not be in order to discuss the contents of the Bill.[117] Following this announcement Marcus Lipton (Brixton) expressed his opposition to the measure and commented that there could be no good argument for consolidating bad law. He found it particularly inappropriate that this should be done while a departmental committee was considering the matter of homosexuality and prostitution.[118] Three years later the *News Chronicle* observed that the Street Offences Act 1959 (which embodied the recommendations of the Wolfenden Committee on prostitution) was 'a sad example of British hypocrisy rather than of British justice or common sense' and that it conflicted with the British tradition that a prisoner was innocent until found guilty. It went on to argue that the sponsors of the law were concerned only with appearances, which would be achieved at the cost of justice and at the risk of spreading police corruption.[119]

As we have seen, the Street Offences Act 1959 provided only a temporary respite from the problems of street soliciting and actively contributed towards the expansion of off-street prostitution and kerb-crawling. Indeed, as early as 1961, welfare workers in Stepney were reporting an increase of soliciting from doorways, while a police sergeant giving evidence at the West London Court on 1 July 1960 reported that there were 'more prostitutes operating in Kensington Road than before the Street Offences Act came into force'.[120] The situation had not been helped by the absence of debate in 1956, which meant that the issue of the sexual harassment of women and children was not opened up to parliamentary scrutiny or public discussion and an opportunity was lost for addressing the issue of prostitution within the wider context of protective legislation. So although the Macmillan government stifled aspects of the discussion in 1956 and may have gained electorally in 1959, the final outcome was an accumulation of new problems, some of which were addressed through the Sexual Offences Act in 1985, while others, such as the issue of the abuse of children through prostitution, were not addressed at all.

After the 1985 Act came into force the nuisance continued, and new strategies were developed for dealing with the situation. Initiatives included 'multi-agency policing',[121] video recording of kerb-crawlers followed up by warning

letters,[122] traffic management[123] and imposing curfews on known prostitutes.[124] The unsatisfactory nature of this Act from a policing point of view
led to renewed police lobbying for legislative change. Their demands for
reform included dropping the requirement to prove persistence by the man,[125]
providing the power to arrest kerb-crawlers and withdrawing driving licences.
It was argued that tackling the prostitute in isolation did not strike at the root
of the problem as, 'To do this fairly and equitably requires police to deal with
kerb-crawlers.'[126] But these measures would not address the emerging nuisance of the male 'cruiser'[127] who merely drove endlessly around an area on a
voyeuristic excursion without stopping to solicit women.[128]

When looked at in retrospect it appears that the 1959 Street Offences Act
contributed towards, or was responsible for, the creation of a diverse spectrum
of more serious problems than the ones it was enacted to solve. And notwithstanding the continuous criticism of the measure and the numerous attempts
at reform, succeeding governments responded by appointing more conserva-
tively inclined committees and by enacting further legislation, which created
new problems of implementation for the police and left others (such as cruising) unsolved .[129] The only relief from the prostitutes' point of view was the
dropping of the penalty of imprisonment.

The reason for this continued conservatism is open to discussion, but in
my opinion it has its roots in the mid-century politics to which I have referred,
and in the ideological stance taken by Maxwell Fyfe as revealed in his Cabinet
memorandum of 1954. It would appear that through the long drawn out
process between 1954 and 1959, during which the government was obliged to
await the Wolfenden Committee's report, the Home Office remained committed to enacting legislation that would provide the police with effective powers
for clearing the streets of prostitutes. This determination was demonstrated
by the government in 1956 when it consolidated a contentious and emotive set
of sexual offences (rape, buggery, incest and the sexual exploitation of women
and children) without opening the debate to parliamentary scrutiny. To have
done this would have provoked an alternative discussion about women as
victims of male abuse, which would have been the antitheses of the impression
of female depravity that the government wished to capitalise upon. And given
that most of the law on sexual offences had been enacted as a result of public
campaigning (especially by women's organisations), it seems likely that the
government of the time was determined to prevent any confusing debate from
interrupting the smooth passage of the Street Offences Bill. Moreover, it is
significant that the introduction of this Bill was delayed until it was seen to
provide the advantages of a popular 'law and order' issue just before a general
election. During the succeeding years new government committees reaffirmed
the general principles set out in the Wolfenden Report. And since the 1959 Act
had been shown to be functional, it would have taken a very brave and liberal-
minded committee to recommend a measure that would have weakened the
effectiveness of the Act by removing the identifiable prostitute from the heart
of the statute. So although succeeding governments have perceived a largely

intractable set of problems, they have evaded confronting them by resorting to the British device of appointing committees that were, on the whole, equally reticent and fearful of change.

Therefore, I maintain that the difficulties posed by prostitution (for prostitutes, residents and pedestrians) cannot be assessed properly without looking at the impact of the legislation as a whole upon the women who work in prostitution, because the purposes of the different Acts contradict each other (ie. protection and repression) and create a situation in which the vulnerability of prostitutes to violent abuse is increased. So far there has been no serious attempt to assess the corpus of legislation as a whole in the light of the prostitutes' perspective or the working conditions that pertain in what we now refer to as the 'sex industry'.

NOTES

1. Much of the correspondence used for Miss Priceman's report is preserved in draft form, unsigned and undated. Some references are in the form of notes taken down as a result of telephone conversations. They are at present part of the JBS private archives but will be made available to the new National Women's Library, Aldgate, London, where they will be added to the 3/JBS2 collection.
2. *The Times*, 2 October, *New Statesman*, 7 October; *Sun*, 8 October 1970. A motion to close the society was carried by 15 votes to 13 during a Special General Meeting on 27 February 1975. The treasurer, Henry Toch, subsequently maintained that: (a) three of the people who had voted were not members of the society and not entitled to vote, and (b) that the constitution contained no provisions for winding up the society. The treasurer stated that he was unwilling to hand over the assets and books of the society unless ordered by the High Court. The matter was discussed at the AGM held on 29 October 1975, and again on 16 November 1976, when it was decided to alter the terms of the constitution and continue the work of the society. Following this débâcle Lord Chorley lost patience and fell out with the executive members of the now non-existent organisation, which refused to wind itself up.
3. Letter of offer dated 1 January 1972, signed on behalf of the JBET by the secretary, Margaret Schwarz, and returned with signature of acceptance by Miss Priceman on 4 January.
4. This was a private contract. As with Rosalind Wilkinson's work for the BSBC, the records of Miss Priceman's research work, and the copyright of any publication based upon the material gathered, were to be invested in the Josephine Butler Educational Trust.
5. Miss Priceman to Mrs Prince (assistant to Professor Gibbens), draft letter dated 1 February 1972, giving an explanation of the aims of her project. Miss Prince replied that she had conducted work in connection with women in Holloway Prison, many of whom were casual or occasional prostitutes. She believed that the legislation served no useful purpose and ought to be repealed.
6. Among the welfare workers involved was Miss E. M. White JP, who was a very active member of the JBS. She ran a campaign in Liverpool against the Street Offences Act and conducted her own research project on the conditions in Liverpool. For a report of the project see *Shield* (1967), pp. 8–11.
7. Josephine Butler Educational Trust, 'Research into Prostitution: The Report of an Investigation' by Miss Priceman (1972). Letters of reply are kept together with the report and documents concerning the research project, JBS collection.
8. Priceman (16 February 1972), notes on interview with Commander Becke, New Scotland Yard. JBS collection.
9. Priceman 'Report' (1972), p. 8.
10. Ibid., p. 9. The rota system was cited by the Wolfenden Committee as one of the practices that brought the law into disrepute, but its existence was denied in its final report. See Cmnd. 247, para. 271.

11. Accusations against the police of this nature cannot have come as a revelation to the discerning. As Morton has shown, they merely reflected established practices among some officers that had been in operation for many decades. See J. Morton (1988), *Bent Coppers: A Survey of Police Corruption*, Warner Books, London, p. 257. The 1959 Act meant that they could not be so easily challenged by the general public.

12. Both Commander Becke and Inspector Williams reported that the liberalisation of the legislation concerning children had removed their powers to return children to their parents or to the establishments they had left, leaving them prey to exploiters. See Priceman, 'Report', p. 15. See also Children and Young Persons Act 1969 [Eliz. C. 54].

13. Priceman 'Report' (1972), Appendix.

14. Priceman, notes on Professor Gibbens' views resulting from correspondence with his research assistant, Mrs Prince (3 March 1972).

15. Priceman, notes on interview with Dennis Powell, Principal Probation Officer, Brixton, London. Powell found that girls took a certain pride in their profession and considered themselves business women (13 March 1972).

16. Priceman, notes on interview with Captain Hutchinson, Salvation Army, Argyle St, London (17 January 1972).

17. Priceman, notes on interview with Brigadier Scott, Salvation Army, Hope Tower St, London (13 January 1972).

18. The London Haven was an old-established hostel and mission, founded in 1857, which remained on the same site opposite King's Cross Station, London. The paper submitted to Miss Priceman from the London Haven states that 'girls are increasingly young – 15, 17 etc, and come either by train or by lorry from the Glasgow area or North England'.

19. Rev. J. Williamson to J. Priceman (4 February 1972). Williamson specialised in caring for prostitutes and founded the Wellclose Trust, which was set up to help women and girls caught up in prostitution. He was an active speaker and campaigner, expressing views that were a mixture of compassion, disgust and racism. He wrote a number of pamphlets and three books, including *Friends of Father Jo.* Williamson pathologised the women, writing of them as 'dim-witted, mentally weak girls, caught up in this terrible racket'. See also 'The Rev. Joseph Williamson and Miss Edith Ramsay as delivered to the London Diocesan Conference on Monday, 13 February 1961', p. 5.

20. Priceman, notes on interview with Mr Cox, Solicitor, Great Marlborough St, London (21 Feburary1972).

21. Priceman 'Report' (1972), pp. 16–17.

22. *Daily Telegraph*, 13 January1971.

23. *Daily Mail*, 2 April 1971.

24. *Guardian*, 24 August 1972.

25. *Evening News*, 2 February 1972.

26. L. Baston (2000), *Sleaze: The State of Britain*, Macmillan, London, p. 111.

27. *Sunday Times*, 20 April1975.

28. Allan H. Mankoff (1975), *Lusty Europe: The Only All-Purpose Guide To Love And Romance*, Penthouse Mayflower Book. Pinned together: Letter from M. Schwarz to the DPP asking if a prosecution could be brought against the book under the provisions of the Obscene Publications Act 1959 or for living on immoral earnings (16 June 1975). Reply from the DPP (25 June 1975). Copy of feature article based upon interview with Mankoff by Timeri Murari, *Sunday Times* (20 April 1975), 3 /JBS2, WL.

29. *The Times* (5 April 1984) reported that the Archbishop of Westminster, Cardinal Basil Hume, opposed Mrs Gillick's court action despite her being a Roman Catholic. The issue was being considered by the Church of England Board of Social Responsibility, which was expected to uphold the importance of doctor–patient confidentiality. The debate concerned whether or not it was desirable for the state to enforce Church morality through the courts. *The Times* (27 April 1984) reported that Prime Minister Margaret Thatcher supported Mrs Gillick (as did most Conservative MPs). A deputation of 'agony aunts', including Claire Rayner, Marjorie Proops, Anna Raeburn and Katie Boyle, visited Downing Street with a strongly worded petition, stating that the existing guidelines offered vital flexibility to doctors in giving help to young people. Mr Terence Davis, MP for Birmingham, stated that the number of pregnancies in girls aged 15 had significantly reduced since the guidelines had been introduced.

30. For a discussion of the Gillick case, see J. Lewis, (1992), *Women in Britain since 1945*, Blackwell, Oxford, pp. 27–8 and 109–10.

31. Hall Williams (undated, most likely 1965), 'Memorandum on Research into Prostitution and the Law', 3/JBS2, WL, pp. 1–3.
32. Ibid.
33. The Vagrancy and Street Offences Committee (VSOC) was a Home Office committee made up of seven internal members (including one woman), a representatives from the Department of Health and Social Security, a member from the Department of the Director of Public Prosecutions, the Deputy Commissioner of the Metropolitan Police, the Chief Constable of Staffordshire and the Deputy Chief Constable of West Yorkshire. Under this committee the problem of prostitution was coupled with a review of vagrancy rather than with homosexuality, suggesting that soliciting was perceived as a matter of public order rather than as a sexual offence.
34. See R. Maudling (1978), *Memoirs of Reginald Maudling*, Sidgwick & Jackson, London. Reginald Maudling became Home Secretary in the 1970 Conservative Government led by Ted Heath. He was determined to follow in the illustrious footsteps of R. A. Butler and to ensure that the police were given the necessary conditions to bring their establishment and recruitment to a satisfactory level. He affirmed his belief that the maintenance of law and order was an overriding priority for any civilised society. But despite Maudling's adherence to the law and order principle he was described by Lewis Baston as 'too easy-going and liberal-minded' to want to lead a counter-revolution against the excesses of the 1960s 'permissive society'. He resigned dramatically in 1972 while the Metropolitan Police Fraud Squad, for which he had responsibility, was investigating a number of financial scandals (including the 'Poulson affair'), which led finally to the House of Commons voting for a public register of members' interests. The Commons Select Committee found Reginald Maudling 'lacking in frankness'. He died suddenly in 1979. See Baston, *Sleaze*, pp. 101–9.
35. Working Party on Vagrancy and Street Offences Working Paper (1974).
36. Report of the Working Party on Vagrancy and Street Offences (1976).
37. VSOC (1974), para. 230.
38. Ibid., para. 234.
39. VSOC (1976), para. 95.
40. VSOC (1974), para. 245.
41. VSOC (1976), para. 88.
42. Ibid., para. 99.
43. Recommended penalties:

> Causing a nuisance by sleeping rough and begging: maximum penalty £50 fine and/or one month's imprisonment.
> Indecent exposure: £100 fine and/or three months' imprisonment.
> Offences of sexually motivated behaviour: £100 fine and/or three months' imprisonment, lesser indecent exposure: £100 fine and/or three months' imprisonment.
> Being found on enclosed premises: £100 fine and/or three months' imprisonment.
> Suspected person: £100 fine and/or three months' imprisonment.
> Prostitution: for a first offence: £25 fine; for an offence committed after a previous conviction: £100 pounds fine; for an offence committed after more than one previous conviction: £100 fine and/or three months' imprisonment.

44. *The Times*, 14 September 1976.
45. Howard League for Penal Reform, 'The Cautioning and Imprisonment of Prostitutes' (1974). Comments and proposals drawn up by Mrs M. Sedgwick, JP, Chairman; Miss Geraldine Aves, CBE, Mrs M. Bligh-Scrutton (late of the JBS); Mr Colin Ferguson, Probation Officer, formerly Welfare Officer, Holloway Prison; Mrs Lucilla Butler, Chairman of Albany Trust, voluntary social worker Soho; Mr Arnold Rosen, barrister; Mr Martin Wright, copy of paper, 3/JBS2, WL.
46. Ibid., p. 3.
47. JBS, 'Written Evidence To Home Office Working Party On Vagrancy and Street Offences' (July 1973).
Summary of Recommendations:

1. That Section 3 of the Vagrants Act 1824 and all remaining local Acts dealing with street solicitation be repealed.
2. That the law relating to Street Offences be based objectively on conduct that is offensive, injurious or a nuisance to the public or to other individuals using the streets.

3. The offence should not be related (a) to the person or category of person who commits it, i.e. there should be no reference to 'common prostitute' or 'known homosexual'.
4. There must be corroborative evidence for a conviction.
5. Section 32 of the Sexual Offences Act 1956 should be amended in such a way as to make clear that it applies to the man or woman who touts on behalf of a prostitute. It should not apply to the solicitation of adults by men for their own sexual intercourse, whether heterosexual or homosexual. The maximum penalty under this Section appears to be excessive. JBS collection.

48. See C. Smart (1995), *Law, Crime and Sexuality: Essays in Feminism*, Sage, London, p. 64.
49. Roger Matthews, 'Beyond Wolfenden? Prostitution, Politics and the Law', in R. Matthews and J. Young (eds), *Confronting Crime*, Sage, London (1986), p. 190. See also Smart (1995), *Law, Crime and Sexuality*, pp. 54 and 64.
50. *The Times*, 27 November 1978.
51. *The Times*, 28 January 1978.
52. The English Collective of Prostitutes (ECP) was founded in 1975 and is based in King's Cross. It campaigns for the abolition of all prostitution laws that punish women. It gives advice on social and welfare issues, and legal advice and help to prostitutes in difficulty.
53. *The Times*, 28 January 1978.
54. Maureen Colquhoun, MP (Northampton North). Ms Colquhoun was deselected by her local constituency on the grounds of bad performance. She maintained that this was because they had heard rumours relating to her sexuality. She was supported by the *Daily Mirror* (28 September 1977), and managed to have the decision reversed, but lost her seat in the1976 election. See S. Jeffery-Poulter (1991), *Peers, Queers and Commons: The Struggle for Gay Law Reform from 1950 to the Present Day*, Routledge, London, pp. 136–7.
55. 'Protection of Prostitutes'. A Bill. 'To amend the Sexual Offences Act 1959; to provide for the better protection of prostitutes from exploitation and victimisation; and for connected purposes', 6 March 1979 [Bill 100] 47/5.
56. Ordered to be brought in by Ms Maureen Colquhoun, Mr Ian Mikardo, Miss Jo Richardson, Mr Martin Flannery, Mr Christopher Price, Mr John Garrett, Mr Sidney Bidwell, Mr Arthur Latham, Mr Tom Litterick, Miss Joan Lestor, Mr Stan Thorne and Mr George Rogers.
57. P.D. 5th Ser. 6 March 1979, cols. 1094–96.
58. Ibid., col. 1098.
59. The Bill provided for the abolition of imprisonment, deleted the term 'common prostitute' in section 1(1) of the Street Offences Act 1959, and reduced the severity of fines.
60. The futility of short-term periods of imprisonment was the subject of an impassioned speech by Lord Stonham during the final debate in 1970 but the matter was not resolved by parliament until the Criminal Justice Act 1982. Lord Stonham, HL Deb, Vol. 307, No. 33, cols. 584–92, 3 February 1970.
61. Criminal Justice Act 1982 [30 Eliz. 2. c. 48], Part V: Miscellaneous, 'Loitering and Soliciting', section 71, Abolition of imprisonment for loitering and (sic.) soliciting for the purpose of prostitution.
62. PD, Standing Committee A. Criminal Justice Bill, Sixteenth Sitting, Thursday 11 March 1982, cols. 523–5.
63. *The Times*, 16 May 1983.
64. *Daily Telegraph*, 14 September 1979.
65. *Daily Telegraph*, 18 September 1979.
66. *Daily Mail*, 4 July 1979; *Daily Star*, 17 November 1980.
67. *Daily Mirror*, 5 July 1982.
68. *News of the World*, 11 September; *The Times*, 12 September 1983.
69. *The Times*, 31 July 1981.
70. *Observer*, 6 November 1983.
71. *The Times*; *Daily Telegraph*, 18 October 1983.
72. *The Times*, 14 January 1983.
73. *The Times*, 12 August 1983.
74. Edwards, 'Red Lights and Red Faces', *Police Review*, 1 July 1988, p. 1371.
75. The CLRC was originally set up on 2 February 1959 by the Home Secretary, R. A. Butler, to be 'a standing committee to examine such aspects of the criminal law of England and

Wales as the Home Secretary may from time to time refer to the committee, to consider whether the law requires revision and make recommendations'.

76. Mrs Audrey Frisby and Her Honour Judge Nina Lowry.

77. CLRC (1980), Fifteenth Report, 'Sexual Offences', Cmnd. 9213; CLRC (1982), Working Paper on Offences Relating to Prostitution and Allied Offences; CLRC (1984), Sixteenth Report, 'Prostitution in the Street', Cmnd. 9329; CLRC (1986), Seventeenth Report, 'Prostitution Off-street activities', Cmnd. 9688.

78. CLRC (1982), para. 1.7.

79. Ibid., para. 1.5.

80. Ibid., para. 1.5.

81. Ibid., para. 1.10.

82. CLRC (1984), para. 18.

83. VSOC Working Paper (1974), para. 234.

84. CLRC (1984), para. 19.

85. Metropolitan Police, 'Evidence Presented to the Home Office Criminal Law Revision Committee Appointed to Review the Laws Concerning Offences Relating to Prostitution and Allied Subjects of the Commissioner of Police of the Metropolis', February, 1984, New Scotland Yard (1984), Metropolitan Police Library, p. 1.

86. Richard Edgington, 'Policing Under-age Prostitution: A Victim-based Approach', in David Barrett (ed.), *Child Prostitution in Britain: Dilemmas and Practical Responses*, The Children's Society (1997), p. 29.

87. Metropolitan Police (1984), para. 5.16.

88. Ibid., para. 5.23.

89. The order of publication and the final recommendations of the committee were influenced by a Home Office request that, in view of continuing public concern, a short report on kerb crawling could be published in advance of the full report on offences related to prostitution.

90. CLRC (1984), para. 2.

91. Ibid., para. 16.

92. CLRC (1984), para. 7.

93. CLRC (1982), para. 1.13.

94. There had been an increase in convictions for 'loitering or soliciting' (3,167 in 1979; 3,482 in 1980; 4,342 in 1982; 10,674 in 1983 levelling off at 8,836 in 1984). See Edwards, 'Prostitutes: Victims of Law, Social Policy and Organised Crime' in P. Carlen and A. Worrall (eds), *Gender, Crime and Justice*, Open University Press (1987), p. 43.

95. CLRC (1982), paras. 3.29–3.30.

96. CLRC (1984), para. 16.

97. Quentin Campbell, 'Prostitution and the Courts', *Justice of the Peace*, 15 September, 1984, Vol. 579, p. 148.

98. In 1981, 54 women were received into prison for default of fines, in 1982, 83 women. In 1983 it rose to 172. See CLRC (1984), p. 11, fn.

99. CLRC (1984), para. 25.

100. Ibid.

101. Ibid. 'Recommendations'.

> 'The accosting of women'
> It should be an offence for a man to use a motor vehicle in a street or a public place for the purpose of soliciting a woman for prostitution.
> It should be an offence for a man in a street or a public place persistently to solicit a woman or women for the purpose of prostitution.
> It should be an offence for a man to solicit a woman for sexual purposes in a manner likely to cause her fear. (p. 18.)

102. CLRC (1984), paras. 44–9.

103. CLRC (1986), Seventeenth Report, 'Prostitution Off-street activities', Recommendation. Living on the earnings of prostitution

> (2) 'It should be an offence for a person for gain –
>   (a) to organise prostitution, ie, to organise the services of more than one prostitute or to control or direct the activities of more than one prostitute;
>   (b) to control or direct the activities of a prostitute,
>   (c) to assist a person to meet a prostitute for the purpose of prostitution.

104. The Sexual Offences Act 1956 was said to have 'given a spurious air of modernity to the relevant legislation . . . What makes the situation worse is that in some instances judicial decisions have given a wider meaning to the statutory language', CLRC (1982), 1.5.
105. CLRC (1986) Recommendations.
     Brothel keeping

> (5) It should be an offence for a person –
>   (a) to manage or assist in the management of premises or other accommodation in connection with their use, in whole or in part, for the purpose of prostitution by more than one prostitute;
>   (b) to let the whole or part of premises or other accommodation for use, in whole or part, for the purpose of prostitution by more than one prostitute, or to be knowingly a part of such a use continuing;
>   (c) being the tenant or occupier or person in charge of any premises or other accommodation, knowingly to permit the use, in whole or in part, for the purpose of habitual prostitution by one or more prostitutes.
> (6) It should also be an offence for a person to provide, occupy or manage or assist in the management of premises equipped for the purpose of prostitution involving the infliction of pain.
> (7) The common law offence of keeping a brothel should be abolished. p. 20.

106. The Sexual Offences Act, 1985 [32 Eliz. 2. c. 44]
107. P.D. 5th Ser. Vol. 82, col. 670, 5 July 1985.
108. Ibid., col. 661.
109. CLRC (1984), paras. 21 and 44.
110. P.D. 5th Ser. Vol. 82, col. 665, 5 July 1985.
111. Edwards, 'Kerb Crawling and Allied Offences – The Criminal Law Revision Committee's Proposals, *Justice of the Peace*, Vol. 148, 13 October 1984.
112. 'solicitation of at least two women on the same occasion or the same woman at least twice'. See Home Office Circular, 'Sexual Offences Act 1985', HOC 52/1985, s.9.
113. For comparisons of prosecutions see, Edwards (1996), *Sex and Gender in the Legal Process*, Blackstone Press, Oxford, Ch. 4.
114. ECP (1997), 'Campaigning for Legal Change', in G. Scambler and A. Scambler (eds), *Rethinking Prostitution*, Routledge, London, pp. 89–91.
115. HL Deb, Vol. 307, No. 33, col. 579, 3 February 1970.
116. While he was soliciting prostitutes, Sir Allan Green, Director of Public Prosecutions, was apprehended by a plain-clothes Metropolitan Police officer in the King's Cross area in 1991. Sir Allan was not prosecuted but he resigned from his job soon afterwards and his wife committed suicide some months later. See S. Boyle (1995), *Working Girls and Their Men*, Smith Gryphon, London, p. 42. See also Hillary and Garry Mason (1991), 'Man at the Kerb', *Police Review*, 11 October 1991.
117. The Speaker explained that it was not in order to criticise the existing law, except on a motion or bill to repeal or alter the law. Such a bill was not before the House. See PD. 5th Ser., Vol. 555, cols. 1750–51, 6 July 1956.
118. Ibid.
119. Quoted by A. Greenwood in *Shield* (1961), p. 10.
120. Ibid., p. 11.
121. See Roger Matthews, 'Policing Prostitution: A Multi-agency Approach', *Centre for Criminology*, Paper 1 (1986). Matthews, 'Kerb-crawling, Prostitution and Multi-Agency Policing', *Police Research Group Crime Prevention Unit Series*, Paper 43 (1991). R. Matthews (1992), 'Regulating Street Prostitution and Kerb-Crawling: A Reply to John Lowman', *British Journal of Criminology*, 32 (1), Winter: 18–21.
122. *The Times*, 29 September 1995 and *Evening Standard*, 28 September 1995.
123. See Robert Golding, 'Policing Prostitution', *Policing*, Vol. 8, Spring 1992, pp. 67–9.
124. *The Times*, 13 December 1994.
125. A government-backed Sexual Offences Bill was introduced to the House of Commons in 1990 by the conservative MP Sir William Shelton (Streatham), which would have removed the word 'persistently', doubled the fines and made soliciting an arrestable offence. The Bill was talked out by Ken Livingstone MP. It was argued that a man could be arrested for approaching a woman on one occasion.
126. G. Edwards, 'Policing Street Prostitution: The Street Offences Squad in London', *Police*

Journal, July 1998, pp. 209–17. See also 'Evidence provided by the Metropolitan Police to the All-Party Group on Prostitution'. See also 'Report of Parliamentary Group on Prostitution' (1996), Middlesex University, Bounds Green, London, passim.

127. In the case of *Darroch* v. *DPP* (1990) 91 Cr. App. R 378, it was held that the act of cruising did not constitute soliciting.
128. 'Report of the Parliamentary Group on Prostitution', pp. 25 and 37.
129. In January 1995 a Home Office Steering Committee was appointed to review sexual offences. The stated aim was to be recommendations which are to 'be fair and non-discriminatory in accordance with the ECHR and the Human Rights Act'. The review has not included the Street Offences Act 1959. Home Office leaflet, 'A Review of Sex Offences' (1999).

CHAPTER FIFTEEN

Conclusion

From my daughter I have learned never to judge by outward appearances. Many women in prostitution are portrayed by the media as 'slags' and 'tarts'. I know that I have been guilty in the past of judging these women as if they were some sort of different species. My experience has taught me differently. (Irene Iverson, mother of Fiona)[1]

Fiona Iverson was 17 when she died in December 1993 at the top of a windswept multi-storey car-park. The frustrated client beat the young woman's head against a concrete floor and strangled her when he failed to achieve orgasm. The punter was arrested and is serving a life sentence, but the pimp who persuaded Fiona to prostitute herself is still at large.

Fiona's death was the consequence of a series of unhappy circumstances that placed her in a highly vulnerable position. She had been an idealistic child from a middle-class family who became obsessed with the evils of racism. She was bullied at school and retaliated by absconding and taking drugs, eventually moving in with her Rastafarian boyfriend. Her mother struggled to keep her daughter in check and protect her from a harmful lifestyle but appears to have been frustrated at every turn, gaining little help from either the police or the welfare system. To Irene the law appeared to be ineffectual, leaving her powerless to shield her lively, clever daughter from pursuing a course that was to lead to disaster. It is not surprising that the media concentrated on the salacious side of the story rather than on the failure of the welfare and legal systems to protect a vulnerable young woman from a predatory adult.[2]

When prostitute murders come in bunches, as with the Jack the Ripper and Peter Sutcliffe crimes, they create fear among the general population, but many individual murders fail to hit the headlines and frequently remain unsolved crimes. A further example of this phenomenon is the series of 7 drug-related murders of prostitutes that took place in Glasgow between 1982 and 1999.[3] These murders were described by Detective Chief Inspector Nanette Pollock from Strathclyde Police during a presentation at the National Police Vice Conference in 1999. She stressed that the police were not looking for a serial killer and that the sex workers' partners ought not to be viewed as pimps as they were too heavily addicted to drugs to exercise any control over the women. She confirmed that drug addiction and related activities had greatly increased the vulnerability of prostitutes.

Similarly distressing stories can be found in the history texts. For example, Angus McLaren's book on the serial killer Dr Thomas Neill Cream demonstrates the way in which a combination of inflammatory rhetoric, social exclusion, criminalising legislation and police incompetence played into the hands of Cream: 'Because the disappearance of a prostitute like Matilda Clover drew little public attention, Thomas Neill Cream was in effect *allowed* to become a serial killer.'[4] It was the prostitutes themselves who amassed the evidence that finally led to the murderer's conviction. In a similar way today's prostitutes take protective action by compiling and distributing 'ugly-mug' lists of violent punters. I am suggesting here not that the police are less concerned about the murder of prostitutes but that the criminalisation of prostitution-related activities increases the physical and mental isolation in which the women work and consequently makes a criminal investigation more difficult.

When the Wolfenden Committee was discussing the consequences of clearing the streets of prostitutes Mrs Cohen commented, 'Any objection that driving prostitutes off the streets would make life unbearably hard for them, and incidentally draw an unjust distinction between one and two-girl flats, could be answered by pointing out that the streets were the ultimate of degradation and that being a prostitute in a brothel was not aiding and abetting the management.'[5,6] Mrs Cohen seems to have accepted the premiss that brothels, despite their illegality, would increase in number and provide a preferable alternative to street work. When people such as Councillor Dyas recommend the establishment of brothels, they usually support their argument by claiming that indoor work is safer than soliciting on the streets. This might be true of some well-organised brothels, but it cannot apply to the solitary call-girl as present legislation makes it necessary for her to operate in isolation, which in turn increases her physical vulnerability.[7]

Concern over the violence inflicted upon prostitutes has stimulated recent research. One such project was conducted by Claudia da Silva (Middlesex University) who has highlighted what she describes as an 'explosion of violence' against indoor sex workers.[8] Her information was gained from 97 women, and included 40 face-to-face interviews and two extended interviews. In addition she analysed all of the Praed Street Project's[9] available 'ugly-mugs' reports, which revealed 299 incidents of violence between 1990 and 1999. The weapons used for these attacks included handguns, shotguns, hammers, swords, machetes, metal bars, knuckle-dusters, bottles, belts, meat cleavers, scissors and razor blades.

Crimes against prostitutes are, of their very nature, difficult to police as sex workers are reluctant to report them and fear that they will not be taken seriously by the police or the courts, or that they may be charged with prostitution-related offences.[10] This is an area that could usefully be researched further, but there are still a number of reliable references. For example, in 1993 an outreach worker reported on the alarming incidence of rape, assaults and other serious crime against sex workers. She had found that these crimes, 'even when reported and accompanied with good information were ignored by the police'.[11] Similarly in a survey conducted by the ECP it was found that in 17 cases out of 23, where women had reported violence from punters, they were told by the police that they should expect to be attacked because of their occupation. Consequently the majority of attacks were not reported.[12] During 1995 the ECP gave legal assistance to two prostitutes who brought a private prosecution for rape against Christopher Davis (who already had previous convictions for abduction and violence) after the Crown Prosecution Service had decided not to prosecute on the alleged ground of insufficient evidence. Davis was convicted and the incident was widely reported in the press.[13]

A more recent survey (November 2000) was conducted by the Criminal Policy Research Unit at South Bank University, London.[14] The team, which had interviewed 36 sex workers, found that sex workers generally felt that the criminal justice system failed them when they were reporting violent men. However, ten out of the 36 women reported positively about their relationship with the police. It was also found that relationships between police and prostitutes varied from one area to another and were better where a vice squad had been established. The police themselves, who have made efforts to improve their practices in recent years,[15] maintain that it is the prostitute's fear of reprisals from pimps or customers that is generally the limiting factor preventing the women from reporting violent crimes. And although I am sure that this is often the case (since violent men may take revenge when thwarted), I have argued that criminalising legislation increases the vulnerability of prostitutes and therefore I must conclude that the solution lies in the decriminalisation of prostitution-related activities rather than in the continual additional of *ad hoc* measure and expecting the police to achieve the impossible. To say this is not to deny the very real aggravation that can be caused to residents through street soliciting, but to suggest that we ought not to apply different standards of justice to some individuals as opposed to others on the basis of deep-seated prejudices.

As I have shown, murder is an ever-present hazard. Hilary Kinnell of the European Project for HIV/STD Prevention in Prostitution (EUROPAP-UK)[16] is currently engaged in research on prostitute murders.[17] She has collated records of 50 women and girls involved in prostitution who have been murdered, unlawfully killed, or reported missing and presumed dead between 1990 and 2000. She writes: 'In only 16 of these 50 cases do we know that a conviction has been secured. In eight of these 16 cases, the men convicted had previous convictions for violence, including murder, manslaughter, rape and assault.' Clearly, given the acknowledged high clear-up rates in homicides, there is a problem here that goes beyond the incidence of domestic violence and is related to the vulnerability of prostitutes. This vulnerability is increased through the criminalisation of their activities and the conditions of isolation within which they are obliged to work.

The motivation of men such as Thomas Cream and Peter Sutcliffe[18] is thought to be that they perceive themselves as 'having a mission' to rid society of its effluent. This becomes their personal contribution to 'cleaning up the streets'. In this context McLaren quoted the verdict of a French prosecutor who in 1886 had commented that, 'the isolation into which their abject profession drives them delivers them all the more easily into the hands of murderers',[19] in other words, the women become easy prey for violently inclined men. It may seem that the case of Sutcliffe was exceptional, but the much-quoted remark of the Attorney-General, Sir Michael Havers, when he observed that, 'Some women were prostitutes, but perhaps the saddest part of these cases is that some were not', revealed familiar attitudes towards prostitutes. This prejudiced viewpoint was repeated when the West Yorkshire Acting Assistant Chief Constable, Jim Hobson, commented on Sutcliffe's hatred of prostitutes: 'He has made it clear that he hates prostitutes. Many people do . . . But the Ripper is now killing innocent girls.'[20] Since Havers and Hobson were in authority they had a duty to appear neutral rather than reflect what they may have considered to be popular prejudice. It is to be hoped that these attitudes are less prevalent in the third millennium, but unlike the 'common thief', the law which incorporates the stigmatising category of the 'common prostitute' has remained in place.

The historical span of my work has been framed by the legislation, but 1985 is a somewhat arbitrary date at which to finish as the narrative continues unabated. The most significant subsequent development has been the appointment of the Home Office Steering Committee on Sex Offences 1999, whose remit was to 'examine the most personal and contentious area of the criminal law and recommend how it should be structured to deliver protection and help achieve a safe, just and tolerant society'.

In more detail the terms of reference were, 'To review the sex offences in the common and statute law of England and Wales, and make recommendations that will:

- provide coherent and clear sex offences which protect individuals, especially children and the more vulnerable, from abuse and exploitation;
- enable abusers to be appropriately punished; and
- be fair and non-discriminatory in accordance with the ECHR and Human Rights Act.'

The committee's report, 'Setting the Boundaries', was published in July 2000.[21] It noted that: 'The European Convention on Human Rights (ECHR) provides us with a dynamic policy-making framework that enables us to look at the role of the state in protecting its citizens, particularly the more vulnerable, from harm; the need to ensure a fair trial and that the interests of justice are upheld (Article 6), the right to a private life (Article 8) and the right to non-discrimination in the enjoyment of ECHR rights (Article 14)'.[22]

However, the promotional leaflet distributed by the Home Office prior to the work of the committee stated quite explicitly that: 'The review will *not* [their emphasis] be looking at decriminalising prostitution [*sic*] or pornography, at

reducing the age of consent below sixteen, or at procedural or evidential issues.'
The consequence of this confusing strategy was that although the Steering
Committee was obliged to review the sections of the1956 Act pertaining to
prostitution, it steadfastly denied that it was reviewing the issue of adult prostitution, stating in answer to numerous letters from organisations such as the
JBS and EUROPAP, that the committee's remit only included, 'offences which
concerned sexual exploitation and abuse which may lead to or perpetuate prostitution, such as section 28 of the Sexual Offences Act 1956' (causing or encouraging the prostitution of a girl under the age of 16, etc.). Therefore the
committee was not looking at the legal provisions governing the regulation of
voluntary prostitution and was excused from having openly to consider the
implications under the ECHR of a law that had a presupposition of the guilt
of the accused built into its structure, and that empowered the police to arrest
without warrant on the basis of their own evidence.[23] Nor was it obliged to look
at the regulatory consequences of a body of law which illogically sought to push
women both off the streets and out of accommodation. Nevertheless the committee did recommend 'that there should be a further review of prostitution',[24]
but at the same time it suggested that section 1 of the Street Offences Act 1959
might be used to regulate male soliciting on the same basis as female soliciting
and it endorsed a government commitment to strengthen the Sexual Offences
Act 1985 regarding kerb-crawling by incorporating a power of arrest.
Although I recognise that there is some logic in the separation of voluntary and
exploitative prostitution, it seems that the Home Office was reticent with regard
to the subject of voluntary prostitution and unwilling to embark upon a contentious issue that would undoubtedly have opened up numerous human rights
issues that would come within the ECHR.

In the meantime, and despite Home Office concern over the accumulation
of piecemeal legislation, a variety of new measures have been put into place.
The use of 'anti-social behaviour orders' was added to the armoury of the
police in 1989, and although ASBOs were not originally intended for this
purpose, they have been seen by the police as a useful tool to use against
women who persist in soliciting.[25] This is a worrying development as failure
to comply with an order can result in a penalty of up to five years' imprisonment, far exceeding the three months' imprisonment available before repeal
under the Street Offences Act 1959. The power to arrest kerb-crawlers was
incorporated into the Criminal and Justice and Police Act 2001, which also
banned the placing of prostitutes' cards in telephone boxes.[26] In addition, a
new law on trafficking attracting a custodial sentence of up to 14 years is to
be incorporated in the Nationality, Immigration and Asylum Bill 2002.[27]
Further legislation on sexual offences is anticipated in 2003. This is expected
to include new offences for the protection of children from sexual exploitation, gender equalisation of the offence of 'living off the earnings of prostitution (sections 30 and 31) and the repeal of section 32 (male importuning).

Throughout this book I have written of the regulation of prostitution, but
it is necessary to recognise that the regulatory aspect of the law substantively,

although not formally or legally, transforms the practice of prostitution into a criminal activity. And once it has done so it disregards the consequences. This is because the Acts were put into place in a piecemeal fashion, first as a public order mechanism (vagrancy laws) and second as protective measures for 'innocent' women against the dangers of sexual abuse and trafficking for the purpose of prostitution. Hence the contradictory aims of the legislation create hazards for prostitutes which provide a contiguous regulatory framework. Indeed the exposure of prostitutes to vulnerable situations has been 'sanctioned' by law through the device of incorporating the concept of the 'common prostitute' into the 1959 Act and underpinning it with an administrative cautioning system in a way that has made it pointless for the woman to plead 'not guilty'. In this respect the law, with its contradictory aims, has become part of the problem rather than the solution.

NOTES

1. Irene Iverson (1997), *Fiona's Story*, Virago, p. 32. Fiona's story is not intended to reinforce another stereotype, i.e. middle-class girl and black pimp. In the context of this study it is used merely as an illustration of a violent fate that befell one young woman who became involved in prostitution.
2. Ibid.
3. Detective Chief Inspector Nanette Pollock, Strathclyde Police, National Police Vice Conference Report (1999), p. 11. An eighth non-drug-related murder occurred in 1982.
4. A. McLaren (1993), *A Prescription for Murder: The Victorian Serial Killings of Dr. Thomas Neill Cream*, University of Chicago Press, Chicago, p. 142.
5. PRO. HO. 345/10/Misc. 9.
6. Sexual Offences Act 1956, Section 33: 'It is an offence for a person to keep a brothel, or to manage, or act or assist in the management of, a brothel.' It would appear that Mrs Cohen felt that it was preferable for a young woman to work in an illegal establishment than solicit on the streets.
7. Most 'prostitutes' working on their own employ a maid, but it can be argued that the maid is living on the earnings of prostitution.
8. Claudia Ferreira da Silva, 'Prostitution in the Nineties: Changing Working Practices, Changing Violence', MA Criminology, Middlesex University (2000).
9. The Praed Street Project offers outreach and clinical services to 'prostitutes' in London. It is based at St Mary's Hospital, Paddington, and was set up in 1986 to look at HIV infection and other sexually transmitted diseases in women working in prostitution.
10. Hilary Kinnell, who is the National Coordinator of the 'European Network for HIV/STD Prevention in Prostitution' (EUROPAP), states that this type of experience is intrinsic to the working life of sex workers. Interview, 25 June 2001.
11. 'Soliciting for Change: Report on Soliciting For Change Forum', Nottingham, 25–26 September 1993, p. 4.
12. English Collective of Prostitutes (1999), *Some Mother's Daughter: The Hidden Movement of Prostitute Women Against Violence*, Crossroads Books, London, pp. 31–47.
13. *The Times; Telegraph; Guardian* and *Independent*, 18 May 1995; *Daily Mirror*, 20 May 1995.
14. Tiggy May, Alex Harocopos and Michael Hough (2000), 'For Love or Money: Pimps and the Management of Sex Work', Police Research Series Paper 134, Home Office Reducing Crime Unit, Clive House, Petty France, London.
15. Since 1994 the police have made efforts to coordinate their operations and establish 'best practice' by holding yearly 'Vice' conferences to which members of organisations outside the force are invited, including the JBS, EUROPAP and a variety of academics engaged in research. In recent years particular attention has been given by the police to the plight of children caught up in prostitution, with special projects being conducted in Wolverhampton

and Nottingham. These projects have uncovered hitherto unsuspected crimes against children, including kidnap, rape, unlawful imprisonment, assault and witness intimidation. This work was found to be very time-consuming and resource-intensive, but operations have been assisted by the adoption of a multi-agency approach, which includes assistance from statutory and voluntary bodies. The Association of Chief Police Officers has submitted new guidelines to the Home Office for the care of children involved in prostitution, since when the Home Office Department of Health have published draft guidance on children involved in prostitution, 17 December 1998. The Metropolitan Police, Charing Cross, London, have a specialist unit dealing with trafficking and the sexual exploitation of women and children: The Vice Office of CO14 Clubs and Vice Branch has a staff of 14 officers.

16. EUROPAP's European Coordinating Centre is based at the Department of Epidemiology and Public Health, St Mary's Hospital, Norfolk Place, London.

17. Hilary Kinnell and Rosie Campbell (2000–01), ' "We Shouldn't Have To Put Up With This": Street Sex-work and Violence', *Criminal Justice Matters*, 42, Winter.

18. Peter Sutcliffe was eventually sent to Broadmoor Prison for the criminally insane after spending a period in an ordinary prison following his conviction, but that does not invalidate McLaren's explanation for the ease with which Cream (and later Sutcliffe) had perpetrated their crimes.

19. McLaren, *A Prescription for Murder*, p. 142.

20. See S. S. M. Edwards (1987), 'Prostitutes: Victims of Law, Social Policy and Organised Crime', in P. Carlen and A. Worrall (eds), *Gender, Crime and Justice*, Open University Press, Milton Keynes, p. 49.

21. *Setting the Boundaries: Reforming the Law on Sex Offences*, Vol. 1, Home Office, July 2000.

22. Ibid., paras. 0.1 and 0.3.

23. This final point reflected a long-term concern of the AMSH/JBS since the time of the CD Acts, as they saw the police power to define *who* was a prostitute as the moral policing of women.

24. Sue McLean-Tooke to Helen J. Self, 7 June 1999.

25. Crime and Disorder Act 1998 (Eliz II c. 37), section 1. See H. Jones and T. Sager, 'Crime and Disorder Act 1998: Prostitution and the Anti-social Behaviour Order', *Criminal Law Review*, 2001, pp. 873–85.

26. Criminal Justice and Police Act 2001 (Eliz. II. c. 16): section 46, Placing of advertisements relating to prostitution.

> (1) A person commits an offence if –
> > (a) he places on, or in immediate vicinity of, a public telephone an advertisement relating to prostitution, and
> > (b) he does so with the intention that the advertisement should come to the attention of any other person or persons.

section 71 Arrestable offences, includes the incorporation of the power of arrest for 'kerb-crawling' in the Sexual Offences Act 1985. See M. Wasik, 'Legislating in the Shadow of the Human Rights Act: The Criminal Justice and Police Act 2001', *Criminal Law Review*, 2001, pp. 931–47.

27. See Home Office White Paper 'Secure Borders, Safe Haven: Integration with Diversity in Modern Britain', February 2002, CM 5387.

Appendix 1: List of Statutes

Aliens Act 1905 [5 Edw. 7. c. 21.]
Aliens Restriction Act 1914 [4 & 5 Geo. c. 12]
Aliens Restriction Act 1919 [19 & 10 Geo. 5, c. 92]
Children Act 1908 [8 Edw. 7. c. 67]
Children (Employment Abroad) Act 1913 [3 & 4 Geo. 5 c. 7]
City of London Police Act 1839
Consolidation of Enactments (Procedure) Act 1949
Contagious Diseases Act 1864 [27 & 28 Vict. c. 85]
Contagious Diseases Act 1866 [29 & 30 Vict. c. 34, 35]
Contagious Diseases Act 1869 [32 & 33 Vict. c. 96]
Crime and Disorder Act 1998
Criminal Law Amendment Act 1885 [48 & 49 Vict. c. 69]
Criminal Law Amendment Act 1912 [2 & 3 Geo. 5 c. 56]
Criminal Law Amendment Act 1922 [12 & 13 Geo. 5 c. 56]
Criminal Justice Act 1948 [11 & 12 Geo. 6. c. 58]
Criminal Justice Act 1982 [30 Eliz. 2. c. 48]
Criminal Justice and Public Order Act 1994
Criminal Justice and Police Act 2001
Criminal Law Amendment Act 1951 [14 & 15 Geo. 6]
Defence of the Realm Act (DORA) 1914
Disorderly Houses Act 1751 [25 Geo. 2. c. 36]
Incest Act 1908 [8 Edw. 7. c. 45]
Indecent Advertisements Act 1889
Industrial Schools (Amendment) Act 1880 [17 & 18 Vict. c. 14–16]
Immoral Traffic (Scotland) Act 1902 [2 Edw. 7. c. 11]
Justice of the Peace Act [34 Ed. 3. A. D. 1360–1]
Late Night Refreshment House Act 1969 [17. Eliz. 2. c. 53]
Licensing Act 1953
Licensing Act 1961 [9 & 10 Eliz. 2. c. 61]
Licensing Act 1964 [12 Eliz. 2. c. 26]

London County Council (General Powers Act) 1910
London County Council (General Powers Act) 1915
London County Council (General Powers Act) 1920 (by-laws 28 July 1921)
Mental Deficiency Act 1913 [3 & 4 Geo. 5. c. 28]
Mental Health Act 1959 [7 & 8 Eliz. 2. c. 72]
Metropolitan Police Act 1839 [2 & 3 Vic. c. 47]
Obscene Publications Act 1959 [7 & 8 Eliz. 2. c. 66]
Parks Regulation Act 1872.
Protection from Harassment Act 1997 [45 Eliz. 2 . c. 40]
Punishment of Incest Act 1908 [8 Edw. 7. c. 45]
Town and Police Clauses Act 1847 [10 & 11 Vic. c. 89]
Refreshment Houses Act 1860 [23 & 24 Vict. c. 27]
Refreshment Houses Act 1964 [12 Eliz. 2. c. 88]
Refreshment Houses Act 1967 [15 Eliz. 2. c. 38]
Sexual Offences Act 1956 [4 & 5. Eliz. 2. c. 69]
Sexual Offences Act, 1967 [14 Eliz. 2. c. 60]
Sexual Offences Act 1985 [Eliz. 2. c. 44]
Street Offences Act 1959 [7 & 8 Eliz. 2. c. 57]
Unemployment Insurance (No. 3) Act 1931 [21 & 22 Geo. 5. Ch. 36]
Vagrancy Acts, 22 Hen. VIII. (1530–1) c. 12
     27 Hen. VIII. (1535–6) c. 25
     1 Ed. VI. (1547) c. 3
     3 & 4 Ed. VI. (1549–50) c. 16
     5 & 6 Ed. VI. (1551–2) c. 2
     5 Eliz. (1562–3) c. 3
     14 Eliz. (1572) c. 5
     18 Eliz. (1575–6) c. 3
     39 Eliz. (1597–8) c. 3
     43 Eliz. (1601) c. 2
Vagrants Act 1824 [5 Geo. 4. c. 83]
Vagrancy Act 1898 [61 & 62 Vict. c. 38 & 39]
Venereal Diseases Act 1917 [7 & 8 Geo. 5. c. 23]

Appendix 2: List of Regulations, Statutory Instruments and Home Office Circulars

Aliens Orders, 1920, No. 448; 1920, No. 2262 1923, No. 326, and 1925, No. 760
Hyde Park General Regulation Acts 1872 & 1926
Home Office Circular No 108/1959. Street Offences Act 1959
Home Office Circular No 52/1985. Sexual Offences Act 1985

MISCELLANEOUS HEALTH REGULATIONS

National Health Service, 'Control of Venereal Disease'. Memorandum distributed to Regional Hospital Boards, Hospital Management Committees and Boards of Governors, Ministry of Health, Alexander Fleming House, London [HM(68)84]
Statutory Instruments (1968) No. 1624
The National Health Service (Venereal Diseases) Regulation 1968 [M.H. 806]

WORLD WAR I (EMERGENCY REGULATIONS)

Defence Regulation 13, 1914
Defence Regulation 13A, 1916
Defence Regulation 40D, 1918

WORLD WAR II (EMERGENCY REGULATIONS)

Defence Regulation 33B. Statutory Rules and Orders (1942), Volume 11, Emergency Powers (Defence), HMSO
Defence (General) Regulations, Amendments: Nov. 5 (1942), No. 2277 (Compulsory Treatment of Venereal Disease)

Appendix 3: List of Bills

Criminal Justice Bill 1982
Criminal Law Amendment Bill [HL] (1914) [4 Geo. 5]. 'A Bill to amend the Criminal Law Amendment Acts 1880 and 1885, with respect to indecent assault on Young Persons, and the Defilement of Girls under eighteen years of age, and for other purposes'
Criminal Law Amendment Bill. 'A Bill to make further provision with respect to the punishment of sexual offences and the prevention of indecent advertisements; and matters connected therewith.' (15 February 1917)
Criminal Law Amendment Bill 'A Bill to make further provision with respect to the punishment of sexual offences and the prevention of indecent advertisements; and matters connected therewith' (29 March 1917)
Control of Venereal Disease' Bill. 'A Bill to provide for the compulsory examination and treatment of persons suspected of suffering from venereal disease by the restoration of provisions formerly contained in Defence Regulation 33B' (3 July 1962), Richard Marsh
Control of Venereal Disease Bill (1968), Sir Myer Galpern
Imprisonment of Prostitutes (Abolition) Bill (1981), Clive Soley MP
Nationality, Immigration and Asylum Bill (2002)

Prevention of Certain Contagious Diseases and for the Better Protection of Women Bill (1832), Bruce's Bill

Protection of Prostitutes Bill, 'A Bill to Amend the Sexual Offences Act 1959; to provide for the better protection of prostitutes from exploitation and victimisation; and for connected purposes' (6 March 1979 [Bill 100] 47/5)

'Public Places (Order) Bill' 1923

Sexual Offences Bill, 'An Act to make further provision with respect to the Punishment of Sexual Offences and the treatment of Venereal Disease and the Prevention of Indecent Advertisements' (11 April 1918)

Sexual Offences Bill (1990) 'An Act to Amend the Sexual Offences Act 1985', Sir William Shelton

Street Offences Bill [H.L.] 'An Act to Amend the Street Offences Act 1959', *The Lord Chorley* (30 November 1967)

Street Offences Bill [H.L.] 'An Act to Amend the Street Offences Act 1959', *The Lord Chorley* (23 January 1969)

Street Offences [H.L.] 'An Act to Amend the Street Offences Act 1959', *The Lord Chorley* (18 December 1969)

Appendix 4: List of Cases

Behrendt v. *Burridge* [1976] 3 All E.R. 285
Belascose v. *Hannant, Barton* v. *Hannant* (1862) 3 B & S 13, 26 JP 823
Chapman (1959) QB 100, [1958] 3 All ER 143, CCA (s. 19 (1))
Christine Elliott and Natanya Kuhn v. *DPP*
Crook v. *Edmondson* [1966] 2 Q.B. 81
Darren Jones and Christopher Wood v. *DPP* [1992] QB
Darroch v. *DPP* (1990) 91 Cr. App. R. 378
Dixon and Frank Dixon (1995) 16 Cr. App. R (S) 779
Dodd (1978) 66 Cr. App. R. 87
Durose v. *Wilson* (1907) 96 LT 645
Doherty (1959)
Donovan v. *Gavin* (1965) 2 Q.B.
DPP v. *Bull* [1994] 4 All. E.R. 411
Donoghue v. *Stevenson* (1932) A.C. 562; 1932 S.C. (H.L.) 1
Farrugia Borg, Agius, and Gauchi (1979) 69 Cr. App. R. 108
Ford (1978) 1 All E. R. 1129
Goddard (1991) 92 Cr. App. R. 185
Gorman v. *Stanton* (1949) 1 Q.B. 294
Greig v. *Bendeno* (1858) E.B. & E. 133
Ioanna Dublidis and Others v. *DPP* [1989] QB
Kelly v. *Purvis* [1983] 1 All E.R. 525
King v. *de Munck* (1918) 13 Cr. App. R. 113, [1918] 1 KB. 635
Knuller v. *D.P.P.* (1973) AC. 435

Mattison v. *Johnson* (1961) 85 LJKB 714
Quinn and Bloom (1962) 2 QB 245
R v. *Jones* (1973) Crim LR 710, CA (s. 17 (1))
R. v. *Sabrajeet Ruprah, Prasanna Rajapaksa* [1992] Cr. App.
R. v. *Silver, Pullinger and seven others*
Shaw v. *DPP* (1961) 45 Cr. App. R 113, [1962] AC 200
Smith v. *Hughes* [1960] 2 All. E.R. 859
Sinclair Smith (1995) 16 Cr. App. (S)
Singleton v. *Ellison* (1895) 1 QB 607
Strath v. *Foxon* (1955) 2 QB 294
Stevens v. *Christy* (1987) 85 Cr. App. R. 249
Stewart (1986) 83 Cr. App. R. 327
Webb [1964] 1. Q.B. 357
Whitfield v. *Bainbridge* (1866) 30 JP 644
Wilson (1983) Cr. App. R. 247
Winter v. *Woolfe* (1930) 1 KB 549
Wies v. *Monahan* [1962] 1 All E.R. 664

Appendix 5: Wolfenden Committee Final Recommendations

(b.) Prostitution.

We recommend:-

(i)   That the law relating to street offences be reformulated so as to elimi-
      nate the requirement to establish annoyance.
(ii) That the law be made of general application.
(iii) That consideration be given to the possibility of introducing more
      widely the more formal system of cautioning prostitutes which is in
      force in Edinburgh and Glasgow.
(iv) That maximum penalties for street offences be increased, and that a
      system of progressively higher penalties for repeated offences be intro-
      duced.
(v)   That courts be given explicit powers to remand, in custody if need be for
      not more than three weeks, a prostitute convicted for the first or second
      time of a street offence, in order that a social or medical report may be
      obtained.
(vi) That research be instituted into the aetiology of prostitution.
(vii) That magistrates courts be empowered, on convicting a tenant or occu-
      pier of
         (1) keeping or managing, or acting or assisting in the management of
             a brothel; or
         (11) knowingly permitting the premises to be used as a brothel; or

(111) knowingly permitting premises to be used for the purpose of habitual prostitution, to make an order determining the tenancy or requiring the tenant to assign the tenancy to a person approved by the landlord.

(viii) That the landlord have the right to be heard in regard to the making of such an order.

(ix) That the courts be empowered to require a tenant or occupier charged with any of the offences mentioned in recommendation (vii) to disclose the name and address of the person to whom he pays his rent; and that there be similar power to require each lessor of the premises, in turn, to disclose the name and address of his superior lessor.

(x) That a landlord letting premises at an exorbitant rent in the knowledge that they are to be used for the purpose of prostitution be deemed, in law, to be 'living on the earnings of prostitution'; and that the same apply to any agent knowingly taking part in the transaction.

(xi) That prosecutions in respect of premises used for immoral purposes, be undertaken, as a general rule, by the police.[1]

NOTES

1. Cmnd. 247, pp. 116–17.

Bibliography

MANUSCRIPT SOURCES

Public Record Office (PRO), Kew, London

Wolfenden Committee papers (HO 345)
Cabinet Papers (CAB)
Metropolitan Police Office Police Orders (MEPO)

Fawcett Library (Women's Library), Castle Street, London

Association of Moral and Social Hygiene (AMSH)
Josephine Butler Society (JBS)
National Vigilance Association (NVA)
League of Nations Documents (LN)

Modern Records Office, University of Warwick

Young Women's Christian Association (YWCA)

Personal Papers and Letters

Papers and letters referenced as 'Josephine Butler Society' or 'Beverley Grey' collection will be made available through the Women's Library under 3/JBS/2. If any difficulty arises the Josephine Butler Society may be contacted.

BOOKS

Abbott, P. and Wallace, C. (1990), *An Introduction to Sociology: Feminist Perspectives*, Routledge, London.
Acton, W. (1968) [1887], *Prostitution*, ed. Peter Fryer, MacGibbon and Kee, London.
Addy, J. (1989), *Sin and Society*, Routledge, London.
Amos, S. (1877), *A Comparative Survey of Laws in Force for the Prohibition, Regulation and Licensing of Vice in England and Other Countries*, Stephen and Sons, London.
Anon. (1959), *Street-Walker*, The Bodley Head, London.
Armstrong, K. (1986), *The Gospel According to Women*, Font, HarperCollins, London.
Banks, O. (1964), *Feminism and Family Planning in Victorian England*, Liverpool University Press, Liverpool.

Barrett, M. and M. McIntosh (1987), *The Anti-social Family*, Thetford Press, Thetford.
Barry, K. (1979), *Female Sexual Slavery*, Prentice Hall, Englewood Cliffs, NJ.
— (1995), *The Prostitution of Sexuality*, New York University Press, New York .
Bartley, P. (2000), *Prostitution Prevention and Reform in England, 1860–1914*, Routledge, London.
Baston, L. (2000), *Sleaze: The State of Britain*, Macmillan, London.
Benjamin, H. and R. Masters (1964), *Prostitution and Morality: A Definitive Report on Prostitution in Contemporary Society and an Analysis of the Causes and Effects of Suppressing of Prostitution*, Souvenir Press, London.
Bland, L. (1995), *Banishing the Beast: English Feminism and Sexual Morality, 1883–1995*, Penguin Books, London.
Bolt, C. (1993), *The Women's Movements in the United States and Britain from the 1790s to the 1920s*, Harvester Wheatsheaf, New York.
Box, S. (1989), *Power, Crime and Mystification*, Routledge, London.
Boyle, B. (1995), *Working Girls and Their Men*, Smith Gryphon, London.
Braybon, G. (1987), *Women Workers in the First World War*, Croom Helm, London.
Bresler, F. (1977), *Lord Goddard: A Biography of Rayner Goddard, Lord Chief Justice of England*, Harrap, London.
Briar, C. (1987), *Working For Women? Gendered Work and Welfare Policies in Twentieth Century Britain*, UCL Press, London.
Bristow, E. J. (1977), *Vice and Vigilance*, Gill and Macmillan, Dublin.
— (1982) *Prostitution and Prejudice: The Jewish Fight against White Slavery 1870–1939*, Clarendon Press, Oxford.
British Social Biology Council (1955), *Women of the Streets*, ed. C. H. Rolph, Secker & Warburg, London.
Bronowski, J. (1974), *The Ascent of Man*, British Broadcasting Corporation, London.
Brownmiller, S. (1997), *Against Our Will*, Secker & Warburg, London.
Buckland, E. (1984), *The World of Donald McGill*, Blandford Press, Pool, Dorset.
Bullough, V. and B. Bullough (1987), *Women and Prostitution: A Social History*, Prometheus Books, New York.
Burford, E. J. (1976), *Bawds and Lodgings: A History of the London Bankside Brothels c. 100–1675*, Peter Owen, London.
Burford, E. J. and S. Shulman (1994), *Of Bridles and Burnings*, Robert Hale, London.
Burt, Sir C. (1952), *The Young Delinquent*, University of London Press.
Butler, R. A. (1971) *The Art of the Possible: The Memories of Lord Butler K.G., C.H.*, Hamish Hamilton, London.
Butler, A. S. G. (1953), *Portrait of Josephine Butler*, Faber and Faber, London.
Caine, B. (1992), *Victorian Feminists*, Oxford University Press, Oxford.
Chambers Biographical Dictionary, Centenary Edition (1999) ed. Melanie Parry, Chambers Harrap Publishers (1999).
Chesney, K. (1991), *The Victorian Underworld*, Penguin, London.
Cohen, S. (1985), *Visions of Social Control: Punishment and Classification*, Polity Press, Cambridge.
Corbin, A. (1990), *Women For Hire: Prostitution and Sexuality in France after 1850* (trans. Alan Sheridan), Harvard University Press, Cambridge, MA.
Coote, W. A. (1910), *A Vision and its Fulfilment*, NVA, London.
— (1916), *Romance of Philanthropy*, NVA, London.
Costello, J. (1985), *Love, Sex and War: Changing Values 1939–45*, Collins, London.
Davenport-Hines, R. (1990), *Sex, Death and Punishment: Attitudes to Sex and Sexuality in Britain Since the Renaissance*, Collins, London.
Dawson, J. (2000), *Fred and Edie*, Hodder and Stoughton, London.
Denning, Lord A. (1963), *John Profumo and Christine Keeler 1963*, H. M. Stationery Office, London.
Delacosta, F. and P. Alexander (1988), *Sex Work: Writings of Women in the Sex Industry*, Virago, London.
Devlin, P. (1965), *The Enforcement of Morals*, Oxford University Press, Oxford.
Drake, B. (1920), *Women in Trade Unions*, George Allen and Unwin, London.
Drenth, A. van and F. de Hann (1999), *The Rise of Caring Power*, Amsterdam University Press, Amsterdam.
Downs, D. and P. Rock (1988), *Understanding Deviance: A Guide to the Sociology of Crime and Rule Breaking*, Clarendon Press, Oxford.

Dworkin, A. (1997), *Life and Death: Unapologetic Writings on the Continuing War Against Women*, Virago, London.

Edwards, S. S. M. (1981), *Female Sexuality and the Law: A Study of Constructs of Female Sexuality as they Inform Statute and Legal Procedure*, Martin Robertson, Oxford.

— (1984), *Women on Trial: A Study of the Female Suspect, Defendant and Offender in the Criminal Justice System*, Manchester University Press, Manchester.

— (1996), *Sex and Gender in the Legal Process*, Blackstone Press, Oxford.

Ellis, H. (1890), *The Criminal*, London.

Emsley, C. (1991), *The English Police: A Political and Social History*, Harvester Wheatsheaf, New York.

English Collective of Prostitutes (1999), *Some Mother's Daughter: The Hidden Movement of Prostitute Women Against Violence*, Crossroads Books, London.

Evans-Gordon (1903), *The Alien Immigrant*, William Heinemann, London.

Fabian, R. (1950), *Fabian of the Yard: An Intimate Record by Ex-Superintendent Robert Fabian*, The Naldrett Press, London.

Faulks, S. (1997), *The Fatal Englishman: Three Short Lives*, Vintage, London.

Fawcett, M. and E. M. Turner (1927), *Josephine Butler: Her Works and Principles, and Their Meaning for the Twentieth Century*, Association for Moral and Social Hygiene, London.

Feinberg J. (1985), *Offences to Others: The Moral Limits of the Criminal Law*, Vol. 2, Oxford University Press.

— (1988), *Harmless Wrongdoing: The Moral Limits of the Criminal Law*, Vol. 4, Oxford University Press, Oxford.

Ferris, P. (1993), *Sex and the British: A Twentieth Century History*, Michael Joseph, London.

Finnegan, F. (1979), *Poverty and Prostitution: A Study of Victorian Prostitutes in York*, Cambridge University Press, Cambridge.

Fisher, T. (1995), *Scandal: The Sexual Politics of Late Victorian England*, Alan Sutton, Stroud, Gloucestershire.

— (1997) *Prostitution and the Victorians*, Alan Sutton, Stroud, Gloucestershire.

Flexner, A. (1914), *Prostitution in Europe*, Bureau of Social Hygiene, New York (reprinted 1917).

Foucault, M. (1971), *Madness and Civilization*, Tavistock Press, London.

— (1977), *Discipline and Punish: The Birth of the Prison*, Penguin, London.

Giobbe, E., in D. Leidholdt and J. Raymond (eds), *The Sexual Liberals and The Attack on Feminism*, Pergamon Press, New York (1990).

Glueck, S. and E. Glueck (1934), *Five Hundred Delinquent Women*, New York.

Gregory, J. and S. Lees (1999), *Policing Sexual Assault*, Routledge, London.

Grey, A. (1992), *Quest for Justice: Towards Homosexual Emancipation*, Sinclair-Stevenson, London.

Griffith, J.A.G. (1985), *The Politics of the Judiciary*, Fontana Press, Cornwall.

Hall, G. (1933), *Prostitution: A Survey and a Challenge*, Williams and Norgate, London.

Harris, J. (1977), *William Beveridge: A Biography*, Oxford University Press, Oxford.

— (1984), *Sex, Ideology and Religion: The Representation of Women in the Bible*, Barnes & Noble Books, New Jersey.

Hart, H. L. A. (1968), *Law, Liberty and Morality*, Oxford University Press, Oxford.

Haskins, S. (1993), *Mary Magdalene: Myth and Metaphor*, HarperCollins, London.

Hay-Cooper, L. (1921), *Josephine Butler and her Work for Social Purity*, London Society for Promoting Christian Knowledge.

Heidensohn, F. (1985), *Women and Crime*, Macmillan, London.

— (1989), *Crime and Society*, Macmillan Education, London.

Hennessy, P. (1986), *The Great and the Good: An Inquiry into the British Establishment*, Policy Studies Institute, London.

Henriques, F. (1962), *Prostitution and Society: A Survey*, MacGibbon & Kee, London.

— (1963), *Prostitution in the New World*, MacGibbon & Kee, London.

Higgins, P. (1996) *Heterosexual Dictatorship: Male Homosexuality in Post-War Britain*, Fourth Estate, London.

Hill, C. (1964), *Society and Puritanism in Pre-Revolutionary England*, Secker and Warburg, London.

Hite, S. (1987), *The Hite Report: Women and Love: A Cultural Revolution in Progress*, Penguin Books, London.

Hoggett, B. M. and D. S. Pearl (1987), *The Family, Law and Society: Cases and Materials*, Butterworth, London.

Hollis, P. (1979), *Women in Public, 1850–1900*, George Allen and Unwin, London.

Holmes, C. (1979) *Anti-Semitism in British Society, 1876–1939*, Holmes & Meier, New York.

Hopkins, E. (1890), *The Power of Womanhood*, Wells Gardner, Darton & Co.

Hufton, O. (1995), *The Prospect Before Her: A History of Women in Western Europe*, HarperCollins, London.

Humm, M. (1989), *The Dictionary of Feminist Theory*, Harvester Wheatsheaf, New York.

Illich, I. (1971), *Deschooling Society*, Penguin, London.

Itzin, C. (1992) (ed.), *Pornography, Women, Violence and Civil Liberties*, Oxford University Press, Oxford.

Jackson, M. (1994) *The Real Facts of Life: Feminism and the Politics of Sexuality, c. 1850–1940*, Taylor & Francis, London.

Jaget, C. (1980), *Prostitutes, Our Life*, Falling Wall Press, Great Britain.

Jeffery-Poulter, S. (1991) *Peers, Queers and Commons: The Struggle for Gay Law Reform from 1950 to the Present Day*, Routledge, London.

Jeffreys, S. (1985) *The Spinster And Her Enemies: Feminism and Sexuality, 1880–1930*, Pandora, London.

— (1997), *The Idea of Prostitution*, Spinefex, Melbourne.

Jenkins, R. (1993), *Portraits and Miniatures*, Macmillan, London.

Johnson, G. W. and L. A. Johnson (1909) *Josephine E. Butler: An Autobiographical Memoir*, J. W. Arrowsmith, London.

Jones, A. (1991), *Women Who Kill*, Victor Gollancz, London.

Jones, J. H. (1997), *Alfred C. Kinsey: A Public Private Life*, W. W. Norton, New York.

Jones, T. E. (1951), *Prostitution and the Law*, Heinemann, London.

Kamm, J. (1965), *Hope Deferred: Girls' Education in English History*, Methuen, London.

— (1966), *Rapiers and Battleaxes: The Women's Movement and its Aftermath*, George Allen and Unwin, London.

Keeler, C. with D. Thompson (2001), *The Truth at Last: My Story*, Sidgwick & Jackson, London.

Kennedy, H. (1992), *Eve Was Framed: Women and British Justice*, Vintage, London.

Kennedy, L. (1964), *The Trial of Stephen Ward*, Victor Gollancz, London.

Kinsey, A. (1948), *Sexual Behaviour in the Human Male*, W.B. Sanders, New York.

— (1953), *Sexual Behaviour in the Human Female*, W.B. Sanders, New York.

Kingsley Kent, S. (1989), *Sex and Suffrage in Britain, 1860–1914*, Routledge, London.

Law, C. (1997) *Suffrage and Power: The Women's Movement 1918–1928*, I.B. Tauris, London.

Lee, S. (1986), *Law and Morals: Warnock, Gillick and Beyond*, Oxford University Press.

Lees, S. (1997), *Ruling Passions*, Open University Press, Buckingham.

Lewis, J. (1992), *Women in Britain since 1945*, Blackwell, Oxford.

Lombroso, C. and W. Ferrero (1895), *The Female Offender*, Peter Owen (1959 edn).

Lyndon Shanley, M. (1989) *Feminism, Marriage and the Law in Victorian England, 1850–1895*, I.B. Tauris, London.

McKeganey, N. and M. Barnard (1996), *Sex Work on the Streets: Prostitutes and their Clients*, Open University Press, Buckingham.

McHugh, P. (1980), *Prostitution and Victorian Social Reform*, Croom Helm, London.

McLaren, A. (1993), *A Prescription for Murder: The Victorian Serial Killings of Dr. Thomas Neill Cream*, University of Chicago Press, Chicago.

McLeod, E. (1981) *Women Working: Prostitution Now*, Croom Helm, London.

Macmillan, H. (1973), *At the End of the Day*, Macmillan, London.

Macmillan, Rt. Hon. Lord Hugh (1953), *A Man of Law's Tale*, Macmillan, London.

Mahood, L. (1990), *The Magdalenes: Prostitution in the Nineteenth Century*, Routledge, London.

Mankoff, A. H. (1975), *Lusty Europe: The Only All-Purpose Guide To Love And Romance*, Penthouse Mayflower, London.

Malthus, T. R. (1926) [1798], *First Essay on Population*, Macmillan, London 1926.

Mason, M. (1994), *The Making of Victorian Sexual Attitudes*, Oxford University Press, Oxford.

— (1995), *The Making of Victorian Sexuality*, Oxford University Press, Oxford.

Maudling, R. (1978), *Memoirs of Reginald Maudling*, Sidgwick & Jackson, London.

Maxwell Fyfe, D. (1964), *Political Adventure: The Memoirs of the Earl of Kilmuir*, Weidenfeld and Nicholson, London.

Melling, E. (1964), *Kentish Sources*, Kent County Council, Maidstone.

Moberly Bell, E. (1962), *Flame of Fire*, Constable, London.

Montgomery Hyde, H. (1970), *The Other Love: An Historical and Contemporary Survey of Homosexuality in Britain*, Heinemann, London.

Moore, S. and D. Rosenthal (1993), *Sexuality in Adolescence*, Routledge, London.
Morris, A. (1987), *Women, Crime and Criminal Justice*, Basil Blackwell, Oxford.
Mort, F. (1987), *Dangerous Sexualities: Medico-moral Politics in England since 1830*, Routledge and Kegan Paul, London.
Morton, J. (1998), *Bent Coppers: A Survey of Police Corruption*, Warner Books, London.
O'Connell Davidson, J. (1998), *Prostitution, Power and Freedom*, Polity Press, Cambridge.
O'Donovan, K. (1985), *Sexual Divisions in Law*, Weidenfeld and Nicholson, London.
Olafson Helerstein, E., L. Parker Hume and K. M. Offen (1981), *Victorian Women*, Harvester Press, New York.
Orwell, G. (1945), *Animal Farm*, Penguin, Middlesex.
— (1953), *England, Your England*, Martin Secker & Warburg, London.
Pahl, J. (1989), *Money and Marriage*, Macmillan, London.
Pankhurst, C. (1913), *The Great Scourge And How To End It*, Lincoln's Inn House, London.
Parent-Duchatelet, Dr A. (1836), *De la prostitution dans la ville de Paris*, J. B. Bailliere.
Pascall, G. (1986), *Social Policy: A Feminist Analysis*, Routledge, London.
Petrie, G. (1971), *A Singular Iniquity: The Campaigns of Josephine Butler*, New York.
Petrow, S. (1994), *Policing Morals: The Metropolitan Police and the Home Office, 1870–1914*, Clarendon Press, Oxford.
Pheterson, G. (1989), *A Vindication of the Rights of Whores*, Seal Press, Seattle.
Phoenix, J. (1999), *Making Sense of Prostitution*, Macmillan Press, London.
Pinchbeck, I. (1977), *Women Workers in the Industrial Revolution 1750–1850*, Frank Cass, London.
Pollack, O. (1950) [1939], *The Criminality of Women*, New York.
Poovey, M. (1989). *Uneven Developments: The Ideological Work of Gender in Mid-Victorian England*, Virago, London.
Porter, R. and L. Hall (1995), *The Facts of Life: The Creation of Sexual Knowledge in Britain, 1650–1950*, Yale University Press, New Haven, CT.
Pugh, M. (1992), *Women and the Women's Movement in Britain, 1914–1959*, Macmillan, London.
Randall, V. (1987), *Women and Politics: An International Perspective*, Macmillan Education, London.
Ranke-Heinemann, U. (1990), *Eunuchs for the Kingdom of Heaven: The Catholic Church and Sexuality*, Penguin Books, New York.
Rendall, J. (1990), *Women in an Industrializing Society: England, 1750–1880*, Blackwell, Oxford.
Reynolds, D. (1995), *Rich Relations: The American Occupation of Britain 1942–1945*, HarperCollins, London.
Roberts, N. (1992), *Whores in History: Prostitution in Western Society*, HarperCollins, London.
Robertson Elliot, F. (1986), *The Family: Change or Continuity?*, Macmillan, London.
Rolph, C. H. (1974), *Living Twice: An Autobiography*, Victor Gollancz, London.
Rook, P. and R. Ward (1993), *Sexual Offences*, Criminal Law Library 13, Sweet & Maxwell, London.
Roper, L. (1991), *The Holy Household: Women and Morals in Reformation Augsburg*, Clarendon Press, Oxford.
Rose, L. (1988), *Rogues and Vagabonds: Vagrant Underworld in Britain, 1815–1985*, Routledge, London.
Rossiaud, J. (1984), *Medieval Prostitution*, Basil Blackwell, Oxford.
Rover, C. (1969), *Women's Suffrage and Party Politics in Britain, 1866–1914*, Routledge & Kegan Paul, London.
— (1970), *Love, Morals and the Feminist*, Routledge & Kegan Paul, London.
Rowntree, S. B. and G. R. Lavers (1951), *English Life and Leisure*, Longman, London.
Rupp, L. J. (1997), *Worlds of Women: The Making of an International Women's Movement*, Princeton University Press, Princeton, NJ.
Russell, B. (1929), *Marriage and Morals*, George Allen & Unwin, London.
Russell, D. (1986), *The Tamarisk Tree: My Quest for Liberty and Love*, Virago, London.
Sachs, A. and J. Hoff Wilson (1978), *Sexism and the Law: A Study of Male Beliefs and Judicial Bias*, Martin Robertson, London.
Saint Augustine, *De Ordine* II, IV. 12 PL XXXII, col. 1000.
Scion, A. A. (1977), *Prostitution and the Law*, Faber and Faber, London.
Scott, B. (1890), *A State of Iniquity: Its Rise, Extension and Overthrow*, Kegan Paul, Trench, Trubner, London.
Shorter, E. (1977), *The Making of the Modern Family*, Fontana/Collins, London.

Showalter, E. (1977), *A Literature of their Own: British Women Novelists from Bronte to Lessing*, Princeton University Press, Princeton, NJ.
— (1995), *The Female Malady: Women, Madness and English Culture, 1830–1980*, Virago, London.
Simpson, A. W. B. (2001), *Human Rights: The End of Empire*, Open University Press, Milton Keynes.
Sinfield, A. (1997), *Literature, Politics and Culture in Post-War Britain*, The Athlone Press, London.
Skelley, A. R. (1977), *The Victorian Army at Home: The Recruitment and Terms and Conditions of the British Regular, 1859–1899*, Croom Helm, London.
Smart, C. (1977), *Women, Crime and Criminology: A Feminist Critique*, Routledge & Kegan Paul, London.
— (1989), *Feminism and the Power of the Law*, Routledge, London.
— (1995), *Law, Crime and Sexuality: Essays in Feminism*, Sage, London.
Spiers, E. M. (1980), *The Army and Society, 1815–1914*, Longman, London.
— (1992), *The Late Victorian Army, 1868–1902*, Manchester University Press, Manchester.
Spender, D. (1981), *Man Made Language*, Routledge & Kegan Paul, London.
— (1983), *There's Always Been a Women's Movement this Century*, Pandora, London.
Stafford, A. (1964), *The Age of Consent*, Hodder and Stoughton, London.
Stanley, L. (1995), *Sex Surveyed, 1949–1994: From Mass Observation's 'Little Kinsey' to the National Survey and the Hite Reports*, Taylor & Francis, London.
Stevens, R. (1979), *Law and Politics: The House of Lords as a Judicial Body, 1800–1976*, Weidenfeld and Nicolson, London.
Stopes, M. (1995) [1918], *Married Love*, Victor Gollancz, London.
Strachey, R. (1928), *The Cause: A Short History of the Woman's Movement in Great Britain*, G. Bell & Sons, (reprinted 1987, 1988, 1989, Virago, London).
Summerfield, P. (1998), *Reconstructing Women's Wartime Lives*, Manchester University Press, Manchester.
Symonds, R. (1999), *Inside the Citadel: Men and the Emancipation of Women, 1850–1920*, Macmillan, London.
Tannahill, R. (1980), *Sex in History*, Hamish Hamilton, London.
Terrot, C. (1959), *The Maiden Tribute: A Study of the White Slave Traffic of the Nineteenth Century*, Frederick Muller, London.
Thane, P. (1982), *The Foundations of the Welfare State: Social Policy in Modern Britain*, Longman, London.
Thompson, R. K. P. (1991), *William Thompson (1775–1833): Pioneer Socialist*, Pluto Press, London.
Tong, R. (1989), *Feminist Thought: A Comprehensive Introduction*, Unwin Hyman, London.
Trible, P. (1978), *God and the Rhetoric of Sexuality*, SCM Press, London.
— (1984), *Texts of Terror: Literary-Feminist Readings of Biblical Narrative*, Fortress Press, Philadelphia.
Trollope, J. (1994), *Britannia's Daughters: Women of the British Empire*, Pimlico, London.
Trudgill, E. (1976), *Madonnas and Magdalens: The Origins and Development of Victorian Sexual Attitudes*, Heinemann, London.
Turner, B. S. (1995), *Medical Power and Social Knowledge*, Sage, London.
Uglow, S. (1988), *Policing Liberal Society*, Oxford University Press, Oxford.
Ungerson, C. (1987), *Policy is Personal: Sex, Gender and Informal Care*, Tavistock, London.
Van de Velde, T. (1931), *Sex Hostility in Marriage: Its Psychology and Technique*, Heinemann, London.
Walby, S. (1986), *Patriarchy at Work*, University of Minnesota Press, Minneapolis.
Walkowitz, J. R. (1980), *Prostitution and Victorian Society*, Cambridge University Press, Cambridge.
— (1992), *City of Dreadful Delight: Narratives of Sexual Danger in Late Victorian London*, Virago, London.
Ward, B. (1987), *Harlots of the Desert*, Cistercian Publications Inc., Kalamazoo, MI.
Warner, M. (1976), *Alone of All Her Sex, The Myth and Cult of the Virgin Mary*, Picador, Pan Books, London.
Weeks, J. (1989), *Sex, Politics and Society: The Regulation of Sexuality Since 1800* (2nd edn), Longman, London.
Whittick, A. (1979), *Woman into Citizen*, Athenaeum, London.

Wilson, E. (1977), *Women and the Welfare State*, Tavistock Publications, London.
Wilson, C. and R. Odell (1987), *Jack the Ripper: Summing up and Verdict*, Bantam Press, London.
Wolfenden, Lord J. (1976), *Turning Points. The Memoirs of Lord Wolfenden*, The Bodley Head, London.
Wollstonecraft, M. (1985) *A Vindication of the Rights of Women*, Everyman Classic, Dent, London.
Woolf, L. (1966), *Collected Essays by Virginia Wolf*, Vol. II, Hogarth Press, London.
— (1972), *A Room of One's Own*, Penguin Books, London.

ARTICLES IN BOOKS

Benson, C. and R. Matthews (2000), 'Police and Prostitution', in R. Weitzer (ed.), *Sex For Sale*, Routledge, London.
Bland, L. (1985), ' "Cleansing the Portals of Life": The Venereal Disease Campaign in the Early Twentieth Century', in M. Langan and B. Schwarz (eds), *Crisis in the British State, 1880–1930*, London.
Chapman, R. (1973), 'The Fulton Committee on the Civil Service', in R. Chapman (ed.), *The Role of Commissions in Policy Making*, George Allen & Unwin, London.
Coxon, T. (1988), 'The Numbers Game: Gay Lifestyles, Epidemiology of Aids and Social Science', in P. Aggleton and H. Homans (eds), *Social Aspects of AIDS*, The Falmer Press, London.
Davidoff, L. (1983), 'Class and Gender in Victorian England', in J. L. Newton, M. R. Ryan and J. R. Walkowitz (eds), *Sex and Class in Women's History*, Routledge & Kegan Paul, London.
Edgington, R. (1997), 'Policing Under-age Prostitution: A Victim-based Approach', in D. Barrett (ed.), *Child Prostitution in Britain: Dilemmas and Practical Responses*, The Children's Society.
Edwards, S. S. M. (1987), 'Prostitutes: Victims of Law: Social Policy and Organised Crime' in P. Carlen and A. Worrall (eds), *Gender, Crime and Justice*, Open University Press, Milton Keynes.
— (1997), 'The Legal Regulation of Prostitution: A Human Rights Issue', in G. Scambler and A. Scambler (eds), *Rethinking Prostitution: Purchasing Sex in the 1990s*, Routledge, London.
English Collective of Prostitutes (1997), 'Campaigning for Legal Change', in G. Scambler and A. Scambler (eds), *Rethinking Prostitution: Purchasing Sex in the 1990s*, Routledge, London.
Jeffreys, S. (ed.) (1987), *The Sexuality Debates*, Routledge & Kegan Paul, London.
Hay, D. (1977), 'Property, Authority and the Criminal Law', in Hay et al. (eds), *Albion's Fatal Tree: Crime and Society in Eighteenth Century England*, Penguin Books, London.
Kempadoo, K. and J. Doezema (eds) (1998), *Global Sex Workers, Rights, Resistance and Redefinition*, Routledge, London.
Nield, K. (ed.) (1973), 'Introduction', in *Prostitution in the Victorian Age*, Gregg International Publishers, Farnborough.
Matthews, R. (1986), 'Beyond Wolfenden? Prostitution Politics and the Law', in R. Matthews and J. Young (eds), *Confronting Crime*, Sage Publications, London.
Mill, J. S. (1985) [1869], 'The Subjection of Women', in *Mary Wollstonecraft: A Vindication of the Rights of Women. John Stuart Mill: The Subjection of Women*, Everyman Classic, Dent, Everyman Library, London.
Monto, M. (2000), 'Why Men Seek out Prostitutes', in Ronald Weitzer (ed.), *Sex for Sale: Prostitution, Pornography and the Sex Industry*, Routledge, London.
O'Donovan, K. (1979), 'The Male Appendage – Legal Definitions of Women', in S. Burman (ed.), *Fit Work for Women*, Croom Helm, London.
— (1993), 'Gender Blindness or Justice Engendered' in R. Blackburn (ed.), *Rights of Citizenship*, Mansell, London.
O'Neill, M. (1996), 'Researching Prostitution and Violence: Towards a Feminist Praxis', in M. Hester, L. Kelly and J. Radford (eds), *Women, Violence and Male Power*, Open University Press, Buckingham.
— (1997), 'Prostitute Women Now', in G. Scambler and A. Scambler (eds), *Rethinking Prostitution: Purchasing Sex in the 1990s*, Routledge, London.
Poovey, M. (1990), 'Speaking of the Body', in M. Jacobus, E. F. Keller and S. Shuttleworth (eds), *Body Politics: Women and the Discourse of Science*, Routledge, London.
Smart, C. (1981), 'Law and the Control of Women's Sexuality: The Case of the 1950s', in B.

Hutter and G. Williams (eds), *Controlling Women: The Normal and the Deviant*, Croom Helm, London.

Storch, R. (1986), 'The Plague of Blue Locusts: Police Reform and Popular Resistance in Northern England, 1840–57', reprinted in M. Fitzgerald, G. McLennan and J. Pawson, *Crime and Society*, Routledge, London.

Szasz, T. (1983), in R. E. Vatz and L. S. Weinberg (eds), *Thomas Szasz, Primary Values and Major Contentions*, Prometheus Books, Amherst, NY.

Walkowitz, J. R. (1983), 'Male Vice and Female Virtue: Feminism and Politics of Prostitution in Nineteenth-Century Britain', in A. Sinitow, C. Stansell and S. Thompson (eds), *Desire: The Politics of Sexuality*, Virago, London.

Ward, W. and S. Day (1997), 'Health Care and Regulation: New Perspectives', in G. Scambler and A. Scambler (eds), *Rethinking Prostitution: Purchasing Sex in the 1990s*, Routledge, London.

CONTEMPORARY JOURNALS

Campbell, Q. (1984), 'Prostitution and the Courts', *Justice of the Peace*, 579, 15 September: 579–80.

Davidson, R. (1994), 'Venereal Disease, Sexual Morality, and Public Health in Inter-war Scotland', *Journal of the History of Sexuality*, 5 (2): 267–93.

Davidson, R. (1993), '"A Scourge to be Firmly Gripped": The Campaign for VD Controls in Inter-war Scotland', *Social History of Medicine*, 6, February: 213–35.

Edwards, S. S. M., (1984), 'Kerb Crawling and Allied Offences – The Criminal Law Revision Committee's Proposals', *Justice of the Peace*, 148, 13 October: 644–8.

— (1988), 'Red Lights and Red Faces', *Police Review*, 1 July: 1371–3.

— (1988), 'Policing Street Prostitution: The Street Offences Squad in London', *Police Journal*, July: 209–17.

Ericsson, L. O. (1980), 'Charges Against Prostitution: An Attempt at a Philosophical Assessment', *Ethics*, 90, April: 335–66.

Holloway, W. (1981), '"I Just Wanted to Kill a Woman." Why? The Ripper and Male Sexuality', *Feminist Review*, 9, Autumn.

Golding, R. (1992), 'Policing Prostitution', *Policing*, 8, Spring: 61–71.

Kelly, L. (1985), 'Feminist', *Trouble and Strife*, 7, Summer: 4–9.

Kinnell, H. and Campbell, R. (2000–01), '"We Shouldn't Have to Put Up With This": Street Sex-work and Violence', *Criminal Justice Matters*, 42, Winter.

Matthews, R. (1992), 'Regulating Street Prostitution and Kerb-Crawling: A Reply to John Lowman', *British Journal of Criminology*, 32 (1), Winter: 18–22.

Mort, F. (1999), 'Mapping Sexual London: The Wolfenden Committee on Homosexual Offences and Prostitution, 1954–57', *New Formations*, 37, Spring: 92–113.

Miller, J. and M. D. Schwartz (1995), 'Rape Myths and Violence Against Street Prostitutes', in *Deviant Behaviour: An Interdisciplinary Journal*, 16 (1).

O' Hara, M. (1991), 'Making Feminist Law?' *Trouble and Strife*, 21, Summer: 33–9.

Pheterson, G. (1990), 'The Category "Prostitute" in Scientific Inquiry', *Journal of Sex Research*, 27 (3), August: 397–407.

— (1993), 'The Whore Stigma: Female Dishonour and Male Unworthiness', *Social Text*, 37: 39–64.

Rich, A. (1980), 'Compulsory Heterosexuality and Lesbian Existence', *Signs*, 5 (4).

Thomas, K. (1956), 'The Double Standard', *Journal of the History of Ideas*, 20: 195–216.

Woodeson, A. (1993), 'The First Women Police: A Force for Equality or Infringement?' *Women's History Review*, Vol. 2: 217–32.

GOVERNMENT PAPERS, OFFICIAL AND SPONSORED REPORTS

Beveridge, W. (1942), 'Social Insurance and Allied Services', HMSO, London, Cmnd. 6404.

Criminal Law Revision Committee (1980), Fifteenth Report, 'Sexual Offences', Cmnd. 9213.

Criminal Law Revision Committee (1982), Working Paper on Offences Relating to Prostitution and Allied Offences.

Criminal Law Revision Committee (1984), Sixteenth Report, 'Prostitution in the Street', Cmnd. 9329.

Criminal Law Revision Committee (1986), Seventeenth Report, 'Prostitution Off-street Activities', Cmnd. 9688.

Edinburgh Corporation Order (1933).

Home Office Research Unit (1972), 'Girl Offenders Aged 17 to 20 Years', HMSO, London.

Home Office Circular, 'Sexual Offences Act 1985', HOC 52/1985.

Home Office (1999), 'A Review of Sex Offences'.

League of Nations (1927), 'Report of the Special Body of Experts on Traffic in Women and Children, Part I' [C. 52. M. 52. 1927], Geneva.

League of Nations (1930), Advisory Commission for the Protection and Welfare of Children and Young People, 'Minutes of the Ninth Session', 9 April [C. 246. M. 121].

League of Nations Advisory Committee on Social Questions (1943), 'Prevention of Prostitution: A Study of Measures Adopted or Under Consideration Particularly with Regard to Minors' [C. 26. M. 26.]

League of Nations Records on the International Conference on Traffic in Women and Children, Geneva 1921 [C. 484. M. 339]

London County Council Medical Officer of Health (1927), 'Common Lodging-Houses and Kindred Institutions'.

Matthews, R. (1986), 'Policing Prostitution: A Multi-agency Approach', *Centre for Criminology, Paper 1.*

Matthews, R. (1991), 'Kerb-crawling, Prostitution and Multi-Agency Policing', *Police Research Group Crime Prevention Unit Series*, Paper 43.

May, T., M. Edmunds and M. Hough (1999), 'Street Business: The Links Between Sex and the Drug Market', *Police Research Series Paper* 118, Home Office Reducing Crime Unit, Clive House, Petty France, London.

May, T., A. Harocopos and M. Hough (2000), 'For Love or Money: Pimps and the Management of Sex Work', Police Research Series Paper 134, Home Office Reducing Crime Unit, Clive House, Petty France, London.

Metropolitan Police (1984), 'Evidence of the Commissioner of Police of the Metropolis, Presented to the Home Office Criminal Law Revision Committee Appointed to Review the Laws Concerning Offences Relating to Prostitution and Allied Subjects', New Scotland Yard, February.

National Health Service (1968), 'Control of Venereal Disease Memorandum' [HM(68)84].

National Police Vice Conference Report (1999).

Report of the Cambridge Department of Sexual Offences, ed. L. Radzinowicz, Macmillan (1957).

Report of the Royal Commission upon the Administration and Operation of the Contagious Diseases Acts (1871).

Report of the Committee on the Employment of Women on Police Duties (1920), Cmd. 877.

Report of the Departmental Committee on the Employment of Policewomen (1924), Cmnd. 2224.

Report of the Street Offences Committee (1928), Cmnd. 3231.

Report of the Committee on Homosexual Offences and Prostitution (1957), Cmnd. 247.

Report of the Committee on the Employment of Women on Police Duties (1920), Cmnd. 877.

Report of the Departmental Committee on the Employment of Policewomen (1924), Cmnd. 2224.

Report of the Departmental Committee on Sterilization (1933) Cmnd. 4485.

Report of the Committee on Children and Young Persons (Ingleby Committee, 1960), Cmnd. 1191.

Report of Parliamentary Group on Prostitution (1996), printed and published by Middlesex University, Bounds Green, London.

Report of the Departmental Committee on Sterilisation (1933), Cmnd. 4485.

Working Party on Vagrancy and Street Offences Working Paper (1974).

Report of the Working Party on Vagrancy and Street Offences (1976).

Royal Commission on the Sanitary State of the Army in India (1863).

Royal Commission on the Care and Control of the Feeble Minded (1908).

Royal Commission on Venereal Disease (1916), Cmnd. 8189 XVI.

Royal Commission on Police Powers and Procedures (1929), Cmnd. 3297.

Royal Commission on the Law Relating to Mental Illness and Mental Deficiency (1957).

Royal Commission Upon the Duties of the Metropolitan Police (1908), Cmnd. 4260-3.

Royal Commission on Population (1949), Cmnd. 7695.
'Setting the Boundaries: Reforming the Law on Sex Offences', Vol. 1, Home Office, July 2000.
Royal Commission on the Care and Protection of Young Girls (1881).
Secure Borders, Safe Haven: Integration with Diversity in Modern Britain (2002) CM 5387.
United Nations Programme for HIV/AIDS, 'Handbook for Legislators on HIV/AIDS: Law and
    Human Rights', UNAIDS/IPU, Geneva, Switzerland (1999).

CONFERENCES AND CONGRESSES

International Medical Congress, Paris, 1867.
International Medical Congress, Florence, 1870.
International Medical Congress, Vienna, 1873.
International Medical Congress, Brussels, 1875.
International Labour Conference of the League of Nations, Washington, October 1919.
London Diocesan Conference (1961).
NVA/IB Conferences and Congresses: Amsterdam (1890); Frankfurt (1902); Zurich (1904); Paris
    (1906); Madrid (1910); London (1913); Warsaw (1930); Berlin (1933); Paris (1937); London
    (1949); Brussels (1958); Geneva (1965).
'International Conferences on Obscene Publications and the White Slave Traffic. Held in Paris,
    April and May 1910.' Presented to Parliament by Command of His Majesty, (HMSO, 1912).
National Police Vice Conference (1999).
'Soliciting for Change: Report on Soliciting For Change Forum', Nottingham, 25–26 September
    1993.

INTERNATIONAL AGREEMENTS AND CONVENTIONS

International Agreement for the Suppression of the White Slave Traffic, signed at Paris on the 18
    May 1904, ratified at Paris, 18 January 1905 by Great Britain, Germany, Denmark, Spain,
    France, Italy, Russia, Sweden, Norway, Switzerland, Belgium, Netherlands, and Portugal.
    Treaty Series No. 24. HMSO [Cd. 2689].
International Convention for the Suppression of the White Slave Traffic, signed at Paris May
    1910. Signed by Austria and Hungary, Great Britain, France, Belgium, Brazil, Denmark,
    Spain, Italy, Netherlands, Portugal, Russia, Sweden. Treaty Series 1912. No. 20. [Cmnd. 6336].
League of Nations Convention on the Traffic in Women and Children, (Geneva, 18 October
    1921). [A. 125 (1) 1921. IV.]
League of Nations Convention on the Traffic in Women and Children, Geneva, 18 October 1921.
    [A. 125 (1) 1921. IV.]
League of Nations Convention for the Suppression of the Traffic of Women of Full Age, 1933.
    Copy in NVA archives, WL.
United Nations Convention for the Suppression of the Traffic in Persons and the Exploitation of
    the Prostitution of Others, 1949.

PRIMARY SOURCE PAPERS, PAMPHLETS, ESSAYS,
BOOKLETS AND REPORTS

Bullock, F. S. (1913), 'White Slave Traffic', New Scotland Yard, 12 June.
Burt, C. (1926), 'Causes of Sex Delinquency in Girls', pamphlet from *Health and Empire*.
Butler, J. (1870), paper on 'The Moral Reclaimability of Prostitutes', read by Mrs Butler at 'A
    Conference of Delegates from Associations and Committees formed in Various Towns for
    Promoting the Repeal of the Contagious Diseases Acts', held at the Freemason's Tavern, 5 May.
— (1871), ' "The Constitution Violated": An Essay', Edinburgh Edmondson and Douglas.
— (1871), ' "The Constitutional Iniquity": Speech of Mrs Josephine Butler at BRADFORD,
    January 27th 1971', Douglas, Edinburgh.
— (1879), ' "Government By Police". An Essay: Respectfully Dedicated to The Town Councillors
    of the United Kingdom', printer unknown.

Catterall, R. D. (1967), 'Prostitution and the Venereal Diseases', Summary of Tenth Alison Neilans Memorial Lecture given at the House of Commons, November.

Chorley (1970), 'The Reform of the Street Offences Act 1959: An Account of an Attempt that Failed', *Shield*.

Church of England Moral Welfare Council (1959), 'The Street Offences Bill. A Case for its Amendment', published for the Church of England Moral Welfare Council by The Church Information Board, Church House Westminster (1959).

Gibbens, T. N. C. (1956), 'Juvenile Prostitution', *British Journal of Delinquency*, VIII.

— (1959), 'Supervision and Probation of Adolescent Girls', *British Journal of Delinquency*, X (2) 84–103.

Hall Williams, J. E. (undated, 1965?), 'Memorandum on Research into Prostitution and the Law'.

— (undated, 1971–72?), 'The Reform of the Law of Sexual Offences: Offences Connected with Prostitution'.

— (1976), 'Report on Discussion About Research Into Prostitution and the Law'.

Glover, E. (1945), 'The Psycho-Pathology of Prostitution', London.

Greg, W. G. (1850), 'Prostitution', *Westminster Review* 53, (1850).

— (1862), 'Why are Women Redundant?', *National Review*, 14.

Heasman, K. (undated), 'Josephine Butler House: A History'.

Howard League for Penal Reform (1974), 'The Cautioning and Imprisonment of Prostitutes'.

International Bureau (1955), 'A Century of Cooperation'.

Jones, A. E. (1960), 'The Law Versus Prostitution', *Criminal Law Review*, October.

London Public Morality Council (1924), '"Women's Courts": Committee of Enquiry 1924, Report', Vacher & Sons Ltd, London.

Mathieson, D. A. and A. J. Walker (undated, 1910?), 'The Royal Commission on the Metropolitan Police: The Truth About the Enquiry', Social Enquiry Reports No. 7, Police and Public Vigilance Society.

Neilans, A. (1941), 'The Unity of the Moral Law', *Scottish Women's Temperance News*.

Penal Reform League (1912), 'Prostitution: its Nature and Cure', London.

Power Cobbe, F. (1894), 'Wife Torture in England', *Contemporary Review*, 32.

Priceman, J. (1972), 'Research into Prostitution: The Report of an Investigation'.

Timwell, J. (undated, 1910?), 'The Royal Commission on the Metropolitan Police: The Truth About the Enquiry', Police and Public Vigilance Society.

Tredgold, A. F. (1918), 'Mental Deficiency in Relation to Venereal Disease', National Council for Combating Venereal Disease, London.

Thomas, K. (1959), 'The Double Standard', *Journal of History of Ideas*, 20.

Wilson, H. J. (1907), 'A Rough Record of Events and Incidences Connected with the Repeal of the Contagious Diseases Acts, 1864–6–9 in the United Kingdom, and of the movement against state regulation of Vice, in India and the Colonies, 1858–1906', Sheffield Parker (1907).

CONTEMPORARY BOOKLETS

Barnardo's (1980), 'Whose Daughter Next? Children Abused Through Prostitution', Barnardo's.

James, S. (1984), 'Hookers in the House of Lords', in J. Holland (ed.), *Feminist Action*, Battle Axe Books.

Lee, M. and R. O'Brien (1995), 'The Games Up: Redefining Child Prostitution', Children's Society (1995).

Mavolwane, S., S. Miller and J. Watson (1989), 'Policing Prostitution', Rights of Women, 52–54 Featherstone Street, London.

United Nations (1992), 'Basic Facts About the United Nations'.

PH.D. AND MA THESES

Taithe, B. O. (1992), 'From Danger to Scandal, Debating Sexuality in Victorian England: The Contagious Diseases Acts (1864–1869) and the Morbid Imagery of Victorian Society', Ph.D. Thesis, University of Manchester.

Ware, H. (1969), 'The Recruitment, Regulation and Control of Prostitution in Britain from the Middle of the Nineteenth Century to the Present Day', Ph.D. Thesis, University of London.
Silva, C. F. da (2000), 'Prostitution in the Nineties: Changing Working Practices, Changing Violence', MA Criminology, Middlesex University.

MISCELLANEOUS

Kinnell, H., J. Bindel and A. Lopes (2000), 'Violence Against Sex Workers', press release, EUROPAP, Justice for Women and Safe in the City, 6 December.

NEWSPAPERS AND PERIODICALS

Birmingham Post (1967)
Catholic Herald (1967)
Church of England Newspaper and the Record (1961)
Daily Express (1972)
Daily Herald (1962)
Daily Mail (passim)
Daily Mirror (passim)
Daily Sketch (1960)
Daily Star (1980)
Daily Telegraph (passim)
Evening News (1967)
Evening Standard (1952)
Guardian (passim)
Independent Magazine (1999)
Kensington Post (1959)
Lancet (1963)
Leader (1885)
Lynn News and Advetiser (1953)
*London Gazette (*1918)
Morning Post (1858)
National Review (1862)
New Statesman (1961)
New Society (1969)
News of the World (passim)
Observer (1962)
People (passim)
Reynolds News (1950)
Shield (passim)
Sun (passim)
Sunday Pictorial (passim)
Sunday Times (1959)
Suffragette
The Times (passim)
Time and Tide (1942)
Tribune (1959)
Vigilance Record (passim)
Vote
Votes for Women
Westminster and Pimlico News (1953)
Westminster Review (1950)
Yorkshire Evening Post (1968)

Index